Dandelion
Growing Wild

A triumphant journey over astounding odds
to become an American marathon champion

Kim Jones

The events in "Dandelion Growing Wild" are based on my memories, supported by documented events and extensive research. My grandmother Helen was an invaluable resource of information regarding my family's heritage and humble beginnings, as well as the early years of my life. I've truly enjoyed learning about my clan through her lively family stories. I have used dialog throughout my book. Many of the quotes are not word-for-word, but from what I recall, taken from letters or journals, or have recreated through discussion with family and friends ~

Author, Kimberly Anne Jones

Copyright © 2012 Kim Jones

Library of Congress Cataloging in Publication Data

ISBN: 0615597424
ISBN-13: 978-0615597423

Dedication

I dedicate this book to my daughters who have enriched my life with love, laughter and hope.

My shining stars
Jamie Suzanne Roth ~ the strong and resilient
Rachel Lynn Jones ~ the wild and adventurous

This is our story

Author's note

The writing process is as personal as childbirth. And that is even truer when writing about your own life. I wrote and rewrote these words over a three-year period, even though I had conceived of the book at an earlier time. Every serious writer wants to find a voice that is true. My effort to find that voice came as I remembered events and then committed them to words. In my case the act of writing was also an act of catharsis, the spiritual healing that must come with any tragedy. I have tried to capture my life within the context of a career as an elite runner. This book, however, is not so much about the running life but rather my endurance and triumph within that life. As Faulkner wrote: "Between grief and nothing, I will take grief." This book has allowed me to move beyond even that.

My story is connected to the lives and deaths of many loved ones. I hope that my memoir honors both their memory and the dedication and courage of the loved ones they had to leave.

Prologue

One sunny day when Dad was busy working on our old prostitute house, he sent Mom to borrow a paint sprayer from my grandparents.

"Take all the kids and spend some time," he told her. "There's no hurry."

When we came back, our house was on fire. We stood there and watched it burn to the ground. There was smoke everywhere, stinging my eyes, making my throat hurt and my chest tight. The blaze crackled and roared. I couldn't take my eyes off it.

Everyone around me was crying and dashing around, trying to find our pets. I could hear everyone, but their voices were muffled. I could see them, but they were blurry. I was in a trance as the fire seemed to draw me in, closer and closer. I stood frozen as I stared into the flames. I heard Dad yelling, "Get back, Swede! Get away from the house!" Then he grabbed me and carried me back.

Mom was screaming at Dad. "What happened? What did you do?" Dad was angry and tried to spray water on the house with one small hose. The fire department never came. We lived on the border of two districts and neither fire department felt it was within their jurisdiction.

I knew my comfort blanket was in the house, burning. I loved that blanket more than anything in the world. Even though I was 7 years old and knew I was getting too old for it, my blanket with its special smell was always there for me when everything turned crazy. It was there for me when Dad acted up, it was there for me when I was hungry and it was there for me when I killed My Blondie. *Now ... it's on fire!*

I wished I had taken it with me to my grandparents' house. Debbie cried for the useless turtle in the bathtub. Charlie was upset about his catfish swimming in the big laundry sink on the back porch.

My blanket was gone. Debbie's useless turtle died in the bathtub and Charlie's catfish was dead. We had nothing left. Dad was sick and couldn't work. There were seven kids to take care of.

Chapter 1

Laurie, Debbie, and Kimmie ~ 1959

I was born with a crooked toe. It's the one next to the little toe on my right foot, and it bends straight sideways all the way under my other toes. The doctors wanted to cut it off, but my mother was horrified and told them "No!" Then they suggested taking the bone out of my toe so it wouldn't break when I stepped on it. But my mother said, "Let's just see how she does once she starts walking."

With my blond hair, blue eyes and turned-up nose, I looked a lot like my mother, Geraldine Anne, but I wasn't beautiful like Mom was. She was stunning, with wide-set eyes that lit up with laughter when she was happy. She was still happy a lot back then.

By the time I turned a year old, my hair was almost white and so fine that it stood straight up, like a dandelion gone to seed. My family teased me and called me "Dandelion Head" when they blew on my hair. When we went anyplace important, Mom would water it down so it would stay put for a little while.

I walked on my crooked toe just fine, as long as I didn't wear shoes.

They called me "Swede" or "The Throwback" because I was the first child in our family who took after my mother's Scandinavian grandmother, who migrated to Leadville, Colorado, in the late 1800s. That's where she met Great Grandfather Carlson, who came from Sweden to work in the lumber industry.

Grandma Helen was born soon after. When Grandma Helen grew up, she married Jack Jeffries and moved to Sonoma, California. Grandpa Jeffries was part Cherokee because his Scottish father had fallen in love with a Cherokee girl, sweeping her up from the stairs of the Trading Post and carrying her away. Grandma Helen says that was probably why he couldn't handle his liquor.

Grandpa Jeffries was always out drinking, carousing and having affairs, never home except to ask for – or more likely steal – the money Grandma Helen made working at the plywood factory during a time when a woman's place was to stay home and take care of her family. Mom says that Grandpa Jeffries was always dressed to the hilt, wearing $20 shoes. That really impressed Mom back then.

He never paid attention to his kids, except when he came home in a drunken rage to belittle them. Grandma Helen says they were better off when he stayed away. He died of a heart attack before I was born.

My father's side of the family was dark with brilliant brown and hazel eyes, except for Dad's mother. Ma Seelye was fair skinned with wavy red hair, and must have been a very brave and strong woman because she had 15 babies. Dad's father, Pa Seelye, just like Grandpa Jeffries, couldn't handle his liquor either.

Dad's family lived on a sugar beet farm in the Dakotas, where he was born. They had no plumbing, or much of anything else. Dad and his 11 brothers and 3 sisters worked hard in the fields without shoes and weren't allowed to go to school until all of the work was done, which meant they didn't go to school much. Even though he went until he was 16, Dad never made it past sixth grade.

When Dad was a child he spent many months in the hospital, where they tried to fix his clubfeet. It wasn't easy, because he was 9 years old before anyone took him to the doctor. By then, he'd been hobbling for so long on the outer edges of his feet instead of walking on the soles that the tops of his feet were where the bottoms should have been. The doctors had to perform a painful operation on both feet and put them in casts "while he stayed in the hospital being spoiled rotten by the nurses," as Pa Seelye put it. Pa was not very happy. Dad should have been out in the fields working.

Dad walked funny for the rest of his life, on the outsides of his feet, and could hardly stand to wear shoes because it hurt so much. Maybe that's a result of not going back into the hospital every few years for re-bracing, even though the family being dirt poor meant treatments were free. After all, Dad was needed in the sugar beet fields.

My dad was tough. He was sad, too, and so were his siblings. You could see it in their eyes. Pa Seelye beat and tormented his 15 kids and walked all over Ma Seelye, who never stood up for herself or her children. She was afraid of him. He even sexually abused some of his kids. I hope he didn't do that to my dad, though.

Dad and his family eventually moved to Sonoma, where I was born. This is where my story begins.

Mom and Dad on their wedding day ~ 1954

Mom met Dad when she was 17 and dating Dad's younger brother, Pat. On one date, Pat and some of his friends had too much to drink and ended up in jail. Dad came to bail them out, and that's how Mom met Dad.

Dad was 11 years older than Mom, and had been married before. He had two children, Murphy and Lorna. Mom says he seemed so responsible. She had been planning to go to college for a degree in fashion because she loved studying all the new designs and then sewing versions of them for herself and her friends. But her real dream was to get married and live in the perfect house with the perfect white picket fence and have many babies, so she married Dad when she was 18, right after she graduated from Sonoma Valley High School.

Pat committed suicide shortly after that, but Mom said it wasn't because of Dad and her. He was sad and troubled, and that's why he attached a hose to the tailpipe and then put the other end into his car as he sat there while it was running with all the windows rolled up. Before that, their older brother Finn had committed suicide also. And Dad's twin brother Warren, also sad and troubled, had put a hose in his car and committed suicide a year earlier.

"There's been another accident," that's what the Seelyes felt better saying after everything that happened. Another brother Ken drowned in a lake, even though he was the best swimmer in the family. He just jumped right into the lake to drown. And just before I was born, there was still another accident. Dad's youngest brother drove his car right off a cliff, even though he could drive just fine. He must have been sad and troubled, too.

I was just a toddler when we lived in Sonoma, so I don't remember much without help, but I know that Dad worked on actor Fred MacMurray's cattle ranch. Mr. MacMurray was playing the father on "My Three Sons" on TV at the time. Later Dad worked on the Duncraggan Ranch after one of the owners, Mr. Ewing, hired him to be one of two head herdsmen. The ranch doctor had to constantly treat the calluses and corns Dad developed from walking funny. Dad hurt all of the time with his bad feet, but he didn't complain. Mom said he was a trouper.

While Dad was there, he was responsible for designing a feeding program for many of the prize-winning cattle that he showed in the Cow Palace arena in San Francisco. The owners of the ranch called his feeding formula "magnificent." He even worked with a prize-winning breeding bull named Old Mole. Dad said Old Mole was worth over a million dollars. I'm not sure if that's true, but I do know that the three owners had a lot of money invested in him.

Mom's dream came true right away. We were put up in a beautiful ranch house right next to the owner and given all the food, milk and beef we needed, even medical care. Everything was free. Mom had her house, with a white picket fence Dad built for her, and three babies. Dad even made her a rose trellis, and soon the most beautiful red and pink roses were growing over it.

Dad was so good with carpentry that he had a shop in a small building next to the house, where he worked in his spare time. Everything was sparkling clean. His tools were in perfect order and nothing could be out of place, not even a nail. He had pinup girls on the walls and that made Mom mad, so she hung a photo of Sal Mineo over the kitchen sink to get back at him. He was a sex symbol back then, and her favorite actor. That didn't please Dad, but Mom told him, "Why shouldn't I have my own pinup man if you have your girls?" Her plan worked – she made him jealous.

One day some nice people knocked on the front door. Mom had a friendly way about her, so she graciously invited them in and looked at the booklets they brought. Not long after that, she and Dad became Jehovah's Witnesses.

Life couldn't have been better. Mom said we were living high on the hog, right up until the day Dad discovered Old Mole was getting lopsided from laying way too long on his left side. Buckey, the other herdsman, tied a big block with nails to Old Mole's left side to keep him from laying on it and getting even more lopsided, ruining their chances for another first prize. Unfortunately, Buckey was lazy and didn't check on Old Mole, who ended up lying on his left side anyway. He couldn't get up by himself with the nails in his side. He died.

Dad was distraught and depressed after Old Mole died. Then, while he was working with the ranch vet, a rabid dog bit him and he had to go through the painful rabies treatment. His bad luck didn't stop there.

Mom had four babies in five years in Sonoma. First came three girls: Laurie, who is 2 1/2 years older than I am; then Debbie, who's just 11 months older; then me. Debbie and I are the same age for a week.

A year later they had their first son, Timmy. As soon as Timmy was born, the doctors told Mom and Dad that he needed a blood transfusion right away or he might die.

The doctors told my parents that their blood had the Rh factor, which meant their children were at risk of life-threatening complications, even death. Under the circumstances, they would likely need a blood transfusion right after they were born. A firstborn is not affected, but the risk grows worse for every child after that.

Even though I was the third child I had no problems, but Timmy wasn't so lucky and was in desperate need of a transfusion. Jehovah's Witnesses don't believe in taking in blood of any sort or in any way, and my parents fought with the doctors refusing to let my brother have it. The doctors pleaded with them and finally took Timmy away and gave him the transfusion anyway.

Timmy survived the blood disorder, but died of hepatitis from the transfusion one week later.

Uncle Harold always said about my dad, "If Laurin didn't have bad luck, he wouldn't have any luck at all."

When I was 3, we moved to a small town called Enumclaw, near Seattle. Most of my relatives lived nearby, not that you could always tell which side of the family they were on. For example, Dad's older brother, Uncle Harold, married Mom's widowed mother, Helen – so he was Uncle/Grandpa Harold and she was Aunt/Grandma Helen. They moved from Sonoma to Enumclaw just after I was born and lived there on a dairy farm with Mom's younger sister, Jan, and Harold's four daughters. When Dad's and Harold's parents – who we called Ma and Pa Seelye in an attempt to keep things straight – moved up from California shortly after we did, Uncle/Grandpa Harold and Grandma Helen remodeled their garage into a small apartment for them.

Eventually Mom's younger sister Jan married Dad's nephew Ron, and Uncle Jim, Mom's brother, married one of the daughters of Uncle/Grandpa Harold. So, my uncle is my grandfather and my grandmother is my aunt and most of my cousins are also my aunts and uncles. If you're confused about this, you can imagine how confusing it was for us as we were growing up. At least there was no incest involved.

My parents were very much into being Jehovah's Witnesses by then. They had two more sons the first few years in Enumclaw, and faced the same situation they had with Timmy. Charlie was born 3½ years after I was, and Bradley was born about 2 years after that, both with the same Rh incompatibility that Timmy had, and were also taken away from my parents against their will to have blood transfusions, but they both survived.

Our first home in Enumclaw was a little farm, with a lot of chickens. Mom said it was "way out in The Boondocks," and for a long time I thought that was actually the name of the place where we lived. Mom enjoyed her babies and had fun playing cards and spending time with the intricate extended family. Dad worked hard at a cattle feed and grain company, wanting to make a good life for his growing family.

And he did. Those first few years in Enumclaw were the best we would ever have together.

Things took a turn for the worse just before my 5th birthday, when Dad fell off a grain silo and severely injured his back. Then, after spending many weeks in the hospital he came home addicted to morphine. He would yell and scream and throw things at Mom, demanding and pleading that she make the pain go away. Sometimes he would get out of bed or stagger off the couch in a rage and try to hit her, then fall and need her help.

Aunt Jan used to come and take care of us when Dad went berserk begging for more morphine, so Mom could tend to him. She would try to distract us from his screams with funny stories and sometimes it worked. Once I went to peek at Dad when he was screaming at Mom and he looked so demonized that I ran out of the room frightened to death. Mom rushed out, grabbed me by the shoulders and began shaking me, "Don't you EVER go near your dad when he's sick! Do you HEAR me?" she yelled. In the next breath, she softened, "Honey, your dad would never want you to see him this way."

"What's wrong with him, Mommy?"

"He needs his medicine, sweetheart," she said, blinking away tears.

I don't know how she did it, but Mom would leave and then come back from the doctor's office with more morphine.

About a year after the silo accident, Dad fell down our well in the backyard. His back still hadn't healed from the first accident and now he hurt it again, along with jamming his leg and clubfoot into the side of the well as he went down. He went back on morphine, full time. Mom wondered if Dad didn't have some "accidents" on purpose so he could get more morphine.

While he recuperated at home, Dad had a lot of time on his hands and enjoyed playing tricks on Mom, like the time when he was taking care of my two sisters and me while Mom went to visit her Uncle Rollie. "Let's pretend we're not here and hide, not a single peep," he told us. We were so excited while we huddled together on the living room floor, quietly giggling as Mom was pounding on the door. When Mom finally broke into the house she hugged us girls so tight I could barely breathe while she screamed, "How dare you, Laurin, how dare you! What were you going to do to my babies?"

There was a loaded gun on the coffee table. We thought Dad had his gun handy to protect us, but Mom didn't.

When Dad was finally able to go back to work, he found a job at a lumber mill but would run off with his paycheck and leave us alone on the farm with no food, no money to pay the electricity bill, and no telephone to call for help. One time, after he left us alone for too long, Mom gathered us all up to hike to a house several miles away. She told the distant neighbors, "I'm sorry to bother you, but we need to use your telephone to call for help. Laurin's left us again and hasn't been home for months."

Then she broke down, telling them between sobs, "We haven't had a thing to eat in days. My children are starving."

The neighbors heard that and gave us tuna sandwiches, ham sandwiches, tomato soup and snacks. I ate them so fast, my throat and stomach felt like everything was going to come back up. Then I had a tummy ache.

Mom called Uncle/Grandpa Harold to help us. He drove out to The Boondocks to pick us up, and told Mom, "I think Laurin may have run off and committed suicide, just like his five brothers." Mom says that's how the two sides of our family became so close that they married each other a lot – attending all those funerals and then partying together afterward.

Uncle/Grandpa Harold must have been scared for Dad, and for himself, coming from a family where so many siblings had already killed themselves. Fortunately, he found Dad in San Francisco with their younger brother, Bill, but unfortunately he was drinking and shooting up heroin.

We lost our farmhouse and had to start over.

I was 6 when we moved into a big old house, way out on the border of the city limits on Muskrat Lake. It had a lot of bedrooms, and each of them had a number on the door. My room was behind door number 3! I ran through the house, so excited to see all of those bedrooms. I told Debbie, "Pick door number 2, right next to me!" I thought it was very special having a number on my door. I couldn't figure out why there were so many tiny bedrooms with no closets until much later. "It's nothing but a dilapidated old whorehouse," Mom told Dad between sobs when she was in one of her sad moods.

The prostitute house needed a lot of work. When summer came, Dad was fixing it up in his spare time, while working two jobs off and on as a cabinetmaker and driving a truck. He built us a really nice swing set, where we spent a lot of our time. Dad told us that we needed to stay out of Mom's hair because she was pregnant again, throwing up and spending most of her time on the couch. Sometimes she couldn't move she was so sick, and Laurie had to help her with the housework and the younger children even though she was only 9.

There was a lot of land, with a scary wooded area and no neighbors nearby. Down a long, long, winding pathway, there was a small lake with catfish and tons of little frogs jumping around everywhere. We snuck down there to catch the small frogs and put them in a wagon, but they jumped out before we could bring them back to our house to visit. Mom didn't enjoy that place as much as we did. I heard her crying to Dad, "How can you leave me and the kids all alone in this creepy place, while you're away doing who knows what?" She was very nervous while Dad was away driving trucks, or away maybe doing things we didn't know he was doing. It seemed like he was gone more than not. Still, we had a lot of fun playing and just being kids, even though I didn't have many friends. Actually, I can't remember having any at all, but I had my brothers and sisters.

I was lucky to have Blondie, too. Everyone said she looked like me, so I called her "My Blondie."

I loved My Blondie more than anything, and I told her so. "You're the best cow in all The Boondocks," I would say, while hugging her big giant neck. Blondie was my best friend, other than my sister Debbie. Blondie was sweet and caring, and would come up to us right away when we went out into the field to find her. She nuzzled me and looked at me like I was special. She would lie down a lot, and I knew she did it to get closer to me so I could sit on her and hug her and talk to her. "I love you so much, Blondie," I would tell her. "You're my best friend ever, and I will always be here for you, every day."

I could tell Blondie anything while we sat together – she would listen and I knew she understood. She made me feel better when Mom and Dad did things that confused us kids. At times I didn't know whether I was being bad or good.

Mom was mad and yelled and yelled one day when we made a fort in the house during one of our usual rainy days out in The Boondocks. We used a clean bed sheet. She had Dad spank us for it when he came home. I didn't think making a fort was so bad, but then I spilled a full glass of milk, which was really bad, and I thought for sure I was in for it but all Mom did was say, "Oh Kimmie," in a sad voice and she even cleaned it up for me. My stomach hurt, unsure of how to behave sometimes.

I would take my special blanket and lie next to Blondie to stay warm and visit, especially when it was cold. We didn't have heat in our big old prostitute house and the fireplace didn't keep us very warm, especially when Dad forgot to chop wood before he left us for days. Blondie's big fat body always warmed me up and I was very happy and felt safe cuddled up next to her. She liked it, too.

My Blondie was the gentlest being in our world and we all loved her. Even Laurie.

There were more animals. We had a little goat named Mary Louise and a few chickens that ran around in the big open yard and laid eggs everywhere. We had an egg hunt every day, which helped make up for us not celebrating Easter because we were Jehovah's Witnesses. Debbie claimed the turtle and took care of it, even after I told her, "It's just a big giant useless turtle." We chased our dogs around the yard and took them out for adventure walks in the scariest part of the woods.

I did everything with Debbie. We played together day in and day out. We fought a lot and were best friends. I always wanted to spend time with Debbie and would ask her, "Do you want to go sit on Blondie with me and relax?" She usually said, "OK, but then we're going to do what I want." She usually got her way and could convince me of anything.

Debbie looked a lot like me except a little more Native American, with light brown hair. Mom named her after Debbie Reynolds, the famous actress at that time. She was very slight, and looked so innocent and precious. Yet even though her eyes were blue instead of brilliant hazel/brown, they looked a lot like my father's. I could always tell when Debbie was lying, because her eyes would get big and wide, and she would talk a mile a minute. She seemed to lie a lot, even about things that really didn't matter. I always wondered why.

Debbie and I shared the same bed throughout our childhood. Even when we had our own rooms – like in the prostitute house – we would climb into bed together for comfort. We had many adventures together and even though we fought more than any of our other siblings, I didn't feel complete unless she was a part of what I was doing.

While sitting on Blondie, we would watch my brother Charlie running around the field chasing the chickens. He was only 3 years old when Debbie and I were 6 and 7, so we always had to watch him while we were playing outside. He was my dad's pride and joy – another son after Timmy died. Charlie was special, and I enjoyed holding him because he looked just like an angel and I loved him very much. Charlie was a healthy blue-eyed baby with big squishy cheeks, along with wavy auburn hair and the temper to go with it. He turned into a piece of work when he was angry.

None of us played much with our goat. She was mean and I was afraid of her, but Laurie loved her. I would sit with Blondie and laugh while we watched Laurie chasing Mary Louise around the yard when it was time to milk her. We had plenty of milk from Mary Louise and Blondie, and if the chickens weren't too upset from being hugged and chased around we had a few eggs. Sometimes the eggs and milk were all we had to eat and drink. Then one day someone came and took Mary Louise and the chickens away. It turns out Dad had written a bad check to buy them.

"We still have My Blondie, and we still have our swing set," I told Debbie. "We can play on it anytime you want, or we can catch frogs or ride Blondie around the field." To cheer her up even more, I smiled nicely and said, "You still have your useless turtle."

It was an especially warm day when they took our animals away; the sun was shining after a heavy rain and the air was so clean that we could see Mount Rainier far off in the distance. Mom knew we were sad and she had tears in her eyes, too. "Why don't you kids take your lunch outside and enjoy this beautiful day," she said. "See if you can spot the reindeer made from the shadows of the mountain."

While searching for that reindeer, Debbie and I were sitting with Blondie eating peanut butter and jelly sandwiches when some hornets boldly flew at us before latching onto my shirt. A big swarm of them began circling us just as we jumped up and started running toward the house. They were stinging me all over. As I began swatting at them I dropped my sandwich in the dirt! I really needed that sandwich.

After we reached the house, Dad and I marched right back down to the hornets' nest attached to an old woodpile and he set it on fire. I felt so safe and secure standing there with my dad, hand in hand, watching the nest burn and hearing it crackle and pop. We were in charge of those vicious hornets.

—

Lorna and Murphy, Dad's children from his first marriage, lived part of the time at our house and part of the time with their mother in Sterling, Colorado. When things were good, they lived with us. When we didn't have any food or Dad was acting up, they lived with their mother. They weren't around much during that time.

Lorna was in her early teens, dark and lean just like Dad. I thought she was beautiful. When she had friends over they played records and talked about things that were fascinating to see and hear from my secret spots. I would hide behind the couch, or when Debbie and I were really brave we'd hide under her bed. Sometimes she would catch us. "Get out of here you two little brats, go back to the sewer where you belong," she would snap. Lorna didn't like us. I don't think she liked Mom, either, and Mom didn't like her much. They were jealous of each other over Dad. Lorna was spooky, and as much as I tried, I couldn't figure her out. "You girls stay away from her," Mom warned us on several occasions. "She's a wicked one!"

Murphy had blond hair and startling blue eyes. He was a year older than Lorna and I looked up to him, but I didn't trust him. While Dad was away driving trucks, he seemed to spend an awful lot of time helping Mom.

I was surprised that Murphy gave me shoulder rides and paid attention to me. I didn't get much attention, being the middle child, but I would try hard to get it. When I did I would try to hold on to it for as long as possible by being silly and doing special tricks. But with Murphy I didn't have to act silly. Maybe he knew what it was like to be lonely. He seemed sad and troubled, like Dad, and he cried a lot when he thought no one would see. He was good to us, but he scared me. I didn't like the energy I felt from him when I was getting those shoulder rides.

Lorna and Murphy weren't there to help us the afternoon in early fall when Dad drove up in a truck, opened the door and fell out. We all ran to him, crying and calling for Mom. He was just lying there with his eyes wide open, but he couldn't move or speak. He looked so frightened.

Laurie told us, "Dad's comatose." I asked, "What's that?" and she said, "He's demonized and will stay this way forever." I cried and cried, thinking of my dad like that forever. Mom was eight months pregnant, and still in her nightgown when she ran out of the house. She told Laurie, "Take care of the kids, I need to get help." Then she shouted, "and stay away from your father!" She didn't know how to drive the truck and we didn't have a telephone so she ran over a mile through the woods and an open field – pregnant and in her nightgown – to a neighbor's house to call for help.

Dad was taken to the hospital. That is when he was first diagnosed with a "hereditary progressive" neurological disorder called Charcot-Marie-Tooth disease. He always had an unsteady walk but he thought it was his clubfeet. Now there was something else he had to deal with.

Later we went to visit Dad in the hospital and waited outside while Mom went in to see him first. He waved out the window, and looked so happy to see us. We couldn't figure out why the windows were covered in wire mesh. He was in the psychiatric ward.

The doctors suspected he had schizophrenia.

At first, Mom didn't understand how serious the situation was. She thought he had some kind of nerve damage from falling off the silo and down the well, until the doctor tried to explain that he also was behaving like a paranoid schizophrenic and they needed to observe him for a while. She didn't understand that schizophrenia was not going to go away.

Dad was gone for weeks. After he came home, sometimes he was nice and normal. Other times he would sneak around the house with crazed eyes, as if he were in a war and hiding from the enemy, sometimes crawling on the floor while peeking around the furniture. Once he threw a rock through a window and hurt Debbie, who was sleeping in a bed under the window. He told the police that somebody was trying to kill him. He didn't realize that he was the one who threw the rock.

I didn't like the worry and uncertainty every day of which Dad I was going to get. "He's unpredictable and crazy," Mom told us, which didn't make us feel any better. He cried for no reason. I didn't want him to be sad, so I tried hard to be funny and do cute things to make him laugh. Once I did somersaults down the long winding path right into the lake. The frogs were scattering in every which direction, frantically trying to jump out of my way. Dad laughed, saying, "Swede, you are something else."

Mom was nice most of the time if she wasn't sad, and even read to us at night just before bedtime. Our favorite storybook of all time was "Little Orphan Annie." We would all gather just before bedtime and sit on Charlie's bed and wait, scared but excited, when Mom would read the frightening fun parts as she walked toward us using a scary voice as she read very slowly, "And ... the ... goblins ... will ... get ... YOU!" – grabbing one of us – "if you don't watch out!" I always wanted her to grab me because then I would laugh from deep down in my tummy. My laugh came out loud. It was fun to watch Charlie and my sisters get scared and laugh, too.

Sometimes Dad would come home and ruin my happy thoughts as I lay in bed with Debbie after story time, waking us with his "real" scary voice yelling at Mom downstairs. "Laurin, please, our kids," Mom would say, and that made him scream more before going outside with his gun. Then we would hear the gunshots. He did it to scare Mom. That's what Mom said. I would cuddle closer to Debbie and wait for it to be over.

After one of his episodes, I asked Dad when he was normal again, "Why did you shoot your gun out there in those scary woods?" He looked puzzled. "I didn't shoot my gun last night, Swede. You have quite an imagination, don't you?" But I knew he shot it.

Aunt Jan came to stay with us several times when Dad was away to help Mom, who was so pregnant she looked as though she would pop. Mom was always happy when her sister was there, and it was the only time that she really laughed. They slept with hammers for some reason. I knew Mom was afraid to be left alone with us kids, but I didn't think anybody would come all the way out in The Boondocks to hurt us. I was hoping Mom and Aunt Jan weren't planning to hurt Dad with those things.

I knew Mom was afraid of Dad at times, like when we were all sitting quietly and watching our favorite television shows and he would sneak up by the window and drop an armful of boards, making it sound like a gunshot. We would all jump and poor Mom would scream. Dad never let Mom or any of us relax and have a quiet moment for long – unless I went to room #3, or to My Blondie to sit quietly for some private time by myself. Mom was always jumpy when Dad was around. She didn't have a special place for herself. I was sure lucky to have My Blondie.

The only time I wet the bed was when Dad had crazy eyes and used his scary voice at night, but I didn't do it by accident. I never wet my own bed, either. I wet Debbie's bed in room #2. I was afraid to go downstairs to use the bathroom during those scary nights, so I would snuggle up next to Debbie as close as possible and wet her side. The next morning I asked in surprise, "Deb, why did you wet your bed?" She believed that she did it until Laurie became suspicious and tricked me with some Good & Plenty candy that Aunt/Cousin Billie Anne gave her. Billie Anne was a year older than Laurie and very spoiled; she got everything. We didn't get much food, let alone candy, and I was surprised that Laurie even had a box.

Laurie and Debbie confronted me in room #3. "Kimmie, have you been wetting Debbie's bed?" Laurie asked. I turned bright red and my cheeks felt like they were on fire but I said, "NO!" Then Laurie said while shaking the box of candy, "I'll give you this box of Good & Plenty's if you tell us the truth."

"OK, I did it," I declared. Debbie was really mad and Laurie didn't give me the box of Good & Plenty's, either. I told Blondie about that mean trick.

Debbie still let me sleep with her when I was scared, though, and she even held my hand and led me downstairs to the bathroom on those scary nights. I loved Debbie more than ever. She was so brave.

Charlie, Debbie, Laurie, Bradley and me

During that frightening time, my brother Bradley was born. Just like Charlie and me, he was a fat baby, and just like me he was all Swede. I felt sorry for Bradley. He was the baby of the family, but by the time he came along, Dad was really sick and Mom was burned out. She was only 19 when she had Laurie, and Bradley was her sixth baby in nine years. Even though he was the most beautiful of all their children, he didn't get the attention he deserved. I thought he was more beautiful than the "Gerber Baby" and I tried to make up for the neglect by holding and feeding him and showing him some special tricks, but later even I ignored Bradley as I tried to fend for myself. There was a lot going on – nothing was ever normal, nor did things move along smoothly for long. Mom said, "We live a schizophrenic life because that's what you do when you live with a lunatic."

Dad wasn't always a lunatic, though. There were times when he was a good father, and even read from his Bible. One afternoon, in late autumn, I was feeling blue after a big fight with Debbie. The leaves were golden yellow and apple red with the sun shining low in the sky when I found Dad sitting on the dilapidated front steps of our old prostitute house. I scooched as close as I could, right next to him, hoping Debbie would walk by and be jealous. "What're you doing, Dad?" I asked.

"I'm reading Romans 5: 3-4," he said. Then he put his arm around me and explained, "We rejoice in our sufferings because we know that suffering produces perseverance; perseverance character; and character hope."

"That's *really* silly," I giggled. "*Why* would I rejoice from suffering?"

He grabbed me and started tickling me until I laughed from deep down in my belly. "Because suffering will make you my *tough little Swede*," he said.

"And... with... *hope*," I squealed between my laughter.

"With hope," he chuckled. Then he tickled me more and laughed from deep within his belly, too.

That winter, when Dad went away for what seemed to be a long while, Debbie and I realized that Blondie hadn't been fed for several days. I was worried about her being hungry and miserable, and told Debbie, "We should feed her ourselves." We didn't realize that we gave her rabbit grain. Blondie loved to overeat, and by the time we fed her she was so hungry she overstuffed herself. Laurie said she popped.

We should have waited just a little longer. Dad came home that night. He took one look at my cow and said, "Blondie's suffering and needs to be put out of her misery." I cried and begged him, "Please don't hurt her. Don't shoot her." Dad had tears in his eyes when he said, "Don't worry Swede, she'll be much happier and everything will be peaceful in her New World." Debbie said, "Kimmie, Blondie will be in Jehovah's New World with us when she's resurrected from the dead. Then we'll be happy and live together in a perfect paradise, with all the food we want!"

Then Dad took his gun and Blondie into the scary woods.

The next morning we went to see what really happened to Blondie. Laurie was right – she popped, split right open. I cried and cried over what I'd done, and over losing my best friend ever. I hated those woods, and I had nightmares for years.

We often left the dinner table hungry, but one night we sat down at the table and could hardly wait for Dad to finish the prayer. The table was loaded with more food than we had seen in a long time, and the smell of the delicious meal promised the first full stomachs in a long time.

"This is the best dinner ever!" I told Mom, and we all thanked her as we ate our fill. We noticed that she looked sad and tired, and didn't seem to be enjoying her meal. I whispered to Debbie, "She must be having morning sickness again," even though it was night.

We finished eating, laughing and joking and feeling happier and more satisfied than we had in months.

Finally, we asked to be excused. While everyone was getting up from the table, Laurie said, "You know that we just ate Blondie for dinner, don't you?"

"You're lying! You're mean and you are lying!"

I was horrified, looking into her eyes for the signs that she was lying. There weren't any.

"Mom had her in the freezer for months and finally decided to cook her for dinner," Laurie said.

I ran to my room, crying into my comfort blanket, feeling sick to my stomach. I felt so bad about killing My Blondie, *and now ... I ate her.*

That was Laurie. She was the first of the Jeffries/Seelye offspring and so special to my parents that they named her Laurie Helen Laurine Francis Seelye, after my father Laurin and both grandmothers. She was the center of their attention and loved it. She was very spoiled and could make our lives miserable. Laurie was beautiful, tall and thin with dark blond hair, and she had my father's eyes. Those eyes scared me. She had the look of someone who is about to do something really crazy. Laurie was smart and manipulative; I was afraid of her, yet I wanted her approval and for some reason needed to please her. It wasn't just me. She had some kind of power over all of us.

I cried and cried into my comfort blanket. Then Dad came in to room #3. "Don't feel bad, Swede. Blondie would've wanted us to have her for dinner. She knew we were hungry." Then he held me tight and rubbed my back while we talked about all of the special things Blondie used to do and then I felt better, knowing Blondie was in the New World frolicking in the fields with all the other cows and happy that we'd had a good dinner.

Dad stayed around more after My Blondie died. When he was taking care of himself and staying home, we had a good life and went to Jehovah's Witness meetings. We had a really good few months after Bradley was born, and even though we were hungry at times we were always clean and cared for. Mom kept the house clean and tidy and cooked great dinners even when she didn't have much food to work with.

We'd had some tough times, but I knew that Mom and Dad loved us and would always be there for us. I knew Dad would never make us sad or hurt us when he was normal. I knew it. I just knew it.

Then one day, just after my 7th birthday, Dad was working on the old prostitute house and sent us to my grandparents to borrow a paint sprayer ... our house burned to the ground ... my blanket was gone ... Debbie's useless turtle was dead.

Soon after the fire, Grandma Helen was going through her photo album to give Mom some of her favorite pictures. "It's a crying shame that Laurin burned down the house," she said while sorting.

"Did Dad really burn our house down?" I asked Mom later.

"Yes, Kimmie, he did."

"Why would he do that?"

"I don't know. I just don't know."

Mom was looking off into the distance. She looked worried. I wasn't so worried. Everything was gone, but I had Mom and Dad and all my brothers and sisters. As long as we were all together, everything would be OK.

chapter 2

Uncle/Grandpa Harold and Grandma Helen didn't have much money and couldn't take care of us. But they also didn't know how bad off we were. Dad always pretended that things were fine and wouldn't let Mom tell the truth, either. Dad could lie very well. Maybe that's where Debbie learned it. Dad would rather have us starve to death than let any of his family know he wasn't taking care of us.

When the Jehovah's Witnesses stepped in, Uncle/Grandpa Harold and Grandma Helen were relieved, even though they didn't approve of Mom and Dad belonging to the church. Mom was a devoted Jehovah's Witness at the time, and on his good days Dad tried to be. We went to meetings at the Kingdom Hall three times a week and Bible study at least once. The Jehovah's Witnesses were Mom's only friends. I remember Grandma Helen and Mom arguing over the religion many times. Grandma Helen told Mom, "It's not right, keeping your kids from celebrating any of the holidays or enjoying their birthdays. They deserve to grow up like other kids."

But we would've been in a lot of trouble without the church people then. They came to our rescue, and moved us into an old house they rented, fixed up and cleaned. They made curtains, brought furniture, found us clothes and fed us for months after the fire.

Grandma Helen was a kind woman. I loved her almost as much as I loved Mom. She said funny things and made everyone laugh even when she wasn't trying to be funny. She got her metaphors, clichés and idioms mixed up all the time, and passed that down to Mom and me, just like my Swedish great-grandmother passed it down to her. I say the wrong things all the time, like: "I'm as pleased as a big pie," "That cakes the top," and "My muscles are tighter than a doorknob." It gets worse when I'm around them. Grandma Helen was innocent and very proper, but tried to swear every once in a while like all of Uncle/Grandpa Harold and

Dad's family. She would get flustered and come up with watered-down swear phrases ("You can shove that in your deep dark place") and everyone would laugh. I picked some of those up, too, like "you are the ass of all asses in the stink weeds."

Grandma Helen was 5'4" and thin, with dark hair, and her deep-blue eyes were gentle. She chuckled a lot and made everyone feel at home. She always knew what I was thinking and what I was up to. She would smile and say, "Kimmie, you're going to be something special some day. I feel it. With all that bottled-up energy and your kind heart, you're going to go a long way."

Except for being much bigger than Dad, Uncle/Grandpa Harold could have been his twin, dark and handsome with thick black hair. He was upbeat, but acted nervous and talked so fast he almost stuttered over his own words, trying to get everything he wanted to say out as fast as he could. Even during the bad times he laughed a lot, and I felt comforted when I was near him. Still, his hazel eyes were sad and haunted. It seemed as if he could look right through me and into something that was troubling him. I always wondered if he was sad because he fought in World War II, and one time I asked him about it. He told me, "No, Swede, it's something more disturbing than that and I hope you never have to fight through your demons like I do. Be happy and try very hard to understand that you're not to blame for any of this craziness in our family."

Maybe he was thinking about the cold winter night when he and Dad were little, and Dad was late getting to bed after using the outhouse. Their father, Pa Seelye, whipped Dad, dragged him outside, and made him sit in the outhouse all night. Things like that happened all the time.

They were still happening. Pa Seelye always tricked us into coming into his garage apartment behind Uncle/Grandpa Harold and Grandma Helen's house when he was there alone. He would ask me through the open window, "Swede, do you want some chewing gum?" Pa was weak with emphysema, so I wasn't afraid of him. I always went in. "Do you want to sit on my lap?" he would ask, showing me the chewing gum. I would get closer and closer, and then quickly grab the gum before running out like a blazing bullet. He tried to trick all of us, but I tricked him.

My younger cousin sat on his lap and he molested her. She cried and told me what happened. Being only 7, I wasn't quite sure what that meant but Mom told me, "It's when old people do inappropriate things to kids." So, I told on him.

"Swede, don't you ever go back into that garage again, do you hear me? None of my grandchildren are allowed in there!" said Uncle/Grandpa Harold in a loud voice. Grandma Helen was behind him, tapping her long red fingernails on the kitchen counter, and clicking her tongue as she always did when she was unhappy about something. Pa Seelye had tried to molest most of Uncle/Grandpa Harold's daughters when they were still living at home, and even Grandma Helen's daughter, Aunt Jan.

No one ever confronted Pa Seelye and after having power over the family for so many years, he still frightened them.

Dad continued to do strange things, even after starting fresh in the Jehovah's Witness house. He was becoming more nervous about people and things around him, and was in and out of the hospital with the mesh windows. He thought his friends and especially Mom were plotting against him.

Dad often went to the tavern across the field from our Jehovah's Witness house and sometimes didn't come home for days. He found a Muckleshoot Indian woman who was good company during his crazed times. She drank with him and then took him home with her, keeping him there for days at a time. Sometimes he would shoot up heroin or any other drug to keep from feeling the pain in his body and in his heart. I knew he grieved for Timmy and his five brothers because I heard him cry to Mom about it.

When Dad did come home from the tavern, he would accuse Mom of ridiculous things. Sometimes he hit her. Sometimes he carried on about "somebody" following him home through the field. The scary look in his eyes was all it took for me to tighten up. I couldn't breathe, and wanted to run away before he did something bad.

We never knew whom Dad might bring home from the tavern. Once he brought some Indian friends. They looked shy and embarrassed, and I wasn't afraid of them because I was Dad's tough little Swede with high hopes. Dad called Mom a worthless Jezebel, and Mom threw a big potted plant. The plant hit one of them and dirt flew everywhere. "Get out of here and take your drunken friends with you! Don't ever bring these people back here again!" Dad looked shocked and destroyed. He was trying to be the boss of her, but Mom stood up for herself and embarrassed him in front of his friends. His mother had never done that. He left, and we didn't see him for many days.

When Dad was normal, he would never have acted that way. He had a soft heart and wouldn't hurt a single fly. But he wasn't normal much anymore.

Mom received one of Dad's hospital reports just before we moved into the Jehovah's Witness house:

February 2, 1964
Patient's name: Seelye, Laurin A.
Requested by Dr. Krishnamoorti because of wasting etc. in lower limbs

This patient was born in Motte, North Dakota on May 22, 1925, one of twins and the eighth in a family of twelve boys and three girls. He was born and raised on a farm. He attended rural schools in North Dakota and later in Montana where he quit school at the age of 16 after completing grade six. He gives the reason for quitting school: There was so much farm work to be done that he missed a good deal of school and by the time he completed grade six, he was much too big for the rest of the pupils in the class. He thought that at that age he should have been through High School and was much too embarrassed to continue his studies in grade school where he got along well. He came to Washington State four years ago from California and during the past few years he has been working for a lumber company in Enumclaw. He tells me that he was married ten years ago and has a wife and seven children. He injured his back two years ago for which he was hospitalized four days at Enumclaw, then to Cabrini Hospital in Seattle where he had three different admissions under the service of Dr. Lawrence Knopp. He was told that he had a "slipped disc" although he is unable to give me convincing evidence of root pain. He relates that he had a myelogram done at Cabrini where he was kept in traction for varying periods. He has been drawing around 300 plus per month disability compensation. He has done a good deal of drinking including beer, whiskey and wine for a number of years, and this to excess during the past two. He relates that since he has not been working, because of the back injury, he has nothing much to occupy his time other than visiting local taverns. He also informs me that he joined a crowd of morphine addicts in the Enumclaw area and was using a needle periodically in addition to frequenting taverns. Either his wife kicked him out or he voluntarily separated, one can not be sure. In any event he has been separated from his family for several months and claims that reconciliation has recently been affected.

He informs me that he has had a total of about four years in the Merchant Marines, that he enlisted in the Army but when they saw the state of his lower extremities he was promptly kicked out.

He alleges that three of his brothers committed suicide, one was killed in a car accident and another Brother drowned while fishing. He tells me that he entered our hospital in order to get himself straightened out so that he could get off the booze, earn a living and support his family - who are presently existing on ADC.

Attitude & General Behavior: Patient is cooperative and tidy

Stream of Speech & Mental Activity: Is able to give good account of himself. Does not show any thinking disorder

Emotional Reaction: Depression, Affect is appropriate

Mental Trend-Content of Thought: Patient denies any delusions or hallucinations but admits to having had suicidal thoughts, feels he shouldn't have been taking these dopes or alcohol and he has neglected his family. He desires help.

Summary:

This 38-year-old married male was admitted voluntarily for depression and was recommended to enter hospital for treatment of his addiction. He went to the hospital many times after to receive hypos and after that he was addicted to Morphine, Darvon, and blockbusters. He was spending a lot of money on them. He was depriving his family of food and they were also constantly fighting. His wife spent most of her time on religious projects. Patient states this was a friction at home. Patient became quite depressed and felt sorry for himself. He attempted suicide as a threat to his wife when he took half a bottle of morphine, some sleeping pills and aspirin. He drove his car to the mountains in an attempt at suicide. She saw him taking the pills and sent patrol officers after him. He was taken to the hospital and when released he used this as a threat to his wife. Recently he said he had another fight with his wife and then he left for California. When he was in California he fell down and was hospitalized. He was told he had some kind of a disease in his legs and he was advised to come to this hospital.

Impression: 1. Depressive reaction – 2 Organic brain syndrome, associated with muscular waste of both legs - CMT - (Charcot-Tooth Syndrome)

Physical summary: Wasting of both calf muscles and weakness of the extensor and flexor at left knee more marked than the right ~

Mom had received similar reports but didn't pay much attention to them, so nobody really knew what was going on.

I always knew Dad was an intelligent man by observing and listening to Mom talking with our Jehovah's Witness friends. Despite his lack of schooling, Dad could figure things out that others struggled with. "He was very smart, and manipulative in many ways," Mom said. For instance, Mom tried several times to have him committed to the psychiatric ward, but he always beat her to it. He figured out that if he committed himself, he was able to obtain a release when he wanted.

～

Life was tough while living in the Jehovah's Witness house. Soon after we moved in, Dad started his own carpentry business in our garage and was one of the best carpenters around because he wasn't happy until each cabinet was perfect. He had plenty of work, but Mom said he was too nice to be a good businessman. I heard them fighting a lot about it. "You need to charge people more," Mom would insist, her voice rising. Dad would shake his head. "I could never do that." Then Mom would yell, "You care more about strangers than your own starving family!"

It really didn't matter. Not long after that Dad couldn't work at all anymore. He ran away with the $300 disability check that began arriving in the mail, spending it on drugs and alcohol and leaving us with no money.

Sometimes we had no food. We didn't have to worry about having enough clothes, though. Laurie would give us her hand-me-downs when she was finished with the ones Aunt/Cousin Billie Anne gave her. We were set!

During the breaks at the meetings in the Kingdom Hall, some of the kids made fun of us for having old clothes and funny haircuts, and repeated things they had heard about our father being crazy. Sometimes I took those little girls with the shiny shoes, wearing pretty dresses and nice long hair in ribbons, out back one at a time and spanked them. Then, I warned them in my tough voice, "If you tell on me, my big sister and her friends will spank you even harder next time." They knew Laurie and how mean she could be. Some of those girls were bigger, but they were afraid of me and learned a good lesson about picking on poor kids.

I struggled through second grade during that year in our new home. Unless I was defending myself, or my family, I was so shy I couldn't talk to anybody without blushing and wishing I were somewhere else. I watched the clock, wanting to get out of there as soon as the bell rang. The kids made fun of me for being different. It felt as if they were always picking on me.

On Picture Day, Debbie and I wanted to impress our classmates. Debbie cut my hair. Actually, she chopped my hair off. Mom had to fix it up by cutting it extremely short, in what she called a "pixie" style. Then we made some makeup by crushing old bricks into powder. Debbie made little hair bows out of toilet paper.

When we got to school, Debbie bobby pinned her toilet-paper bows into her hair, and I put the brick powder on my face. I walked into my class-room as proud as could be with my orange face, along with my drastic new "pixie" haircut. The entire class started laughing hysterically. It seemed like that moment lasted forever. I cried, and the white streaks from the tears running down my orange face made the class laugh even more. My teacher took me out of the classroom and washed the brick powder from my face and tried to fix my hair so it wouldn't stick out everywhere.

Debbie had her picture taken with the toilet paper in her hair. I won-dered why she didn't put the brick powder on her face like me.

Along with everything else they did for us, the Jehovah's Witnesses gave us some really nice toys. My favorite was a baby doll and I spent most of my time pretending I was a mother, playing house with my sis-ters and cousins. Baby Doll's mouth had an opening for a bottle, so I used to feed her my brother's baby food and give her real milk. After a while, she didn't smell very good and nobody wanted Baby Doll near them. I tried to wash her but I couldn't get rid of the odor. Whenever I ventured too close to anyone in the family with Baby Doll, they would yell, "Get out of here, and take your stinky doll with you."

My dream when I played with Baby Doll was to grow up and have a nice husband who didn't yell or turn crazy, and who would take good care of my baby and me. My dream included making big meals with meat every night and a big pot of mashed potatoes with gravy. Then we would have pie or cake with ice cream for dessert. I would act it all out so I would be ready when I grew up.

We had "grown up" dolls, too. Laurie had a Barbie doll and Debbie had the brunette Midge. I was stuck with the Midge doll with red hair. I didn't like Midge's hair, so I cut it like mine into a pixie. You couldn't feed her, though.

Debbie and her big feet, me with my crooked toe and
my Midge doll before our pixie-cuts

Mom took care of us the best she could, but she seemed sad. Dad was away most of the time by then. Sometimes when I thought he was away again, he was actually home all the while. He would lock himself in his room with the shades down and stay there for days with migraines. Later, days turned into weeks. Mom would make us keep quiet, but we didn't know why. Maybe she didn't want to worry us or maybe she thought it didn't matter. Either way, he wasn't around.

One time when Dad came out of the bedroom after a bad migraine, I screamed. "Why is Dad's mouth purple?"

"It's OK, Kimmie," Mom explained. "It's purple medicine."

Dad had pyorrhea, which made his gums painful. He had to apply an antibacterial and antifungal cream called gentian violet. "Your dad and his family never went to the dentist or took care of their teeth when they were children, and now he's forced to make up for it." Still upset, I asked, "We don't go to the dentist. Will this happen to us?"

"No, no, you're clean and tidy and always brush your teeth. You'll be fine."

I washed my face and brushed my teeth extra after that. "I don't want purple teeth when I get old," I told Debbie.

As the year went on, Mom became so desperate to feed us that she broke down and sought help from the welfare department. They gave us what we called "free boxes of food." I was happy to have anything. There were times I hid behind the couch to eat dog food.

Uncle/Grandpa Harold once caught me eating cattle grain in the barn while we were visiting. He scolded me. "Swede, why in the world would you eat cattle grain?"

"It's really good," I told him, "especially the corn pieces. The hard kernels taste just like licorice."

I couldn't tell him the other reason – that I was starving and we didn't have any food at home. He left the barn, shaking his head. Then, I ate some more.

Grandma Helen would make Swedish coffee rolls and enjoy coffee with the women while the men were out on the farm talking and taking care of things. Sometimes I would take a baking pan of rolls, hide behind the couch and eat them. All of them. There were 24 rolls in a pan. Grandma Helen didn't yell at me. Instead, she would smile when I came back with the empty pan and ask, "How were my rolls, Kimmie?" I wondered if she knew I ate the whole batch because we didn't have any food at home and I didn't know when my next chance would be.

With the free box of food, we had either Cream of Wheat or Roman Meal for breakfast almost every morning, along with powdered milk. For lunch we had canned tuna so cheap that it still had the bones in it. The bones were soft enough that we could chew them, but just barely. If we didn't have any more tuna with bones left, Mom would make us grilled cheese sandwiches out of a big log of processed cheese.

Grandma Helen said I was a sweet and happy baby with "rolls and rolls" of fat down my legs and from the time I was born, weighing nine pounds, I've always needed more food than almost everyone else.

I loved going to my grandparents' house more than anything. There was plenty to eat, plus my cousins came over and we would play war, tag and red rover. I was always the weak link in red rover. Anyone could bust through my arm, even if I was holding the hand of a strong cousin/uncle in his early teens. When the other team called, "red rover, red rover, send Kimmie on over," I went barreling across the yard, head down, and with all my might tried to break through the arms of the weakest people on their team, only to make contact and fly backward, inevitably landing on my backside. I didn't like landing on my backside, but I liked the fast running.

Those were the happiest times for us kids. Our parents were inside, mostly playing poker, smoking and drinking. Sometimes a fight would break out. But we didn't care because we were outside, together, having fun away from the unhappy adults.

When we were leaving their farm to go home one night, Grandma Helen gave Mom a big meaty bone for our dogs, Tippie and Mittsie. They were the two cutest dogs in the world, fluffy Samoyeds with yellow fur. They had pointed ears and big brown eyes, and were always wagging their tails and happy to see us. Tippie had a white tip on her tail, and Mittsie had little white paws, like mittens.

Mom cooked the meaty bone and made stew for us the next day because we were out of food again. I felt bad for Tippie and Mittsie because they missed out on their treat. Later that month, Mittsie was run over by a car right in front of our house. We cried and cried. I wished she could have enjoyed her meaty bone before she died.

When Dad came out of the bedroom after being in there for days, he was worn out. But when he came home from really being away, his eyes were crazed and things would turn frightful for all of us.

I had a secret hiding place behind our house, a grassy clover patch covered in dandelions, with tons of ladybugs crawling all around. The clean smell of the clover and the beautiful yellow dandelions made me feel good when there was chaos everywhere else around me – the fighting, terrifying threats, and the strange things that were about to happen after Dad walked back from the tavern across the field with his crazed look.

If it was raining or the weather was cold when the scary strange things were about to happen, I would turn on the television and watch cartoons like "The Flintstones" or "Bozo the Clown." Sheriff Taylor on "The Andy Griffith Show" always made me feel better, too. He never did strange things, and Opie always had enough to eat. Sometimes I would pretend I was Opie's sister.

Mom would deal with it all by yelling at us, and the more disturbed and violent Dad was the more she yelled. I had my secret hiding place with the dandelions, or the nice TV families. She had the yelling. That's what her father did to her, so that's what she did to us. With a houseful of kids, a schizophrenic husband, no money, no food and no heat unless the Jehovah's Witnesses paid the bill for us, what else was she supposed to do?

After weeks of being away with drug users or some Muckleshoot woman, Dad would come home and accuse Mom of being a no-good Jezebel. One time, he lined all of us kids up, even Murphy and Lorna, and pulled Mom into the room. He called her terrible names and then started reading from the Bible, screaming out all of her "sins," calling her a Jezebel and telling us what an evil woman she was. Dad even accused Mom of sowing some wild oats with Murphy. I was frightened to death.

Mom said that Dad's first wife was a real Jezebel, embarrassing him by running around town with other men and leaving him to take care of Murphy and Lorna for days at a time. Only I was confused, Dad was accusing Mom of doing all the things that he was out doing, while she was home on her own trying to take care of us. Mom was friendly and beautiful, and men loved to help her out, but she didn't flirt, or at least didn't mean to.

Finally, it all backfired. His good friend Mike used to come over to play cards. Dad would find a reason to leave Mom and Mike alone for a couple of hours, trying to trick them into doing something inappropriate together when he came back. That went on for months.

One day, she left us all with Dad and ran away with Mike.

I watched Dad, hoping he wouldn't get that crazed look. I kept hoping. He tried to do the right thing. "You girls need to be good," he told Debbie and me. "I want to keep you forever and take good care of my kids." We tried, but one day we started fighting like we always did. He came into the room with that look and his belt in his hand, and spanked me until I went numb, wetting my shorts. The humiliation was worse than the beating. Debbie didn't get spanked because Dad broke down and cried. "I'm sorry, Swede ... I'm so sorry." He cried so hard he had to lie down.

I ran to my secret hiding place with the ladybugs and dandelions. I cried and wanted to run away somewhere, but there was no place to go. I was shocked that Dad could do such a thing. I felt destroyed.

Then Dad came to me. I was surprised that he knew about my secret hiding place. He held me tight and sobbed, "I'm so sorry, I'll never hurt you again my little Swede, never again." I was happy to have him there with me enjoying the beautiful dandelions. I felt wanted and loved for the first time I could remember.

As the month went on, Dad was taking good care of us, and we were adjusting while Mom was away. One morning Debbie, Laurie and I were on the back porch playing with our Barbie and Midge dolls. Laurie was being nice, giving Barbie's hand-me-downs to our Midge dolls and sharing her tiny Barbie shoes with us so that Midge could have a new look, but I needed to do something with Midge's bad pixie cut. Suddenly I remembered how good Mom looked when she covered her hair curlers with her beautiful silk scarf with the bright little flowers. If I cut just a tiny corner off that scarf, I could use it for Midge. Mom certainly wouldn't miss just a corner when she came back.

I was so excited to show Laurie and Debbie how great Midge looked that my hands were shaking as I tried to tie her new little scarf around her tiny chin.

We heard a horrific scream. I dropped Midge. All three of us ran toward the scream. Dad was on the floor of the garage. There was blood everywhere.

I stood frozen in my bloody tracks, the sound of blood thundering in my ears, the musty odor in the air, as I watched blood gushing from my father's hand.

Dad was so desperate to get Mom back that he used a power saw to cut off three of his fingers.

"Get a towel," he told Laurie weakly. She rushed to the kitchen, then came back and wrapped his hand in the towel, holding it tight. I think Debbie called the ambulance when Dad started crying; I'm not sure because I felt dizzy and couldn't breathe very well.

"Pick up my fingers, pick up my fingers," Dad said over and over. Everything was spinning, sweat popped out on my brow and I thought I would throw up, but I remember that someone picked up his fingers. I think it was Laurie.

Dad fainted.

The ambulance came and took Dad and his fingers away. The doctors couldn't sew them back on, though. Mom came back home to take care of us. She wasn't mad about her fancy scarf with a missing corner.

—

It is Thursday, February 3, 1966 – several months after Dad cut his fingers off. I am at school. At 1:45 the teacher decides we will start our valentine project early because we had voted to make two valentines, one for each parent, instead of just one valentine. The plan is to draw three hearts on construction paper for each card: a giant heart on red paper; a slightly smaller heart on pink paper; and then a smaller one on white paper. We are to cut out the hearts, then glue the pink heart into the center of the red heart and the white heart into the center of the pink heart.

I leave the classroom. Because I am a Jehovah's Witness, I always have to leave the classroom when there is anything to do with a holiday. As always, I get up and pick out a book from the bookshelf on my way out the door. Some of the nice kids feel sorry for me. "Poor Kimmie, she always has to leave when we finally get to have some fun." Other kids laugh and say mean things.

I walk into the school office and sit in my usual chair. The secretary looks at me but doesn't say anything. I open my book and pretend to read, but I'm not reading. I'm thinking about our class project. If I could make those cards I would make them perfect for my parents. I would paste tiny red hearts all over the pink part of the card, then I would write Mom on one and Dad on the other with glue and then pour those fun colorful sparkles on the glue so their names would come out pretty and shiny on the white heart. I would glue some of that pretty lacy paper around the border of the red heart to make it look even more beautiful. I would make the best cards in the class. I know I would ... if I could.

I look at the clock: 2 o'clock, a half hour until I can go home. I look out the window. It's raining, just like most winter days. I think how nice it will be in a few months, when the sun comes out and makes the flowers grow. I think about how nice it will be when the dandelions and lady-bugs come back to me in my secret hiding place. When it's spring, I will turn 8 years old. I can't wait to be 8 years old. Seven sounds so young, but 8 sounds older and I will be responsible then. Whatever that means. Without thinking I begin to write 8 all over the pages of my book as I daydream. 8 8 8 8 8 8. The office lady yells, "Stop that this instant!" and takes the book from me. I look at the clock. It says 2:10.

Now I have nothing to look at to escape making eye contact with people who walk into the office. The principal walks in and smiles at me but I quickly look to the ground. I wonder why he smiled at me. I didn't do anything funny. I notice my old, tattered shoes are way too big for me. I know they must have looked pretty and shiny when Debbie wore them last year. We are close to the same size everywhere else, but Debbie's feet are huge and mine are average. I'm glad they're too big for me. My toes have some room to spread out so the bigger toes don't step on my crooked toe all at once. It hurts when that happens. I go barefoot all the time except to school and the Kingdom Hall. I can't wait to take my shoes off. I look at the clock. It says 2:20.

I can't wait for the bell to ring at 2:30 so I can get out of this place and onto the bus with Debbie. She will make me feel better after a rough day. I watch the second hand on the clock. Tick, tick, tick. Tick. Tick. Finally the bell rings and I am out of there like a bottle rocket, racing to collect my things and then jumping on the bus. Laurie isn't on the bus because she is going to a friend's house. I am so relieved to see Debbie and really want her to hold my hand, but we can't do that with all of those mean kids around because they'll make fun of us. At least I can sit next to her on our short bus ride, as close as I can.

Bradley and Charlie are too young to go to school, so they are waiting for us. It is good to be home.

Friday, February 4, 1966. I wake up dreading having to go back to school, knowing I will have to spend the afternoon in the office while my classmates work on their fun Valentine's Day project. I wish I could stay home with my brothers, but I can't. I get up, get dressed and sit at the big round table in the kitchen, eating our usual free hot cereal with powdered milk. Damn Ass in the Stink Weeds, it's Roman Meal this time. Why couldn't it be Cream of Wheat? I hate Roman Meal. I know I'm going to hate this day.

Dad walks into the kitchen with hugs and candy. We haven't seen him since he sawed his fingers off and then went to the hospital with the wire mesh on the windows. His hand is still in a bandage and he has that look he gets when he's about to do something crazy. He goes into the hallway to talk with Mom. They fight for a long time and suddenly Mom screams, "Get under the table!"

Mom is struggling with Dad for a gun. Mom rips her hand and thumb on the gun and blood is gushing. They're in the bedroom now. There's a gunshot ... then another one.

The neighbor lady rushes over to help before Mom gets into the ambulance. A little while later Uncle/Grandpa Harold and Grandma Helen come for us. While driving to their house I ask Grandma, "Is Mom OK?" Grandma says Mom is fine. "She just has a bad cut on her hand and needs to have the doctors at the hospital sew it up." I'm relieved. I'm not concerned about the gunshots because we're used to Dad shooting his gun when he looks crazy. He does it all the time. Sometimes out in the yard, other times out the windows while in the house. I don't know why everyone is making such a fuss. Dad hurt Mom all the time, but she's going to be OK.

Debbie and I are sitting on the cushiony couch watching "Tarzan" on Uncle/Grandpa Harold's really nice TV. There's a candy dish on the coffee table. Debbie and I decide to behave, and take only one piece. The next thing I know, we eat all of it – "uh oh Debbie, we're going to be in huge trouble!"

Grandma and Grandpa come into the living room. Grandpa turns the TV off. We're in for it now for eating all the candy. They look as if they've been crying. Grandma sits between Debbie and me on the couch and puts an arm around each of us. "Girls, your dad died today." That's all she said.

My stomach has a giant rock in it. I am being stung by millions of hornets all over my body. Debbie is crying and crying. Grandma Helen holds her and tries to soothe her. I run to Uncle/Grandpa Harold and climb into his arms. He holds me tight in his big oversized chair and rubs my back as I begin to cry. "It will be OK, Swede, it will be OK." Uncle/Grandpa Harold looks so much like Dad that I feel better.

Grandma tells Debbie and me to go lie down on her bed to rest while she makes a late dinner. We sit there in the dark room. Debbie says, "Kimmie, Dad shot himself in the bedroom." I begin to cry again but this time I am wheezing and struggling to breathe. Debbie holds me and rubs my back and sings "Angel Baby," our favorite comfort song. Then she sings her special version just like an angel:

"You're my sweet Angel ... Ohhhh sister dear
I'm so very happy ... whenever you're near
Dad will never leave you ... I know this is true...ue
Ohhhh how I love you ... Dad loves you, too...oo
Angel Kimmie ... my Angel Kimmie ..."
I go to sleep for the rest of the night.

That was the last I heard about my father. No one ever talked about Dad again.

Dad spent so much time away with drug people or in the hospital with the mesh on the windows that I was used to missing him, but he always came back, so I kept hoping he would come home this time, too. And because no one ever told a funny story about Dad at family get-togethers, or ever said they missed him, I thought he might still be alive. We didn't go to any funeral. *Maybe he is just in the hospital again.* Sometimes I thought he might be watching me, so I would show off and try to make him proud.

It kept me going and trying to be good.

Lorna and Murphy moved back with their mother. We never heard from them again.

Mom was disassociated from the Jehovah's Witnesses because of her adultery with Mike, whose wife had been in Mom's Bible study group. Mom wasn't allowed to have any contact with any Jehovah's Witnesses or even speak of Jehovah. Those are the rules. We were outcasts. We lost our only friends, and the only people who had ever been there to help us.

Even Uncle/Grandpa Harold and Mom's own mother, Grandma Helen, were angry and upset with her for making bad choices and leaving Dad for his friend Mike.

We didn't stay in Enumclaw long. We packed up our few belongings and Mike moved us to the Olympic Peninsula, a place he lived as a child, and loved. Mike drove around the Puget Sound and across the Hood Canal in a U-Haul truck and Mom followed, driving the car. The trip only took a few hours, but seemed to be the longest day of my life.

Tippie was carsick. Yohan, our parakeet, made so much noise we had to cover his cage, but he escaped anyway and flew away when Debbie opened the car door at a rest stop. We cried and made a huge fuss because we didn't want to leave him all alone and afraid, but we called for him and called for him and finally we had to leave. I pretended he flew into a car with really nice people who would take good care of him, better than we could. I was sort of wishing I could have flown away with him.

Near the end of our drive, I noticed that Baby Doll was missing. I looked everywhere in the car. Nobody knew where she was. I cried and hoped that someone had just hidden her as a joke. "You still have your Midge doll," Debbie said, trying to make me feel better. I was miserable and afraid of moving to a new place and now I couldn't find my doll.

Later Debbie told me they threw my Baby Doll out. "She smelled so bad, we couldn't stand it any longer."

Chapter 3

At the next rest stop of the trip, I asked Mike, "Where *is* this Port Townsend?"

"Kimmie," he said, looking up to the sky like he was looking toward heaven. "You won't believe it when you see 'this Port Townsend.' It's a chance for a new start, and the most amazing place on earth."

He was right.

When we finally arrived, we were silent. It was like driving into a fairy tale. No, even better. I'd never seen anything so beautiful, even in a picture storybook. Water and trees were everywhere. We could see the snow-capped Olympic Mountains to the west and the Cascade Mountains to the east from across the waterways that surrounded us. Everything was green and clean. I didn't think any place like *this* existed.

As we drove past a courthouse and hotel that looked liked castles and an old clock tower that looked like it had been there forever, it was as if we had taken a step back in time. Block after block we saw beautiful old buildings. We drove past the Crown Zellerbach Paper Mill, past the boat harbors, through the downtown, right along the waterfront and past the ferry dock just as the ferry was pulling out for Whidbey Island.

We drove past the schools we would soon attend, magnificent three-story historic buildings sitting on top of a big hill, right up to a little white house with three small bedrooms, one bathroom, and a tiny kitchen and living room.

It may have been a new world, but it was still the same family.

Mom and Mike took one bedroom. Debbie, Charlie, Bradley and I shared a bedroom crammed with bunk beds and another small bed. As the oldest, Laurie was given her own room. Mom and Mike said she deserved some privacy because she had more responsibilities, like babysitting us when they went out. There were times when we were home alone for many hours of the night. Laurie prepared dinner, put us to bed and made sure we were safe. She would be 11 in August.

Laurie took good care of us that first summer in our new house but would also turn on us in an instant. One time, while we were sharing a bowl of popcorn and watching "Bonanza," she said I could sleep with her in her bed that night. I was so excited, and even though I had a special snack and was watching my favorite TV show, I couldn't wait for bedtime. When I finally climbed into her bed, Laurie growled at me in an evil voice, "Get out of here right now. You smell like popcorn." She screamed, "I hate you!" as she chased me out of the room.

Another time, Mom and Mike were missing $5. "Who took it?" they asked us three girls. We all said we didn't, and Mom sent us to our rooms until someone confessed. Laurie peeked into our room and asked Debbie and me if we wanted to come to her room for some candy. "Do you want some licorice, too?" she asked. Of course we did. Then she said, "One of you needs to go out there and tell Mom and Mike that you stole the money. There's no reason all three of us should suffer." I drew the short straw and went out to confess. I was sent to my room for the rest of the day while Laurie and Debbie were allowed to go out and play.

A few days later, Mom found $5 behind a framed photo on Laurie's dresser.

Laurie, Debbie and me ~ below: Charlie and Bradley ~ 1966

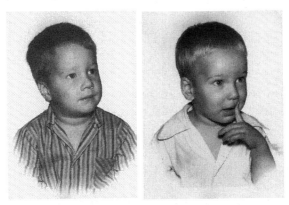

About 5,000 people lived in Port Townsend when we moved there. To grownups, it was a historic Victorian seaport on the northeastern tip of the Olympic Peninsula, a gateway to the region. To me, it was a historic amusement park and the gateway to happiness and a normal life.

We settled into the little white house and explored our new territory. It didn't take us long to find our way to Chetzemoka Park, with swings, a merry-go-round, slides and places to picnic in the grass surrounded by more kinds of trees than I had ever seen. Below the huge park was a beach that we could walk along for a half-mile to go downtown, to the ferry dock and to the boat harbor. Or, we could go the other way for a mile and end up at Fort Worden and the lighthouse at the tip of the peninsula. On the other side of the lighthouse and another mile away was North Beach. All that and we never had to leave the waterfront.

We figured out short cuts from our house to uptown, downtown, to Fort Worden and to North Beach. We discovered beach glass, then found out we could collect it and sell it in jars to the antique dealers. We learned how to find clusters of clams along the beach by spotting clam "shows" in the wet sand. Clam shows look like a dimple or hole in the sand, and sometimes like a donut. We learned how to run over them as they sprayed us with water from the opening of their long necks when they retreated back into the sand. The huge horse clams were the best to run over, spraying high into the air like a small geyser and showering us with seawater as we screamed in delight from the shock of the freezing cold water.

Jehovah's Witnesses called anyone outside the congregation "worldly" and we weren't allowed to socialize with them. Since we weren't Jehovah's Witnesses anymore, we had a lot more time to do things with worldly people. We were set free!

We liked to save our pennies and walk the half mile to Aldrich's, owned by the Aldrich family for many years and the only grocery store uptown. We went straight to the penny candy to buy as much as we could. But we didn't always buy it. Laurie and her new friend taught us how to steal. Sometimes we took our dolls wrapped in blankets into the store, making sure "Old Man Aldrich" wasn't looking from his office window way up above. He could see everything that was going on in the store from up there. We waited and watched. When he stepped away from the window, we would put ice cream bars, candy and little toys into our doll blankets. It was way too easy. We were so good at it that Laurie and her friend talked us into stealing cigarettes. Not just a few packs, but cartons of them.

One day Laurie decided that we older kids should have a picnic at the beach in Chetzemoka Park. Laurie said, "Kimmie, you're in charge of the hotdog buns and potato chips." Laurie took the big job of stealing the hotdogs because they were in the meat department and just below Mr. Aldrich's window. She told Debbie, "You're in charge of the condiments" and told her friend Deb, "You steal the beans and cookies." We all fulfilled our assigned tasks, and then went to the beach to have our picnic and play in the water. Mostly, though, we tried to be cool by smoking cigarettes and skipping rocks through the waves. I couldn't smoke because it hurt my lungs and it made me cough. I felt like I was going to pass out. But I could hold a lit cigarette, put it close to my lips and pretend. We did that a lot.

We made a clubhouse in an old barn across from our little white house. It was used to store nice antique furniture. Most of it was closed up, but there was a small window we could crawl through. We painted the walls with some paint we found in the barn, uncovered the furniture that we wanted to use, and then decorated the place. It was dark in there with the windows boarded up, so we added candles. We decided to stash the candy, cigarettes and snacks galore from Aldrich's in the clubhouse. We were set. Or so we thought.

Mike was a heavy smoker, and one weekend he ran out of cigarettes. We knew we could help him out, and we wanted so much for him to like us. So Debbie and I ran over to our clubhouse and brought back whole cartons of several different brands so he could choose his favorite. "Here Mike, you can have whatever you need," we said proudly.

Sitting up quickly in his recliner, Mike's eyes got big. Then he smiled. "Why," he asked, "do you have so many cigarettes?"

Debbie and I looked at each other. Now our eyes were big. We waited for each other to tell a lie. We couldn't. He tricked us by acting so nice.

"We are thieves," we both said at the same time. Just like the thieves we'd read about in the Bible.

I was spanked first. Mike used a belt, just like our dad. Worse, getting spanked made me laugh, even if it hurt a lot. I often laughed when I was feeling uncomfortable, and at the worst possible times. After Mike finished spanking Debbie, we ran into our room and I couldn't stop laughing. So Mike had to give me another one, even harder. It worked out much better for me if Debbie went first; then she would get the worst of it. I hated waiting my turn, though – I couldn't win.

Mike and Mom marched us down to the police station and made us tell the coppers what we'd done. "We were thieves," we admitted. After that, we had to go way up into Old Man Aldrich's office. My cheeks were bright red. "We've been taking cigarettes from your store," I said. "We are bad thieves." Mr. Aldrich scolded us and looked at us really mean. Mom gave him $20 that we couldn't afford, to cover all the cigarettes we stole, along with everything else they suspected we took. It wasn't even close to being enough. Old Man Aldrich knew that, I bet, but he didn't ask for any more.

I always wondered if Mike smoked any of those cigarettes, though, before we went back to the store. *He'd really wanted a cigarette before this all started.*

We had so much fun in that barn. We ended up burning it down when one of us left a candle burning. It was a shame. The owners never found out we'd made it our clubhouse or set the fire. Instead they blamed our neighbors, a family with even less money and more kids than we had. They were the most-worldly kids I had ever met. Their clothes were dirty, they smelled awful, and worst of all – they were mean. They lived in a huge Victorian home that was falling apart. Unfortunately, their yard was a shortcut to Aldrich's and we couldn't resist taking it. They would yell at us, calling us filth and spastic, using swear phrases that I didn't even know. Then they would sic their wild dogs on us. We had to sprint through that big old yard as fast as we could. When I was alone, I would take the long way around and I didn't care if it took 10 more minutes.

The older kids in our family weren't the only ones to have adventures that summer. One night Mom got a call from the manager of the Safeway downtown. He asked if she had 3-year-old and 5-year-old boys. "Yes," said Mom.

"They're in my store eating ice cream from the cartons."

Safeway was all the way downtown, almost two miles from our house, and the only way to get there was to walk down a huge hill from uptown. I guess my little brothers paid attention when we took them down there without permission, and snuck out on their own. Bradley was wearing his white underwear and T-shirt with no socks and cowboy boots that were two sizes too big for him – on the wrong feet. Charlie was barefoot and in his pajamas. They just walked out the door, straight downtown, into Safeway, up to the ice cream section and started eating. They were too young to get in real trouble, but they cried when the Safeway manager caught them and cried again when Mom and Mike spoke to them after the coppers brought them home. Then they had to go straight to bed, but it was way past their bedtime anyway.

Soon after we moved in we made friends with our neighbors, the Levels. Betty Level was in the process of getting a divorce from Al, who lived a half mile down the street. She and their six kids – Kathleen, J.D., Duke, Sarah, Mary and Pippi – lived in a small house identical to ours. We shared the same yard and played on their swing set. Most of them had blond or red hair and freckles, and they were all close to our ages. Sarah was a few years younger than I was, but quickly became my best friend. Their little sister Mary not only copied everything we did, she followed us everywhere, and worse – she and Pippi, the youngest, ran around naked, chasing us. We would run away screaming, and they would end up having the swing set all to themselves. Maybe that was their plan.

Kathleen was the oldest and did things with Debbie, Sarah, J.D., Duke and me. Laurie wanted nothing to do with us after becoming popular and making her own friends. My brothers were so young they couldn't leave the yard except when Mom made us take them along when we went anyplace important, which would have ruined everything except we could usually persuade them to stay and play with the little naked girls while we went off on our own.

Betty always offered to watch the younger kids while we went off for our adventures, knowing they would cramp our style. She was the kind of mother who let kids make butter and sugar sandwiches and didn't mind having crumbs on her floors. Mom wasn't happy with her one time when she helped Debbie and me clean our room so we could go to the beach. She showed us how to sweep all the toys under the bed and put all the clean clothes into the laundry hamper rather than waste time folding them and putting them into drawers. I didn't like just hiding the mess, but we were in a hurry. That wasn't so good for Mom, who had to wash all of our clothes and bedding in one of those laundry tubs with the hand wringer and then hang everything out on the clothesline.

We usually made our way to Fort Worden beach, my favorite place in the summer. We couldn't really swim for long, because the water stays around 50 degrees all year, so we would jump off a gigantic dock shaped like a "U" and swim to shore as fast as we could. As if the high dock wasn't high enough, I would climb up what looked like an old crane attached to the end of the dock and jump off when someone bet me I couldn't do it. I had to jump between two jagged, broken-off poles standing upright in the water. Mike yelled at me a couple of times from out in his fishing boat when he saw me, but I could see his fishing buddies smiling. I think they were impressed.

We also caught jellyfish with sticks and then set them out on the lower dock to dry out and melt. Kathleen once accidentally sat on one of the stinging jellyfish. She cried in pain and her butt swelled up and broke out in welts. That time we were lucky that Mike was fishing near the beach. We called him in for help. Kathleen was fine after a few days, but we were told not to catch jellyfish anymore.

The Levels had a bike that didn't work and we had a bike with many missing parts. We decided to put the two bikes together and make one working bike. Our parents were out again and Laurie was in charge. Even she helped work on the bike, and together we all did a pretty good job. Problem was, we all wanted to be the first to ride it.

While everyone was arguing, I jumped on the bike, pedaling as fast as I could before anyone realized what was going on. Ha! When they did, they started chasing me. I pedaled down a steep hill toward a busy street. But we'd forgotten to fix one thing: the brakes. I rode right out into the street and hit a car. I flew off the bike and into the air as high as the telephone lines before I hit the ground and landed on my knee. I couldn't bend it.

An ambulance came and took me to the only hospital in Port Townsend. Mom and Mike soon arrived and were angry about our stupid idea of putting the two bikes together, but even angrier that I was taken to the hospital in the ambulance. We didn't have any health insurance.

The doctor was concerned about my knee and wanted to do some tests, but Mom told him I would be fine and took me home. I walked around all summer with a stiff leg. I couldn't bend it at all and everyone laughed, calling me "peg leg." It's funny, but I didn't think twice about not being able to bend my leg, and just figured it would always be that way. I adjusted and learned how to play and do everything with my peg leg.

Life may have been more fun in Port Townsend than it was in Enumclaw but we still ended up back on welfare food. In the mornings we had hot cereal, and for lunch we were back to having tuna with bones in it and the big block of cheese. It was a treat when Mom let us have cold cereal, usually puffed wheat or puffed rice, on Saturday mornings while we watched cartoons.

Mr. Level — we called him Al — wanted to get back together with Betty, so he went over on the weekends and made his family the best breakfasts and lunches. I was always still hungry so after my breakfast I would go sit on their picnic table and wait for Sarah to come out to play. I timed it so they were all just about ready to sit down at the kitchen table, where they could see me from the window. They always invited me in to eat.

In the fall, I started third grade. I wasn't sure about going to school in Port Townsend. I was always afraid of doing something wrong and was the perfect target for kids to make fun of. It certainly didn't help gimping around on my peg leg – I hated looking like a fool. Whenever anybody noticed me, I would turn red and my cheeks would get so hot they might as well have been on fire. The more I was determined to stop it, the redder and hotter they would get. To make matters worse, I had a small space between my front teeth, so I whistled when I tried to pronounce any word starting with "thr." I hated answering questions in class. It was bad enough that I would turn red as soon as my classmates looked at me, but if I had to use a "thr" word to answer a question it was a nightmare.

Mrs. Morton was my first teacher in Port Townsend. She was an older lady with a very rough voice. I was afraid of her and didn't want her to even notice me. I *really* didn't want her to talk to me.

A few months after school started, she asked me to answer a math question. The answer, to my horror, was "thirty three." I told her, "no."

She insisted.

"I don't know."

"Look at the problem and figure it out while I stand here to help you."

She wasn't going to move until I answered it correctly. By then everyone in the classroom was watching. My cheeks were on fire. I finally answered "thirty three" with two big whistles. Everyone laughed. I thought Mrs. Morton was the meanest teacher ever and I never wanted to go back to school again.

The next day I pretended to be sick. I did that for two more days before Mom caught on and made me go back. But instead of going to school, I hid in the sticker bushes near our house until everyone was gone, and then went to play on the beach until school was out. I loved going to the beach by myself because it was the only "alone" time I had. After leaving the dandelion patch and ladybugs in Enumclaw, it was my new secret place. I did that for a few more days.

Then one morning, Tippie followed me to the sticker bushes. Her tail was wagging and she was barking. I managed to get her to stop barking but she wouldn't leave. Mom looked out and saw Tippie wagging her tail and my hand coming from the bushes, pushing her away.

Mom knew I wouldn't skip school for so many days without a good reason. She came with me the next day and told Mrs. Morton, "I'm concerned that Kimmie won't tell me why she's skipping school." Mrs. Morton smiled. "I have a good idea why," she said. "I had throat cancer and my voice is very coarse. I think it frightens her." She also told Mom about the "thirty three." Then Mrs. Morton took me aside and talked to me for a long time. "You're one of my favorite students and I want you to be happy." She went out of her way to make me feel special and never made me answer out loud again unless I raised my hand, which I never did. After that, she was my favorite teacher ever and I wanted to go to school every day.

Mike and Mom ~ 1967

From the time Mom was banished from the Jehovah's Witnesses, she and Mike were drinking a lot more. They would go out for hours and then have huge fights when they came home. Mom turned into a crazy woman, accusing Mike of flirting with other women, and she just wouldn't stop badgering him until he took her into their bedroom and hit her to calm her down. But that only made it worse. "Hit me again and show me what a big, strong man you are," she would taunt him, and then it would turn really horrible.

We stood outside the bedroom door crying and wanting to help. I would say to Debbie, "Why doesn't she just be quiet? Then he would stop." During one of their fights, all five of us – Laurie, Debbie, Charlie, Bradley and I – grabbed iron skillets of different sizes hanging on the kitchen wall and were ready to hit Mike when he walked out of the bedroom. Fortunately, he stopped hitting her and then stayed in the bedroom a long time before coming out. By then we'd put the skillets away.

Another time, Mom came home from partying late one night when we were all in bed. I woke up to her in our bedroom yelling and demanding to know who was responsible for drying and putting away the dishes that night. I told her it was me. She took me by the shoulders and marched me into the kitchen, showed me a damp dish, and then took every plate, bowl, cup, glass, pot and pan we owned out of the cupboards. She watered them all down and made me dry every one of them perfectly. It took me a long time to dry all of those dishes, and I knew that if she found even one damp spot anywhere once I finished, I'd have to start all over.

That wasn't the only time one of us was awakened in the middle of the night to clean something or put something away. It was as if the house had to be spotless and orderly to make up for the drinking, fighting and chaos in the rest of their lives.

Mom craved stability and a moral life, but she was easily swayed. Before Dad died, Mom hardly ever drank, only at the parties after family funerals. But soon after, she and Mike went out drinking every weekend. All the while we were growing up, she went along with whatever situation was handed her. When the Jehovah's Witnesses came to the door, eager to tell her about Jehovah and how to live an honorable life, she followed. When temptation came to the door, she followed that. Back and forth, back and forth.

It was easy to forget they were so young, yet Mom was still barely 30, and Mike was only 22. One of the many times I hid under the big wooden kitchen table sneaking a snack – that time it was uncooked spaghetti noodles – I heard Mom talking with Grandma Helen when she showed up for a surprise visit and caught Mom in one of her usual muumuus with big colorful flowers and with her hair in curlers, washing a big pile of clothes in the wringer washer. Grandma shook her head and clicked her tongue.

"Mom, all I do is clean, cook and wash clothes," she said to Grandma Helen. "I love my kids, but sometimes I just want to run away forever."

Grandma wasn't sympathetic. "You had your chance Geraldine, but instead you just *had* to marry Laurin and have all these babies."

But Mom had the weekend nights for her adult time. "It's my chance to get away from it all," she would tell us in a bubbly way, while kissing us and giving us extra hugs. She changed into a different person – so happy to be with Mike, going out all dressed up with a sparkle in her eye.

She didn't come home that way. Mike would always shush her as we heard them coming in late at night, but we could hear her just fine. "I hate my life," she would say, crying.

"Mike was brave to move our big family to live with him and take care of us. He must love us a lot," I would tell Debbie as he dragged Mom into the house.

Laurie had turned 12 by then and was in charge when Mom and Mike were out, and it wasn't an easy job. On a cold winter night the rain was coming down in buckets when we heard noises and saw faces looking in through the window. We thought they might be demons or, maybe worse, the older boys from that crazy poor family with the wild dogs. Laurie gathered us into the large closet off the kitchen where Mom had her wringer washing machine. Tears ran down my face and I couldn't breathe very well. I wheezed and tried to be quiet. Debbie, as always, put her arms around me and rubbed my back. Then I wasn't so scared, and I could relax and breathe. We must've hid in the washing room for an hour before we dared come out.

We learned about the demons at the Jehovah's Witness meetings. They work for Satan, trying to control and turn people into Satan worshipers by doing bad things like stealing, lying and not learning or preaching God's word. Demons were once angels before choosing to do wrong and being thrown out of heaven with Satan. Now they are here on earth to torment and create bad situations for anybody who knows God's word but ignores what they've learned. The job of the demons is to turn people away from Jehovah.

Doing bad things invites them into your home, *so now that we weren't Jehovah's Witnesses and were doing bad things, they're after us!*

Occasionally other kids would bring over a demonized toy for us to play with and then leave it behind. When that happened, I would be terrified. Once we played with a friend's Ouija board and then hid it under my bed. That night, I was certain the demons were sitting on me, holding me down and covering my mouth. I was paralyzed and couldn't call out to anybody. I couldn't even say "Jehovah" in a stern and strong voice, which is what you're supposed to do to scare the demons away. I could open my eyes and see everything around me, but no matter how hard I tried I couldn't move or force a sound to come out. I grew more and more panicked. The powerful energy was in total control. It took what seemed like forever to be able to move or speak so that I could finally say "Jehovah" in my tough voice to frighten those demons away.

Even though life was better in Port Townsend, we were still trying to live on about $300 a month from my father's Social Security. Mom told Mike that he needed to get a job or it wasn't going to work out for them, so Mike signed up with the Merchant Marines for a six-month hitch hauling war supplies to Vietnam.

After he left, Mom found her first job. "Crazy Eric's" was one of the few burger joints in Port Townsend. Mom's sister Jan and her young daughter Rhonda came to stay with us while Uncle Ron was away in the Navy. Rhonda was as close to a sister as possible, since her mom was my mom's sister, and her dad was my dad's nephew. With Mike gone and Laurie to watch the rest of us, Mom finally had a chance to be on her own a bit, and she took the opportunity to sow some wild oats. Mom and Aunt Jan would go out dancing at the local cocktail lounges and come back happy and full of life. I found out later that they even danced with some of my soon-to-be schoolteachers. I'm not sure what else.

I do know that we loved to watch them get ready for their nights out. Mom and Jan had matching dancing outfits. Mom wore orange pin-striped pedal pushers and a white tank top with orange trim around the arms and neck, and Jan wore the same outfit in green. Both wore white sneakers and had beehive hairdos. Side by side on the hallway floor, with a full view of the bathroom and Mom's bedroom, Debbie and I would lie on our stomachs, propped up on our elbows, and watch them sip their drinks as they prepared for their nights out. It sure took a lot of bobby pins and hairspray to get their hair to stay up like that.

"Let's do that when we get old!" said Debbie, her blue eyes blazing with excitement. "OK," I replied calmly as I watched closely. "That looks like a lot of fun."

Except for the Levels, I didn't like any of the neighborhood kids. When she wasn't working at Crazy Eric's, Mom babysat a couple of them; two boys who lived near the barn we burned down. They had all the signs of becoming serial killers, and Mom wouldn't let us be alone with them, especially after the oldest boy, who was Debbie's age, posed naked for us so we could draw his private parts.

One afternoon, I came home from the beach with the Levels to find our plastic toy airplane, about the size of a breadbox, in the middle of the yard. That wasn't where we'd left it. Something inside the airplane seemed to be moving. When I reached inside, I felt something furry. It was my favorite kitten! Those boys had stuffed Lucy into the airplane and threw it against the wall, then crushed it with a bat and kicked it over and over. We managed to pull her out but blood was coming from everywhere. I fainted, woke up, and then fainted again. Lucy died.

I was feeling blue after Lucy was killed. Even watching "Leave it to Beaver" that evening didn't help me feel any better. Afterward, I went into the kitchen to find Mom with her hair in curlers under her beautiful flowered scarf with the missing corner, kneading bread dough. I loved the smell of the warm yeast mixed in with the dough, and it tasted even better. As I sat at the table and watched her knead, I asked, "Mom, why don't good things happen to us like they do for Wally and the Beav?"

"Oh, they will sweetheart," said Mom as she pulled off a piece of dough, handing it to me. "You need to pray to Jehovah every day and wonderful things will happen. You'll see."

Mom was right! I prayed extra long for days, and something wonderful happened, a miracle just like in the Bible. After a year of hobbling around on my peg leg, I was taking a warm bath and suddenly realized that my knee was bending a little. Over time it slowly started moving properly and I was able to use it again. I could swing with both legs, run faster and climb better than ever. Then, when summer arrived, Mike came home.

When Mike returned home from his Merchant Marine duty, he brought Debbie and me baby china dolls as presents, but Mom said they were too fragile and locked them in her china cabinet for safekeeping. He also gave me a Japanese doll the same size as Midge. She was made from fabric and looked delicate and beautiful in her bright purple kimono with her hair pulled back into a tight bun. Japanese Lady had a colorful face, with bright red lips and makeup on her eyes and cheeks, and held an elegant purple umbrella. I took her everywhere and couldn't look at her enough. I wanted to look just like her.

First, I wet down my hair and pulled it back tightly with a rubber band. Then I crushed a raspberry and rubbed it on my lips before making little circles on my cheeks and even rubbing it on my eyelids. I took tiny, dainty steps while carrying my umbrella – a paper plate stuck on top of a stick. Everyone laughed, but I knew they were just jealous.

After that, I liked Mike more than ever, so much that I would lie and tell everyone he was my dad. Mike was well over six feet tall, with dark hair, piercing blue eyes and a mustache. He looked just like the actor Tom Selleck.

I couldn't wait to show Mike off to some kids when he and Mom took all of us kids swimming at Fort Worden beach that summer. Not only was he the most handsome man in all of Port Townsend, he also had some cool tattoos, like birds on his chest and a nice design on his arm, even a beautiful girl with a colorful face like Japanese Lady covering his lower leg.

Mike and all of us kids climbed across the pilings and rafters under the dock to a platform several feet above the water and 100 meters from shore, being sure not to rub against the pilings covered in tar. With all of us rushing to reach the platform first in the underbelly of the dock, we looked like a bunch of scurrying rats.

Mike dove in first, perfectly, with the rest of us right behind him. There was only one problem though: Mike was used to swimming in the warm water of the Orient. He forgot that the water in Port Townsend was only 52 degrees – on a good day. He screamed like a girl while we all swam back to shore. Mom was on the beach laughing with those kids I had wanted Mike to impress.

A few months later, Mike found a job working in a gas station – and shortly after, an even better job at a lumber mill – and Mom decided it was time to go to the Jehovah's Witnesses meetings again. She talked to the elders of the Port Townsend congregation to see if she could be reinstated. They told her she first had to prove that she was sorry for committing adultery and could live a wholesome life of which Jehovah and his people would approve. So we started going to the Kingdom Hall again for meetings, three times a week for two hours each. We also had a weekly Bible study, along with a Bible scripture reading every morning.

The next step was for Mom and Mike to get married. On their wedding night, Mike's dad told him, "You must be out of your mind, taking on this big family."

So I had a stepbrother and sister, Jeff and Sissy, who lived with us off and on depending on what their mother was up to. Plus, my three cousins – Jimmy, Julie and Jolene – came to stay with us for a while when their parents (Mom's brother and my real dad's niece) were having trouble taking care of them, but "a while" went on and on so Mom and Mike decided it was best to obtain legal custody. Then we had three more kids in the family, which made 10 counting Jeff and Sissy.

Chapter 4

When I was 10, and after two long years in the little white house, we moved a half mile away from the Levels to a nice house in a nice neighborhood with nice people. Mike and Mom managed to rent the perfect house from the Chandlers, the sweetest older couple I had ever met. It was an old green Victorian with a long walkway leading up to a big front porch. As you walked into the front door, there was a big living room with bay windows all around. There was a middle room that we used as a playroom and where Mom would do her sewing and ironing. We used that room a lot in the winter because it had an oil-stove so warm that it heated the entire house.

Beyond the middle room was a huge kitchen, and right off the kitchen was the only bathroom in the house. It was small and pink with only the bare necessities: a toilet, sink and bathtub, but no shower. Out in the hallway a big mirror on the wall between the bathroom and kitchen, with a dresser and washbasin beneath it, helped keep the fights down over the busy bathroom.

Mom and Mike had one large bedroom downstairs and Charlie and Bradley shared the other big bedroom with our cousins Jimmy and Jolene, and Jeff and Sissy when they stayed with us. We older girls – Laurie, Debbie, Julie and I – were upstairs. We had to climb a steep wooden attic stairway behind a small door off the kitchen to get up there.

At the top of the stairs there was a hallway with a big closet, where Julie slept. Around the corner was half of one large bedroom. The walls were sunny yellow and the ceiling was bright green – my favorite colors, like the dandelions in my secret hiding place in Enumclaw. Debbie and I shared that half of the room and Laurie had the other side. She had her own door, through Julie's closet, and a green bamboo screen divided her side from ours. When her light was on, we could see through it and spy on her. To top it off, the ceilings were so low that grownups never went up there. We loved it.

The house was just across the street from the lower field of the historic grade school and high school, with basketball courts, monkey bars, ball fields and even tetherball courts. The two schools were directly above the fenced playing field. We had to walk up a long, steep hill to get to the upper playground and the grade school building. The high school buildings were just above that.

The Chandlers' house was on the other side of a road, across a small field. They thought my parents had a few kids and wanted to help a young family start a new life in a nice place, so they gave us a break on the rent, only $75 a month. One day soon after we moved in they came over to say hello. We were all heading out the door on our way to school when they arrived. Laurie walked out first. Then came Debbie and me. Charlie and Bradley marched out, followed by cousins Jimmy, Julie and Jolene, one right after the other like a regular parade.

The Chandlers looked as if they couldn't believe it. But they gave us a chance and seemed pleased to find out how well behaved and polite we were, always saying "please" and "thank you" and respecting other people's property.

Mr. Chandler was tall and a little bent over, with a huge nose. He was quite serious, and when he did try to smile it seemed awkward for him. But he and his wife fell in love with us kids. After awhile, Mr. Chandler asked Mike if he wanted to buy the house. "There's no way I could afford that!" said Mike. So Mr. Chandler said, "Let's put the past months of rent toward a down payment, and you can buy it for $7,000." Mom said it was a blessing ... our $75 a month was a house payment.

Not only did we have a nice house, we also had plenty to eat. The Chandlers gave us vegetables from their garden. Finally, I wasn't desperately hungry all the time. We ate tons of green beans, beets, carrots, squash and potatoes. It's not what "normal" kids would choose, but of course with my appetite I loved even the beet greens. Mike caught salmon, halibut, crab and shrimp, and dug for clams, so we ate tons of fresh seafood – really fresh, less than an hour after it was caught. Mike hunted with his dad and friends, which meant we had a lot of venison and sometimes, even moose on the dinner table. For a while, there was a moose tongue in the freezer. Mike used to take it out and chase us around the house with it while we screamed and ran away. Eventually Mom cooked it and we sliced it up like a roast and ate it.

It took months for Mom to prove she was deserving of being reinstated as a Jehovah's Witness. Three times a week, she would pack us all up into the big blue station wagon like a bunch of crabs trapped in a crab pot and take us to the Kingdom Hall. When you've been disassociated it's as if you don't exist, so we weren't able to talk to anyone as we all walked in and took up an entire row. It wasn't easy to be on our best behavior for over two hours, but Mom wanted to make a good impression so we tried really hard. Every now and then, though, Debbie would hog the armrest and elbow me until I couldn't take it anymore. I would elbow her back and sometimes bite her. We wouldn't be at it for long before Mom pinched us behind our upper arms. It hurt horribly, and that would end that. Everyone in the congregation thought we were the most well behaved kids they had ever seen.

Eventually, my mother proved herself worthy and was once again a Jehovah's Witness. Mike wasn't interested in the religion and didn't like her being so into it, although I do think he liked the fact that she took all of us kids away for hours at a time during meetings. With so many kids around all the time, I always wanted to run and hide someplace quiet and just be alone. I'm sure Mike felt the same way.

Because we were Jehovah's Witnesses again, we had to come straight home from school and couldn't dillydally with our old worldly friends. The Levels – my only friends – were a thing of the past. Mom had plenty of chores for us. The girls had to fold and put away the laundry, dust, vacuum, and help her get dinner ready. It takes a lot of potatoes to feed 10 or 12 people, so we did a lot of peeling. We would set the table, clear it after we ate and then wash, dry and put away the dishes. We older girls would rotate chores every week. The boys were still little and only had to feed the dogs and take out the trash.

There were times when I had to do all the chores as punishment for playing baseball or football too long with worldly kids, or getting back from the beach a little late, or just forgetting that I had a chore to do at all. My sisters loved it when I was bad because they were free from housework for a week, sometimes longer.

Before bed, all of us kids gathered in my brothers' room and Mom read to us from the children's Bible storybook the Jehovah's Witnesses published.

My favorite story was Jezebel. The Bible storybook showed big color-ful pictures of Jezebel in her beautiful lacy skirt and skimpy golden top with jewelry everywhere – on her ankles, arms, neck, ears, and even in her belly button. She had bright red lips with all kinds of colorful makeup, much better than my old orange brick powder. I wanted to look just like her when I grew up. I wanted everyone to notice me as I walked down the street in beautiful flowing clothes and jingling with all that shiny jewelry. She seemed like a special and very important person. When it was my turn to choose, I would always say, "The Jezebel story." All the other kids would moan, "Not again!" Mom would read it but would also remind me not to miss the point, that Jezebel was an evil woman, not a role model.

It was nice when Mom read to us since we had to read plenty of Jehovah's learning books on our own, even more than school reading.

We were expected to study a lot of material so we'd be ready to answer at least one question during each meeting, but once I figured out that the perfect answer to almost every question was "Do God's will," I didn't have to study anymore. I had to be tricky sometimes and add a few words to make that answer fit the question, but it worked like a charm. No one ever caught on.

When you're a Jehovah's Witness, you don't worship or celebrate anything in this world except Jehovah and the death of his son, which is called The Memorial of Christ's Death. No holidays, no birthdays, no saluting the flag. I always wanted presents for my birthday and Christmas, and I really wanted valentines. I wanted to go on Easter egg hunts and trick-or-treating on Halloween. Even a Thanksgiving dinner with family and friends would have been nice.

So I would do my best to participate in some of the worldly activities. Once in a while I stood up at school for the Pledge of Allegiance, but the other Jehovah's Witness kids would tell on me. On Halloween, Debbie and I would sneak out for some trick-or-treating when we could get away with it. In one of Debbie's typical con jobs, she would guard the bedroom door while I jumped out of our window and brought the ladder for her to climb down safely. Then it was time to score some candy.

Mom said that we were very lucky to have our one celebration, not that The Memorial of Christ's Death was festive or exciting with presents or fun and games. Instead, we dressed up and went to the Kingdom Hall during a spring evening around the full moon. It wasn't much different than our usual meetings, really. We listened to a brother talk, only that time it was about the Passover, when Jesus and his Apostles share bread and wine. Then we passed wine and bread down each row, giving each congregation member a chance to partake, but nobody was allowed to take it unless they were one of The One Hundred and Forty Four Thousand Anointed Ones. That's 144,000 in the entire world, from the day of Jesus Christ's death and ascension to heaven at Pentecost – 33 AD – until now. These chosen ones join Jehovah, along with Jesus, to rule a new earth in his Kingdom up in heaven once they die.

I really wanted to enjoy some of that delicious-looking red wine and snack on those crackers, but as they were passing through our row Mom would watch me closely and harshly whisper "Kimmie" if I seemed too interested. The only good part was the chance to watch the one brother who did partake. I was fascinated, maneuvering my way into a seat with a good view to watch him enjoy his snack. In total silence, he would reach for the dried bread as it passed and nibble on it importantly. Then he'd wait for the wine to come around, slowly taking the small glass from a tray and bringing it close to his face before giving it a sideways glance. Then he would carefully bring the wine to his lips and sip, all the while aware that we were watching him. It was quite a show, and he knew he was the star.

"How can we have an 'Anointed One' right here in our congregation?" I asked Mom. "It doesn't seem like there would be many around." Mom always said, "Our congregation is blessed to have such a special man in our presence." *Hmmm*, it seemed odd to me. I often wondered if maybe he made a mistake a long time ago when he first became a Jehovah's Witness, taking the wine and crackers before he knew the rules, then decided to go with it each year to save face knowing that Jehovah would forgive him.

We learned that once the Anointed Ones are in place, the rest of the Jehovah's Witnesses will live in a perfect paradise after Jesus the "Lamb" returns to earth and defeats Satan the "Beast" in the battle of Armageddon, throwing Satan and his demons into a bottomless pit, the "Abyss." Everything undesirable in the world, the people who have ignored or turned their backs on Jehovah, the world leaders and the corrupted government will be destroyed by earthquakes, floods, famine, everything you can imagine. All evil will be wiped off the face of the earth. That's what they told us.

These teachings can make a kid who has learned about Jehovah very nervous. I had to be good, otherwise! I would worry myself sick when I sinned, but then hurry to be good right away. They warned us, "The end is near." The pressure was on.

After Armageddon, all of mankind from the beginning of time who have good hearts and haven't had a chance to learn about Jehovah will join the Jehovah's Witnesses in the New World. Then there will be a resurrection from the dead and everyone will rejoice while turning, plowing and returning the earth into the perfect paradise Adam and Eve were responsible for before they messed up by forsaking Jehovah and falling into temptation.

Everyone will be rewarded with everlasting life while living in this New World. No more pain, sorrow or illness. No more death.

That's why we needed to preach this good news to everyone.

However, it didn't help our reputations when we had to "go out in the service" delivering good news every weekend. We were supposed to get in a certain number of hours every month preaching God's word, going door-to-door to spread the good news to people within our service territory. For us, that was everyone in the Port Townsend area, including our classmates. Of course they would tease and make fun of me the next school day. It was always best when we had a territory to work in some other nearby small town.

An adult would usually drive us through the neighborhoods, but then we were allowed to go to the door on our own. That was good. While out in the service, we were supposed to tell the person answering the door something that applied to the articles in the *Watchtower* and *Awake* magazines that we were trying to leave, or "place," with them. If they asked, "How much?" – probably to get rid of us – we were supposed to say they could keep the material "for a contribution of 10 cents." But I would say, "One buck, please." If Debbie was with me I would have to share it, but I still made some pretty good money going out in the service.

The Jehovah's Witnesses print their own literature at Watchtower Farms in Wallkill, New York, employing people in the religion plus feeding and housing them as well. They print Bibles, all the study books, Bible storybooks and, most importantly, the *Watchtower* and *Awake* magazines. Congregation members from all over the world buy the literature at a low cost and then place it with people in their service territory. Some will ask for a contribution of 10 cents and others just place the literature with the householders for free. I don't know if anyone else ever asked for a dollar.

Certainly no one ever did what we did next. Getting a dollar for the literature when we asked for it gave Debbie and me the bright idea to make pincushions out of extra material we found in Mom's sewing room. We had Mom sew three sides of a square inside out, then we turned it right side out and stuffed it full of scrap fabric before hand stitching the last side. When we started to run out of scraps we went to making pot-holders, which were lumpy with hardly any stuffing. Mom thought we were making pillows for our doll beds.

We went door-to-door, showing householders our pathetic creations and asking if they wanted to make a contribution for a pincushion or pot-holder of their choice. People usually smiled and gave us a dollar, sometimes more. One woman asked whom the contribution was for. "Us," we answered. She still gave us a dollar.

Then one day a man who looked just like Dad answered a door in an apartment complex we decided to work. He was putting on his shirt as the door swung open, and we saw a scar near his heart. He smiled Dad's smile and said hello in Dad's voice before giving us five bucks. Debbie and I looked at each other with huge eyes, but didn't say anything. We were silent as we walked away. Debbie finally asked, "Did that look like Dad?" and I said yes. She started to say, "Did you see that scar on his ..." and I said, "yes." *This is where he went after they told us he died!* We ran home scared out of our wits.

Mom said it was our imaginations, but Debbie and I insisted. "Honest to Jehovah God!" I said. Whenever we wanted someone to know that we were really telling the truth, that's what we said. We truly believed in Jehovah and would never use his name in a lie.

The next day, Mom sent Laurie with us to the apartment to put an end to our fantasies. When we arrived, the man was gone and the apartment was bare. Then nobody believed us, but it made us even more certain that our father was alive. We told stories to each other about how he'd been following us around over the years to make sure we were being taken care of, and that we were being good.

But after that, we didn't go door-to-door asking for contributions for "us" anymore.

There was only one other thing I was required to do as Jehovah's servant, and it was even harder than going out in the service. Every few months at the Friday night meetings, it was my turn to give a talk in front of the entire congregation. We had to use certain scriptures in the Bible that pertained to a required subject, and were given a report card afterward listing things we could improve on: gesturing, speaking loud enough, using the allotted amount of time, getting the message across, enunciating clearly, and so on. We would earn an "E" for excellent or a "G" for good and then move on to another task the next time, or get an "I" for improved, which meant you were getting better but still needed to work on something. "W" meant you didn't do very well at all, and had to work on it again until you got it right.

We usually had to fill six minutes in covering a subject. Six minutes! That was torture, or would have been if I hadn't found a way around it. I made up skits pretending I was talking with a friend or going out in the service, so that one of my friends or sisters would have to be up there on stage with me and have a part in my talk. I would usually pretend to be visiting a friend or householder, looking up Bible scriptures and then explaining what they meant and how they pertained to our discussion. I would write a *big* part in for my householder and have them read some scriptures, too, so I didn't have to do all the work up there. My face still turned red, and my report card would usually say, "slow down," but I often earned a G and sometimes an E.

Going to meetings, having home Bible study and going out in the service didn't leave much time for fun. Plus, I missed all the good TV shows. "The Brady Bunch" was on Friday nights during our 7-9:30 p.m. meetings. Still, we managed to have some good times, having big picnics with the congregation, hosting pinochle parties at our house or playing baseball with the other Jehovah's Witness kids as long as we had chaperones.

I loved baseball enough that I would risk getting into trouble and having to do all of the chores for a week just to play with worldly kids. Since the baseball field was just across the street from our new house, I could go and play a few innings after dinner and then hop the fence to be home in time to prepare for evening meetings. And I did, many times.

One night, the District Overseer was visiting our congregation. He would travel to all of the congregations around the Northwest, checking up on them. Everyone admired and respected that important man, and our congregation wanted to impress him. We were expected to be well dressed and on our best behavior for the meeting that night. "No fighting or fidgeting," Mom warned, and we knew she meant it even more than usual.

I needed a "quick fix" as Dad used to say before taking a couple belts of whiskey to face his stressful times – something to lift my spirits and ready myself for what was looming that evening – so just after dinner, I sneaked over the fence to play a couple innings of baseball with my worldly friends, rushing back home just in time to put on my nice skirt and blouse. Mom loaded us all into the station wagon and off we went to the Kingdom Hall. When we arrived, Mom had all 10 of us line up for inspection before we walked in. My face was dirty, so she spit on a Kleenex and wiped it. I was 11, almost a teenager, so I was mortified but knew better than to complain.

Then she told me to pull up my knee socks. When I did, there were dirt rings all around them from playing baseball in the dirt after they had fallen down. Mom was horrified, and in an angry whisper ordered, "Push them back down!" In we marched, with everyone else in the family looking neat and tidy and me with my socks scrunched down around my ankles. I thought I'd be in serious trouble with Mom after the meeting, but she was so excited about the overseer's visit that she forgot about me and my dirt rings.

~

We were blessed to have Chuck, who lived across a busy street from us. We met him right after we moved in. I was still inside helping put things away when I looked out the window to see that all of my brothers, sisters and cousins had treats. I dashed out the door.

"Where did you get those ice cream bars?"

"The nice man across the street just gave them away, for nothing!"

I really wanted one, so I went over to the house they pointed out and bravely knocked on the door. When Chuck answered, I said, "My mom told me to thank you for all those ice cream bars you gave my brothers and sisters. They must be really good because they're enjoying them a lot." He smiled and asked, "Would you like one? It seems you missed out." I got my ice cream bar and was very happy.

Chuck looked just like Mr. Cunningham from "Happy Days." His wife was also nice, but smelled like old alcohol and was always in her bathrobe, even in the afternoon if she wasn't downtown working at Don's Pharmacy. Chuck was the best neighbor any kid could dream of having. When we went over for what I called a "Chuck visit" he would always offer us some candy. His candy drawer had every type you could imagine, making it a dream situation for us. Then he would sit and have us tell him about our day, asking questions as the stories went along. I felt important around Chuck.

We would often wait on our front steps for Chuck to come home from work at 3:30, and would run across the street to greet him as soon as his truck turned into the driveway. He did special things for all us kids, but Debbie and I were his favorites. Every few months, he took us on an outing to Port Angeles. There was even a McDonald's there!

On the 45-minute drive, we talked and laughed and sang our favorite songs. After spotting a perfect parking space for Chuck, we watched the ferry pull in and load for the next trip to Victoria, British Columbia, then headed to the department store. Chuck told us to pick out whatever we liked. Debbie and I couldn't figure out what we should get. We both had good manners and knew we shouldn't fill the basket with everything we really wanted, although he would have probably let us. I told Debbie, "We should only pick out five things each." I chose two troll dolls – the larger one had flaming red hair – along with a nurse's kit, a paper doll set and the game "Operation" to share with my brothers and cousins. Debbie picked out one troll doll, three paper doll sets and a doctor's kit. We were set.

Once we finished shopping, Chuck took us to the McDonald's, where we ordered burgers, fries and chocolate milkshakes. *This is the happiest day of my life!* After we finished, Chuck asked, "Would you like anything else?" I said, "Yes, another burger, fries and chocolate milkshake for the ride home, please." He laughed and ordered me another round.

When Chuck dropped us off, we rushed into the kitchen, still excited, and told Mom all about our day, and then Debbie started showing her what Chuck bought for her at the store. *Uh oh.* Mom took one look at her troll doll and screamed, "Get rid of it! It's demonized!" Debbie cried when she threw it into the garbage. I showed Mom my paper doll set, the Operation game and the nurse's kit, but I hid the troll dolls. I would take them out and play with them during my quiet time under the plum tree or in our room with the low ceiling where Mom didn't come. I gave Debbie the little troll doll and I kept the big one with the fiery red hair for myself. My favorite secret game was to play troll dolls with my worldly friends, for hours and hours.

Many months later, Mom caught Debbie, me, and a worldly friend playing with those troll dolls. She told us, "You're calling the demons into your lives and are probably demonized along with the dolls." She ordered us to throw them into the rusty old oil drum we used for burning trash. It was blazing with fire. I cried and told her "no" but underneath I was afraid that the demons would attack me, so Debbie and I threw them into the burning barrel. Nothing happened. With big eyes, we looked at each other and then at Mom, screaming, "They aren't burning! They're demonized!"

But we couldn't help going back to look, and by then the plastic was turning black and the hair was melting off. It was scary looking. We ran away screaming, but came back. They looked more and more like the demons every time we dared take a peek. Mom seemed pleased.

We were frightened to death for a long time, and from thereafter I felt there were demons trying to attack me when I was alone in the dark.

We didn't get much snow in the winter, but we had the next best thing, a steep hill right next to Chuck's house. Year-round we could slide down on dry, slippery grass on old cardboard boxes, then run right back up again, over and over. Chuck watched from his house, looking concerned, but would always smile and wave back when we waved from the top of the hill with our cardboard. When we crashed and skinned ourselves up, we would run to Chuck to have him take a look at our wounds. Once I took an especially big tumble at the bottom of the hill and Chuck ran over to see if I was OK. He said he was amazed none of us had broken any bones on that hill.

"Nobody in our family has ever broken a bone, not even when I ran into a car on a bike," I proudly told him.

"That's a miracle," said Chuck, surprised.

"No," I said. "It's from eating all that tuna with the bones in it when we were poor."

Mike didn't like Chuck. "He's too nice to you kids," he would tell us. "There must be something wrong with him," he'd say to Mom.

But Chuck didn't stop at just buying us burgers or listening about our daily adventures. He made good money as a supervisor on the Indian

Island Naval Base nearby, and eventually asked Mom if Mike would be responsible enough to take on a good job working on Indian Island. Ships were loaded there with weapons before being sent off to war zones, and you couldn't mess up on a job like that. Chuck wanted to recommend Mike for a position if Mom thought he was capable of holding down the job and wouldn't disappoint him.

Chuck knew what went on in our house across the street. Mike was out a lot, sometimes until all hours of the night. Every so often he came home staggering after getting into fights. Once he was so badly beaten that we didn't recognize him when he stumbled home. He was fighting his own demons, not the demons from troll dolls but from his rough childhood. Mom said he never got over the abuse he took as a child because he was already an alcoholic by the time he joined the Navy when he was 17. He had to work hard to manage his anger and not hurt Mom, or us. The spankings he gave us were harsh, beyond a normal spanking, but when he was a boy he was more than just spanked so he didn't know any better.

Mike didn't like spanking us, though. I heard him tell Mom many times, "I don't want to spank them, they're good kids." But Mom was on the sidelines telling him to be sure to teach us a lesson for our bad behavior, while she boldly quoted a few scriptures from Proverbs: "He who spares the rod hates his child, but he who loves him diligently disciplines and punishes him early," and "Foolishness is bound up in the heart of a child, but the rod of discipline will drive it far from him."

Later that year, I noticed that Mike became more easygoing and relaxed after his mother, Pat, moved to Port Townsend. She had some wild oats to sow when he was a young boy, and had been living far away, in Vermont.

But finally Grandma Pat was back in Mike's life and paid special attention to him, showering him with gifts and always calling him Michael Jon. I could tell he liked that because he would hunch his shoulders slightly while looking around sheepishly with his "Tom Selleck" grin. Some of his demons began to go away.

I liked Grandma Pat. She dressed well, had good manners and was very proper. She was striking – thin with platinum blond hair and dark brown eyes, and she had an elegant way about her. I enjoyed watching her and listening to her talk in her Vermont accent. I loved it when she came over to visit. She always asked me about my day and made me feel special. "You're so smart and pretty, darling," she would say in her accent. "You're going to grow into a beautiful woman." I knew I was going through an awkward puberty stage, feeling homely and stupid and never saying or doing anything right, but she gave me hope for better things to come. Mom usually told me to go outside and get out from under their feet so they could have some adult time. I think it was Mom who really needed the adult time, not Grandma Pat.

Like most small towns, Port Townsend had an annual celebration. Ours was the Rhododendron Festival, held on the third weekend of May to celebrate the flower that grows like crazy in the area. On Thursday after school, there was a pet parade with kids walking a shortened parade route through uptown, dressed up in costumes with their pets. On Friday there was a kiddie parade over the long parade route for kids who wanted to dress up and try to win a prize. Saturday was the big Rhododendron Parade, the biggest event of the year – especially if you liked candy. The people on the floats, the clowns and especially the grand marshal, who was The Most Important Person in Town, threw a lot of it to the crowds. We loved that time of year.

The organizers of the pet and kiddie parades gave out free tickets for rides at the carnival, which set up downtown in the street next to Memorial Field. One year we all entered, trying to win a good prize as well as those free tickets. We made a big purple shoe out of crepe paper and put it on top of our wagon to make a small float. Mom helped Laurie dress up as an old lady, while the rest of us dressed as ourselves. Laurie looked really old and tired with a straw hat, a long skirt and a cane. Our sign read: "The Old Lady Who Lived In the Shoe, With So Many Kids, She Didn't Know What To Do." We all walked along beside the wagon as Laurie limped along with a cane in one hand while pulling our float with the other. We won a prize!

Another year I didn't have any money saved up, so I decided to enter the pet parade to get free tickets for the rides. I wrote "Hobo" on the front of an old T-shirt with a felt tipped pen, and wore it with old torn-up jeans. Then I chased down our black and white tomcat, Sambo, who had a missing strip of hair all the way down his tail. I tried carrying him uptown to the parade start, which was over half a mile away. He kept scratching me and running away.

I found an old pillowcase, then chased him down and put him inside, but not before being scratched and bitten. I needed a pet so I could be in the parade, and it didn't say anywhere that it couldn't be inside a pillowcase. I thought I was pretty smart.

All of a sudden, water came dripping out. Sambo was peeing. Everyone in the crowd was laughing and all the kids in the parade started making fun of me – I was so embarrassed. I ran home with Sambo screeching and bouncing around in the dripping pillowcase. Once I was home and let him out, he scratched me up one more time and ran away. I didn't see him for days. I was the joke of the town for a long time and the kids at school made fun of me more than ever.

I was surprised when Mom allowed us to take part in the parades or go to the carnival, even with an adult chaperone present – with all those worldly people around! Then, other years it was forbidden. It was confusing for all of us.

If we weren't busy with parades, chores and all of our Jehovah's Witness activities, we found other things to do. Sometimes things we shouldn't do.

It seemed that Debbie and I were always in trouble together in the green house. That fast talker could persuade me to do anything.

She totally conned me into trouble again one hot summer day when Mom asked us to rush to Aldrich's to buy some Kool-Aid because Mike's mom, Grandma Pat, was visiting and we were out of refreshments. "Get 25 cents out of my purse and you can buy some penny candy with the extra change," she told Debbie. After we picked out the Kool-Aid and were headed to the counter, Debbie told me, "I stole an extra quarter out of Mom's purse to buy some Fudgesicles. Mom will never know." I was happy about having that Fudgesicle, and we even had enough for some extra penny candy.

We had to eat the Fudgesicles before we got home, so we walked extra slowly. It took us so long that Grandma Pat had already left. There we were, with Kool-Aid we didn't need anymore and chocolate all over our faces. Mom was furious.

"How much money did you take from my purse?"

"Just 25 cents," Debbie said, with her big blue eyes as wide as could be before starting to talk a mile a minute.

Mom finally looked at me, and I said right away, "Nuh uh, Debbie, you lied. You stole a quarter."

I thought for sure I would be off the hook for telling the truth, but that wasn't the case. We were sent to our room and Mom yelled at us, "You girls are in big trouble when Mike gets home!" Debbie was so mad at me for telling. We waited and waited, and when Mike walked in, Debbie and I snuck down to the bottom of the stairs to listen through the tiny attic door to hear what Mom was about to tell him.

Mike knew how to laugh, but he had a stern look and gruff voice so we could never tell if he was in a bad or good mood. We were *really* scared that time. We heard Mom tell him, "Debbie and Kimmie stole again, and this is unacceptable even if it was just a quarter. First they stole those cigarettes and now this!" Mike told her, "I'll take care of the girls after dinner."

While everybody else was eating dinner, Debbie and I prepared for our punishment by putting on all of our pajama bottoms, even Laurie's and Julie's, for padding. We even put some shirts in our underwear for a little extra. After they'd eaten, Mike called us down to the middle room and sent away all the other kids. He talked to us about being thieves again. "Why did you steal a quarter from your mother's purse? I thought you two learned your lesson after being punished for stealing all of those cigarettes and who knows what else from Aldrich's?"

Debbie and I stood silently, looking at the floor. My face was burning. Then I finally opened my mouth. "Debbie is the one who stole the quarter. I just helped her spend it."

Debbie gave me a dirty look, but didn't say anything. Mike took the belt from the coat rack. He grabbed me first and tried to spank me, but I kept running away. He pulled me back, held my arm, and whacked me as I ran in circles around him. There was a muffled thud with every strike from all my padding.

Mike gave up after only a few swats. Holding back his smile, he said, "You girls go up to your room and stay there for two weeks." I would have rather endured the spanking and had the punishment over and done with. We could only come down for meals and to go to the Kingdom Hall. For those two weeks, I was happy going to the meetings.

Debbie and I were miserable being stuck in our room. We tied apples to a string, tacked the string to the low ceiling and bobbed for the apples in the air. We played card games. Even though I was 11 and getting too old for them, we played with our dolls, too.

We played all kinds of dodge ball, sometimes throwing our stuffed animals at each other and sometimes throwing plums from our tree as hard as we could. Debbie missed me a lot because I was the dodge ball champion in school. Plus, I was the best thrower in our family and could hit her easily, so she cried and said, "I hate this game! Let's play Oh Play Mate." It's a clapping hand game where whoever messed up was punched by the winner. She was much better in that game and punched me really hard every time I made a mistake. We jumped rope, fought and told stories. You name it. We used our imaginations and came up with a lot of ways to occupy our time.

We called our cousins and brothers to the window every day and begged them to toss up some plums from our tree and apples from Chuck's so we would have enough for our games. Then I asked them, "Would you go to the kitchen and sneak us some good snacks and throw those up, too? We're starving up here."

"What will you give us?" asked Charlie and Bradley.

"I'll give you Dr. Dentist, and all of the money I have," I told them. I gave them my Dr. Dentist, a knickknack of a dog dressed up like either a doctor or a dentist – we never did decide – but I didn't have any money so I tricked them on that one.

On the last day in our room, I told Debbie, "This is what prison must be like. I will never, *ever* go to prison." Debbie looked at me with her big blue eyes and said, "Me either, Kimmie."

Once our two weeks of punishment was over, we ran around our yard yelling, "We're free, we're free!" Chuck was across the street and called to us, "I was wondering where you were." We told him, "We were thieves again and were sent to our room for two weeks, just like prisoners."

An hour later I was behind the house, relaxing under the plum tree and enjoying all of the dandelions growing wild around me, when I saw a hornets' nest. I had a problem with wasps' and hornets' nests. I liked burning them up. The sound of a burning hornets' nest is amazing. They crackle and pop, and burn so quickly. Even the few hornets that escaped had to find a new home because of me. *I am in charge of their fate! I am the boss of them!* I tried to fight the urge, but I set it on fire anyway and enjoyed that powerful feeling. Then I had the devil to pay – I was sent right back to my room for the rest of the day.

When Charlie came by my bedroom window, he threw me up a freshly baked cookie. He felt sorry for me but said, "That was so stupid. Why did you do that? You just got out of trouble."

It was worth it.

That wasn't the only time we were restricted. Debbie and I spent many days in our room together. We would get so fed up with each other when we were stuck up there that sometimes we said and did mean things. We loved each other very much, but we couldn't help ourselves, either. One night Debbie was still angry with me for telling on her about something – I was always the one "telling" in the family – and we were sent to bed early for fighting. As we were lying in bed, she drew a line down the middle and said, "You can't cross the line to my side or I will punch you hard."

I stayed on my side. Just as I was falling asleep, Debbie found a new way to get even.

"We're sleeping in the bed Mom and Dad had in Enumclaw and your side is where Dad died after he shot himself," she whispered eerily.

I started crying and wheezing, struggling to breathe.

Debbie suddenly felt so guilty that she told me in a kind voice, "You can sleep right next to me, on my side," and then she rubbed my back and sang "Angel Baby" to comfort me.

After Debbie and I turned 11 and 12, we could wander farther away from the house. We would take acceptable friends or gather up our brothers and cousins and spend most of our time down at Fort Worden. The Fort, high above the beach, had been a military post built to guard the Puget Sound during both World Wars. No one ever attacked, but Fort Worden along with Fort Flagler and Fort Casey were what they called the "Triangle of Fire" that supposedly could thwart any invasion by sea. Fort Worden sits on the bluff, on the northeastern tip of the Olympic Peninsula where Mike fishes all the time off Point Wilson, near the lighthouse. In 1953 it closed as a military installation. From 1957 to 1971 it housed a juvenile detention facility, and we would go to the beach there and sneak into the fort and the bunkers.

The Fort Worden bunker area was a great place to play and explore. The old moss-covered roads leading up to the off-limits bunkers were still guarded by the military. To avoid them we had to either take trails and bushwhack our way through the thick brush and forest or climb up a 300-foot cliff from the beach. Either way took more than an hour, but was worth any amount of effort.

Once there, we could run through the chalk tunnels, go deep inside the bunkers, and explore hidden rooms. We found strategy rooms with old nautical maps, bits of rusted weapon parts and something that looked like an old dismantled switchboard. There were even a few old guns and what looked like rusted cannons on the very top of the bunkers, overlooking the big waterway that separates the Olympic Peninsula from Canada called the Strait of Juan de Fuca. It was as if we were back in the 1940s and the enemy was about to attack.

We ran through the dark tunnels, playing war games, shouting and screaming until somebody fell into one of the uncovered manholes, which led to more tunnels underground. The manholes had never been sealed because no one thought it was possible for anyone to get up there. They hadn't met us, though. When one of us fell into a manhole, we had to yell for help since most of the shafts had no ladder to climb back up from the six-foot drop. Then the game would turn into search and rescue. Sometimes it would take us 20 minutes or more to find the person who fell in, using their cries as our guide, kind of like the "Marco Polo" game only scarier. Sometimes we scraped our ribs, backs and shins during our falls, but we were never seriously hurt. Or at least not what *we* would call seriously hurt.

After hours of escaping into the bunker play land, we would suddenly realize what time it was. We were allowed to play around town as long as Mom and Mike approved of our friends and knew where we were, but the only way they could be sure we would be home before dark was to insist we be there in time for dinner at 6 o'clock. If we walked in late by even one minute, we were sent to bed without dinner and put on restriction from the beach and friends for a week. So, as soon as we realized it was late, we scurried down the cliff or dashed through the overgrowth of trees and bushes. I usually ran as fast as I could to get way ahead, and then took a rest so I wouldn't get a tight chest and struggle to breathe.

But that time, I didn't rest. I was feeling unbeatable as I ran through the bushes, down the pathway and onto the road. I had never felt so powerful, not even when I was burning up the hornets' nests. It seemed as if I was invincible and could run forever.

Once I hit the road, which was still almost a mile from our house, Mr. O'Meara drove up alongside. He was a nice milkman from the town. Mr. O'Meara told me that I was running over 10 miles an hour, which didn't really mean anything to me but sounded good. My chest was getting tighter and it hurt to breathe, but I was running fast and for the first time I was determined to see how far I could go without stopping.

The next thing I knew, I was lying on the side of the road, panicking because I couldn't breathe. I didn't think I would ever be able to breathe again. Mr. O'Meara helped me relax and gave me what must have been some kind of CPR, pushing on my back and forcing the air out of my lungs so I could inhale some fresh air to breathe again, just as my brothers and sisters did when I played too hard or was upset about something. Once he was convinced that I was OK, he helped me into his car and drove me home.

When I walked into the house, Mom said, "You're late. Go to your room."

I'd just experienced my first serious asthma attack, but I was more concerned that I was missing dinner.

After that, Mr. O'Meara started leaving free milk at our doorstep every morning.

Chapter 5

It was summer and almost two years had passed since we moved into the green house. Mom and Mike were still going out almost every weekend, and the night would always start out well. They would leave us food for dinner that we could easily prepare ourselves, like hotdogs, beans and potato chips. It was a nice change from the healthy meals Mom usually prepared. Or, they would get takeout from Crazy Eric's, the Five Burgers for a Buck deal. A couple of dollars fed us, and I was in heaven with burgers galore.

Every once in a while, though, they had a drunken fight when they came home. It was nothing like when we lived in the little white house, when it happened a lot, but I still hated those nights. Mom would act nothing like the good Jehovah's Witness mother she usually tried to be. In the Bible, Matthew 26:41 says, "Watch and pray so you will not fall into temptation. The spirit is willing, but the body is weak." When we kids were bad, Mom told us to read that verse, over and over. But she fell into temptation as often – or more – than any of us. We were confused.

I hated waiting for the moment when they came out of their bedroom the next morning, unsure of what to expect from them. I knew they would waste most of the day recovering. I usually had the house cleaned perfectly, which made Mom less likely to lash out. Mike's routine was to get up and give us "the look" before settling into his recliner and having a cigarette while we watched cartoons. I was getting too old for them but liked to watch with my brothers. Mike didn't say much, but he looked sad. There were still some demons left to fight and now he was hung over, too.

A lot of Mike's anger around that time was about Mom's return to the Jehovah's Witnesses. Mike was against it from the beginning. Soon after

Mom was reinstated, they had a terrible fight and she asked him, crying, "How can you know what we believe, criticizing everything we do, unless you learn our ways?" After that he began studying the Bible and the religion with our congregation's overseer. It didn't last long. "I just had too many unanswered questions," he explained.

So the fights continued. All the fighting made Mom drink more, and soon she was screaming and yelling at us, too.

That fall, when Debbie started seventh grade, she moved into the junior high school with Laurie, who was in ninth. They started spending more time together and became best friends with two Jehovah's Witness cousins, Pam and Carla. The four of them were a tight group that didn't include me. "Get lost and find your own friends," they said when I tried to follow them around, but my only friend was Debbie. I was terribly lonely back in our old school in sixth grade by myself.

I found a new friend, Rene. There was one problem though – since she didn't worship Jehovah, I was allowed to play with her "only at home." That way Mom could keep an eye on us. I watched with envy while Debbie and Laurie went out for the day with their JW friends while I was stuck at home with Rene. They were starting to develop, too, so boys began paying attention to them. I was very thin, with no hips or any sign of anything else. Even Rene was growing hips and breasts, mildly.

Rene was a redhead with snow-white skin. She looked a lot like my Midge doll before I gave her the "pixie cut." Rene's mother didn't want her spending a lot of time with us because she always came home skinned up and sunburned. Before winter set in we played outside almost every day in cutoffs and T-shirts, or less, and we were always barefoot. We were all darkly tanned in my family and we didn't know about sunscreen. Poor Rene would go home red and miserable with sunburn.

Since my cousins Julie and Jolene were a couple of "goody two shoes" and wouldn't take part in fun, worldly endeavors, I started doing more daring activities with my younger brothers and cousin Jimmy. We took adventure trips downtown to the boat harbors and any other place that had abandoned buildings, to work on our throwing skills by hurling rocks at the windows. I taught the boys how to work on their aim and they became very good. The police chased us a few times, but they didn't come close to catching us. Just like the other times, my heart was racing with the thrill of possibly being caught by the coppers.

The only time we got into trouble was when we brought Rene along. She was a bad thrower and not very fast, either. One time when the police chased us, my brothers and I ran away, but they easily caught Rene. When the police brought her home and talked to her parents, she didn't tell them who the other kids were, but she didn't really have to. "I'm sure it was those Seelye kids who live down the street," her mother said instantly. When Rene told me that, I had to reassure the boys. "Don't worry. They can't prove a thing."

When I had the chance, I'd follow Laurie and Debbie. They hated having me around because they worried I might "tell," and I often did, so they took to pushing me into the closet and locking it before going off to have fun. Usually someone else in the family would hear me screaming and come to my rescue after a few minutes, but there was one time nobody heard my cries for help. I was so frantic that my heart was pounding and even my arms were tingling. Everything was spinning. There was a knot in my throat, and every time I cried out the knot grew tighter and tighter. It was the beginning of horrible claustrophobia that would follow me for a long time.

Finally, I sat down and tried to relax because I didn't want one of those attacks to come on. Eventually I fell asleep until Laurie and Debbie came home hours later. "We're so sorry, Kimmie," they said, but quickly added a warning, "Don't you *dare* tell on us."

Every once in a while, Laurie and Debbie included Rene and me in their plans. Usually, it was when they needed us for something. One night they had Pam and Carla over for a slumber party. Rene had permission from her parents to spend the night, too, but because she was worldly mine said no and I had to sneak her in through our bedroom window.

Rene and I went to play on my side of the room with the latest pet crabs I'd caught down at Chetzemoka Park beach. I made a nice home for them in a roomy paint can, with sand, seaweed and a pretty rock to sit on and relax. It was an idea I picked up from the bottle where Jeannie lived in "I Dream of Jeannie."

I knew something was up when Laurie asked us in a sweet voice, "Kimmie and Rene, do you want to join us for some fun?"

The older girls were planning to pierce their ears and wanted us to go first. I was so pleased to be included that I said OK, even though I knew they only wanted to start with me for practice. They cut a potato in half, burned the end of a needle to sterilize it, soaked a thread in rubbing alcohol and then put the thread through the needle. *I'm not feeling good about this.*

We were set to go. They put the potato behind my earlobe and pushed the needle through the front of my ear into the potato. It hurt a lot, and I was trying hard to be brave and not to cry. Then the needle went through. It happened quickly. Even so, I didn't want them to do my other ear. They persuaded me to be strong and go through with it, but the second time was worse and took longer. Sweat popped out on my brow, and I thought I would faint and throw up at the same time. It was the same feeling I had when Dad cut off his fingers, and when I found my kitten beaten to death.

Rene, who covered her eyes during my ordeal, was excited about having pierced ears and eager to be next. My sisters went through the same procedure, but that time the needle became stuck. Rene's earlobes were thicker than mine. Tears ran down her face as they poked and struggled. It was almost like trying to work the needle through gristle. I had that fainting/throwing up feeling again.

I guess Laurie and Debbie learned something. They used ice to numb their earlobes first.

We all walked around with loops of thread through our ears for weeks. Every few hours we would put alcohol on the thread and turn it to be sure the hole didn't close up, because we heard from other girls that it hurt a lot if your ear grew attached to the thread.

Of course, Rene's ears became infected. Her mom, a nurse, was furious. She came over and told Mom what happened. We got into trouble for a long list of things and went on restriction for two weeks. At least we were getting too old to be spanked.

Me, Rene and Debbie with Morgan Hill in the background

Rene was a prissy only child with over-protective parents. She was given everything she wanted and had a perfect pink bike. She didn't have to walk or run everywhere like we did, meaning Rene didn't know how to run fast to get away from things. When we jumped from rock to rock along the bank of the downtown waterfront, making our way where we weren't supposed to play behind the buildings, Debbie and I would land lightly on each rock but Rene would miss or slip and fall into the deep water, then go home soaking wet and we would end up in trouble, again. Debbie and I would sneak out of the house by jumping from our bedroom window, landing lightly on our small camper parked just below. We barely made a sound, but Rene landed so hard you could hear a loud thump. Finally, she crashed right through the camper roof. We ran to the beach and hid until my parents came to find us.

We had two bikes in our family, one that worked and one we used for parts to keep the first one working. Rene's prissy bike had even better parts, so my brothers took all the good parts off her bike to fix ours. We thought that was a great solution but Rene's mother said that was the last straw. We didn't play with her much after that, which was OK by me because she was way too much trouble.

I hated grade school without Debbie there because friends were scarce – that's what Mom said to make me feel better about not having any – and the kids always found a reason to pick on me. I had to show them, beating all the girls – and boys – in races on the monkey bars at recess. Winning their milk money was a bonus. Not only was I the monkey bar champion, but I always won at tetherball, was the last one in the dodge ball circle and nobody could beat me in the basketball game H.O.R.S.E. I could even jump rope longer and faster than any girl in school without messing up, usually to the skipping rhyme "Blue Bells Cockle Shells," throughout the entire recess if needed. The other kids had to show me a little respect for that.

It didn't help that my sixth-grade teacher was one of the men Mom and Aunt Jan danced with back when they were sowing their wild oats. The only time he paid any attention to me was when he asked, "How's your Mom?" at least once almost every single day.

As I struggled through my year, I was sad for myself but even more so for my brothers. If it was hard for me to be singled out for not being allowed to celebrate holiday parties, or take part in school activities, or be teased for wearing hand-me-down clothes, it was harder for them. At least I was good at sports, which gave me some relief from the taunting and ridicule they had to endure for being different. That kind of thing can toughen you up, but sometimes it breaks you instead. My brothers would come home crying. I wanted to do more than just hug them. I wanted to teach them how to survive.

Grade school wasn't much fun for any of us.

Once I started junior high, things seemed to settle down for our family, and thanks to Chuck, Mike had a good job. Life wasn't perfect though, Mom was still very strict and meetings and Bible study took up a lot of our time. Plus, we couldn't go to any worldly functions or play worldly sports after school, and to make matters worse, I didn't have any JW friends my age.

The junior high school was a mile from our house. We had to walk down a steep hill and then along the golf course every morning, which wasn't bad, but the walk home was more challenging. There was a short-cut straight through the golf course, and the angry golfers would yell and wave their clubs at us when we took it. But I liked junior high. For one thing, the school had an indoor swimming pool. Better yet, I made some friends right away, with a group of popular girls who came from Grant, the other elementary school in town. I couldn't associate with any of them except at school or I would surely be in big trouble, but they understood my situation and always included me in everything anyway. I felt sad and disappointed knowing they were getting together and having fun without me.

Then Kim O'Meara came along, and finally I had a real friend.

Kim and I were in the same classroom at Lincoln elementary, but Kim was in the popular crowd of girls and we didn't become friends there. I'm not sure why. Maybe I had more self-confidence being that I was back in the same school with my sister Debbie, or maybe Kim started to think I was cool after noticing that other popular girls liked me.

Kim wasn't a baptized Jehovah's Witness, but her parents had studied the religion and sometimes came to meetings so Mom "approved" her even though she was technically worldly. Her father was the nice milkman who stopped and helped me the time I was running home for dinner and had my first big asthma attack. Kim knew I couldn't be a part of her worldly activities. Instead, she joined us in our little world by going to the Jehovah's Witness meetings and attending Bible study with us. Mom loved her and allowed Debbie and me to associate with Kim and her sister Karen, even outside of our house and yard. I could hang out with Debbie and my best friend at the same time. Nothing could be better.

Even though Kim's long, blond hair was a little darker and her eyes were brown, we were the same height and looked a lot alike. We enjoyed the same things, like playing football, baseball and basketball; going to the bunkers, the beach and downtown; and even just sitting and relaxing while talking for hours about nothing. Her uncle owned the uptown movie theater, meaning I could go to movies for the first time ever, for *free*, even though I had to sneak out for all of them except "The Ten Commandments."

About that time, we started liking boys. Kim's cousin Ron was our age and along with his brother, Rick, worked the film projector at their father's theater. A group of their friends hung out on the theater steps, teasing everyone who walked by. Naturally, we always found a reason to visit Ron. Kim and I managed to attract their attention many times. Once in a while we would bring Debbie and other girls along so they would *really* notice us.

Kim's mom, Joan, had a dance studio across the street from Aldrich's and a few buildings down from the movie theater, which gave us another good reason to walk by the boys. The studio was above an antiques shop and a tiny family-owned Mexican restaurant.

Joan taught ballet and tap dancing to all ages. Kim persuaded Debbie and me, along with our other good friend Patsy, to take a tap class. Joan talked to Mom about it and promised she would keep a close watch over us. Mom said OK, but that we would need to figure out a way to pay for it ourselves.

Debbie and I decided to get a paper route together. We wanted to tap dance with our friends and be able to go uptown twice a week for our lessons, close to the action. We also wanted to be in the big dance recital the last week of school and show off our dancing skills in front of everyone.

We found a paper route near our house, delivering the *Peninsula Daily News* out of Port Angeles. The route was large, starting at the top of the hill next to the high school. Two flat roads paralleled each other with rows of houses side by side. That was the easy part. Then there was the other part. That section went up and down hills and around the courthouse, had houses that were more spread out, and took twice as long to cover. Debbie convinced me that she needed to take the flat portion of the route.

"Kimmie, I'm not as quick as you and it would take me so much longer to do the hills." Then she added, "It would be best if I use the bike. You'd have a hard time riding it up and down all those hills with those heavy papers." As usual, I agreed.

Every morning at 4:30, Debbie and I crawled out of bed and went out to the corner of our yard where the papers had been dropped off. We cut the string tied around the bundle with my pocketknife, then folded the papers and put them in our packs. Debbie walked the bike up the hill with me to the start of her easy route, then hopped on and tossed the papers as she went along.

I walked up and down the hills, delivering papers on foot while carrying my heavy pack. Delivering to the early houses, until I got rid of some of the heavy papers, was really tough. Debbie zipped through her route and then rode the bike down to pick me up when I was about finished, riding me home on the handlebars. I guess that was better than nothing. We did that six days a week and then usually went over to Chuck's for hot chocolate and donuts. "It makes my mornings, knowing you will be by to enjoy a hot drink with me before the birds come out," he told us.

We made more than enough to pay for our dance lessons, and all the rest went for snacks. Lots of them. We were always hungry, especially after getting up so early and working so hard to deliver papers before going to school all day and then to our Bible study or dance lessons in the afternoon. Having Aldrich's close by came in handy. I loved Susie Q's and Hostess Cream Pies. Debbie loved Twinkies and the fruit pies. The Jolly Rancher sticks were always a must. As if we didn't buy enough for ourselves, we were generous and bought snacks for my brothers and friends, too, right after we collected the money from customers on our route. There were times when we barely had enough to pay for the papers.

Joan was good to us, but she was stern and didn't let us get away with goofing off. We learned so much from her, and actually became decent tap dancers. Joan would get frustrated with us at times, but stayed calm and made us keep trying.

After dance class, we waited for Joan to finish up with her last class so she could give us a ride home after dark. While waiting, we either went down to the Mexican restaurant for a few tacos or across the street to Aldrich's for some treats before flirting with the boys in front of the movie theater.

I never danced in the recital. A few weeks before the big day I found my way into some mischief and Mom punished me by not allowing me to be a part of it. Joan was not happy.

Kim had two horses, a big white one named Taboo and a Shetland pony named Shamrock. She rode Taboo all the time and I rode the pony to make her happy, giving both horses some exercise. Kim was a good rider, but I had never ridden a horse before and was scared to death of riding even a wimpy Shetland pony.

Kim decided to give me some lessons on how to ride the pony without falling off. Shamrock was mean, stubborn and knew how to show who was in charge. He either walked really slow or trotted, which made riding him very uncomfortable and he knew it. We didn't use a saddle, so I usually ended up falling off, sliding down his side to the ground. Kim worked with us for a long time before taking us out on the road, getting him to gallop smoothly and walk normally without suddenly putting his brakes on. We could ride those horses all over Port Townsend, even along the soft shoulder of the small town roads, but first I had to learn how to stay on.

On our first time out, Shamrock followed Taboo. Kim rode along gracefully on her big white horse and I bounced all around on Shamrock, trotting to keep up. I'm sure it was a sight to see. We decided to ride past the movie theater in case the boys were there. As we were riding past and saying hello, Shamrock took off like a blazing bullet. I had no control but was trying to look cool in front of the boys, so I went with it while Kim chased us down on Taboo. All of a sudden, Shamrock went from a fast gallop to a sudden stop and put his head down. I went flying off over his head. The boys were laughing and making fun of me, just as they did when we were in grade school. I told Kim, "Shamrock did that on purpose and I'll never ride him again!" I got to ride Taboo after that, and she rode Shamrock.

We spent a lot of time on Taboo together, doing tricks in front of Chuck and anybody else who would watch us. Kim galloped Taboo around the lower school field across the street from our house while I stood up behind her and held on to her head, sometimes lifting one leg up in the air. We were quite daring. Chuck was worried. "This is too dangerous, and even eating tuna with bones in it won't protect you from breaking your neck," he warned me.

Chuck felt better when Debbie, Karen, Kim and I played football on the lower field. I would hike the ball to Kim and run down the field so fast to catch her perfect pass that Karen and Debbie barely had time to react. We were brutal on the field, even with just the four of us playing. Karen was strong and powerful like her sister and Debbie could throw a decent pass. When they were on offense Debbie usually handed off to Karen, who could put her head down and plow right through Kim and me. It was great fun. The boys' high school football team, which practiced on the other end of the field, would watch us and clap when we did something impressive.

Mr. Brink watched us a lot. He was the high school football coach and boys' track coach as well as the history teacher. He told me, "You should think about running for the track team when you start high school," and told Kim, "You would make a great javelin thrower."

—

I didn't pay much attention to what everybody else was doing unless it involved me or somebody was in need of my help. I did know that Mike had one night a week to himself and I always looked forward to the outcome.

On weekends, Mike played poker with his buddies. Sometimes he would win more than just money; for instance, the camper that Rene jumped through under our bedroom window. Another time he came home with a hunting dog named Pot Licker, who was always licking his empty pot that we used for a bowl. Pot Licker was a big old hound dog that howled for hours at a time. It was hard to sneak out of our bedroom with him around because his doghouse was just below our window and he howled at any kind of noise. Mike collected guns, and won plenty of them in card games, too. I heard Mom scold him about the guns, "Mike, the kids will be frightened to death with all these guns around!"

The best prize from his poker playing was Kayla, a beautiful, blond Afghan hound. Tall and graceful, Kayla could run beautifully for miles without stopping after she escaped from the house, which was often. Every time Kayla found an escape route, she would tear out of the house and run as fast as she could. "Kimmie, Kayla is loose again! Go get her," Mike would call. He laughs about the time he watched Kayla running with her long legs and long blond hair flying behind her, while I chased after her barefoot and wearing cutoffs with my long legs and long blond hair flying behind me.

Kayla would run all over town with me right behind her. Sometimes she slowed down just enough to turn around, checking to see if I was still there, and then take off again. Everyone in Port Townsend saw us out there at one time or another, running through the streets, up and down the hills, even out on the country roads, at times for over an hour. Some townspeople would wave as we ran by. "So Kayla got away again, did she?"

I paid extra attention to Mom, though, because she was pregnant with Stanley and we were all eagerly awaiting his arrival. Mom was pretty good about being pregnant. By then she'd had a lot of practice. She craved beer, which she said kept her from feeling queasy, and would ask one of us to run over to Chuck's to buy a few bottles since Chuck's wife, Doris, liked beer, too, and had a refrigerator full of the stuff. I would always volunteer to go because Chuck would share his candy and ask about my day, making me feel special. He never took Mom's money but would send me back with a six-pack. Mom seemed more relaxed after a few beers.

I was 12 when Stanley was born. Mom and Mike came home from the hospital with a big giant bundle of baby, bigger than any doll I ever had. Stanley weighed 10 pounds when he was born. My poor mother must have had a rough time of it.

We couldn't look at Stanley enough. I wanted him all to myself and loved him even more each time I was near him. I wanted to hug him, hold him and never let him go. We girls took turns dressing him up and taking care of him during the meetings. When it was my turn, I walked into the Kingdom Hall so proud, with Stanley looking absolutely adorable. My parents loved him more than anything, but I couldn't imagine anybody loving him more than I did.

Stanley was very long. As he grew a little older, he became a beautiful baby in an awkward way, which made him even more adorable. He wasn't the picture perfect baby with the cute button nose and perfect smile; instead, he had a rather large nose, and when he smiled he scrunched up his tiny shoulders and leaned forward a little. His eyes would crinkle up and the right corner of his smile was higher than his left, making his dimples uneven. I just wanted to pick this precious baby up and hold him, smell his soft baby hair, and kiss his rosy cheeks. He was so happy, laughing and smiling most of the time. It was comforting to be near him, hold him and be a part of his life. I loved his soft chubby cheeks and the beautiful blond baby hair that had the same comforting texture as my blanket that burned in the fire. It even smelled like my blanket. I would rub his hair to make it fluffy, and then tell him in a silly high-pitched voice, "You have blankie hair," and he would hunch over, and laugh and laugh while I smelled it.

I rushed home from school every day to see Stanley. Even Kim enjoyed spending time with him. We taught him how to say our name and do little tricks, like "Samson the Strong Man." Little Stanley would sit there in his highchair and do the muscleman pose with his upper body, fists in the air and grunting with strength. We laughed, so of course he would do it again. With so many siblings encouraging him, he walked and talked at nine months. He could do the puzzle blocks and the size-and-space puzzles before any baby his age. I was so proud of him.

Mike laughed more after Stanley was born. He came home from work happy and became more involved with all of us. My brothers started calling him "Dad." I really wanted to, but I wasn't ready yet.

As the year went on, Mom seemed to mellow, too. The partying slowed down, though it didn't cease entirely. Mom and Mike got together on weekends with Mom's sister Jan and my Uncle/Cousin Ron, after they moved to the Bangor Navy Base, across the Hood Canal Bridge about 20 miles from us. Ron was a diver in the Navy.

Besides Rhonda, Jan and Ron also had a little boy named, Timmy, who was Stanley's age. They were two of the most charming baby boys I had ever seen and could have passed as twins with their blond hair and sparkling blue eyes – both were good natured and played well together. I asked Mom, "Did they name Timmy after my brother Timmy?" She didn't answer as she looked off into the distance, but not at anything in particular.

Ron and Jan would often bring Rhonda and Timmy over for Laurie to babysit, and then go out dancing with my parents. They would come home late and make something delicious to eat, often steak. I loved steaks and could smell them broiling from my bed. After the adults ate and had their fun, Jan and Ron would wake up their kids and take them home.

When Mom and Mike finally went to sleep, I leapt out of bed, finished their leftover steak and then cleaned up the big mess they'd left. I couldn't sleep knowing there was a mess in the house, especially half-empty glasses of wine, rum or whiskey, along with full ashtrays and cigarettes everywhere. I hated the smell of whiskey and the stench of cigarettes floating in the old stale drinks in the morning. I certainly didn't want Stanley waking up to such a thing and maybe even trying one of those horrid drinks with the cigarettes floating in it. Once everything was sparkling clean I would go back to bed and sleep well that night without worry, sure that everyone would be happy in the morning.

Stanley

Mom and Mike partied with other couples as well, playing records and dancing. Other times they played poker or just sat and talked for hours while they drank and smoked. Occasionally a drunken fight would break out between couples.

Sometimes those fights could be entertaining. One night the two couples came in from a night of dancing and made hamburgers. As they were sitting at the kitchen table, Uncle Ron and Aunt Jan started arguing about something. We girls heard the loud voices and tiptoed to the bottom of the stairs to peek through a crack in the door that led to the kitchen. Jan was so mad at Ron that she grabbed a bottle of beer and poured the whole thing on top of his head. Mike and Mom started laughing hysterically, and Mike said, "You look like a big giant hamburger." Ron, who resembled Hoss Cartwright on "Bonanza," sat there with the funniest expression on his face, and he really did look like a big giant hamburger. We couldn't help ourselves and started laughing, too.

One night when Mom's brother, Uncle Jim, came to visit Julie, Jolene and Jimmy – his kids – he came home from partying and drove straight onto our lawn, crashing into a plum tree. When everyone ran out to see what the commotion was, he was sitting in his car smiling in a drunken stupor as plums rained onto his car in a loud plock plock plock. It looked just like a skit from "The Carol Burnett Show."

In the old days, I thought drinking was a horrible thing that only made everyone nasty, mean and sick. But, I was beginning to think it must be a fun thing to do after all, since everyone was laughing and having a gay old time.

—

My house was a mile down the road from Kim's, and from there all we had to do was cut across a big field and make our way down a steep hill to the beach at Fort Worden. During the summer, wearing cutoffs over my swimming suit and carrying my beach towel, I walked or ran barefoot to Kim's. I enjoyed running barefoot because my toes would spread out, giving my crooked toe some relief from being crushed under the bigger ones. My feet were so hardened and calloused that I could walk over glass or the hottest sand without feeling it, while everybody else winced and quickly tiptoed across or found a better route to reach the cooler sand near the water.

We had a big snack at Kim's before heading to the beach for the day, hoping the boys would be there. Then, after our fun and games at the beach we would go back to Kim's and have a few more snacks before I headed home. If nobody was using them, I rode one of our bikes. Things had changed with our bike supply. Mike, who was the best fisherman on the Olympic Peninsula, took the boys out during the annual kids' fishing derby and over the years they all won bikes as prizes. By then we had plenty of them.

Mike's favorite everyday place to fish for salmon was Point Wilson, just off of Fort Worden Beach. From there, he could also keep an eye on us while we were playing on the beach and jumping off the dock. Sometimes he caught us doing something we weren't supposed to be doing, like jumping off the crane on the high dock. Over the years, I perfected the jump and made lots of money from dares. At age 13, I was a dock jumping pro.

It was rare for Mike to come home without a salmon. Sometimes he came home with other things ... one time, a huge octopus. It became tangled in his line and came onto the boat with its legs grabbing every-thing in sight, wrapping one around Mike's fishing pole, another around his head and a third around his leg, even reaching out to get his friend. They were both screaming and yelling, embarrassing themselves in front of the other fishermen on their boats nearby. In the end, they knocked it unconscious and brought it home for dinner. It was tough and chewy, but I loved it. Then Mike put it through the grinder for mincing clams, and we had octopus fritters. Other days he pounded it with a meat ten-derizer to flatten it before dipping it into batter and frying it. Like I said, it was a huge octopus. We ate it for many days in many ways. Best of all, my brothers and sisters weren't too impressed with it so I could eat as much as I wanted.

Mike's talent at fishing almost made me forget the days when I had to eat dog food and cattle grain. We had my favorite – fresh oysters – all the time, along with all the Dungeness crab we wanted. I would go into the refrigerator and find a mixing bowl full of crabmeat already cracked out of the shell and ready to eat. I could sit down and eat the entire bowl if I wanted, and usually did because there was plenty more, along with shrimp and clams. I relished all of it. Mike was a great hunter, too, and of course poker player, and we all reaped the benefits.

At the beach, when Mike wasn't looking or was too busy with his catch of the day, Kim, Karen, Debbie and I jumped off the high dock to show off for the boys with synchronized jumps and tricks. When we hit the icy cold water, we swam like crazy to the hot sandy beach and would lie there until we warmed up. Then we would do it again. Other times we sat with our friends talking, laughing and flirting with each other, without a care in the world. If it was a cold day, we made a beach fire to stay warm as we looked out on the water, watching the ferry heading to Whidbey Island and the boats and barges passing by, with the beautiful snowcapped Cascade Mountains in the background. Sometimes a pod of Orca whales swam by. Even as young teenagers, we were in awe of our surroundings. It was our own little paradise.

Of course, whenever a bunch of kids get together to enjoy life and each other, somebody always comes along to ruin things. There was a mean boy named Don, whose only friends were the few idiots who encouraged him in his meanness. After our fun and games one late afternoon, we were just getting ready to head home when Don grabbed Kim's black cockapoo and threw him off the high dock. Poor Precious spun several times before hitting the freezing water. Kim freaked out and screamed, jumping in right after him. But Precious went the wrong way, and instead of swimming toward shore he swam toward the piles under the dock, where it was dark and gloomy with barnacles on each pile, stinging jellyfish, and even a few octopuses. We'd even seen fish that looked like stingrays. It was a place we never went.

Kim was muscular and cramped easily in cold water. When I saw her swimming in the danger area, away from the warm beach, I knew she was heading for trouble. I jumped in and swam toward Precious, yelling to Kim, "Go back to the low dock and wait." Precious was frightened, and kept swimming deeper and deeper into the piles and toward the rough current on the other side of the dock. Kim was screaming, "Precious, come back!"

The little dog was terrified, swimming in circles and lethargic from the cold by the time I grabbed him. He was ready to go down. I was frightened as well and I hated that feeling of being cold and afraid of what I might touch next to me. I started to feel dizzy from the smell of tar on the pilings, and it was so dark it was almost like being locked in the closet again, but I knew the only way to save Precious was to get out of there. Scraping my legs on the painful barnacles, I swam back to the lower dock with the poor, scared dog. At least I avoided the jellyfish. Kim grabbed Precious and hugged him for a very long time. I was quite proud.

That fall, Debbie and I decided to invite our dance buddies – Kim, Karen and Patsy – to join us on our paper route, figuring that if they helped us work through it quickly we could all have some fun early in the morning when it was still dark, before the townspeople started their day. On our first day, we rushed through the paper route and then decided to go downtown to the Arden milk warehouse, where Kim and Karen's father picked up milk for his deliveries. Kim and Karen knew how to get into the building, which the milk company shared with the local Rainier Brewery Company.

We climbed to the flat roof of the two-story building and pried open the tiny secret door. Once in, we climbed down a ladder and went to the refrigerator where they kept the outdated chocolate milk that we were allowed to drink. As we were looking around, we decided it would be nice to take some beer, too. A few cases would be enough. The five of us carried them out through the main door and across the street before ducking under the fence of Memorial Field, which was used for the high school football and baseball games. We lugged the beer across the playing field and then through a few loose boards to get out to the other side before ditching it in the sticker bushes and long grass next to the fence. Nobody would find it there.

A few days later, we hurried through the paper route again and headed back to our stash. Before we got there, Debbie said, "Maybe we should snitch a keg this time!"

"Yeah," I said. "We could have a keg party at North Beach. Just like the older kids!"

We went through the same routine to sneak into the warehouse but, wow, was that keg heavy! We couldn't lift it, but wouldn't give up. Finally, Patsy took off her coat and spread it on the floor, and we rolled the keg onto it. Then we all grabbed a corner of the heavy-duty coat, lifted it and walked out. We scurried across the street as fast as five kids balancing a heavy keg on a coat could scurry. We rolled the keg under the Memorial Field fence and across the football field, then managed to push it through the loose boards on the other side. We stashed it with our cases and decided to get back to it all later when we had more energy. Besides, it was almost daylight.

We were set. That next weekend we rounded up the gang again and rushed through the paper route. Then we got greedy, deciding we might need another few cases of beer, because you never know. We were enjoying the challenge of acquiring and then stashing it. My heart raced, shockwaves shot through my body, the thrill gave me a surge of energy – fearing we could be caught if we didn't execute our daring plan to perfection.

By that time my accomplices figured out that it only took one person to climb up to the roof, crawl inside through the tiny door, and then unlock the main door for the rest waiting in the ditch below. As I scaled the two-story building and pulled myself onto the roof, though, I discovered that the secret door was shut tighter than usual. With the little pocketknife I used for cutting the string from around the newspaper bundles, I started prying it open. Just then, a spotlight came shining from below. Coppers!

"I think somebody's up there. Let's go take a look. It might be them."

I lay flat on my stomach, breathing hard and sweating like crazy. My whole body throbbed with each heartbeat. I knew the others were waiting below, so I yelled, "Run! Run!" In an instant, I jumped up and ran right off the roof, my legs still churning as I flew through the air. I hit the ground without losing stride and kept running straight across the road. I dove under the fence arms and head first, then sprinted across the football field as fast as I could, slipping through the loose boards and hiding there in the bushes against the hill, not making a sound. The coppers didn't stand a chance.

It turns out that my faithful buddies had seen the police before I did and hightailed it out of there. They were hiding in a nearby bush waiting for me. We laughed and talked about our adventure as we cracked our first beer ever and drank it to celebrate our escape. I looked at my partners in crime and proclaimed, "That was fun!" After two beers, we hid the rest to save for another time.

As we were walking home, Patsy started acting strange. We were all feeling pretty good and a bit tipsy, but Patsy was so drunk that when we told her to put her face in all the mud puddles along the way home to sober up, she actually did it.

"Another time" came soon enough. In the dark again, after delivering our papers, we managed to move the keg from downtown, up the big hill and across uptown to an old abandoned barn that we used as a clubhouse, in the same field as the barn we burned down a few years before. It was over a mile, so it took awhile. After all that ... everything was ready.

We told some boys about our plan and we all met at the barn the next night. I had to sneak out for *this* one. Poor Debbie was called away on a babysitting job and would have to miss out on the fun. The boys brought a tap and knew how to open the keg. After my first glass of beer, I was acting tough and feeling good. After my second and third, I was feeling even better. We started playing drinking games and of course I had to keep up with the boys, even though that was the first time I'd ever had more than two beers. It seemed like the drinking games went on for quite some time before I started feeling strange. *I need to go home!* I don't think I ever threw up, but I definitely wanted to. Kim and one of the boys who hadn't been drinking dragged me the half-mile home. Then the boy ran away. All the boys were afraid of Mike.

Kim went inside to get Debbie and Laurie to help sneak me upstairs from the back porch through the kitchen, while the rest of the family was in the living room watching TV. It was late, and they thought I was up in my room all the while. The three of them guided me to the steep attic stairway to our bedroom as quickly as they could while I was hugging them and slurring things like, "You're the best sisters in the world! I love you so much." They pushed and shoved me to the top of the stairs just as my parents came into the kitchen to see what the commotion was all about. Laurie and Debbie went running down when they were called, closing the attic door behind them. *Whew, just in time!*

Unfortunately, I came tumbling down the stairs right behind them, scraping my backbone on every sharp edge of every wooden stair until I reached the bottom. I crashed through the door and landed in a heap on the kitchen floor.

Mom started screaming, yelling and asking Kim what happened, grabbing me and shaking me. She was shouting so many questions at me so fast that I couldn't possibly answer. Even Mike told her to leave me alone. Kim was sent home and I don't remember too much after that.

The next morning, I woke up feeling miserable. At first I wasn't sure why, but I had a sick feeling in my stomach as I slowly remembered bits and pieces of what had happened. My spine was hurting worse than my head. I didn't want to get up and face the music. I never wanted to get up again. I stayed in bed until I had to use the bathroom. I tiptoed down the stairs, through the kitchen and into the bathroom, where I washed up and took a look at my backbone. Every vertebra had a big, red, bloody mark.

But that was the least of my worries. The house was silent, which was more nerve-wracking than any amount of yelling.

I walked into the middle room, where Mom was sewing. She didn't even look up. Stanley was playing blocks on the floor, so I picked him up and sat on the couch, holding him tight and trying to comfort myself by smelling his blanket hair. Mike was in the living room watching TV in his recliner and smoking a cigarette. All the kids were gone. *I'm feeling very uncomfortable about this.*

Time passed by. I was getting tired of waiting for my punishment, so I bravely went into the living room and sat on the couch next to Mike's recliner. He said good morning, but nothing else. Nothing. Mom was quiet and not very friendly, but they acted as if the previous night had never happened. Maybe they realized they hadn't been ideal role models when it came to drinking. Or maybe they assumed I'd learned my lesson. Either way, they were right.

Kim came over later that afternoon with wide eyes and looking a bit timid as she walked in the door. She was relieved to find I was "let off the hook."

Then she told me, "The good news is … you were much better off than the boys in the contest. Most of them threw up and the rest passed out in the barn. You won!"

———

Winter turned to spring, and our concern turned toward Tippie. She had been with us for many years, even before we started eating free boxes of food – and sometimes her food – back in Enumclaw. Tippie was still the best dog in the world. Her ears were small and pointed upward, especially when she was excited, and her round, dark brown eyes always looked eager and ready to go. In good times and bad, Tippie was there for us, sitting with us when we cried or chasing away any person or thing she thought could harm us.

Tippie followed us everywhere, and we often had to send her home when we went downtown or to a place where she shouldn't be. Or where *we* shouldn't be. Mom would watch from the house as we all marched up the hill toward school as Tippie tried to sneak behind us, her stomach dragging on the grass as she hovered low to the ground so she wouldn't be noticed. She would drag herself up the hill skillfully, only to be caught and sent home. Disappointed, her head down in defeat, she trudged home and waited at the end of the yard until we were in her sights again after school. She would come running toward us, so happy, as if we were what she lived for.

It was when Tippie became sick that I realized just how special and kind Mike could be. She started bloating, just like Blondie did when we fed her too much rabbit grain. When Tippie tried to eat or drink, she bloated more. She was growing old and wasn't going to live much longer no matter what, but we all cried and loved her so much that Mike agreed to take her in for a $100 operation even though we still didn't have much money and would have to make small payments for months. After the surgery, Tippie seemed much better for a while but eventually we had to put her to sleep.

Losing Tippie made me think of Dad, and then I started missing them both. When Chuck came home from work, he found me crying under his apple tree. He came over and tried to cheer me up. He knew about Tippie and loved her, too.

Chuck always knew what to say to make me feel better about bad and unfair things over the years, and he made me feel better about Tippie's death. He said he had never seen a happier dog. "Tippie had a good life, and was loved 13 times over by everyone in the family. She was very lucky."

After feeling sorry for myself a bit more, I asked him, "Chuck, why do you like us? We're nothing special." He sat down next to me and said, "You kids have made an old man very happy. I look forward to waking up in the morning, knowing you and Debbie will be over early to bring in a new day with our hot drinks and good company, if you aren't out getting into mischief after your paper route."

He loved having us come over before dinner and our Jehovah's Witness meetings to say hello, and said he enjoyed sitting on his front porch watching all of the activity across the street in our yard, like our little skits and plays. His favorite was "The Wizard of Oz." We needed our whole family plus a few friends to act out the movie, and even then we all had to play several parts. I was usually the Cowardly Lion and a Lollipop Kid. We used our long and winding sidewalk next to the house as the yellow brick road. Chuck said it was brilliant.

One summer afternoon shortly after Tippie died, we kids were sitting with Chuck on his front porch when a big treat was brought out.

"Why are we having cake and ice cream?" Laurie asked him.

Chuck smiled. "I want you kids to share my birthday with me. Don't worry ... it's not a celebration. We're just sharing a special day together." He knew we couldn't celebrate birthdays, but we could enjoy a day together with a friend. Bradley asked him how old he was.

"I just turned 50."

"Man, Chuck, you're half a hundred!" said Bradley.

We all laughed and ate more cake and ice cream.

As the summer stretched on, our family went through more changes. After they'd lived with us for a few years, Julie and Jolene's mother came back for them. Poor Jimmy, his mother told us that he would be too much trouble and asked if we could keep him. Jimmy was blond and blue-eyed with a turned-up nose like mine, but his was pointed. He talked with a high-pitched voice and we all teased him way too much. He was always rambunctious, but after his mother left him behind he became angrier. It didn't help when we teased him for wetting the bed.

Jimmy often waited until our parents went out, then he would chase us around with a sharp butcher knife that Mike used to cut up the venison.

He was trying to stab us, and he wasn't joking around. I was a wimp when it came to defending myself and all I could do was run from him. If he cornered me, I would lie on my back and kick frantically. Debbie was strong and quick, always getting between us, protecting me by grabbing his arm as he wildly swung the knife. Once he cut my legs before Debbie stepped in. He was acting like those neighbor boys who killed my kitten.

When he wasn't terrorizing us girls, Jimmy got my brothers into trouble. Jimmy, Bradley and Charlie started sneaking out late at night and vandalizing property, even stealing cars and sometimes crashing them. They were finally caught after stealing Judge Grady's car and driving it all over Port Townsend. Once they finished cruising through town, they put the car in neutral and pushed the car off a cliff, from uptown straight to downtown. They were just 9, 12 and 13. To top it all off, Jimmy stole checks out of a neighbor's mailbox and then tried to cash one of them, at Aldrich's of all places. Mom and Jimmy ended up getting to know Judge Grady very well.

After that, Jimmy went to live with my grandparents in Enumclaw. Uncle/Grandpa Harold thought that if he lived in a home as an only child he would feel special, gain some confidence and behave. He didn't. Things only got worse.

We went back to Enumclaw several times to visit. It was always the same. We played games with all of our cousins and young aunts and uncles, while our parents, grandparents and our older aunts and uncles and cousins played poker, drank and carried on. There was always a big cloud of dark smoke when we walked into the kitchen where they played cards.

Ma and Pa Seelye, my father's parents, were still living in Grandma Helen and Uncle/Grandpa Harold's garage apartment. During one visit back to Enumclaw, Pa was showing his age and I could see he wasn't well. I looked at him from across the room and it was like seeing what Dad would have looked like in his mid 70s, those sad hazel/brown eyes, the dark skin and the half smile that didn't seem happy.

I couldn't feel hatred or anger toward Pa. When I looked at him, I saw a poor, feeble man who had emphysema but still smoked like a fiend. Seeing him again after so many years, all I wanted to do was ask him, "How could you have been so cruel to my dad? How could you do such horrible things?" But I wasn't brave enough, nor did I have the heart. He was so sad and I was sure he must have endured a lot in his lifetime to have put his 15 kids through such agony.

Pa Seelye died soon after, of his emphysema. My other grandparents sold their house and moved with Ma Seelye to Port Ludlow, a beautiful resort town only 20 miles from Port Townsend.

That was my last visit to Enumclaw.

When I started eighth grade in the fall, I noticed a new boy in my class who just moved in from Chicago. Blond and brown-eyed, he wore cool jeans with peace-sign patches and was much bigger and more muscular than the other boys our age. He was the best looking boy I had ever seen. He walked around with cool confidence, so sure he was special. Even his name, Brad, was cool. I liked looking at him. Brad went out with the high school Jezebels and was the best athlete in school, even though he was only in junior high. He was very worldly.

Brad seemed to notice me. I thought maybe it was just my imagination. *Is there something wrong with me? Or maybe he's staring at my turned-up nose?* He always said hello and smiled. He watched as Kim and I did things a little "differently." We weren't prissy, like the girls trying to impress him.

Things hit a snag toward the end of the school year when I noticed Brad smiling at Debbie, who strutted down the hallways like a bad Jezebel. In the mornings she stood in front of the mirror for a long time looking at herself before getting dressed. She started waking up extra early to spend more time on herself while preparing for school or the Jehovah's Witness meetings. She wore a normal bra that she filled out and nice silky bikini underwear. I wore a small Playtex bra called "Thank Goodness it Fits," with white high-waist cotton underwear.

As she was admiring herself one morning, Debbie asked me how she looked. She was turning in the mirror, checking herself out from every direction. She asked me if she looked good, knowing darn well that she did. I sat up in bed and said, "You look pretty good, but you have thick thighs, and your thighs and butt make you look like you have sidesaddles."

She looked destroyed as she walked away from the mirror and rushed to get dressed. Then she left. I felt terrible.

When I saw Debbie in the halls that day at school, there was no skip in her step. I could tell she wasn't feeling confident or happy with herself. My stomach hurt. *How could I have said such a terrible thing?* That night I told her I was just jealous and that she was the most beautiful girl in the school. I went out of my way to make sure she knew how beautiful she was. It didn't take long before Debbie was back at school flaunting herself to everyone in sight. But she still took a little extra time looking at her thighs and butt, and wasn't quite as proud of herself in front of that mirror every morning.

Debbie wasn't too much trouble once she went on to high school the next fall. I moved up to ninth grade but was still stuck in junior high. At least I had Kim with me, and the new boy made it interesting. I started liking boys even more. After school, Kim and I often walked by the movie theater to pass by the boys and that year there was one more to impress, Brad. His parents bought an old Victorian building uptown, across the street from the dance studio and a block away from the theater. They turned it into an antiques shop, and behind it was a smaller building for his father's construction company. Above the antiques business and showroom was an upper level, where they lived. Brad became good friends with Kim's cousin Ron, which meant we saw even more of him.

Although I had my eye on Brad, my first kiss was with Ron. It happened on North Beach during one of the many times Kim and I sneaked away for some fun. Ron was almost as inexperienced as I was, but he wasn't as shy. It was a nice kiss but that was the extent of it. It was rushed, and given nervously. Ron went back and told everyone at the movie theater about kissing me, and I believe he even exaggerated a bit.

The morning after one of the many parties I wasn't allowed to go to, Kim came over early and told me all about being with Brad. "He had the choice of any girl at the party and he chose to be with me!" she said.

"What did you do?" I asked eagerly, wanting to hear about everything I missed.

"We were kissing a lot and wrestling around." Then she told me he chased her into the living room where everyone was sitting. Bad timing – she had gas, and was holding it in with all her might. As he grabbed her around the waist in a bear hug to wrestle, she erupted long and loud. Brad dropped her where he stood. "Everyone laughed and I was so embarrassed," she sighed.

Kim really liked Brad, but he lost interest in her after the gas incident. He started liking me more, and always managed to be in the same place I was at school. Everyone knew I wasn't allowed to go to worldly parties or basketball and football games. I sneaked out occasionally but not very much after my drinking incident. It seemed strange that he would want to be around me when there was no chance of going out. I didn't have time for boys with all of the meetings and Bible studies anyway.

But Brad was brave. He came to my house. When Mike came to the door looking big and mean, Brad still asked, "Can Kimmie come out and talk?" Mike said, "No." Brad tried again, and again. "Can I visit her here?" Mike said, "No." When Mom or Mike answered the telephone, they told him to quit calling. I liked him a lot but it was useless. I couldn't see him except at school, and couldn't talk to him on the phone unless my brothers or sisters answered before my parents did.

Near the end of the school year, our ninth grade class went up to the high school for a tour and then stayed for the senior class play. It took place in the huge auditorium, with a big stage and row after row of comfortable seats, great lighting on stage, and the audience sitting in the dark. It was just what you would expect for a big important play in an auditorium that was 100 years old.

As we were waiting for the play to start, Brad came over and sat down next to me. I was nervous. I never had a boy so close, except when Ron gave me that quick kiss. When the play started and the auditorium went dark, Brad held my hand. I don't think I sweated so much in my life ever again. My hands were clammy and my armpits were soaked. My face was flushed and felt like it was on fire. I was so glad it was dark.

After school, while walking down the hill to my house, I told Kim what happened, and how embarrassed I was for sweating so much and turning bright red.

She laughed. "It's better than blasting him with gas."

Chapter 6

The summer before my sophomore year, some charismatic young men moved to Port Townsend. Mel and Eric were Jehovah's Witnesses from another congregation, brothers in their early 20s and handsome with their strong, fair Norwegian looks. They both lifted weights on a machine set up in their garage. They looked alike, and even walked and talked alike, sometimes finishing one another's sentences. They both had gorgeous smiles. Mel had the whitest teeth I'd ever seen.

The brothers had a great life, living in their bachelor house with their younger brother, Daryl, and a peculiar but nice guy named Corky. Like us, the three brothers came from a large Jehovah's Witness family whose father had died. Their mother, another brother and three sisters lived across the Hood Canal Bridge and were members in the Bremerton congregation.

Mel and Eric started coming over a lot to see Laurie and Debbie, but seemed to enjoy spending time with all of us. That was a good thing, because they weren't allowed to be alone with the older girls. I looked forward to them coming over for dinner even more than Laurie and Debbie did, knowing that after dinner I would get to play pinochle while I chaperoned.

We played for hours. I loved the game and practiced every free minute. Mel or Eric would say, "Good move, Kimmie" or "nice trump," and I would feel so smart and clever. They were remarkably good at saying things to make us feel special. I practiced all the time, because I really wanted to show off for them and "Shoot the Moon," where you win big or lose everything. The only way to do it is play a perfectly executed strategy and hope for good cards. I shot the moon with Eric as my partner several times and was so proud.

They seemed like nice guys, but Mike wasn't very polite to them. After dinner, when they started to tell funny stories about their teens – like acting out scenes of fixing their cars only to have them break down again at the most inopportune times – Mike would get up from the table and go have a cigarette in his recliner.

Charlie and Bradley wanted to look like Mel and Eric, their new role models, so they started lifting anything heavy they could find around the house. Then they would walk by the hall mirror in the middle room and strike a Popeye pose, admiring their biceps and their tall, lean, muscular physiques. Even 3-year-old Stanley was doing the muscleman pose whenever he had the chance.

The Jehovah's Witness parties and picnics were more fun with Mel and Eric around. They were great baseball players, which meant Laurie and Debbie were finally playing baseball. I was perfectly happy being a Jehovah's Witness that summer. I didn't care about having to miss all of the worldly functions. I didn't even care about walking past the movie theater to see all the boys, and neither did Kim. Debbie and I even quit our paper route. She was more interested in grownup activities like trying to impress Eric, and I decided I'd rather babysit for extra money than get up so early in the morning by myself. People liked having me babysit because I hated a mess and cleaned their house until it was spotless after I put their kids to bed. They told me their houses had never been so clean.

Laurie was kept busy fighting off all of the young JW women who were after Mel. Even her good friends were vicious, trying hard to outdo one another and talking bad behind each other's backs. Before every meeting, Laurie made really cool dresses and fixed herself up. She started to spend more time in front of the mirror. Even more time than Debbie.

By then I was the best pinochle player in town, but Mel started coming over way too much for even me to sit and chaperone all the time. When I couldn't, they had to sit on the couch in the middle room where everyone could see them from anywhere in the house. Stanley was always in there playing with his toys, anyway. We could see them kissing a lot, and Mom said, "They're getting way too friendly to continue on this way."

It only took a few months for Mel to propose to Laurie, and their engagement wasn't long, either. Laurie said they needed to get married before they did something "unacceptable." Jehovah's Witness girls were always marrying really young, before they could do anything "unacceptable." I kind of knew what that was, but none of us ever talked about sex.

The word didn't exist in our household. We learned "the facts of life" from our Bible study book, which basically said never be alone with a boy you desire, always have a chaperone, and if you get a warm and exciting feeling go to your parents or the Elders and talk about it.

Things moved fast, and Laurie's wedding date was set for late summer, two weeks after her 17th birthday. She was ecstatic. We were all excited. Even Mike, I think, but you never knew with him. Over time I was figuring out that Mike was a pretty nice guy on the inside, even though he still acted all gruff.

Mom and Laurie made all of the bridesmaid dresses as well as Laurie's wedding dress, which looked better than anything they could have bought in a store. It was a simple and traditional long gown, white lace with a high neck and a long veil. The Jehovah's Witness women made all kinds of tasty food, and a Jehovah's Witness neighbor named Fletice made a spectacular three-layer wedding cake. I couldn't wait for the wedding so I could try it.

There was a lot of teamwork involved to make things easier on Mom and Laurie, but Laurie got totally stressed out anyway. She was barking orders all the time and yelling at everyone in her way. I warned her, "You're going to give yourself a heart attack." She ended up growing a huge pimple on her forehead, which was just as bad if not worse. I laughed and told Debbie, "That's what she gets for being such an ass." Laurie was frantic and tried everything to get rid of that pimple, which made it even bigger. By her wedding day, she was so stressed that it turned into a huge breakout. Then I started feeling sorry for her.

The wedding was held in the Kingdom Hall. The girls who'd lost out on Mel were bridesmaids along with Debbie. Kim and I were dressed alike in beautiful blue and orange dresses with small white and yellow flowers, which Mom made for us, and we each wore a corsage – even though we were only in charge of welcoming everyone as they entered the Kingdom Hall. I thought maybe Mom wanted us to feel important.

Mike in his suit and tie and Laurie in her wedding dress looked stunning walking down the aisle together. When Mel lifted Laurie's veil after the vows to kiss her, I noticed that she'd managed to do a pretty good job of covering up all of her pimples. The reception was in Chetzemoka Park, and I couldn't wait to eat all of the delicious food and try that cake I had been admiring.

Laurie and Mel bought a white Victorian house out on the same country road where I chased Kayla, using money Mel had saved from his job at the lumber mill. There was plenty of room for the big family they wanted. Mike always used to say, "This family is so fertile, all a man has to do is throw his pants over the bedpost and the women get pregnant." He was so right. Laurie got pregnant right away. She became moodier than ever, and I was glad Mel was responsible for her from there on out.

Instead of finishing high school, Laurie decided to stay home and take care of their house and Mel. She learned to be an excellent cook and was the perfect homemaker, just how I wanted to be, but she became overzealous about the housework. I still felt she should have finished her last year of high school and graduated, but she insisted she was plenty educated from going to the Kingdom Hall meetings and attending Bible studies. She became overzealous about that, too.

Besides visiting Enumclaw, the only time I traveled outside Port Townsend and off the Olympic Peninsula was for an International Assembly of Jehovah's Witnesses held in Vancouver late that summer. I was excited about traveling to Canada, and for such an important event! Every Jehovah's Witness we knew was planning to go.

Even though I was looking forward to it, I knew there would be at least one challenge. Over the years we had attended tons of Circuit Assemblies, which were all nearby, and it was always torture to sit still for hours – and the circuit events lasted only three days, Friday night and then all day Saturday and Sunday. I would doze off and then jerk awake before Mom caught me. Those were tough enough, but *this* would be a five-day ordeal.

Joan O'Meara, who was studying the religion again, brought Kim, Karen and their younger brother Shawn, and the four of them climbed into our station wagon with Debbie, Charlie, Bradley, Stanley and me. Mom did the driving. With the 10 of us, and all of our gear, that station wagon was packed.

We passed a lot of fast-food restaurants on our drive through Vancouver. Stanley was excited about seeing a McDonald's, but beside himself when he saw a Kentucky Fried Chicken. Whenever we passed one, he would sing out "Fucky Fied Chicken" at the top of his lungs. He was only 3 and couldn't say Kentucky. Or his R's. We all laughed, which only encouraged him to do it again. Mom was angry because we couldn't be making a good impression, but I noticed that Joan had a smile on her face each time Stanley sang his little tune. Mom finally gave up on scolding us.

We planned to camp at a park next to a lake with a lot of other Jehovah's Witnesses from our congregation. I had never been camping before and was looking forward to a new adventure. It wasn't what I expected. The park was jammed with campers, and I had no space. People were coughing on me, and things weren't too clean. There weren't any showers, so we had to jump into an ice-cold lake to bathe, and I used that dry powder shampoo for the first time, spraying it in and then combing it out. I wouldn't have minded it all so much except that we had to wake up at 6 a.m. to be ready for the morning session at 9 a.m. sharp.

The assembly was full of people from all over the world, all different colors and races and speaking many languages. I loved that part. But the sessions were long and tiring, without many breaks. It was hot, and I felt dirty and sticky and nauseous. I was trying hard to be good and sit still, but I thought I would faint.

The first few days were tolerable but I was so miserable the last day that I couldn't even listen to the speakers. Eventually, I just laid down on the hard bleacher and felt every aching muscle begin to relax and melt into the bench. I was stunned when Mom gently lifted my head into her lap to let me sleep. It felt so good to lie there, knowing I wasn't going to get into trouble. Mom began to sift her fingers through my hair, maybe just trying to get the dry shampoo powder off but it felt so soothing.

It was the first time I remembered feeling comforted by my mother. I slept all afternoon. To please Mom I decided I would listen to the evening session.

I couldn't wait to climb into our crowded car, listen to Stanley sing "Fucky Fied Chicken" on our drive to the ferry, get back to Port Townsend and stay there forever. I had enough of travel and roughing it.

~

My first year of high school was about to start, and I was more excited than nervous. I had my friend Kim for confidence, plus I would be in the same school with Debbie again.

I didn't have to work hard to get good grades, but Debbie struggled and would bring home C's and D's. She wasn't real pleased with that, even though she put no effort into her schoolwork and skipped class a lot.

I ended up in her typing class, and would do her assignments when she skipped class by quickly finishing mine and then going to her typewriter to do hers. We looked so much alike it was no problem. People often couldn't tell Laurie, Debbie and me apart unless we were all together.

I helped Debbie's friends when there was something in it for me. My sister had made new JW friends during her first year of high school, and was already popular with some classmates who had cars. They didn't like me following them around or trying to be a part of their group, but allowed me to join them every so often if I did something like take their typing tests. The class was huge, and the teacher's attention was always somewhere else. Once, after I finished my test and then Debbie's as usual, I just kept going to the next typewriter and the next while she and her friends were all off somewhere. I wasn't a great typist but I would give them a passing grade.

One day after school, Debbie and her best friend, Carla, let me cruise around with them. They decided to go to North Beach and smoke some marijuana. I didn't even know they were doing that kind of thing, but I tried to be cool and fit in. When it was my turn, I took the biggest, most impressive puff I could manage, inhaling everything possible into my poor unsuspecting lungs.

A strange noise came out of me, a noise I had never heard before and never want to again. I started to cough violently. Then the wheezing began, followed by a terrible asthma attack. I thought I would suffocate. I panicked, which made everything close down – my lungs, my throat and even my stomach muscles.

Debbie yelled, "Start breathing or we'll be in huge trouble!" Instantly, she made me lie flat on my stomach as she had done many times before, and forcefully pushed on the middle of my back with the rhythm of my wheezing. Every time I wheezed, she pushed to help me exhale. Once I was able to breathe normally again, they finished getting high and started laughing. "We should give her the brownies next time," said Debbie. I laughed, too. At least I could entertain them. They never took me to North Beach again, and I never wanted to go back with them, either.

I didn't need to get high to make friends anyway.

While getting to know the other students and gaining popularity, I noticed Cathy, one of the many poor and crazy neighbor kids with those scary dogs back when we lived in the little white house. She didn't have any friends, and people laughed at her old tattered clothing and told her to take a bath. I smiled and said "hello" whenever I could, trying to make her feel better about herself, and she smiled back.

Another girl, named Deanna, was teased even more. Deanna wore cheap clothing and always had a frown on her face as she carried around a big bag of coins for no reason we could figure out. She was also in the process of writing out every word in the entire dictionary to practice being left-handed even though she was right-handed. I asked her how it was going one time and she said she was up to the letter "C."

The day she dropped all of her coins in the middle of the cafeteria everyone started laughing and calling her a social misfit. I hadn't forgotten how often I'd been teased when I was little, and how bad it felt. It must have been worse at *this* age. *These kids should know better!* I got up from the lunch table and helped Deanna pick up her coins, which had rolled everywhere. Once I started, some of the other kids began to help. Deanna always smiled and said hello when we passed in the hall after that. It was nice to see her face without a frown.

I was grateful to be popular, and a little surprised. Because of my religion I still couldn't go to important places and do the things I wanted with friends; however, people accepted it after awhile. Plus, we didn't have much money so I had to be resourceful to put together a "stylish" wardrobe. I saved my babysitting money and bought quality clothes, spending a little extra on nice things that I could wear several times a week by being tricky with the outfits. For instance, I had a short black jumper that I wore over a blouse, with knee socks. I would change it by wearing a top over the jumper to make it look like a black skirt, and then sometimes I wore a long-sleeved black leotard top under it with black tights to make it seem like a nice black dress. I mixed and matched the few outfits I had and nobody could tell that I had very few clothes. Girls would ask me where I shopped.

Late in the winter, Mr. Brink, the boys' track coach, was preparing his team extra early – "for strength," he said – with a 10-mile time trial out on the country roads. Some of the seniors on the girls' team had crushes on the boys, so conspired to put together a relay team to race against them. The girls asked Kim and me to join the relay after Mr. Brink told them they needed to recruit us for the track team in the spring.

The boys ran the whole 10 miles, with the girls each running a mile. I ran the first leg for the girls, and was ahead of all the boys by halfway. It was easy, even though I ran well under a 6-minute mile, uphill. I was in the lead when I handed off to the next girl. Then the other girls took their turns. I ended up running Mile 7 when one girl didn't show up, just as fast as Mile 1. The boys barely beat us.

After that, Kim and I decided to take track in the spring, if my mother would agree to such a thing. The girls' track coach was the physical education teacher. Over 6 feet tall, with short, slicked-back blond hair, she talked in a deep voice and walked like a gangly basketball player. I liked her even though there were tons of rumors about her sexuality. That kind of thing didn't matter to me one way or the other, even though homosexuality was against the Jehovah's Witness religion.

That spring, Mrs. Kuehl asked if I planned to turn out for the track team. "I'm not sure if my mother would allow it," I admitted. "She's very religious and doesn't want us doing worldly things."

"Would you mind if I go to your house and ask for your parents' permission?"

That night I was anxiously awaiting her visit. I appreciated her interest and really wanted to be on the team, but I didn't have the nerve to tell my parents she was coming over. When she rang the doorbell, Mike and little Stanley, who was almost 4, let her in. As she and my parents were walking into the living room, Stanley announced, "He's a big guy!" Mike kept ignoring him, hoping he would stop, but Stanley kept saying, "He's a big guy, isn't he, Dad?" When Mike didn't answer, he would go to Mom. "He's a big guy, isn't he, Mom?" No answer. But he was not going to be ignored. Finally, he came over to me. "Kimmie, he's a big guy, isn't he?"

"Yes Stanley, he is." That was all he needed. He sat quietly next to me and listened while the big guy wearing bright red lipstick talked to my parents.

At first Mom was against me taking part in any sport. "I don't want Kimmie associating with kids outside our congregation," she told Mrs. Kuehl. "They could be a bad influence on her. Bad association spoils useful habits."

It was a phrase from 1 Corinthians 15:33 that she liked to use. My heart sank.

But Mrs. Kuehl promised she would keep things under control and make sure the girls all conducted themselves properly. Mom was softening, and finally said she would let me join the team if the girls came to our house on Wednesday afternoons for our weekly Bible study.

Mrs. Kuehl nodded. "I'll see what I can do."

To my surprise, the girls agreed to do it. I guess they really wanted me on the team.

Debbie, for one, was not pleased – she was stuck with my chores. I liked going from class to the track without going home and having to dust, vacuum or fold laundry, even though I missed not being able to rush right home to see Stanley. That was OK, though, because he was even happier to see me when I eventually made it home.

Besides the Bible study on Wednesdays, we had two meetings on the weeknights. Tuesday was the book study meeting, a casual gathering where a small group of Jehovah's Witnesses met at a neighbor's home. The McKay family lived a short walk away, meaning I didn't have to rush to get ready after track. The Friday night meeting was another matter, and it didn't help with Mom yelling, "Shake a leg!" as I scrambled to clean up and eat dinner in time for the drive to the meeting at the Kingdom Hall.

The team met every weekday afternoon but we really didn't train much, just running a few laps around the track and doing some jumping jacks, sit-ups and leg kicks. "You girls need to train harder," said Mr. Brink, a tall, well-built man with dark hair, a mustache and a twinkle in his eyes. He told us to run a lap as fast as we could, and had us run some hill repeats with the boys, up and down the big hill by my house from the lower field up to the grade school and high school.

I kept up with the boys. It all seemed much easier than running up Morgan Hill after we slid down on our cardboard.

We had a 330-yard dirt track behind the gymnasium and locker rooms. I wanted to run barefoot, but Mrs. Kuehl told me I needed to wear shoes. Everyone else on the team had special track shoes, but my P.E. sneakers were all I could afford. I didn't like wearing them, either, and slipped them off whenever I could get away with it. That worked out just fine, for a while anyway.

Every Wednesday after we ran our two laps my teammates and I jogged down to my house for my mother's weekly Bible study. We would read a paragraph aloud out of one of the learning books, and then Mom asked us questions before moving on to the next paragraph. We had to answer by using Bible verses that corresponded with the information. I was glad there were others to take up the slack, and some of the girls really enjoyed it. Three of them ended up becoming baptized Jehovah's Witnesses.

The boys' and girls' teams trained at the same time. Brad was one of the best 100-yard boys around, and was even better in the discus, shot put and javelin. I didn't pay much attention to the other boys. Kim became a pretty good javelin thrower and during practice Brad would help her throw and give her pointers. *I'm not pleased about this!* Watching from across the track, I gave them "the look."

I was growing concerned about our first meet on our home track. "I'm not sure I can stay in my lane while I'm racing fast and trying to be coordinated," I confided to Mr. Brink. He laughed and told me, "Just practice more."

I practiced and practiced, right up to the meet. Then ... it was time to face my fear. Track racing was all so new to me. I didn't know what to do. I had no idea how fast I could run any of the distances I was about to race. The only experience I had was chasing after Kayla or running to the beach. When the track teams from the other schools arrived, I felt green about the gills. Those girls were bigger and stronger than me. I was about to run my first race ever, and I was afraid. But I knew I had to be a "tough little Swede" and hope for the best.

Kathleen Level was a senior and a good shot putter on our team. Her entire family came to the meets to watch her, and me as well. I was so happy to have the Levels back in my life. Their mom, Betty, short with curly black hair and a great sense of humor, always teased me about my long flyaway dandelion hair, especially when it blew all over the place on a windy day. "You have fine hair, Kimmie, mighty fine hair!" She became our track mom. She came to every meet, bringing snacks and making sure she had all the extra things we might need. Just before my first race, Betty smiled, gave me a pep talk and told me to get out there and run like the wind. I felt a little better.

Mr. Brink was more specific. He took me aside and told me to pace myself in the mile. "Sit back with the other girls and see what they do, and go with whoever takes the lead," he instructed. "Most importantly, stay with them until the final 220 yards. Then take off, because nobody can match your speed."

I felt even better because I had a plan.

The mile was packed with those big, strong girls plus a few other skinny ones like me. We all took off to run five-plus laps around our little 330-yard track. I stayed behind whoever took the lead. Racing was easy after all, just like running to the beach with my slower friends. With 220 to go, I took off and won the race. It felt exhilarating, just like running from the coppers!

I used the same strategy for the 880 (half mile), and *won*. Then the 220 – *Wow!* Those girls were even bigger and stronger. I poured on the speed in the final 50 yards, and felt that same surge of adrenaline as I did the time the coppers almost caught me at the brewery. I won *again.*

I don't know if I was more shocked that I won all of the races in my first meet, or that it seemed pretty easy and even familiar. I loved running fast and I loved everything about racing: pacing myself, running only as hard as I had to, never pushing myself until I needed to, letting the other girls do the work. It was just like chasing Kayla and following her until she grew tired of it all.

People began to notice me more. My photo was in the newspaper a lot and every week an article was written about my wins. I could even take short cuts through the golf course by running right down the middle of the fairways, and instead of yelling at me the golfers would shout, "Great race last week, Kimmie! You make Port Townsend proud."

I was surprised at how much attention I received, and it felt good. I was experiencing real confidence for the first time, and I liked it. There's a saying, "confidence is the child of optimism." I felt so optimistic that I won races I probably shouldn't have. Later, I learned the meaning of the word "sanguine," but back then I just knew I wanted to get out there and race hard and enjoy every step of it. I never obsessed about winning or losing. I did enjoy showing off when Brad would look over from his event to watch my finishing kick.

I especially liked performing for Charlie, who was the only one in my family who came to watch me run. I could tell he was proud of me. When I came home, nobody made a big deal about my winning or breaking track records. I would get cleaned up and sit down to dinner, and when somebody finally asked, "How did the meet go?" Charlie would tell them proudly, "Kimmie won all of her events." Then we ate, and I did the dishes.

When we qualified for the big meets in the Seattle/Tacoma area, running against the largest schools and best athletes in the state, we were a sight to see wearing cutoffs and white T-shirts with Port Townsend written across the front in black felt pen. I even ran barefoot in some of those meets. I would take my shoes off just before the start of my races, before Mrs. Kuehl had time to scold me to put them back on.

I remember lining up with the best quarter-mile runners in the state during our biggest meet. The sprinters in the final had muscles three times the size of mine, and wore bright shiny uniforms that looked like swimming suits. Everyone else used starting blocks, but I'd never even tried them ... I was in a standing start.

Still, I wasn't afraid. I didn't know if I would win or lose, but I knew I would race as hard as I could.

The gun went off and I was left in the dust in the first 50 yards with my pathetic start. I slowly made up ground on the backstretch, catching up to the swimming-suit girls in the final turn, and then, finding a kick I didn't even know I had, passed the leader in the final 50 yards to win. My competitors were shocked that a skinny blond sophomore with hair flying wildly behind her, in cutoffs and barefoot, wearing a silly T-shirt, could possibly beat them. I earned some respect after that, and Mrs. Kuehl called me a gutsy racer.

I was fortunate to have coaches who didn't push me beyond the "fun" level. I didn't train hard like most sophomores in high school. Mrs. Kuehl was there for support and encouraged us to do our best, while Mr. Brink gave us advice and a solid weekly workout to improve our fitness levels. I did three races in every meet, almost every week, and that was my hard training. I ran only as fast as needed to win, saving myself for the other races or just from unnecessary discomfort.

My asthma was never a problem in those shorter races. I was good for a five minute, all-out performance – it was when I had to push beyond five minutes all-out, or when the smoke or pollutants in the big cities bothered me that the asthma intruded. Port Townsend was never polluted. It was a pristine place with clean and fresh air, with a light breeze always coming off the water. It had a wonderful fragrance of sea air and evergreen, and of lilacs blooming during track season. It all made me feel energized and good about waking up in the morning. My bedroom window was always open.

Track season went by quickly. Three of us made the state meet: Jerre O'Brien (our high jumper), Kathleen Level and me. I was glad Kathleen made it. She had the same great sense of humor as Betty and made me feel more secure during my first big adventure away from my family.

I was disappointed to learn that I wouldn't be allowed to race in the state meet unless I wore shoes. However, the school and town were so happy to be sending three of us that they bought us new shoes and uniforms. That cheered me up.

We drove over five hours to Goldendale, in Eastern Washington, where it's dry and hot that time of year, very different from Port Townsend. We didn't have much time once we arrived before I had to start racing. I had qualified in all of my events – the 220, 880 and mile – but it would have been impossible to run all three because of the schedule. Our new assistant coach, Mr. Royce, talked me into choosing the mile and 880.

I hadn't experienced a big meet like that before, with its protocol. For instance, we had to run heats in the 880 to qualify for the final. I was more worried about being disqualified for doing something wrong, like leaving my lane too early to cut into the inside lane after the first 220, than I was about the race itself.

I won both of my events the same way as always, running strong with the pack, being pulled along effortlessly by the leader, then sprinting the last 220 yards for the win. I walked away from each race learning something new about myself, the other runners or the event itself. Winning was always a thrill and very rewarding ... I was a double State Champion! Kathleen placed third in the shot put and Jerre placed fifth in the high jump. There were 79 schools at the meet, and we won the third place trophy despite having only three girls on our team.

The best part was the uniforms. Even though I had to wear heavy shoes, I felt good about myself, looking more like the other runners in their shiny uniforms. Ours weren't shiny or as bright and I didn't fill mine out as well as some of the other girls did, but those uniforms were special. They showed that our town was proud and wanted us to look like stars.

We came back from the state meet as heroes. Cathy and Deanna even had the courage to come up and congratulate me. Brad noticed me more and started asking me to do things again. He was even brave enough to come to my house again to ask Mike if I could go out with him. Mike said, "No!"

I hadn't snuck out of my window in ages, not since my drinking incident, so I thought it was about time to slip out and spend some time with Brad. I knew Mike and Mom would never allow me to go out with a "worldly boy" and he was certainly worldly; the best looking and most intriguing boy I had ever met.

I told Debbie about my plan. She was impressed that Brad was even interested in me, but she had other things on her mind.

Things hadn't worked out for Debbie and Eric, and she was falling for a guy named Mark, a member of the Pasco congregation in the southeast corner of Washington State. He was visiting some relatives in our congregation. Mom and Mike called him an "arrogant ass." He did have a bit of an attitude, but I liked him. He made Debbie happier than she had been in a long time.

Debbie wasn't allowed to see Mark very much, and she was angry about it. She decided to get baptized to try and please him, Mom and the Elders – hoping that, as a devoted Jehovah's Witness, she would be allowed to spend more time with him.

Everyone seemed to be getting baptized: Laurie a year earlier, Kim after that, and then Debbie. The pressure was on. I studied the required books, inside and out, as if preparing to be baptized. But I wasn't ready. I still enjoyed doing the innocent, fun things that Jehovah's Witnesses weren't allowed to do, like kissing a worldly boy or going to a basketball game, even if I had to sneak out. I knew that once I was baptized, I could be disassociated from the congregation for many kinds of misconduct. I didn't know what I would do if I couldn't talk to or associate with my family or Jehovah's Witness friends, especially Kim. I respected the religion and the many good people in it, but I wasn't ready to devote my life to Jehovah.

Debbie was able to see Mark at the meetings and social gatherings, so we did a lot of roller-skating, where they could hold hands. Once again I was the chaperone, back to playing many hours of pinochle and watching movies at our house. Debbie and Mark barely paid attention to me, and I was bored with the job. Mike and Mom still didn't like him and told Debbie she should wait until somebody else came along, or maybe start seeing Eric again. They weren't giving Debbie any slack.

"I hate it here!" she would say. "I want out of this place. This is like prison!"

The night Debbie ran away, I helped her put all of her belongings under a bush outside our bedroom window. After everyone went to bed, Debbie climbed out the window, and she and Mark put her things into his car. Then they were gone! Off to get married in Pasco. My sister Debbie had left me.

For the first time in a very long time, I felt sad and insecure.

After Debbie left, I started doing more things with my friend Sandy, who was strong, responsible and one of the most popular girls in town. Sandy was becoming more involved in the Jehovah's Witnesses and studying the Bible even after our track team Bible study ended, but she still had fun and we spent a lot of time together that summer before she left for nursing school.

I spent almost every day with Sandy and Kim, but I couldn't talk to either of them about my worldly endeavors. Kim was baptized, scolding me when I did anything "inappropriate," and I wasn't sure how Sandy would react, as she was becoming more zealous.

When the date finally arrived to sneak out and meet Brad, I couldn't wait for evening to come. After changing clothes a few times to make sure I looked my best, I climbed out my window and met Brad at the high school. We walked to his house to have a few snacks. I had met his parents at the track meets, but they seemed different in their home with all the nice antiques around. His mom was nice but reserved. His dad told jokes and was quite friendly, seeming like a kind and respectful person.

Once we finished our snacks, Brad and I walked the six blocks to Chetzemoka Park. It was dark, and surprisingly chilly for the end of June after such a warm day. Brad kissed me near the gazebo where Laurie had her wedding reception, and it was the best kiss I could have imagined. Then he started kissing me longer and harder, until I had to push him back. He joked around a little and started again. I was pleased about his attention and all, but confused by his forcefulness.

Before I knew it, Brad was pulling off our clothes and lying on top of me. He was used to being with worldly girls and assumed I was experienced. I couldn't or didn't fight him – I'm not sure which. I didn't know if that was how sex was supposed to happen. I tried to stop, but at the same time, I wanted to please him, and to be what he wanted me to be. It was painful and frightening until I took myself out of the situation, as if

I was watching from another place. I drifted into a strange twilight state, neither awake nor asleep.

Brad walked me home afterward, giving me a lot of attention, saying kind things and asking when he could see me again. I was in shock. He assumed I was fine with the situation. I wasn't. I hated myself, hated being so ready to please him and putting my own feelings and beliefs aside. I was deeply ashamed.

The summer went by as if nothing had happened. I told no one. Kim, Sandy and I had all kinds of adventures. Then Sandy was off to nursing school in Tacoma and Kim and I started our junior year, getting ready to play on the first high school girls' football team. It was a short season with only a few games, and the boys' team coached us. Brad was one of the coaches. I pretended nothing had happened, and it seemed to work. He had so many girls in his life that I wasn't any different from the rest of them. He asked me out a few more times, and I was glad when he gave up.

Our girls' football team won all our local games, along with the final tournament. Kim was the quarterback and I was the halfback. Playing many hours of football with our sisters a few years earlier paid off. She threw well and I could catch, take a good handoff and run fast. The whole town was at Memorial Field watching our team win the championship game. It was like track season all over again. I loved that thrill of winning, and of coming through for everyone who was behind me.

After a few months, I realized that I hadn't had my period for a while. I just figured I was slow to mature, like some other girls I knew whose cycles were sporadic. I ignored it, until the day I noticed a little hard lump in my lower abdomen.

If I were pregnant, I would be five months along! *That couldn't be.* I was still very thin. When Mom and Laurie were five months along they *looked* pregnant. I woke up every morning hoping that even if I were pregnant, which I couldn't be, that it would just go away.

Mom became suspicious after realizing she hadn't bought sanitary napkins in ages.

"Kimmie, are you having regular periods, honey?"

My face turned bright red. "Sometimes," I replied hesitantly. "Not every month." I could tell she wanted to talk more, but I cut her short and she never asked me anything else. Instead, she took me in to see our family doctor.

Dr. Scheyer was the most caring man I knew. He was a runner, and his son was a distance runner on the track team. He reminded me a lot of "Marcus Welby, M.D." with his kind smile and an assured look in his eyes, except he was very thin and looked like one of those healthy people who went to those co-op food stores. He started the Rhody Run road race, held as part of the Rhododendron Festival, and was one of my biggest supporters during the track season.

Mom took him aside and said she thought I might be pregnant. I could hear them from outside the door.

"There's no way Kimmie could be pregnant," Dr. Scheyer insisted. "I just don't believe she could put herself in that kind of situation." Then he came into the exam room and talked to me about my running and checked my heart rate and blood pressure, saying that Mom was worried that I looked tired. I went out to the waiting room while he talked to Mom again. We left.

At first I truly believed it would just go away. Every morning I would wake up alarmed and sickened as reality filtered in. A few weeks later, I knew that I couldn't hide from it any longer.

After telling my parents, I went in to tell Dr. Scheyer I was pregnant.

I started crying, and he had tears in his eyes. "It will be OK, Kimmie, everything will be fine," he reassured me. "I'll help you through this." He told me that I had a few options. I could have an abortion, or put the baby up for adoption. "You have your whole life ahead of you and should think about the baby's life as well as your own – one way or the other."

There was no way I could have an abortion. A girl I knew at school once described her abortion and there was just no way. Plus, I knew I was almost six-months pregnant even though Dr. Scheyer said I was too small to be that far along.

Mike and Mom treated me like a criminal. So did Laurie and Mel. "How could you do such a thing?" my oldest sister asked. I knew I had disappointed them, but I was even more disturbed that my brothers were going to have to endure more than just the usual ridicule for being Jehovah's Witnesses. Heaven forbid ... they had a sister who was unmarried and pregnant at 16, on top of it.

I had to talk to the Elders of the congregation. They were very nice and gave me some good advice. "You need to do God's will," they told me. "Do what's best for the baby and take responsibility for your actions." They told me that Jehovah would forgive me if I did the right thing and prayed for forgiveness. I was so glad right then that I didn't get baptized, or I would have been disassociated from my family and congregation when I needed them the most.

Chuck cried when I told him, and the look on Kim's face said it all. I broke her heart. Then there were all the townspeople who had supported me. I was a disgrace and wanted to disappear forever for disappointing them. I cried every night before going to sleep, every morning when I woke up, and whenever anybody looked at me with that look of disgust. I hated myself.

The hardest part was when Brad and his parents came over. Brad looked miserable. His father looked sad and concerned, and his mother was outraged that her son's future was in jeopardy. "There's no way I'm going to allow Brad to ruin his life for this mistake," she said. "Marriage is out of the question!" Then she brought up abortion. Mom jumped in immediately, "There's no way my daughter would ever have an abortion, it's against Jehovah's will," and then recited several scriptures.

Mike and Claude, Brad's father, were more concerned about my well-being. "Kimmie is too young and has so much more to do in life before raising a child," said Mike, suggesting adoption. Claude agreed.

Brad's mom didn't want Brad involved in any way with the baby. Mom wanted me to keep the baby and raise it on my own. "Kimmie needs to take responsibility for her actions," she insisted.

I was confused and not sure what I wanted. I felt as if I wasn't even there.

We decided that Brad had to pay the doctor and hospital bills by working in his father's construction company after school, which would be his only obligation to me or the baby. I would decide the baby's future. Brad got off easy, but still complained to all his friends that he was stuck working to pay for the bills.

In late November, when I started showing, I didn't want to continue going to school and feeling even more humiliated. Then Debbie called – she was pregnant as well! She and Mark invited me to come and stay with them. So, I happily waddled onto the Greyhound Bus with my little suitcase and traveled over the Cascade Mountains, across the Columbia River, and on to Pasco to be with my sister again.

I walked off the bus and there was Debbie looking bigger and even more pregnant than I was. We laughed at each other, hugged, and then laughed some more. It was the first time I had laughed in months. It was so good to see her. Mark was there, and he wasn't the "arrogant ass" my parents called him. He smiled, shaking his head at Debbie and me and saying we looked cute, like two little girls pretending to be pregnant. We were 16 and 17, which was young enough, but we looked more like 13 and 14.

Staying with Debbie and Mark was like taking a little vacation from real life. It was nice to wake up every morning knowing I wasn't going to get looks of disappointment, anger and disgust. Instead, I woke up to Debbie waiting to share the day with me. After Mark went to work, Debbie and I had a big breakfast, cleaned up, and then watched soap operas for most of the day. For lunch we strolled across the street to the A&W to order our usual: "Mama Burger in a Basket." We craved the burgers, fries and milkshakes, and had them every day. We walked back, laughing at the way the person taking our order looked at us, especially after my second order. He was watching us grow bigger and rounder each day.

During the three months I was there, Mark took us to movies or out to dinner in the evenings. We didn't go to many meetings. Debbie said we didn't have to and Mark went on his own most of the time. I think she was trying to protect me from the stares. I knew it wasn't going to last forever, but I was thoroughly enjoying every moment.

My English teacher was the only one who sent assignments with me so I wouldn't be overwhelmed with work when I went back to school. Debbie did them for me while I cleaned the house really well to make it smell nice and feel good to be there. She wasn't the best housekeeper – let's just say there were a lot of crumbs on her floors. After Debbie went to bed, I corrected the homework she had been working on.

I could have stayed there forever. Maybe I should have.

On the bus ride home, I had to start facing reality again. *This situation isn't going to go away, and it is my responsibility to deal with it. If I hadn't sneaked out to see Brad, if I'd been more honest with him about my inexperience, if I'd fought against him more, this would have never happened.*

Even with all my thinking, it was nice riding back into Port Townsend. I'd never been away so long from that beautiful place, and I missed it. Mom and Laurie came downtown to meet me at the bus station. They hugged me and then looked me over. Laurie cried and Mom had tears in her eyes. I hated the feeling that they, or anyone else, felt sorry for me.

My brothers stared at me, but Mike seemed to have a hard time looking at me at all. I knew that of all the kids, I was "the one" as far as he was concerned, the one who was going to make it big in the world. I'd ruined my chances and his hopes.

Mom kept trying to persuade me to go to the meetings, but I didn't want to go. Finally she insisted, and it was the most humiliating three hours of my life. The disapproving looks and comments made me want to disappear. *Or am I imagining it?* I would have stared at a pregnant 16-year-old who looked 13, too. Either way, I was miserable. I stayed home and in my room as much as possible.

Kim gave me reports about what was happening at school. She told me that Brad was going out with different girls and having a gay old time. It was embarrassing. I hated being and looking like a fool. The thought of me about to have a baby and him going on without a care in the world, then complaining about having to work a few extra hours a day to pay for his mistake made me mad.

The only time I went out of the house was to go to Lamaze classes with Sandy, who was going to be my coach during labor and childbirth. Sandy was the only one I enjoyed being around, and we actually had fun in our twice-a-week classes. I learned everything I needed to know just in time. My water broke the morning of March 30, 1975, as I was getting out of bed. At first I was shocked, then happy to finally be having the baby, then frightened to death over what was about to happen.

Dr. Scheyer was at the hospital to greet me. Seeing his caring face made me feel much better. "Everything is going to be just fine," he said softly. "I'm going to be right here with you to bring this baby into the world." Sandy soon arrived, and then the labor pains started.

It hurt so much, but I knew there was no way out. I tried to relax as I waited for the next wave to begin. Sandy was calm and authoritative while she worked with me during each contraction, making sure I followed the Lamaze breathing exercises when I was certain I couldn't take it any more. She was the toughest girl I knew, but I saw her trying to wipe the tears off her cheeks before I noticed. The pain intensified with every wave of contractions. Dr. Scheyer kept asking, "Are you OK, Kimmie?

Tell me if you need anything." I lay there terrified, bearing the pain without a sound, as quietly as Job.

I thought death would be better than having to go on with it much
longer. At last, after 10 hours, it was time. Out came an 8½-pound baby
girl. I heard the nurses say, "How could this young child have such a big
baby, and deliver naturally? Poor little thing."

Mom and Laurie came into the room. "Kimmie, are you OK, sweetheart?" Mom asked, pushing my hair back and kissing my forehead.
Laurie held my hand. "You did it, Kimmie ... you actually did it! It's over
now." Sandy, who had stood by me through everything, was still crying
but by then they were tears of joy.

I named my beautiful baby girl Rachel Lynn Seelye. Lynn is Sandy's
middle name.

The minute I saw her, I loved Rachel with all my soul. I wanted
her to have everything, more than I could possibly give, more than
the other Port Townsend babies who were born to mothers too young.
I wanted her to have her own clothes, her own toys, and plenty of
self-respect.

I wanted her to have more than just tuna with bones in it.

But she was *my* baby, *my* sweet beautiful baby, and I was confused.

Like everyone else, Mike had tears in his eyes. He was kind and attentive right after Rachel was born, softhearted and more concerned than I
could ever remember him. When I was still in the hospital, all I wanted
was a grape pop and Mike brought me a six-pack. I drank it all, one can
right after the other.

After a few days, we brought Rachel home. I tried to take care of her,
but I was sick with a fever and so weak it was hard crawling out of bed.
Already, I was disrupting my family's life and making them suffer for
my mistake as they helped with a newborn they hadn't asked for. They
had finally started to settle down a bit. My brothers were behaving, living more peacefully, and my parents weren't going out and doing crazy
things as often as they used to. Just as everyone was starting to laugh and
live a more normal life, I was messing it up.

Not that there weren't some precious moments. One morning when I
woke up, Rachel was out of her bassinet. I rushed out of bed and into the
middle room to find Stanley, who was just 4 years old, rocking the baby
while singing his favorite Jehovah's Witness song to her:

"... We're Jehovah's Witnesses.
We sing out in fearlessness.
Ours is the God of true prophecy.
What he foretells comes to be..."

It was the sweetest thing I had ever seen. I loved both of them so much, and there they were together. But I didn't want Stanley to grow up thinking that's what life was supposed to be like, that it's OK to have a baby when you're 16.

Mike may have been proud of me back in the hospital, seeing what I'd gone through during the pregnancy and then the pain of giving birth, but once I was back home he was reminded every day of how I was throwing my life away, of what a disappointment I was.

One night, after he'd had too much to drink, I overheard him tell Mom, "I don't want those damn JW's in this house, and I certainly don't want your whore of a daughter and that bastard child in my house!"

I didn't blame him. I needed to leave for everyone's sake. Mom and Mike didn't protest, so I found a job at the Safeway store as a grocery bagger. Just after receiving my first paycheck I dashed over to the bank to cash it. I was horrified when the cashier told me I had the wrong check. I had grabbed a co-workers check with a name spelled very similar to mine. I was branded a thief even though my paycheck was still at the store and near the time clock in alphabetical order with the others. As humiliating as that was, it was the best thing that could have happened to me, a new chance in life. The child welfare system looked into the situation and after talking with my parents felt I would be better off living in a foster home where I could live with Rachel, where someone could care for her while I went back to finish high school. Maybe then I could still make something of myself.

We found the perfect foster home, just half of a mile from our house across the school playing field. Marsha and Jim had watched me run past their house during track practice, and even back when I chased Kayla. They heard about my situation and offered to take me in.

Marsha and Jim had two small boys of their own. They were very kind and down to earth, with a lifestyle much different than I was used to. They were almost like hippies, eating whole-grain foods, shopping at that co-op food store, and dressing simply and comfortably.

Marsha had long, thick wavy red hair down to her waist, and freckles. Jim and the boys looked a lot like her. That family sure had a lot of freckles. They seemed like nice people but I was apprehensive about moving into another family's home and suddenly being part of it. I didn't know what to expect.

They prepared a cozy room for us, letting me choose the colors of our bedroom and the fabric of the curtains that Marsha then sewed. I chose light lavender, like the lilacs, with bright lilac flowers on white for the curtains. They all went out of their way to make me feel welcome. I felt homesick, but Jim and Marsha's place was going to be the next best thing to being home, I knew that.

Once I started school, Marsha took care of Rachel during the day. I had to make up for most of my junior year, so I was busy taking extra credits and classes, then coming home and taking care of Rachel in the afternoons and evenings.

My first day in school was strange. Everyone stared at me, and the girls I knew who'd had abortions were the ones that stared the most. I walked down the halls and didn't really care what they thought at that point. Having a beautiful baby girl, living with a family so kind and caring, and believing I was doing the right thing for me and my baby was all that mattered. It would have been nice to be like my classmates, without a care in the world other than impressing boys and deciding what clothes to wear for the day, but I had more important things to do.

I did well in my classes and was making up credits from my junior year with ease. My teachers gave me some slack by giving me extra study time and allowing me to go to the gym and locker room by myself, without a teacher, to exercise every afternoon for my missed P.E. credit.

I loved sixth period – my time to be alone. If it was raining or cold, I shot baskets in the gym or played handball against the wall by myself. When it was warm, I went out the gym door and ran barefoot around the track for a while. It felt so good to run again. Then I would lie on the high jump and pole vault mats to enjoy the soothing warm sun on my face. Mrs. Kuehl came to check on me during the last few minutes of my so-called P.E. "class." She smiled and told me, "You deserve a little time to yourself."

After my first few weeks in school everyone seemed to adjust to my having a baby at home. Deanna walked by and said, "I'm glad you're back. You've been through a lot." It took a lot of nerve for her to come up to me, and that made me feel really good. I was glad I helped her pick up the coins in the cafeteria.

The one time that Brad came over to see Rachel he seemed nice and caring, and wanted us to start seeing each other. I actually started dating him, just in case, for Rachel's sake and my own – I was confused and felt contaminated and worthless, thinking no other boy would want to come near me. Maybe we would end up falling in love and getting married. Then Rachel would have a mother and a father. I didn't hate Brad, and I had liked him a lot before everything that had happened. It turned out to be one big mistake and nothing good came out of it. He hadn't changed one bit.

The boys were nervous around me. I ignored Brad and he ignored me, but his friends were very polite and said hello whenever he wasn't around. One good friend of Brad's, a boy named Shawn, went out of his way to say hello and I noticed him staring at me a lot. Sometimes he gave me a quick look and a shy smile, and other times he had a sad look on his face, as if he felt badly for me. He was tall and handsome and if I had a choice, I knew he would be the one for me.

Cathy was happy to see me. She had changed from the poor smelly neighbor kid I knew years ago into a clean and well-dressed girl. "It's good to see you in school again," she said. "Not many people could manage like you have." It was nice to hear that, but even better to see her looking good and fitting in.

During those few months, Rachel was growing like a weed, rosy-cheeked and chubby. She loved to eat – imagine that! She had hair just like mine when I was younger. It smelled so fresh and sweet, and I loved to blow on it and call her "Dandelion Head."

There were times I lay in bed at night after putting Rachel to sleep and thought about how lucky I had been so far in life. So many good people had made up for any bad luck I'd had: the Jehovah's Witnesses to help us when our house burned down; Mike to move us away from Enumclaw to a beautiful paradise town; the Levels and Kim for being good friends; Chuck, who did more than anyone for my family; Sandy, who helped me through my pregnancy and Rachel's birth, and then Marsha and Jim. I was thankful and would always say a prayer.

As grateful as I was, I was still torn about Rachel's future. I loved her so much but knew I couldn't give her everything she deserved and needed. I wasn't ready to get married, and at my age I couldn't find a decent job. All I wanted was for Rachel to have the best chance, without a lot of dysfunction in her life.

One day when I brought Rachel over to visit Mom and Laurie, they told me about a Jehovah's Witness family who wanted to adopt Rachel. "They'll take good care of her, and they have money and a daughter she can grow up with." Plus, they would let Mom and Laurie remain a part of Rachel's life. I was shocked at first, but I knew and liked the family and we all wanted what was best for Rachel. I had to think about it.

Mike had a different idea. He agreed it would be best to give Rachel up for adoption, but not to a Jehovah's Witness family we knew. He said he thought that would be too hard on me. He truly seemed more concerned about me than Mom or Laurie did.

Still, I decided to let the Jehovah's Witness family adopt my baby.

Saying goodbye to Rachel literally made my stomach ache. I was numb, and couldn't stop crying. I moved back home, and then starting missing Jim and Marsha and their boys, too. I was a mess for months.

Once I pulled myself together and started going to Jehovah's Witness functions again, I would see Rachel from afar at the meetings. She was adorable in her beautiful dresses and the silly crocheted hats her new family made her wear. She was their queen, drawing more attention than their older baby daughter. Laurie and Mom held her at the meetings while I stayed back and just watched. I was torn. I wanted her back, but I could see how happy she was with her new family, and that they would give her a better start than I could. She needed to be with them.

I felt sick knowing I would never be a part of her life.

chapter 7

I didn't want to get out of bed. I didn't want to see anyone. It scared me to feel that way. It made me think about Dad and his depression, his addiction to drugs and alcohol, and his suicide. His grief over losing his brothers must have played a part in his suffering and horrible death. I gave Rachel away at the grayest, most dismal time of year, and it was the grayest, most dismal time of my life. The sun would never shine again.

I went through the motions – school, meetings and homework – but the clouds didn't lift. *What have I done? I gave up my daughter. Was it the right thing to do? Was I being selfish? Could I have figured out how to raise her and give her a good life if I'd tried harder?* My mind jumped from one question to the next, and I was nowhere close to any answers.

Stanley was a huge comfort. I would turn on his favorite shows, like "Captain Kangaroo," "Gilligan's Island," and "Mister Rogers' Neighborhood," so that he would come over and cuddle up next to me. He knew I was feeling sad, and having him snuggle up so I could smell his blanket hair was comforting. I loved him as much as I loved Rachel. But then Stanley would get up and run off, and the second-guessing would begin again.

I hadn't run much since my pregnancy began, almost two years earlier. I was too embarrassed, too sorry that I let everyone down. Finally, I went out and ran through the golf course to see how the golfers would react after my disgrace. I was a little uneasy but I had to do it. I had to know.

A couple of golfers, the "old guard" of Port Townsend, were getting ready to tee up. One of them called out, "Hi Kimmie, it's good to see you out running again!" Another group, on their way from one hole to another, joined in to give a wave and welcome me back.

Those golfers probably had no idea how much weight they took off my shoulders. Maybe the townspeople didn't think I was a complete failure after all.

Now I can look forward to track season.

It didn't take a lot to bounce back into decent shape. A week after Rachel's birth I was already at my normal weight – I never gained that much anyway – and I was so young that I didn't lose much fitness. "You snapped right back," Mike told me. The boys on the track team weren't so sure. A few weeks before practice started, one of them told me, "You should try and do something active since you were doing nothing for two years, just sitting around being pregnant and taking care of a baby." *Just?* That got me going.

Mom didn't give me a hard time about joining the track team or even insist the team come down the hill on Wednesdays for Bible study. I think she and Mike realized that I needed to run, and that Mike was feeling badly about his harsh comment to Mom after I came home from the hospital with Rachel.

I wouldn't know until my first race if I really still had the speed and mental toughness to be the best in the state, but at least I wanted to try. Waking up to the birds singing, the sun shining and the sweet scent of the spring air ... my optimism bloomed along with the lilacs. I wanted to enjoy the day and do what I loved – run.

Sarah Level had started high school a year earlier, and I was glad to have her there with me for my final track season. Sarah was one of the best sprinters and long jumpers in the state. Irene Griffith was an excellent miler and Molly Ritter was a good shot putter. We had all the makings of a great team.

Sarah and I were inseparable. We walked around like we were something special, teasing the boys and constantly joking around with our team. I'm sure we fed off one another's confidence. We liked being the center of attention. Especially Sarah, but I went with it.

Mr. Royce joined the track team as Mrs. Kuehl's assistant in 1974, and he pretty much took over the program in 1975, becoming our head coach in 1976. He was built like a football player and looked like Starsky from "Starsky and Hutch." He was perfect for the job, finding a good balance between letting us have fun and working us harder than we'd worked before. He was more vigilant, though, when I tried to sneak my shoes off and run barefoot. "We can't risk a foot injury," he pointed out.

With Mr. Royce coaching, I trained for real a few times a week. I did some interval training for the first time: 6 x 220's (running half a lap as fast as I could and then jogging the second half before doing it again, six times total). It was hard, almost as hard as running down to the dock full speed before jumping into the cold water.

Mr. Royce told me I was plenty fast for my own good, but that I needed to spend the early season working on endurance to build up strength and stamina. He wanted me to go out for 2-mile runs with the distance runners. *What?!* I had never gone out for a long run just to do it. I needed a place to go, and a reason, like running to the beach or my bike being broken or showing off for the golfers.

So Mr. Royce gave me a reason. "Run to Chetzemoka Park with the distance runners and if you run there and back without stopping I'll give you a candy bar," he told me. Then just as we took off, he'd yell in his booming voice, "And no goofing off down at the beach when you get to the park!" We could still hear him as we went over the first hill.

The distance runners were surprised that I needed bribery. They thrived on long slow distance runs, *hmmm.* Irene would go out for miles and miles, sometimes 10 miles a day, which made no sense to me. Of course, I ran miles and miles without realizing it a million times, especially when Kayla decided to take off. Either way, the ploy worked. I ran to the park and back, and earned my Baby Ruth.

At last, it was time for our first meet. I was entered in the 440, 880 and both relays. Mr. Royce said it was time to see what I could do.

Betty was there with all of the Levels to watch Sarah and me. Mary Level, one of the little naked girls when we were little, followed me around everywhere. She made good-luck charms, like little woven-grass people or a pinecone with eyes glued on it, before every meet and expected me to carry them while I raced. I would carry them in one hand, or tuck them in my shorts. That could hurt a little, but I didn't want to disappoint her. She always stared at me, saying, "I'm going to be just like you when I'm in high school." I was annoyed at times but appreciated her, as well. Someone looked up to me.

Of course Charlie was there, and the whole place was packed. We were talked up in the newspapers, which brought everyone out to the meet. Sarah and Irene had made a name for themselves the previous year when I was out, so everyone was there to see them again and eager to see how "The Comeback Kid" would do. I was eager, as well, and so nervous that I felt as if I might keel over.

My first race was the 880. As I went out on the track with the other girls, Mr. Royce stood right there on the starting line, checking to be sure I kept my shoes on. There was no slipping them off seconds before the start with him around.

He didn't say much before the gun went off. "You know what to do," he told me. "It's in you." Mr. Brink gave me a little wink from across the track as he always did. Then everything went strangely quiet, hushed as if everyone in the stands and on the grass was holding their breath. I heard just one voice – Mr. Royce. "Go get 'em, Kimmie," he bellowed. "Run smart!"

The starter gave us the command, and we were off.

I tucked in behind the lead pack and it was like someone threw a switch. Suddenly, I wasn't nervous, I wasn't concerned about letting people down, and I wasn't worried about losing. I was there to run my best and do what I could to win. That's all I had on my mind. I was totally focused on the task at hand.

The leader took off extremely fast for a half-mile race, but it felt good to me. She and I dropped the pack after just 330 yards. Everyone was on their feet cheering, and it grew even louder when the announcer told them we were on pace to set a school record. I followed her for another 220 before throwing in a kick and passing her in the final lap. Charlie left his usual seat in the corner of the wooden bleachers on the homestretch, getting as close to the track as he could. By the time I turned the final corner, he was almost right next to me. "Go, Kimmie!" he yelled.

I won and broke the meet record on my first race back! Mr. Brink was a big man, so big that his nickname was "Bear," but he had tears in his eyes.

I still have it in me. I can make people proud of me again.

The 440-yard race (quarter-mile) was even more thrilling. I went out as if I were being chased by the coppers and felt more powerful than when I burned those hornets' nests. I won that race as well and nobody was close to us in the relays, where I ran the first leg of the 440-yard relay and the last leg of the mile relay. Irene won the mile, while Sarah won the 100, 220 and the long jump. Townspeople were surprised at our times and scores – our tiny "Single A" school had posted faster times than the biggest schools in the state! We were a hit.

After the meet, I looked over at Charlie, sitting in the stands and trying to look his usual cool self again. I walked over and told him, "You should go out for track. You're in high school now, you're Sarah's age and you're built to be a runner." Charlie was a taller and stronger version of me, with the exact same body type.

"I'll race you sometime during the season and show you how it's done," he bragged. We both laughed, and then walked home together. It was a good day.

After earning so much public recognition, my family started to pay more attention to my running. Stanley was almost 5 by then and I would get a big hug from him after Mom showed him my photo in the newspaper. "Good job, Kimmie," Bradley would say in his deepening voice. Sometimes he'd feel so proud of me he would cry – he was the crybaby in the family anyway. Mike was proud, as well, especially when his friends would talk to him about my races after reading about me in the paper. Even Mom started clipping and saving articles from the *Port Townsend Leader* and the Port Angeles newspaper that Debbie and I used to deliver.

Everybody in Washington was talking about little Port Townsend. Our girls' team was ranked #1 in the state, and so was the boys' team. Brad was one of the best shot-putters and javelin throwers in the state, and ran well at 100 yards and on the 440-yard relay. I just sort of pretended he wasn't there. Mark McCready was a great high jumper and looked the part, tall and thin. John Stroeder was an incredibly tall redhead, much taller than Mark. He was an excellent discus thrower and an important part of the boys' 440-yard relay. He grew to 6' 10" and played for three seasons in the NBA, and now coaches the Port Townsend High School basketball team.

"It's unbelievable to have so many good athletes on one small high-school team at the same time," Mr. Brink would say.

Mr. Royce treated us girls more like family than his track stars. He and his wife, Jerrie, had us over for pasta dinners, and he gave out awards for no reason other than to recognize us for something special we did during the week, even if it wasn't running related. I received an "Act of Kindness" Award once for helping a crying girl feel better after her period started in the middle of a race, in front of everybody. And once

I was honored with "The Biggest Eater" Award. He worked us hard, but never pushed us to the point where we weren't enjoying our training and racing. He had all of that talent in his hands and he could have driven us so hard that we ended up hating the sport, but he didn't. Mr. Royce never ruined our joy of running; he encouraged it.

One afternoon at the end of a home meet, Charlie said to me, "You had a great race in the 880, but you need to run with some real competition. You need to push yourself against the best." I began to smile, because I knew what was coming: the dare. "I could give you a race and beat you easily."

"Let's see what you can do," I said as I took my shoes off. *Nobody can make me wear shoes for this race.* We walked to the start of the 880, me in my track uniform and bare feet, Charlie in his jeans and Converse sneakers. "Ready?" I said. He nodded. "Then let's go!"

Right off the bat he went flying, looking like a natural runner with his long, steady stride. I was struggling to keep up, never working so hard in my life. I was barely able to keep up with him for the first half of the race. My teammates, the other teams and the coaches all stopped packing up shoes and equipment to cheer for the underdog – Charlie!

When we came around the corner with a half lap to go, Charlie unleashed a kick more powerful than anything I had. I managed to hang on to him around the final corner and into the straightaway, but after that it was a lost cause. He beat me, and even though I would never have let him win on purpose, I was glad he did. Everyone clapped and cheered his victory. We didn't time that 880 race, but I'm sure it was the fastest one I ever ran.

Afterward, Charlie turned to me and said, "I'll show you how to run the 440 next time." We laughed. I went over to pick up my shoes and we walked home together. I was so proud of Charlie, and I told him so.

In addition to the meets against small schools in our area, there were also invitational meets against the 4A schools – the biggest and best competition around. Our small Port Townsend team usually had eight girls qualify for an invitation to those special meets: Sarah, Irene, Molly and me; along with Terri Purviance, Andrea Mitchell, Marianne Maiden and Nikki Fountain, who were a part of our winning relays. We would face teams with 20 or 30 invited girls, and still win the meet outright because we won almost every event we entered: the mile, 880, 440, 220,

100, 440-yard relay and mile relay, and then Molly always came through in the shot put. We shocked everyone and were the talk of the town.

COMPETING AT ISSAQUAH was the Townsend delegation gathered in the accompanying photo—(front, from left) Terri Purviance, Andrea Mitchell, Kim Seelye, Sarah Level, Irene Griffith, Coach Lorraine Kuehl, (second row) Marianne Maiden, Molly Ritter, Nikki Fountain and Coach Larry Royce. —Leader Photo

Front: Terri, Andrea, me, Sarah, Irene, Mrs. Kuehl
Back: Marianne, Molly, Nikki and Larry Royce
1976 ~ Courtesy of the Port Townsend Leader

Our school and townspeople again were so proud of our track team that they raised enough money to buy us new uniforms for our last few races and the upcoming state meet. We were finally going to wear elegant uniforms, a white ribbed and form-fitting singlet with "P. T." in red velvet on the upper corner, and slim-fitting red shorts with "Port Townsend" written down the side in white velvet.

I didn't wear socks anymore – I hated how they scrunched up inside my shoes and bothered my crooked toe – and I told Sarah to lose her silly tube socks because they ruined the uniform. She agreed and went sockless in the next meet only to develop blisters. Mr. Royce wasn't too happy with me.

In a big Seattle meet, Mr. Royce decided to enter me in the mile so I could run the distance at least once that season, given that I'd won the State Championship two years earlier. I wasn't too excited about running the mile to start with, since I was perfectly happy in the shorter events, but the worst part was that I would have to run against a teammate, Irene, who had one of the fastest times in the state that year. We had such a small team that everyone ran different events, and we'd never had to compete against each other before. Everyone was anticipating the matchup except me.

The fastest milers in Washington State were there, from the smallest Single-A schools like us through huge 4A schools. It was a much bigger and more competitive meet than our upcoming state meet would be, where we would compete against just Single-A schools. I really wanted to take my shoes off for *this* one, but Mr. Royce was right there, as always.

As darkness fell just before the start of the mile, the lights flashed on. I'd never run under the lights before. Suddenly, the many powerful girls in their bright, shiny swimsuit uniforms – plus Irene and me – were in the spotlight. I was glad our uniforms weren't shiny or revealing. They were classy and the shorts were just short enough, but not too short. Even when I was little and wearing nothing but Debbie's hand-me-downs, I would ask my mother to take in or lower a waistline so that things fit well. No matter what, I always liked to feel good about what I was wearing, and I certainly felt special in our new uniforms that night.

We lined up in our lanes and were given instructions: no cutting into the inside lane until after the first 110 yards, around the first corner.

Because I didn't have a mile time that season, I was treated like a slower runner and assigned one of the middle lanes, behind both Irene and another girl. I was nervous, feeling claustrophobic being packed in my lane like a sardine behind the other runners.

It was the big race of the meet and all eyes were on us. *I really want to take my shoes off.*

The gun went off, but we didn't move very fast. Irene took off so slow that I was stuck behind her and the other girl. We crawled around the first turn and when I cut into the first lane after 110 yards, I was in last place. The pack was way ahead. *I'm not used to this!*

I pulled into the second lane and slowly picked up the pace. Irene followed me as we caught and passed all of the struggling runners who went out too fast. We slowly made our way up to the lead pack, catching them with one lap to go. My crooked toe was really hurting by then, but I tucked in behind the leaders until the final half lap, and then sprinted to the finish for the win in 5 minutes. Irene came running in with the others a few seconds later. I was so glad that Mr. Royce bribed me on the long runs with those candy bars. The whole thing seemed effortless.

After the meet Mr. Royce told me, "It was good for you being boxed in with that slow start." He was right. As a result, I did the right thing by slowly moving my way up to the leaders from last place, I learned to trust my instincts: don't panic, don't waste energy by worrying, and don't run too fast trying to catch up right away.

"You did the right thing," said Mr. Royce, "You're a natural distance runner."

Throughout the next several weeks, we would have to make it through the district and regional meets. We trained and worked just hard enough to still enjoy every practice. I can't remember anybody struggling with an injury. Some coaches said we should have trained harder, but those same coaches were the ones with the most injuries on their teams. Mr. Royce was a blessing, our gift that just kept giving.

Betty Level talked Mom into coming along to our district meet on Bainbridge Island. I was so pleased and proud to have Mom at a meet for the first time that I tried not to flirt with the boys or seem worldly. Mom seemed happy to be there, but I made things nerve-wracking during the 880. In the first 220 yards, someone stepped on the back of my shoe and it came right off. I pulled into the second lane as the runners kept racing around the corner, quickly pulled the other shoe off, caught up to the pack, and then went ahead just in time to win the race. *So much for shoes!* I thought as I proudly walked off the track.

"So you finally managed to run a race barefoot this season," Mrs. Kuehl said with a chuckle.

At districts I qualified in all four of my events, and then we had only a week to prepare for regionals. At one practice Mr. Royce brought me a present: a brand new pair of Adidas track spikes. They were velvet red with white stripes and matched my uniform perfectly. I was thrilled and wore them in practice whenever I had the chance. I couldn't wait for a speed workout so I could put them on. I didn't care about running barefoot when I was wearing those spikes.

We couldn't make any mistakes at regionals if we wanted to place well enough to qualify for the state meet. Sarah and I were our usual relaxed selves, walking around in our cool uniforms as I carried my red velvet spikes over my shoulder for an added touch.

"If you two spent half as much time thinking about your races as you do trying to be cool, you might break your own records," Mrs. Kuehl told us. We all laughed, knowing she was probably right. But all of us qualified in all our events and several of the boys qualified as well, so it was a good day and being cool didn't hurt anything. Our photos were in the newspapers again and they even displayed a nice one of me wearing my new spikes.

It was a good time in my life. The track season helped ease my sadness, and at times even forget, but I still missed Rachel, holding her and smelling her sweet baby hair. I actually looked forward to going to the Kingdom Hall three days a week, to admire her from afar. She changed and grew so much during those first months in her new home, and I felt better seeing for myself how happy and spoiled she was. Everyone loved her and she captured more attention than any child in the congregation, except maybe for my precious Stanley. I could tell that she thrived on it, all smiles and laughter.

Mel caught me watching Rachel after one meeting. "She's happy, isn't she, Kimmie? They're taking good care of her," he said as we observed from the corner of the Kingdom Hall. "You made the right decision, you know."

"I can see that," I told him. "I'm at peace knowing she's happy."

"It was a tough decision, but now you have a chance in life," he winked, "and another shot at becoming a State Champion. I'm really proud of you, Kimmie."

A few weeks before the state meet, voters turned down a school levy. It failed by just a single percentage point, and that meant there would be no money in the budget for sports for the foreseeable future. After that year, there would be no more teams. Our 1976 track team would be the last for a while, maybe a long while. It was a long shot, but we hoped we would do so well at state that someone would have to come up with something.

When state came along, Port Townsend was abuzz with excitement. A lot of townspeople made that long trip to Yakima to support us. Some even made bets with fans from other towns, and there was a $100 bet on me to win the 440.

But there were bets against me, too. One girl could run close to the same time as me in the 440, and had been running the 220 in most of her meets to improve her speed. I was concerned, but not worried. All I had to do was power out of my starting blocks without false starting and then let my instincts and skill take over. I was calm, cool and ready to run hard. Whether I won or not was secondary. Mr. Royce came down to the track to make sure my blocks were set, but he didn't have to check to make sure I had my shoes on. I had those beautiful red velvet spikes on, securely laced and double knotted.

There was a delay while they finished removing the hurdles to clear the track for our race. As I was standing near the girl who was supposed to be able to beat me, Brad walked up to her and started flirting. She flirted back. Then he said to her ...

"I hope you beat Kim."

How dare he! I was fuming, and totally lost focus on the race I was about to run. We were finally told to take our places. We got into our blocks, in the set position. The gun went off and I bolted, leaving everyone behind, even the faster girl. I ran on pure anger, not thinking at all. Everyone was cheering and screaming as I came running down the final stretch, far ahead of the others. Little did they know why I was so fired up, but I made some gambling men from Port Townsend pretty happy.

The same girl was in the 880, and I was ready to go at her again. She was flirting and acting like a showoff Jezebel in front of everyone. Brad winked at her and said, "good luck." By then I was calm and ready to race levelheaded. I got away with it in a one-lap race, but I couldn't run fueled on fury for two laps or I would have the devil to pay.

I followed the perfect strategy, even letting the showoff Jezebel lead for a while. After the first lap I was feeling too comfortable, and could hear all of my buddies, coaches, and the townspeople cheering me on from the stands. Jezebel was getting tired and I could tell she wanted me to start doing the work. She tucked in behind me, running right on my heels in the final lap. I knew she was a great 220 runner and was fast in more ways than one, so I had to keep my focus and start pushing the pace. *Faster now ... a little faster ... almost so she doesn't notice ... now a little faster.*

Just after the final turn she took off past me down the straightaway. *This is not happening!* Losing a race to a speedier girl was one thing but losing to Jezebel after Brad wished her luck? I passed her so fast she couldn't react. I'm sure I surprised her, because I definitely surprised myself.

It was the most thrilling of all my races, and maybe the most satisfying. It was perfectly executed. I had no idea I had that extra gear, but I did. I believed I could do whatever it took to win the race. We ran 2:15 for that 880 – the first lap in 77+ seconds and the second lap in 57+ seconds – the same time I ran in my 440 race!

The relays were exciting, as well; we medaled in the mile relay and won the 440-yard relay. Sarah won the 100, 220 and the long jump, and was on the winning 440-yard relay with me. Irene was second in the mile race, while Molly placed third in the shot put.

Our girls' team won the state meet. So did the boys. John Stroeder won the discus, Mark McCready won the high jump, and Brad won the javelin, along with placing in the relay with John.

We came back to Port Townsend as superstars. At a school assembly in the auditorium, both teams went up on stage with the big stage lights on us, and were given beautiful red roses. They were the first flowers I'd ever received.

Not only were we the first teams to ever win a state track title for Port Townsend, but we were also the first school to win both the boys' and girls' state titles in the same year in any sport. A week later, two bank officers – Rennie Bergstrom, a vice president of Seattle First National Bank, and Jerry Iseman, president of Jefferson National Bank – presented a $20,000 check to the school board, which included a $5,000 "shot in the arm" for sports. The track team would be back.

Graduation ~ May 1976

A week later was graduation weekend. I had no trouble completing all of my credits for a missed school year and managed to get good grades, even after having a baby and going through all of that emotional turmoil. I was ready for graduation.

My family was proud. Mike's mom, Grandma Pat, seemed the most excited for me. Maybe she knew more than anyone how important it was to have a good education. Stanley rushed over after I received my diploma giving me a big hug. "I'm going to graduate just like you, Kimmie," he said, beaming with pride. After taking many photos, my family and friends gathered at our house for a big celebration with a potluck dinner and cake. I enjoyed my party, but felt as if there was a big pit in my stomach when I wasn't allowed to join my classmates for the Senior Party and all of the other fun and festivities. Later that night, after pouring myself a large glass of milk, I sat alone at the kitchen table and finished off my graduation cake, to ease that growing pit in my stomach.

Mom wanted me to stay in Port Townsend and marry a Jehovah's Witness just like Kim O'Meara, who was planning to marry Eric – Mel's brother and Debbie's old boyfriend – so no one, me included, paid any attention when many of the top schools around the country offered me track scholarships. I went right to a great summer job in the engineering department at the Crown Zellerbach Paper Mill.

Mr. Royce generously loaned me enough money to buy a 1965 three-speed red Mustang with a black vinyl top until I could pay him back later in the summer, and I started dating an older guy Mike didn't like. He was 22 and had a bad reputation, from what Mike heard through his poker buddies. So instead of upsetting the household yet again, I broke it off with the older guy and didn't go out with boys or do much of anything other than work at the mill and learn how to drive using a clutch. I spent the weekdays with the beautiful and lively secretary of the engineering department, my mentor Connie Stapf, who guided me through my job, taught me to use makeup and fix my hair in fashionable styles – and her brave husband, Richard, gave me driving lessons. On the weekends, my friends and I would cruise through town and hop down the street from one stop sign to another. Everyone would duck and laugh. We had a good time in that Mustang.

Toward the end of summer, Debbie came to visit with her one-year-old son, Jade. It was so good to see Debbie again. I was pleased when she said, "Kimmie, let's go to the track. I want to watch you run," and surprised that Charlie wanted to go with us after watching me the entire track season. I showed off for them while they sat in the wooden bleachers counting my laps. After running for quite awhile I shouted, "How many laps is this?" Debbie calls out, "10!" Charlie hollers, "15!" They were laughing hysterically.

My hands shot in the air. "What?!" I ran closer. They were getting high! *Hmmm.*

The next evening, Debbie and I cruised around downtown in Charlie's souped-up Chevy before it was time for a big family dinner at Laurie and Mel's. As we were driving by the Safeway store, I yelled to Debbie, "There's Shawn!" and took my eyes off the road long enough to soak in the guy I felt could be the love of my life. Crash. I rear-ended the car in front of me, which was merging into the ferry line. Everyone saw the accident, even Shawn. Debbie was laughing. I wasn't. I was embarrassed in front of the love of my life, and then I had to tell Charlie I damaged the front of his car.

For some reason, Charlie wasn't angry. He drove downtown in my Mustang and shook his head while inspecting the damage I did to his Chevy, then said, "Kimmie, I'll tow the poor guy across the ferry. It looks like he needs some help." Debbie and I went to Laurie's for a nice dinner, but I didn't enjoy it much knowing that Charlie was missing out on lasagna, his favorite meal. He didn't seem to mind helping me out, though, using my car to tow the other guy onto the ferry and then straight to an auto-repair shop near his home on Whidbey Island.

Chapter 8

School was just about ready to start that fall when I started second-guessing myself about staying in Port Townsend. I saw Chuck in his yard, and went over to ask him what he thought about me staying on another year at the mill to make extra money before going to college.

"Kimmie," he told me, "you have so much to learn, you need to get out of this small town and experience life as soon as you can. You need to learn the ways of the world and see what it has in store for you."

All that night, I thought about what Chuck said. I decided he was right.

The only college I could find that hadn't used up all its scholarship money for that semester was in Spokane, so I packed up my red Mustang, said goodbye to everyone and headed off to the other side of the state. I hadn't driven that Mustang much so didn't know if I could navigate onto the ferry from Bainbridge Island to Seattle, and I certainly didn't know if I could manage the clutch up the mile-long hill full of stoplights between the ferry port in Seattle and the interstate toward Spokane. Therefore, Charlie went out of his way to help me – again – and came along.

Charlie was the quiet one in the family. He sat back and observed, even more than me. He would say something when he felt it contributed to the conversation but didn't talk just to be heard. Just like Grandma Helen, he smiled and chuckled a lot at things that amused him. When he was younger he'd shown a fiery temper when he was provoked, but it was taming down. He was the calmest, most stable sibling, the one with whom I could always relax and enjoy some quiet time, the only one other than Stanley who wasn't always causing some kind of turmoil.

The drive gave us the chance to catch up after working our separate summer jobs and not seeing much of each other. We laughed for the entire seven hours, taking turns behind the wheel. When it was my turn to drive, he smoked some marijuana and we laughed even more.

Once we arrived in Spokane, I began to feel weepy, realizing how grateful I was to have Charlie in my life, and I tried to hold back my tears. "Thank you, Charlie. I love you," I told him, just before he climbed on the next bus directly back to Port Townsend.

"I love you too, Kimmie," he said, tears welling in his eyes. "I worry about you, so please be careful."

"I will," I promised, and hugged him for an extra long time. Then he sauntered onto the Greyhound bus in his cool manner.

Then ... I was on my own. When I met the coach later that day, he suggested I room with Linda, a top 400/200-meter runner from the Tacoma area. She was in her second year of school and had been temporarily renting a room in a woman's house. We soon found a small apartment a mile from campus.

Linda was a tall, powerful, beautiful black woman with stunning green eyes. It turns out that we'd raced against each other my sophomore year; she was one of the girls in the bright shiny swimsuit uniforms when I was still in cutoffs. We laughed about that. She was dating the quarterback of the football team. Linda took me under her wing and invited me to all of the team's parties and get-togethers. I enjoyed being in their group and felt special because I was one of the few white people invited. They really liked me and seemed to enjoy my way of thinking – I was innocent and came up with the funniest comments without even trying.

By the time I arrived it was early autumn, and cross-country season had already started. Because we didn't have a cross-country team in Port Townsend, the longest distance I had ever raced was a mile on the track, never three miles over rough terrain in the woods. But the coach thought I should run cross country and that I should jump right into training for it.

I hadn't run much over the summer, so my fitness wasn't up to par. For some reason, the coach felt I needed to run with the men's team. I was surprised when he sent me out on their training runs, up to 10 miles. I tried going out with them on one of their five-mile runs, but they ran way too fast. The climate in Spokane was hot and dry, and the air wasn't as clean and clear as in Port Townsend. It was all so new to me. I managed to run the five miles, but it was torture. I couldn't breathe very well, and I hated it.

To top everything, I was shocked to see Jezebel, from the high-school state meet, on the team. She was still a showoff and flirted endlessly with Linda's boyfriend and all of our other friends. "She's flaunting herself, the little ass," said Linda. "Yes, just like a Jezebel," I told her. We laughed, but I knew *this* girl was trouble.

I wanted out. The coach insisted on sending me out on those miserable long runs with the men's team. It didn't take long before I decided to take a rest at the river, just below the trail, about half of a mile from the college. The guys would drop me off there before heading out for their run. I would relax and soak my feet in the cool water, waiting for them to come back and pick me up so I could finish the final half-mile with them. We did that for every run. I managed a mile of running, to and from the river. I did the track workouts once a week because I enjoyed them. Plus, the football team was practicing on the infield where the players liked watching us train and I liked watching JB, one of the cutest and nicest players on the team.

We had our first cross-country meet in the Finch Arboretum. It wasn't a huge meet, only a few colleges, and I was stuck having to run. We lined up together in the beautiful arboretum with the colorful fall foliage all around us. I was in awe and admiring the autumn leaves when the starting gun went off. I took off a little late but quickly caught up to the other girls. They seemed pretty slow, so I took the lead. Big mistake!

There were dozens of short hills on the grassy course, with a maze of twists and turns around trees. There was no path to follow and suddenly I realized I was running alone. I'd gone the wrong way. As I turned around to see which way the other girls went, I ran into a tree and fell to the ground. *Unbelievable!* I jumped up, caught up to the pack, and still won. But it was the most miserable race of my life. I hated it.

I quit cross country. My scholarship was for track anyway. Most of the women on the cross-country team ended up with an injury of some sort – *this is supposed to get us ready for track season?*

Even though I was the first in my family to go to college, it wasn't that important to me. Although, having taken Chuck's advice, it was a way to meet new friends, expand my horizons and learn the ways of the world. I *really* didn't enjoy going to class, but I did like my work-study job in the information booth at the entrance to the college. I could study and watch a small TV that Carl, the campus cop, watched on his breaks. I loved the job during snowstorms. I enjoyed being out there so close to the falling snow but nice and warm in the tiny booth, watching my comfort TV shows, like "I Dream of Jeannie" and "Leave it to Beaver" reruns. Carl liked to watch "Bonanza" too, so we watched that between his patrols.

Linda and I spent a lot of time hanging around in the Student Union. Linda would talk loud and impress everyone and I followed right along, trying to talk just as loud and keep up with her. We were sitting there one afternoon, talking about all the potted palm trees arrayed in a semicircle around the lounge, when one of the football players pointed to a six-foot palm and said, "This would be a great Christmas tree." Linda replied, "Yeah, it would. Kim and I could use a Christmas tree like this for our place."

Then, the dare: "We'll give you 50 bucks if you two can get it out of here and up into your apartment, and then bring it back after Christmas break without anyone noticing."

That night, during evening class hours when things were quiet, Linda and I drove her car onto the sidewalk that led right up to the big front doors of the Student Union building. We went into the building quickly, in dark outfits with our hair in hats trying to disguise ourselves as much as possible without making ourselves look like burglars. Once the coast was clear, we put a school towel around the dirt at the trunk of the tree so it wouldn't spill out, turned the plant on its side, and rolled it out the two giant doors. We had to fold the top of the tree over so it would fit into Linda's bright yellow Fiat hatchback. Then we jumped into the car and hightailed it out of there before Carl the cop was due on patrol in his little green truck. That was my first surge of adrenaline since my last big race in high school. We managed to haul the plant up to our apartment without too much trouble, and then we decorated it.

The next day in the Student Union, everyone was laughing and joking about the vacant spot where the tree was supposed to be. *Oops.* Later I moved another tree over so nobody else would notice anything was missing.

Just before going home for Christmas break, Linda and I were driving up to our apartment when we saw two men carrying the tree out of our building. We couldn't figure out how they knew we had it, and certainly couldn't figure out how they got into our apartment. After worrying all night, we were called into the dean's office the next day. He told us that someone had informed the P.E. department about the theft.

We soon found out from someone who overheard her telling the coaches that it was none other than Jezebel. Apparently, she paused her audacious flirting long enough to actually listen as the guys bragged about what Linda and I had done. She was the third 400-meter woman on our team, behind Linda and me, and the second 800-meter woman on the team, behind me, so she stood to benefit in a big way if we were thrown off the track team.

"There's way too much of this kind of thing going on," said the dean. "I want to make an example out of you two."

Then he expelled us from school for a semester, and he just "had" to press charges. Later, we were taken into jail and charged with theft/larceny, and much later went to court to face the music. We also had to serve many hours of community service. I may have been the first in our family to go to college, but I was also the first family member to go to jail.

That meant I couldn't run indoor track and the spring track season was wiped out, as well. I didn't know what to do other than wait it out for a semester, then go back to school and start again. And we didn't even get our 50 bucks, because we didn't return the plant without being noticed.

I drove home for Christmas break in my Mustang, which I could drive very well by then. For the first time in three months, I would see my family. I'd really missed everyone, especially Stanley. When I pulled into the driveway I could see him through the bay window, leaning over the back of the couch while he watched and waited for me. I was so touched to see his eager little face.

I walked in the door and Stanley came running with a big hug and tears in his eyes. It seemed as if everyone was there to greet me: Uncle/Grandpa Harold and Grandma Helen, Laurie and Mel with Little Mel, Charlie, Bradley, Mom and Mike.

I was telling them about my first semester and the many new and fun experiences, when Grandma Helen asked me, "What have you been up to?"

"Nothing."

She smiled. "You're up to more than you're telling us. I know you too well."

I enjoyed myself for a month over the holidays, and then the month turned into seven weeks. Eventually, Mike and Mom started wondering, "How long are these college breaks?" I decided I'd better head back to

Spokane and figure out my next plan. When our lease was up at the end of January, Linda decided to leave Spokane and go someplace where she was appreciated. I told her we should fight back and make something out of the fact that two detectives went into our apartment without permission or a warrant. She said it wasn't worth the hassle, and left school for good.

I found some new roommates right away, friends I'd met during first semester. Claire, who was on the track team, wanted out of the dorm and Kelley's roommate was boring, so we all found an apartment together directly across the street from the college.

We got along perfectly. Claire and Kelley went to class in the mornings and early afternoons. I stayed home and cleaned our apartment until it was spotless, then watched TV for the rest of the day. I spent some time trying to figure out how to make some money to pay the rent and bills, too.

The legal age for drinking in Washington was 21, so every Thursday night all the kids from the dozen or so colleges in the area drove across the state line to Idaho, where we could drink and enjoy the disco clubs at age 18. It was only a 20-minute drive to the Slab Inn ("All the beer you can drink in one hour for only $1"), where everyone started the evening. Later we would move on to a disco place called the Kon Tiki, where we danced and had a few drinks until the 1 a.m. closing. We went a few times a month, and it dawned on me that I could make some good money at the Slab Inn.

Besides the ability to run fast, I had another talent: I could drink faster and more than anyone around without spilling a drop. The drinking lessons I learned from beating the boys back in my paper route days might finally pay off.

At first, the winner was the person who could drink the most beers in half an hour without spilling. I would take on all comers. Often it was big burly football players who thought they were hot stuff after a few beers. "There's no way you can drink more beer than me," they would say. Everyone bet against me, putting their money on the football players, so there was a lot of cash on the table.

The rule was that you had to drink the whole beer without spilling a drop before moving on to the next one. I practiced with water at home and it paid off. I could just pour them down without even gulping. I was unbeatable, even by the biggest and rudest guys around. Once, against the best guy, I had to drink 20 beers in 30 minutes, which wasn't very pleasant. It was cheap, watered-down beer in 10-ounce glasses, but still. Sometimes I had to loosen my big, stylish belt and undo the top button of my sleek satin-pink disco pants, but I could earn around $500 in 30 minutes.

After my competitions, Kelley and Claire took me to the disco, where they danced and took turns taking care of me. I just sat back and watched. I only "competed" once a month, to win enough money for rent and bills, and the rest of the time I drank very little, enjoying the band and getting out there on the disco floor.

After a while, the regulars caught on to my drinking talent and would egg on their unsuspecting buddies. The demand for competition was getting intense, but I could only drink so much. I had to come up with another plan. So, to make it easier on myself, I perfected the "Montana Chug," which I'd learned somewhere along the way. In this maneuver, you put your hands at your sides, grab a glass of beer with your teeth, then tip your head and the beer back to swallow it, before setting it back down on the table – again, with no spilling allowed.

I could pour a beer down in seconds. As soon as my competitor spilled even a drop, I would win. People from all around came to race against me the first Thursday of every month, right before my rent was due. I was the queen of the Montana Chug. I never lost. That meant I didn't have to drink too much and could finally enjoy my time at the Kon Tiki afterward.

Later I became a pro at the "Montana Chug Upside Down," where you put a glass of beer on the floor, squat down and grab the back of the mug with your teeth, then drink the beer as you tip your chin and beer in toward your chest. Of course it was "no hands." As you slowly stand up, the beer keeps pouring into your mouth. That was a tough one, and took a lot of practice. Nobody else ever came close to succeeding, meaning I had to drink just one mug of beer to pay the rent.

By then, I wasn't interested in the track program, or running at all. I'd always run for the joy of it, and there was no joy in that program.

I went home to visit my family every break, and in the summers often stayed with Laurie and Mel and their boys. Little Mel had a baby brother by then, named Danny. Rachel's family lived a few houses away, and she would come over and play in the sandbox with Little Mel. Her family didn't allow it when I was visiting, but she would make her way over anyway. Rachel looked just like I did in my baby pictures, with the messy flyaway blond hair, rosy cheeks smeared with dirt from playing with trucks in the dirt pile and sandbox, the dirty skinned-up knees.

Rachel seemed very happy, and was talking away. She came over once when Mom was there, excited about the new family car. "Gwamma," she said, "ouw cow is a wabbit."

"What?"

"It's a wabbit."

"Where's the rabbit?"

"No, ouw cow is a wabbit."

"Your cow?"

Mom finally got it.

Laurie had calmed down a lot, becoming an easy person to be around, and had the picture perfect life. Her house was spotless, she made the most delicious meals and Mel and the boys were dressed neatly. Laurie made their shirts and meeting suits, and was busy washing clothes and diapers, hanging them on the line to dry in their perfect backyard. I loved sitting and relaxing with them at night after putting the boys to bed. We had tea or a glass of wine, watched "Dallas," and talked and laughed about everything. Laurie became my best friend.

One afternoon we decided to give each other a permanent. I was wearing the Farrah Fawcett hairstyle and was ready for something more structured. Laurie gave me a perm first and then, as my hair was setting, I rolled her long dark-blond hair into the small rollers. I had no idea what I was doing, but as usual … I was hoping for the best. She took my rollers out first, and my hair came out a bit frizzy but not bad. Then I took her rollers out. Or, rather, I tried to. After pulling and twisting with no success, I finally had to cut them out. I was terrified about what Laurie might do to me for ruining her hair, but then we started laughing. I was so relieved. A beautician fixed up the disaster, although her hair was a lot shorter by the time the fiasco was all over.

Mostly I preferred to just hang out with Laurie and Mel, but I went out on a couple of dates and even went to a few parties. I went to a keg party at the Levels one night, not expecting anything other than to visit with my good friends and enjoy a beer in front of a bonfire on the waterfront. The Levels had moved into a house with a beautiful view of downtown Port Townsend and Indian Island, where Mike worked. I wasn't going out with anybody at the time, and was trying to get away from an obsessed guy who just wouldn't leave me alone after Sarah set me up on a blind date with him earlier that year. As I was standing near the big fire, staying warm on the cool summer night, who came up to me but Shawn.

I was embarrassed, because the last time Shawn saw me was when I rear-ended a car to get a good look at him. He was a little timid at first, and we talked about never having the chance to get to know each other in high school. Then we talked about everything as the night flew by, and fell in love right there. I would finally have my chance. He was charming, kind and strikingly handsome, resembling a young Richard Gere. I knew I could stay in Port Townsend and enjoy the rest of my life with him. That night, I couldn't think of anything better.

We were holding hands and talking next to the fire when Mary Level pulled me aside and whispered, "You're so lucky." She must have had a crush on him, too. I was so in love, and knew that I had been for a long time, from a distance. After the party, he kissed me goodnight for an extra long time. I was floating on air, like a seagull soaring in the sky. Shawn told me he would see me when he was back in town. He was working a summer job at a lumber mill near Seattle, and promised to call the moment he returned. I couldn't wait to see him again.

I waited and waited, but never did receive his call. *How could I be so gullible? I was so sure he was "the one"! Damn, I'm always too hopeful.* I was angry and so disappointed, but went through the summer, dismissing the rest of the world as I tried to put him out of my mind. Until months later ... Mary Level came over to my parent's house and told me the news. Shawn was killed in a head-on car collision on a narrow road in Seattle.

It was a violent blow. I went numb.

As heartbroken as I was, I felt deep sympathy for Shawn's family. It sickened me wondering how they could possibly live through their horrific loss. I wished I could have known him better, but oddly, another part of me was grateful I didn't – his death would have been even more painful.

—

Starting school in the fall helped ease my sadness, as it always did. I found going back to Spokane gave me the distance needed to absorb the pain I felt during my visits home to Port Townsend. My heart ached to see anyone in my family in distress, even over the slightest things. Stanley was being bullied at the school bus stop and Bradley was having a hard time with his grades. Charlie was always upset about Mom and Mike constantly fighting. Laurie seemed sad and Debbie was doing who knows what! I just wanted everyone to be happy at the same time, living perfect joyful lives. I needed for them to be at peace in order to put my worry for them aside and feel content and happy in my own life.

My roommates kept me busy, bringing out my lighter side when I needed it most.

Kelley was a sarcastic, quick-witted Japanese-American girl, about 5' 2", who was always watching her weight because she tended to put it on quickly. She wasn't an athlete, but was a good student and the most responsible of the three of us. She made sure we paid the rent and the bills and still had enough money for food at the end of the month. Claire and I each gave her money the first of every month. Not only would she pay the bills, she also safeguarded a little extra to give back to us when we ran out of money before the month was over.

Claire, with short brown hair and a round, freckled face, was on a track scholarship. A discus thrower, she was a big girl, strong with a little extra weight, so, like Kelley, she was always on some kind of strange diet. Once, Claire fasted on nothing but watered down apple juice. I decided to help her out by joining her on the ninth day. Big mistake. Only a few hours into that day, we were so hungry we cooked a big chicken and baked a chocolate cake, split both of them in half and ate it all.

I enjoyed the times when my friends grew tired of starving themselves and went on their eating sprees instead. Claire usually dieted all week before going to a big party over the weekend, and then afterward we would end up going to a 7-Eleven for bean and cheese burritos at 2 in the morning. We'd heat them in the microwave and down at least four each. On Wednesdays, they took me to "All You Can Eat" night at the Pizza Haven, and of course they pulled the usual college stunt of putting as much pizza as possible into their purses for later. I couldn't do that, not just because it was stealing but because it was so unsanitary.

Our friend Ken, a cheerleader at college, was the funniest guy I had ever met. He was definitely not an athlete and all he had to do was lift the cheerleaders up, but he thought he was amazing, which made him even more endearing. Ken was on the heavy side, so he was dieting, too. He used to scold us and wag his finger, "A shake for breakfast, a shake for lunch and then a sensible dinner!" It was the tagline for a liquid diet called Slim Fast. It was ironic that all my friends were dieting all the time, while I maintained my healthy appetite.

I never had the desire or need to watch my weight, but I'd always been fascinated with nutrition after reading the only other magazine my mother read every month besides the *Watchtower* and *Awake* magazines. *Prevention* magazine covered a wide range of subjects but focused on food, cooking and nutrition, and I was especially engrossed in their articles on homeopathic remedies, health tips and vitamin deficiencies. So, I decided to study nutrition, and with all my friends dieting, I felt I could help them out in the process.

I had a few boyfriends, but nobody seemed right. When I was on a date, I wanted to be back with Kelley and Claire, even if that meant just watching TV in bed and then going to the 7-Eleven in our pajamas to get a half-gallon of frozen yogurt instead of the fattening ice cream. A half-gallon each.

We loved watching "Eight is Enough," "Charlie's Angels," and "Dallas," along with "Quincy," which was our favorite. Quincy was a medical examiner who solved mysteries and made everyone seem important, even the people lying dead on his table. Even though they weren't too fond of it, everyone watched the "The Waltons," knowing I wouldn't go out with them until it was over.

We hardly ever went to the state line anymore. Since I started receiving a bit of money from my dad's Social Security benefits and was able to save from my summer jobs, I didn't have to compete at the Slab Inn anymore. Every once in a while we'd go back and have a competition just for old times' sake, but by then there wasn't much money to be had because the word was out on me.

Instead, Kelley and Claire thought it was a lot of fun to drive to Pasco, two hours south of Spokane, and visit Debbie on weekends, but Debbie was beginning to turn a little wild. She and Mark were doing crazy things with worldly and undesirable people, having affairs with each other's best friends, smoking marijuana and not attending meetings at the Kingdom Hall. Consequently, they were disassociated from the Jehovah's Witnesses for misconduct.

One weekend when I went alone to visit her, I had to worry about being arrested after a few stunts she and her friends pulled when I was along. Somewhere along the line Debbie became friends with two sisters, one who was in a halfway house after being released from prison, and the other who was just plain crazy. I drove with the three of them to a motel, supposedly to pick up the crazy sister's paycheck. She worked there as a maid, and was having an affair with the owner of the motel.

The three of them went into the motel while I waited in the car. And waited. All of a sudden, Debbie and the halfway house sister came running out with all of the money from the cash register. The crazy sister, who had lured the owner into bed while the other sister robbed him, was right behind them, leaving Mr. Motel still in bed. I was shocked that Debbie would be a part of it. I told the halfway house sister, "You're going to end up back in prison, along with the rest of us."

Debbie and Mark were still married, but by then the marriage was a farce. That same weekend, I drove with Debbie and her thieving friends in an old junky car that smelled of mold and rotting food, with fast-food debris piled high, the music blaring and their cigarette smoke billowing out the windows, to the penitentiary in Walla Walla so the sisters could visit their boyfriends. Debbie said, "It won't take long, Kimmie," and it didn't, but when they came back into the beater car they were laughing about smuggling drugs, wrapped in balloons inside crevices of their body, to their boyfriends. That was the last time I visited Debbie in Pasco. I was afraid of her friends, and for her.

———

A couple of years had passed since I quit the cross-country team, and I still had no desire to run. The whole experience just totally turned me off. However, I was very interested in dating competent, runner-type athletes who looked good in shorts and possessed integrity and a strong sense of honor.

Rory was on the tennis team, and we started dating after years of his hearing about me through the campus gossip. For instance, the plant "theft," running fast, the "Montana Chug Upside Down" and every so often chewing tobacco with my friends on the baseball team. I was different, and he was intrigued.

Rory lived with two tennis teammates, Randy and Tom, in an apartment across the street from a park. I really liked Rory. He was romantic, kind, smart and gorgeous, tanned from his days on the court, with longish white-blond hair and startling dark-brown eyes. He would get up in the morning after I'd spent the night with him and run a couple of laps around the perimeter of the park. He asked me to join him one morning and I did, just to impress him. It was wonderful.

Despite enjoying Rory's company, I never really got hooked on him. After the many disappointments with the men in my life, I put up a wall between me and any guy I ever dated, even my friends. Only my family was allowed inside my little bubble. I'm sure Rory sensed that barrier.

I dated Rory off and on, but there was no commitment. He was a bit of a ladies man, and Claire, Kelley and I all thought he was dating another girl. I didn't think I cared that much, to be honest, but they had crushes on Rory's two roommates. Kelley was in love, so she said, with Randy, and Claire was head-over-heels for Tom. Of course Tom and Randy had no idea, nor were they interested.

Claire and Kelley always wanted to spy on Tom and Randy, like we did with all the guys they had crushes on. We watched "Charlie's Angels" and felt we fit their profile, so we would go out on an "Angel Investigation" when we were bored, driving to a guy's house and sitting in the car eating snacks, waiting and watching for hours to see who he came home with. Sometimes we even looked through his windows, or followed him when he left for the evening.

One night, Claire and Kelley wanted me to go with them on an "Angel Investigation" of Rory, Tom and Randy's apartment. At first I told them, "I can go out with Rory whenever, so what's the point?" but then Kelley said, "Yes, but do you know what he's doing when you aren't with him?" *Hmmm.* I was in.

It was a warm spring evening, with a full moon, and the sweet scent of the air smelled fresh and clean. We laid a blanket on the grassy hill in the park across from their apartment, with a clear view of the stairway leading up to their front door. We had two bottles of wine with glasses, along with cheese, crackers and snacks galore. We needed plenty of snacks because it could be a long night and being an Angel Investigator was hard work. I didn't care if the guys showed or not, I was enjoying my friends.

Claire was drinking plenty of Chablis, but she wasn't snacking with us. She was on one of her diets again – allowing no solid food other than raw vegetables. That evening before our investigation, she had chicken broth with peas and was so hungry that she gulped down the broth, swallowing the peas whole. Her goal had been to fit into my baggy, button-up low cut jeans for the night. She managed to squeeze into them while lying on the bed and holding her stomach in as Kelley and I helped get them buttoned up. I wasn't sure that exactly counted as fitting into them, but at least she had them on.

Kelley and I were running out of snacks and Claire was getting bold and impatient, wanting to look through their window to be sure they weren't sitting home, watching TV or something all the while. So we walked across the street and up their stairway. Just as we were looking into their apartment through the big living room window, all three of them came walking up the stairs, right behind us. We were trapped.

We acted as if we'd just arrived and were knocking on their door. They asked us in, and we sat and had a beer with them. Believe me, Claire didn't need a beer – she drank plenty of Chablis on the stakeout. We were having a nice visit until Claire got that goofy grin she always gets when she is drunk or in love, and that time it was both. She sat right next to Tom and said, "Tom, I love you. I'm in love, Tom, with you and only you." Kelley and I didn't know what to do, while Tom looked surprised and embarrassed. We all laughed nervously.

Claire lay down on the couch with her head in Tom's lap. It was getting bad, but it quickly turned a whole lot worse. While gazing up into his eyes, Claire began to throw up whole peas. The peas were rolling all over her face, even into her pug nose. I started laughing. I couldn't help it. When she tried to sit up, all the buttons on her/my jeans started to pop off. I was dying with laughter, and so was everyone else. It was the funniest thing I had ever seen anybody manage to do.

Poor Claire. The guys helped us load her into our car, which was hidden and parked away from their apartment. They were wondering why we parked so far away. When the moon emerged from behind a cloud, they saw our blanket with the cooler and wine bottles on the hill. Then it was my turn to be embarrassed. They eventually hoisted Claire into the car while I gathered up our investigation scene. She looked hilarious in the back seat, her tummy sticking out of our jeans with all the buttons missing.

We maneuvered Claire out of the car, but couldn't get her up to our third-story apartment. We couldn't even move her to the stairs; she was just too heavy. Leaving her on the grass just below the balcony to our apartment, we took our blanket from the car, covered her up, and left her to sleep out there for what little was left of the night. Kelley and I went to bed.

We were awakened by an awful scream and raced to the balcony, fearing Claire was in trouble. She was, sort of – we forgot about the sprinkler system turning on every morning at 6 a.m., and Claire was huddled under her blanket, confused about where she was and getting soaked.

A few days later, Mom called to tell me my brother Murphy was dead, crushed by a piece of machinery while working as a mechanic. My half brother had fought depression, and there was talk that he'd had schizophrenic tendencies, that it might even have been suicide. The facts were murky. Debbie said he had the "Seelye curse."

Murphy's death made me think about my dad, and I cried for both of them. Why did Murphy leave and never come back to us after Dad died? We loved him and he was our brother. I wondered what kind of turmoil he went through after Dad's death.

It seemed I could never stay carefree for long.

~

Summer came after my third year of college, and as always I went home to Port Townsend. My family had moved from our drafty old house into a brand new one a few miles out of town. There, Mike could store his 16-foot Glasply boat and all his fishing gear in the huge garage he had always dreamed of. Mom finally had the new house she'd always wanted, beautifully decorated with new furniture and where she could create her own little paradise with a beautiful garden-park in the backyard.

Mom referred to it as her "Secret Garden," her escape. Colorful perennials sat in pots at each corner of a large deck and along steps leading down to a lush green lawn surrounded by rhododendrons and evergreens. She had transplanted the perky, much-loved daisies from the old house, with flowerbeds and small trees lining a walkway. Antique jugs, more barrels filled with flowers, driftwood in odd shapes and sizes, naked frog statues, little signs that said things like "Only Gardeners Know The Dirt," and rocks collected by her children and grandchildren over the years filled every available patch of bare ground.

Every time I looked, I spotted something new in that garden – even though it had been there all along.

There was an herb garden next to a pathway winding down to a creek where we all played on a rope swing, sometimes jumping into a deep pool of water to join an otter that chose to live there. Our tomcat, named Rat Breath, always tried to take a bite out of him. Poor Rat Breath got the worst of it. Even so, he was right back at the edge of the creek, bandaged and all, for another chance at that otter.

I had never seen my parents and brothers so cheerful and content. I loved seeing Stanley, and went to the meetings with Mom to see Rachel. Mom and Laurie had started babysitting her. Rachel's new family still didn't want me near her, but Laurie would sneak Rachel over to our house. She was just 4, though seemed to sense that I was somebody special.

Many afternoons, I would fall asleep on the couch watching "I Love Lucy" before going to my summer job only to wake up with her lying in my arms, pretending to be asleep after maneuvering her way in. It was so nice to be with her, hold her, and enjoy watching her show off for me. When I purposely paid no attention to her, trying not to become too attached, she did little tricks, inching closer and closer, until I had to laugh. It was much better than I could have hoped for. I was grateful that Mom and Laurie persuaded me to keep her in our lives.

I was working at the Port Ludlow Resort, overlooking the boat harbor and Hood Canal, with the Olympic Mountains as a backdrop. It was just a 20-minute drive from our house. I worked as a waitress in the lavish restaurant, while Charlie and Bradley had summer jobs there as cooks.

The three of us teased each other in the kitchen, laughing and having a gay old time together during our shifts, from 5 p.m. to 11 p.m. After sleeping in, we spent the mornings relaxing with a cup of coffee and enjoying the beautiful Port Townsend summer days on our parents' deck. I didn't do much of anything else before heading to work.

I did go out on a few dates, only because Sarah set me up with friends from my high school days. Sometimes I went out with a guy more than once, but I really wasn't interested in finding anybody yet.

Problem was, I had a hard time hurting a guy's feelings. After a night out, if he asked me to go out again I'd say, "Maybe, we'll see," "I'm busy this week," or something that wouldn't make him feel bad that I didn't want to go out with him again. But sometimes they wouldn't let up. "How about next week?" they'd ask, or "Can I call you tomorrow?"

At times they just showed up at the door, and I told Mom to say I wasn't home. "Kimmie, I'm not going to lie!" I ran and hid in the closet or dove under the bed, telling her, "Fine, then you can tell them to find me hiding here, under the bed." She would come up with something like, "I haven't seen her in a while," or "She's in the middle of something," or "She's not right here at this time."

"She's hiding under the bed," Charlie would say with a smile when he answered the door. The guy would laugh and assume I wasn't home.

At work, Charlie was offered a promotion from cook to the chef's assistant, and a raise as well, if I dated the chef. Charlie asked me several times, even begged me once, telling me how much easier life would be at the restaurant for him and promising to make me special meals after my night shift. I finally gave in and went out with the guy, who was nice enough but not somebody I would normally go out with. He was very skinny with a big Afro, and he looked a lot like Horshak on "Welcome Back, Kotter."

We went to a second-run movie, "Car Wash," at the drive in, and when he tried to kiss me I started laughing, like I always did when I was nervous going all the way back to those spankings as a kid. I couldn't imagine kissing him. I apologized, telling him I liked him as a friend. I figured I'd blown it for Charlie's promotion, but the boss accepted my apology and Charlie was rewarded with his new job and his raise. Charlie made me whatever I wanted after our night shift together. I usually had steak and lobster.

It was a busy Friday night at the restaurant, with the tourists and boaters there in full force. Charlie and Bradley were working in the hot kitchen and I was busy waiting on all kinds of rude, rich tourists who for some reason on that night expected way too much from me. I tried really hard to be nice, but it was getting difficult. Finally, I snapped.

"Why are you so rude?" I asked a woman who tried to belittle me once too often. My hands shot in the air. "You're in a beautiful resort, having drinks and enjoying a wonderful meal with your husband and friends, but you don't seem to be happy unless you're making me miserable, belittling the help, and trying to make life difficult for people going out of their way to take care of you. You're no better than any one of us."

She was stunned. Her husband smiled. "I couldn't have said it better myself."

I needed that job and felt I may have stepped over the line, but when I went to check on an order everyone in the kitchen started clapping, even the owner. To top it off, the husband of the "rude rich lady" left me a $100 tip!

By the end of the long night, my feet were aching and I was exhausted. When I finished with my last table all I wanted to do was go home, take a hot bath and go to bed. Then Charlie, who had just graduated from high school a few months earlier, asked, "Do you want to go to a party with me to unwind after this crazy night?"

"No thanks, I'm beat."

"Goodnight, Kimmie," he said, as I headed home.

"Have fun without me!" I told him.

I woke with a start at 1 a.m., with a terrible feeling that something was wrong. I went to check on everyone in the house. I was relieved to find Stanley sound asleep, then Bradley, Mom and Mike. I wanted to feel better, but Charlie wasn't home yet. I paced the house trying to wait up for him, but eventually I went back to bed for a fitful sleep.

Mom and Mike woke me early in the morning, their eyes swollen. Charlie's car had crashed, at 1 a.m.

He was dead.

I started shaking, cold and in shock. The hornets were back, millions of them, stinging me all over my body just like when they told me my father was dead. Then I went numb. *Maybe this is just a nightmare and I will wake up in a minute.* Waves of guilt made me feel even sicker. *I should have been with him. Or I should have persuaded him to come home with me; we could have gone out together the next night, there was always a party somewhere.* "Have fun without me." Without me there ... he was gone.

Charlie and a friend had been driving home from the party in his new souped-up El Camino when a guy challenged him to a race. Charlie didn't respond, but the guy started passing him around a blind corner anyway, just a mile from our house. He lost control and forced Charlie off the road. The El Camino rolled over as Charlie was falling through the driver's window, and he was crushed.

Charlie's friend wasn't hurt at all. He told us that Charlie was very calm right before he died, and that he hadn't been in pain.

My family pulled together. Uncle/Grandpa Harold had been through so much in his life, and it looked as if our latest blow might destroy him. So much death. Grandma Helen couldn't look at Mom without breaking down. Laurie and Mel came over with their two little boys. Laurie was going to have another baby in several months, which made her even more emotional. We were out on the deck trying to comfort each other with stories about Charlie when Stanley started to laugh, and he couldn't stop. He was barely 8, the same age I was when Dad died, and I knew exactly how he felt. He was just trying to cope with the stress.

"Why are you laughing?" Laurie shouted. "Don't you care that your brother is dead?"

I was crushed to see Stanley's face as he ran away. I found him sobbing in his bedroom.

Bradley was hurting, too, and more than he was letting on. He was the one closest to Charlie, sharing a room and a job ... and almost every moment of every day. He felt as much guilt as I did. Not long before, Charlie had asked to borrow $50.

"I need new tires. I'll pay you back when we get our paychecks."

Bradley said no.

He told us all, "It should have been me, not Charlie."

By then, Debbie had left Mark and was living in Tacoma. She was grieving, but she was angry, too, even belligerent. She wanted to confront the driver of the other car. The fact that she was on drugs didn't help. It took a lot of energy to calm her down.

Mom was despondent. She had lost her father, a husband, a stepson, a baby boy, and now Charlie. Mike fought to keep himself under control for our sakes, but couldn't help breaking down.

It was good to be together. We needed to be together, even though we all mourned in our separate ways.

I woke up sickened each morning realizing Charlie wasn't coming home, that he would never be back. The scriptures in Psalms 103: 15, 16 kept creeping into my mind: "Our days on earth are like grass; like wildflowers, we bloom and we die. The wind blows, and we are gone – as though we had never been here."

I could barely eat for the rest of the summer, and didn't want to get out of bed. I broke down every time I saw anything that reminded me of Charlie. *I thought I had known grief before, but this is new and worse and will never go away.* Mom was worried about me.

"Go out for a run, honey," she urged. "It always makes you feel better."

I had no desire, but finally gave in. Once I started running ... I felt free and alive for the first time in a long while. It was as if Charlie was right there with me. I gazed over the landscape, moved by its beauty, noticing the brilliant green pine trees again. I was awakened to the rhododendrons growing wild on the roadside, their colors deep and rich ... their dark leaves glimmering in the sunlight. The air was fresh and pure, and the sun was so warm and comforting. I thought about Charlie driving with me that first time to Spokane for college, being there for my track meets, showing me how to run a "real race." Now he would be a part of me on every run.

I needed to live my life like Charlie had, appreciating everybody and everything as if every day could be the last day of my life. It was time to grow up.

chapter 9

When I returned to Spokane for my final year of school, things weren't the same. I became more reserved, less willing to join in and have fun. Losing Charlie left a stark emptiness in my heart that I would never be able to fill. I knew my family was feeling the same sorrow and that deepened my pain. His death was hard on everyone, especially my parents, having to stay in Port Townsend. It was better being away from the many reminders of Charlie, expecting him to walk through the door at any moment.

Laurie had her third son several months later. She named him Charlie.

My friends tried to cheer me up and constantly invited me out to do things. I went along when I couldn't avoid it, but preferred to just stay home alone and have some quiet time to brood while the others went out. It seemed I was always trying to come to terms with things: my father's suicide, giving up Rachel, and then Charlie's death.

During a party that winter, a mutual friend introduced me to a guy named Kelly, who was in his second year at Eastern Washington University. Polite and handsome, he was 6 feet tall, strong and lean – his hazel eyes sparkling with gold. I'd never seen anything like those eyes. He looked like a dark-blond version of Little Joe on "Bonanza," and had been a high school football star in Spokane before college. It was love at first sight, or seemed like it in my foggy mind.

We didn't spend a lot of time together. If Kelly wasn't in class, he was working at his family's businesses, either his parents' truck rental/auto dealership or his grandfather's travel agency and bus rental companies. However, Kelly joined us the one night every weekend when 12 friends and I got together to have dinners and small parties, and he fit right in.

None of my college friends besides my roommate Kelley knew I'd had a baby when I was in high school, yet I became comfortable enough with Kelly right away to tell him about Rachel and show him some pictures. He came from a "proper" family and wasn't very happy to learn that I had a child, but he didn't say much about it.

Even with Kelly in my life, for the many months after Charlie's death I retreated into a twilight state, neither in the moment nor connected to the world. I became irresponsible during that time of despair, throwing caution to the wind. Once again Mike was right, that "all a man has to do is hang his pants on a bedpost and the women in our family get pregnant."

I was 21, and pregnant again.

We decided to get married in the spring. Kelly's mom, Karen, helped me plan the wedding. Actually, she did most of the work, talking to me about the colors, the guest list, and all the details. She couldn't have been more helpful. But frankly, most of the time I didn't particularly care one way or the other what she did. Between Charlie and the pregnancy, I was numb. Kelly and I probably would have just slipped away to get married quietly.

Karen was a great organizer but she couldn't plan for everything. Kelly came from a Catholic family and I was raised as a Jehovah's Witness, so where to get married and by whom was tricky. We eventually decided to marry in the Women's Club, an elegant historical building on the South Hill in Spokane. We asked Laurie's husband, Mel, to marry us since he was an Elder in the Jehovah's Witness congregation.

I didn't expect Mike to come to my wedding – he never liked to travel away from the Olympic Peninsula, for anything – but I was overjoyed when the rest of my family drove across the state. Uncle/Grandpa Harold even came to walk me down the aisle. It was almost like Dad giving me away, since they looked so much alike.

It started out as a special day for Karen as well, who was happy to see the results of all her hard work. The Women's Club was beautifully decorated and everything was falling into place perfectly.

Until ... the cross!

Mom and Karen met for the first time that weekend, and I could tell right away they didn't like each other. I knew they both could be fiery if provoked, so I hoped for the best. But as the guests were about to arrive, Karen put her family cross up above the wedding bower. Laurie was fixing my hair in the back room when I heard the fighting begin. Other than a chance to see my family, my main interest in the wedding had been to get through it without an incident. Now we had one even before my hair was done.

"There is no way we can have a cross here! It's a pagan symbol and an idol. We don't believe in the cross or what it stands for!" Mom was shouting.

"It's my family cross and it's precious and holy! How dare you say it's a pagan symbol!" Karen screamed.

The argument went on like that for a while, until Karen insisted she wanted no part of the wedding and stormed off to sit on the top of the backseat of their open convertible, crying and carrying on as the guests walked in. I felt badly for her.

Meanwhile, Mom came rushing into the back room, hysterical. "How can she expect to have a cross displayed above you during this ceremony?" Everyone, including me, tried to calm her down. "I don't care if it's there or not," said Kelly, who had followed Mom into the room. I said I didn't care, either, and Mel reassured Mom, "Gerry, it's OK. I'll talk to her."

Karen held the cross after ripping it from the bower and the ceremony went on with two fuming mothers in the front row. They haven't spoken to each other since.

Several weeks later, my morning sickness was so bad I had a hard time moving from the orange beanbag chair Kelly contributed to our new apartment. I started missing too much school, and finally quit. Kelly quit, too. He was working two jobs, trying to save enough money for a down payment on a house up on the South Hill near his parents, and couldn't keep up with his schoolwork. Kelly was responsible and worked hard, and I knew he would provide a good home for our baby and me, just as Mom pictured Dad providing a good home when she married him in Sonoma 30 years earlier.

I was pleasantly surprised to discover that Kelly was as neat and clean as I was. He liked everything put in its place, and he even moved the furniture when we vacuumed. There was never a crumb on the floor. That part was great. His level of organization, however, was a concern. He kept lists and ledgers of our daily and weekly activities, as well as recording the date and amount of each bill. He even made charts and a time frame for every move we made throughout the day, every detail whether it mattered or not. I tried to brush it off. Everyone has quirks.

Kelly was good to me and attentive, but he didn't want me talking with my friends. He wanted me all to himself and became extremely jealous when he heard me talking, or worse, laughing on the telephone. My friend Ken the cheerleader called a few times. "I don't want you talking to her," Kelly told him, then hung up. Ken called again. Kelly hung up on him again. Ken called one more time and I could hear him right through the phone telling Kelly, "You're a control freak and you'd better put Kim on the phone right now." Kelly unplugged the telephone.

"What was that all about?" I asked. "You can't treat my friends like that!"

There was a long silence. When I looked up into his stone-cold face, he said in a deep, emphatic voice, "You are *my* wife."

"What?!" I yelled, with both hands in the air.

"I don't want your friends coming to *my* house, or calling you on *my* phone."

Hmmm, I'm not feeling very good about this. Still, I was hoping for the best, figuring Kelly would get over it once we were married for a while. Deep down, though, I felt helpless. I was married to a strange man I barely knew, my sole provider. I was pregnant. I had no job, no money. Mom must have felt just like that back when we lived in the old prostitute house out in The Boondocks. *Perhaps she had been hoping for the best? Maybe that's what kept her going?*

We didn't have much furniture in *Kelly's* home, and the only spot I felt comfortable in during my entire pregnancy was that beanbag chair. One sunny May afternoon, I fell asleep there, and when I woke up it was pitch black. At first I thought I'd slept for hours, but when I looked at the clock it showed 3:00. In the afternoon?

I turned on the TV to a warning from the emergency broadcasting system, telling people that Mount St. Helens had erupted, spewing ash and debris into the air. The wind was blowing the ash from the west side of the state into the east, and Spokane was covered in it. We had several inches on the ground, and it darkened the sky for days before turning the city into a dust bowl.

My eyes burned, I couldn't breathe and I wheezed whenever I went outside. I wasn't sure how safe it would be for me, or my unborn baby, to breathe in that ash. Nobody knew. So I was pregnant, miserable and stuck inside for two months, going out only when absolutely necessary. I thought about how nice it would be to go out and run, to feel strong and invincible once again. It wasn't going to happen any time soon.

We weren't in the apartment for long. With the help of Kelly's parents, who knew a lot about real estate, we were able to get a decent loan and move into a really nice house at a great price.

Our new house was on a corner lot with a big fenced backyard and stairs leading up to a large deck and a back door to the kitchen. It was a split-level home with a big kitchen, a cozy living room, and two bedrooms and one bathroom on the upper level. The downstairs had an office and guest room, along with another living room, which we didn't use often, and another fireplace. There was also a big laundry room and a basement door leading to the backyard. It was perfect for starting our family.

Kelly's parents helped us fix up the nursery. We painted the room yellow and white, and used my sewing machine to make yellow and white checked curtains. Karen and Shawnie, Kelly's younger sister, gave me a baby shower and the gifts provided everything we would need to start out.

I was fortunate to have Karen and Terry as in-laws. They were intelligent people, and I was interested in their conversation, ideas and advice. Terry was a kind man with a great sense of humor, stern when needed but very fair. He had a lot of depth to him, tall and handsome with a warm and friendly smile. Karen, a beautiful and strong woman with solid opinions from whom I learned a lot, looked like Elizabeth Montgomery on "Bewitched," and was just 38 when she became a grandmother. Like Kelly, Karen could get riled up easily, yet always seemed to have good intentions.

Karen seemed pleased that I was a neat and clean person with good values. I think she worried, though, that I might become a Jehovah's Witness. I think her worst nightmare was to have a messy daughter-in-law who neglected her son and grandchild, *and* was a Jehovah's Witness.

Meanwhile, Mom continued to encourage me to study the Bible and go to the Kingdom Hall in Spokane, and even called the Spokane congregation to enlist them in her cause. I did end up studying the Bible with a Jehovah's Witness woman named Connie, an older lady who reminded me of those wonderful Witnesses in Enumclaw. If Kelly had known I was studying on Wednesday afternoons after he went to work, he would have been furious.

Our life continued to fall into place as the arrival of our baby grew closer. Thanks to his Uncle Tracy, Kelly got a good position at a produce company and would be able to support us on just one job, working nights, from 4:30 p.m. to 1 a.m.

Laurie asked during one of our weekly telephone conversations, "How's married life, Kimmie? What do you do with your time?"

"It's quite leisurely – too leisurely, really. I make an early dinner before I send Kelly off to work, and then I have plenty of quiet time to clean the house perfectly and bake, then watch TV and go to bed."

"Try to enjoy it. You'll have plenty to do once the baby is born, believe me!"

"I do enjoy the mornings. I wake up at 7 o'clock, have coffee and watch 'Good Morning America,' which I especially enjoy because the co-host, Joan Lunden, is pregnant, too." I went on to tell her that Kelly woke up at 10 and needed a big breakfast, so I made a lot of bacon and eggs with homemade hash browns and toast or pancakes. Waffles were a must several times a week and Kelly needed a lot of orange juice. Laurie laughed, because she knew I would eat as much as Kelly did, if not more. A lot in my life had changed, but not my appetite.

I was eight months pregnant and growing by the minute when I made the mistake of going bowling with Kelly and his friends, not the brightest thing to do. I ended up straining some abdominal muscles, and was stuck in that orange beanbag chair most of the day for almost a month. I had never been so inactive or had such a strong desire to run.

At long last, on October 14, 1980, at 3 in the afternoon during "General Hospital," I went into labor. Kelly and I went to the hospital at 4 o'clock after the show was over. It was Kelly's favorite, and why miss the end of the show when nothing major would happen for hours yet? Karen and Terry came a little later, when the "real" contractions started. It was comforting having Karen there with me since Mom was so far away.

Even though Kelly and I had taken Lamaze classes and I had given birth naturally the first time, toward the end I couldn't endure the searing, stabbing pain any longer and I panicked. "There's something terribly wrong!" I cried out, and was finally given an epidural. As Kelly was coaching me along and breathing with me in the final stage of my labor, I yelled at him, "Back away! You have bad breath!" The doctor laughed and said, "I guess it's time."

After 10 hours of hard labor, at 12:08 a.m. on October 15, 1980, Jamie Suzanne was born. Suzanne is Karen's middle name.

Jamie was a big baby, just like Rachel, well over 8 pounds and extremely long. She was absolutely adorable with her little round head, blue eyes and blond hair, with a slightly turned-up nose.

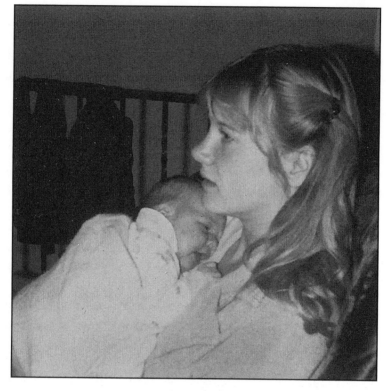

With Jamie at two weeks old ~ November 1980

Jamie slept through the night right away. We were blessed. Once I finished my evening housework, I had time to watch "Dallas," "The Love Boat," "Hart to Hart," and my favorite, "Magnum P.I.," without interruption.

The baby weight came off easily again. I weighed 118 pounds before Jamie was born, went up to 167 at the end of the pregnancy and was back to 118 within weeks. However, the weight came off too rapidly for a reason. I hadn't felt well since Jamie was born, and six weeks later became extremely ill. When I went in for my checkup the doctor couldn't believe what he was seeing. "You've been suffering from a birthing injury! How in the world did you manage the pain and weakness? Most women would be passed out right now," he said, shaking his head. I had to go straight into the hospital for a surgical procedure to repair the damage and stop the bleeding. I'd been hemorrhaging from premature cord traction from the placenta before it naturally detached from the uterine wall.

I was scared to death when the doctor told me I might need a blood transfusion. All I could think of was my brother Timmy dying of hepatitis. I needed my mother, and called her while I was waiting to go into the operating room. She was worried for me, naturally, but more concerned about the transfusion. "Don't you dare! It's against Jehovah's will!" she warned. It wasn't the comforting moment I was hoping for.

Fortunately I didn't need the transfusion, but I was anemic and tired for months and it took some time to gain my strength back. A brisk walk in the chilly winter afternoons was the only thing that made me feel lively. Again I dreamed of going out for an invigorating run, but again that was going to have to wait, and my desire to run continued to grow.

Around that time there was a serial rapist on the streets who regularly changed his appearance and attacked women alone after dark or jogging in the early morning. There was a lot of publicity about the "South Hill Rapist" and women in Spokane were afraid, especially on our side of town. There were 52 rapes in Spokane from 1978 to 1981, and he was the suspect in most of them.

I wasn't too concerned because I didn't go out in the evening alone, nor was I a jogger at the time. After Kelly went to work, I would put Jamie in her stroller and take her for a walk up and down Rebecca Street, just in front of our house and through the neighborhood, but we were in before dark.

As I was recovering from my anemia, a man came to our door several times a week on the nights Kelly was at work. He never came on Kelly's nights off. Sometimes he had slicked-back hair. Other times he had curly hair, or it was long and straight; even so, I knew it was the same man. I looked through the peephole to get a good look at him, but I never answered the door. I never called the police because I didn't want to be another one of the panicked Spokane women who called about every little thing during the scare. Nevertheless, after several weeks of that I was growing concerned. He always came at about the same time, so I asked Karen and Terry to come over a few times. He never showed up on those nights.

One evening, Jamie and I weren't feeling well. Instead of going for our walk, we both took a nap just after Kelly went to work. We slept for hours, right past dinner. Suddenly, I was awakened to a dark house ... noises were coming from the kitchen window! Usually I'm a total coward in the dark and would freeze or hide under the covers, but my precious baby was next to me. I had to protect her. I grabbed Kelly's baseball bat from the closet and turned on the hallway light leading into the kitchen. As I slowly crept down the hallway holding the bat in front of me, I saw somebody's leg coming through the window. I screamed as I raised the bat above my head. The intruder turned around and scurried back out, running down the deck stairs and out of the yard.

That time I called the police right away. They quickly found that the kitchen window had been pried open. With the house dark, the porch light off and the evening newspaper still at the front door, the policemen guessed that the man had assumed I wasn't home and planned to be inside when I returned. The guy knew our routine.

The police planned to keep an eye on our neighborhood after I told them about the mysterious man who usually came to my door at that time of the night. "Your intuition and awareness may have saved you from serious harm," they told me. "It's unlikely, but be sure to call immediately if he shows up again."

I continued taking Jamie for a walk every evening through our neighborhood, coming home and giving her a bath, putting her to bed and then enjoying my quiet time. I was a little nervous during the night, but all the news stories said the rapist never hit the same place twice.

Not long after that, they caught the South Hill Rapist. I recognized him as the guy who had been coming to my porch. He lived four blocks from us, right on Rebecca Street. I had walked past his house with Jamie every evening.

—

Jamie grew quickly in that first year, and before I knew it she had been transformed into a little version of me, with her blond hair that looked like a dandelion gone to seed. She had my height, too, and then some – I'm 5'7" and Karen, her grandmother, is 5'8". Our pediatrician called Jamie's height "off the charts," saying, "From the looks of it, she's going to be close to 6 feet tall." Jamie had my body type and my long and lean muscles, even at a very young age. She had perfect running form and could run faster than most of the toddlers in the neighborhood.

I was amazed at how much everyone adored Jamie, although nobody loved her as much as I did. She was everything to me. I felt guilty because I didn't have that type of relationship with Rachel, but I finally had another chance to do it right and be a good mother. I spent all of my free time reading to her, playing games, and at times just sitting and watching her.

Even when she was tiny, Jamie loved showing off. If we had visitors, Jamie would run to her room, bring out every toy she had and say "watch dis" while showing everyone how she could play with each toy. Our company seemed to enjoy it, although they didn't have to see the routine every single day.

Like her mother, Jamie had an enormous appetite. She had big meals with us, then several snacks just before bed. In her second year, she slept solidly from 8 p.m. until 8 a.m. without even moving. The problem was, she would soak through her diaper every night. I solved it by triple diapering her. I think she weighed an extra 10 pounds from her drenched diapers when I picked her up out of her crib each morning. She looked so cute in her little sleeper pajamas with that big solid backside, greeting me with a cheerful "Hi There!" except it came out more like "Hi Dayew!" Those were her first words, along with "num nums" for snacks and "Baboo" for Karen, and "Papa" for Terry.

Kelly was still working the night shift, which gave me special time alone with Jamie after he went to work. That was just what I was dreaming of when I was a young child playing with my doll with the unpleasant odor, having a husband who took care of us, being a good mother, keeping a clean house and having big meals with meat every night for dinner, along with a lot of mashed potatoes and then dessert and ice cream galore. Just like Mom's dream of a big family and the perfect house with the white picket fence, and just how I had practiced it with "Baby Doll."

Unfortunately something was unsettling and didn't feel right.

On weekends during the fall and winter, we mostly stayed home and watched football. Kelly was obsessed with football and studied each team, college and pro, in great depth. He spent hours poring over the statistics for every team in the newspapers and football magazines, underlining every detail and then writing it all down in a ledger. We entered the weekly contest in the Spokane newspaper, where we had to pick the winning team of every major college and pro game each weekend. The winner at the end of the season would win a trip to Hawaii.

Kelly spent way too much time on the contest. I would just use all of his research, and then in games that looked like they would be close I chose the team with the best field-goal kicker. It worked pretty well.

A few years later I would pick all of the teams correctly, thanks to Doug Flutie's "Hail Mary" pass in the final seconds during the Boston College game against the University of Miami, but I didn't pick the tiebreaker games correctly. Even so, I qualified for the finals only to miss out on the trip in the final round. Kelly came close many times as well, but entering football contests over the years never did win us that trip to Hawaii.

Some nights after Kelly went to work and I'd put Jamie to bed I would catch up with friends and family on the phone. I'd talk to my old college roommate Kelley Kuribayashi, and call Mom and Laurie at least once a week when the rates went down after 10 p.m. – never on Friday nights because that was when "Dallas" was on. However, Kelly would always call me from work, and if the line was busy he'd be furious. He would call back later, yelling and demanding to know whom I had been talking to.

"You shouldn't be on the phone when you know I call during my breaks!" he shouted.

Half the time Kelly had already figured it out; when the line was busy he would call everyone I knew to see whose phone was busy at the same time.

I felt claustrophobic. I used to dream of a husband who would stay around and take care of us, but by then I dreamed of a husband who would leave me alone so I could enjoy my life with Jamie. It was a huge relief when Kelly left for work.

I went to only a few Jehovah's Witness meetings, the important ones like The Memorial of Christ's Death each spring, but had to go in secret. Of course, one of the few nights I went to a meeting, Kelly called on his break and couldn't find me. Later he questioned me until I had to tell him, which only spurred him into a fit of fury. "You are not allowed to go to those meetings and you can never take Jamie there. I forbid you!" he shouted. I was stunned. I wasn't sure how to respond other than, "Ass!" I didn't go to any more meetings, but Connie still came over secretly once a week to study with me when Kelly was at work.

Poor Kelly tried so hard to be in control that he often became irrational. It reminded me of my father when he would do strange things like that to my mother, and the situation was getting worse. Kelly needed to know my every move. If it wasn't on his ledger of our daily activities, I shouldn't do it. I didn't have many friends and he was doing a good job of preventing me from having any life other than seeing to his needs. I felt my life was in a state of stagnation and I was almost to the point of depression.

The more I fought back the more controlling he became. I found it was easier to just go along with whatever he wanted. Like Mom had done with Dad.

Perhaps Kelly will calm down, or maybe he'll find something to curb his desire for control? I even prayed for a miracle, deciding I needed to give him some time.

That spring something awakened in me, kindling my desire and my hopes.

There's a road race in Spokane called the Lilac Bloomsday Run. Don Kardong founded it the year after he missed a bronze medal by only three seconds in the 1976 Olympics. Bloomsday is a 12-kilometer (7.46 mile) race in early May, starting downtown and running through the city streets, up and down several large hills, over the river and back up into downtown to the finish line – in front of the beautiful Riverfront Park where Spokane hosted the World's Fair in 1974.

The television stations and newspapers started covering the race weeks in advance, giving training and racing tips and doing feature stories on people planning to run. As the day grew closer, the media focused on the elite runners who would be competing. The town was buzzing with excitement. My mother-in-law, Karen, was planning to run the race, and a few weeks before tried unsuccessfully to persuade Kelly and me to join her. I was still recovering from the complications after Jamie's birth, but mostly at that point in my life I just wasn't interested in participating in a crowded race fighting for space with thousands of people, nor was Kelly.

I was interested enough on race morning to turn on the TV, though. Coffee in hand, I settled into my comfortable chair. A lively announcer was talking up the race just before the start, saying there were close to 20,000 runners. Most of them were from the Spokane area, running for fun. Everyone on the starting line looked like they were having a gay old time, laughing and joking with the reporter. At home in my pajamas, I felt like I was missing out on something special, just like I did when I had to miss out on the parties when I was in high school.

As the race began, the television commentator on the press truck started talking about the elite runners in the lead pack, all of whom looked beautiful with their perfect and effortless running form. As he described the race, he made it feel as if I were right there with them. I pulled my chair closer to the television.

Afterward Bud Nameck, a sports reporter, along with the same lively commentator, interviewed the top finishers in the race. They all seemed happy and excited, and so full of energy even after running so hard. A cute runner named Jon Sinclair finished second. "Everyone should be out here running these road races," he told the reporter. "It's a great way to improve your health and enjoy the camaraderie of fellow runners. And this is the only sport where people of all ability levels can compete together in the same event."

He was so articulate and passionate that he instantly sparked my desire and gave me a reason to run the following year. I wanted to feel energized like Jon Sinclair and all of those runners I watched on television, to enjoy that excitement and that powerful sense of control – I knew that feeling. I had it when I ran from the coppers, when I burned the hornets' nest and when I ran track in high school. I felt it when I was a child on the beach in Port Townsend, running through the cold water on the wet sand away from the trouble and sadness at home.

I didn't realize how much I missed it until watching that Bloomsday race.

~

The year passed quickly and Kelly decided to join me for my first Bloomsday that spring. Kelly played on a couple of baseball and basketball teams, so he kept in good shape, and we both played wiffle ball, badminton, tag and pretty much everything else with all the neighborhood kids. However, my training consisted mostly of chasing after a 2-year-old all day, which left me exhausted. I didn't run a step before the race. In fact, I hadn't run in years. My only goal was to run the entire distance without having to stop.

That year, 1982, Bloomsday fell on my birthday. Since marrying into Kelly's family, I'd started celebrating my birthday and Christmas. I'd often wondered what it would be like, and I was surprised that it took some getting used to. At Christmas, everyone seemed so stressed, although I always enjoyed Jamie's special Christmas moments. On my birthday, I felt awkward and uncomfortable about people making a fuss. However, running Bloomsday was a perfect way to celebrate. Even though there were thousands of people all around me, it was a private gift to myself.

I had no idea what I was about to unwrap.

The gun went off, but with 17,000 runners on the starting line it took what seemed forever to get going. I was feeling claustrophobic, and began to panic at being stuck in the masses. Once I finally started moving and finding space, I began to enjoy the freedom of running and feeling alive again. I thought about Charlie, and at that very moment I knew he was there with me as I cruised along. I felt at peace for the first time in a long while.

I continued to enjoy every moment even when things became more demanding in miles 3 and 4. I'd been looking forward to the vulture on top of Doomsday Hill ever since I watched the race the previous year. Doomsday Hill is a steep half-mile climb that starts at Mile 5 — as runners in various states of exhaustion reach the top, they're greeted by a man dressed as a gigantic vulture waiting to grab or taunt anybody who stops or walks. I put my head down and tried with all my might to keep going. It was tough, and I was tempted to join the people around me who were taking walk breaks. But if I was going to reach my goal of running the entire race without stopping, I couldn't walk up that hill.

As I ran past the vulture, he gave me a high-five. It was the boost I needed to press on in the final two miles, and cross the finish line without having to walk even one step of the way.

Once I finished – in 1007th place – I went through the finishing chute and made my way to the closest curb to sit down. I needed a rest. Every muscle in my body ached. *That's what I get for not preparing properly, or rather, at all.* As I sat there watching the finishers walk by, a woman with a lovely accent sat down beside me and asked how my race went.

"I ran the whole race without stopping!" I exclaimed, high on endorphins and much more animated than I usually am. "I can't believe I didn't have to walk, even on Doomsday Hill!"

"This must be your first race," the woman guessed.

"No, I was a sprinter in high school but haven't run in years," then I started to tell her about that as well and ... suddenly I felt embarrassed about bragging and apologized for rambling on about myself.

"How did you do?" I asked.

"I won the women's race today."

The woman was Anne Audain. I couldn't believe I was sitting next to the famous New Zealander, one of the best distance runners in the world. Then I was even more embarrassed, and told her so. She laughed and said that she really enjoyed talking with me, adding a bit of advice,

"If you were to train for your next Bloomsday, you would run a lot faster and feel much better during the race, and after the race, too. A lot better than you do right now."

Besides Bloomsday, the only other excitement in my life was traveling to Port Townsend, or when Mom, Mike and Stanley came to visit in Spokane several times after Jamie was born, as did Laurie and Mel and their three boys. For Mike to come along was a big step for him. Considering how much he hated to travel, it made his visits even more special, and it was around that time I started to call him "Dad." Mike had always loved us like his own children, and gave us whatever he could of himself even when he was fighting his own problems and didn't have much to give. It took having Jamie for me to realize the strain that Mike had been under when we were all so young, ten kids, and he was barely in his twenties.

I enjoyed having my family come to visit, and it was especially wonderful to see my little brother. At 13, Stanley had changed from the adorable, awkward baby boy with the crooked smile into a gorgeous young Tom Cruise look-alike, while still being the same joy to be around that he was as a toddler. He loved to take Jamie out in the snow and pull her on her little duck sled for hours. Their laughter warmed our hearts and they both looked so sweet all bundled up with their bright red noses and rosy cheeks. It was a miracle. Instead of turning into a sullen teenager, Stanley brought nothing but delight and comfort to our lives.

Laurie's three boys looked like Huey, Dewey and Louie, Donald Duck's nephews, with their reddish-blond hair and button noses. The boys all maneuvered to be near Jamie and listen to her talk. Jamie couldn't say her R's or L's, so during dinner, they prompted her by asking, "Why do you drink milk?" Jamie would answer, "miwk makes my bones gwow and makes me wun fastew." They laughed, which of course only encouraged her.

Jamie was the only baby girl in the family, and that meant she was the queen. She had a blankie at her side every moment. Not only was it filthy from being dragged around, it was slowly falling apart. But she would panic if I tried to wash it. Just before it was on its last thread, Jamie asked Laurie during one of her visits, "Aunt Wowey, would you sew my bwankie befowe you weave?" Laurie sewed up all the loose ends. Aunt Wowey, like everyone else in the family, would do anything for her.

Stanley and Jamie ~ 1982

Kelly, Jamie and I would go to Port Townsend for two weeks every summer. At the beach, I showed Kelly and the gang all of the special tricks I did as a child. Kelly loved jumping off the dock and swimming quickly back to shore in that ice cold water. All my little nephews/cousins and Stanley laughed and cheered him on while we adults enjoyed watching him scream and holler from the shock. We had many Catch of the Day barbecues after Mike/Dad and Kelly's long day of salmon fishing, shrimping or crabbing. We had big family picnics and we all played baseball. Even Grandma Helen joined in. She could still hit a home run at the age of 68.

There was another baby in the family. Over the course of several years, my brother Bradley had grown into a strong, tall Viking who looked like Brad Pitt after a good session in the weight room. Good humored and kindhearted, he had plenty of female admirers. Right before graduating, he got his high-school sweetheart pregnant. They married and moved just a few blocks from my parents. Bradley went to work at a local sawmill to take care of his family. Even though he had a baby, he still seemed like a big kid himself.

We weren't seeing much of Debbie. She and Mark divorced shortly after my last visit with them in my college days. Debbie moved to the Tacoma area and married a man named John, who was wild and crazy at times, and they had a son named Geno a few months after I had Jamie. As close as we were when we were children, it seemed only fitting that we had both of our babies just a few months apart. She came around to visit my parents during some of our vacations but she still had a wild side, smoking marijuana ("the good stuff," she said), taking amphetamines and other drugs, and always looking for an adventure or a party.

When Debbie made it over for a Port Townsend visit, I would see her change with the different drugs she was taking. There was a time when she was so thin I thought she would end up in the hospital. She was on speed and wasn't eating a thing, yet asked me, "Do I still have saddlebag thighs like I did in high school?" That's when I knew that my jealous "saddlebags" remark years earlier had caused some major damage.

I was worried for Debbie. She seemed insecure and overly nervous around everyone. She was either out doing crazy things or was full of unbelievable stories, always spinning a yarn, just like our father years ago.

By that time, Rachel was 7 and her adoptive family began letting her visit Mom, and especially Laurie, a lot more. They often kept her for days at a time, and I took pleasure in seeing her during our annual visit to Port Townsend. She called me Kim, but she knew I was her mother. Kelly was furious when he found Rachel and Jamie playing together outside my parents' house one day. Jamie was 2, walking and talking and beginning to acknowledge things more. Kelly grabbed Jamie and stalked into the house, yelling at Laurie and Mom, "You'll never see Jamie again if that little girl is here!"

Everyone was shocked. Fortunately Dad didn't see that, or who knows what would have happened. My family had always liked the respectful, fun-loving Kelly, but they had begun to see his possessive, controlling side and how impulsive he could be in lashing out. That was the worst example yet.

A few months later, during a visit to Spokane, Laurie and Mel took me aside to tell me that Rachel's adoptive parents were splitting up and felt Rachel would be better off with her real family. Laurie and Mel loved her, and as her adoptive parents' marriage disintegrated she was with them most of the time anyway. Since Kelly wanted nothing to do with her, everyone assumed I had no hope of having Rachel in my life. Laurie and Mel asked for my approval to adopt her.

Despite wanting so much to have Rachel with me, I had never dreamed it was possible after giving her up for adoption. I finally had a chance. After Laurie and Mel left, I told Kelly, "I want my daughter back."

"I don't want my family knowing about that little girl!" he ranted. "No!" Furious that my sister was planning to adopt her, Kelly didn't stop there. He demanded that Rachel never come with Laurie and Mel when they visited.

"She's not allowed here," he said.

I was crushed. We fought for hours every day, until it started taking its toll on Jamie and our marriage. I had no way of supporting Rachel and Jamie. I was helpless, a feeling I loathe.

I gave Laurie and Mel my blessing, and Rachel was soon the queen of their household the way Jamie was queen of ours, especially as the only girl among three boys. I managed to see her in Port Townsend when I could, hoping Kelly wouldn't find out.

I became silently furious with Kelly, losing any amount of love and appreciation I had for him. I knew that if I had been in a good position, Rachel and Jamie would be with me and Kelly would have been out the back door. *I will find a way out of this. I can't allow a man to keep me from my own daughter.*

———

Winter had come and gone, and before we knew it Bloomsday was coming around again. That year, Kelly and I did a couple of short runs together a few months before the race. It still wasn't quite the training Anne Audain had suggested when she befriended me on the curb the year before, but I figured it was better than nothing. At least the race might not hurt as much.

To my amazement, I ran 44:37, even though my crooked toe was killing me and ended up black and blue afterward. The race still hurt. I had to plop down on the closest curb again when I finished and I could barely walk for a week, but it was well worth it. I ran a minute a mile faster than the previous year and I placed 17th among the women. *If I could perform that well on very little training, what could I do if I really worked at it?*

It was time to take Anne Audain's advice. I would train properly for Bloomsday 1984. Kelly took on the challenge and jumped into training as well. He enjoyed running and was thrilled with his Bloomsday time of 47:14. Kelly was very competitive in everything he did. When he was a boy he would ask his father to time him while he ran around the house over and over, trying to run faster every time around.

Not that running didn't bring out some of his odd habits. From where we lived on the South Hill, we could run a few blocks and be out on country roads. Kelly measured out 34 courses from three to ten miles long and spent days writing out charts with the descriptions of each course, the degree of difficulty, and the best times he hit for each point along the way of each one. I thought it was a waste of time and way too organized, but I went with it to give myself some peace.

Jamie would get her pencil and writing pad, lie on her stomach on the living room floor in front of the TV next to her dad, and pretend to write just what Kelly did. That was the good part – it actually kept them both busy. Between her father's ledgers and lists and my need for a spotless house, Jamie wasn't going to have much of a chance to be disorganized or messy, that's for sure.

Five days a week we ran from three to six miles, with one long run of seven to 10 miles every weekend. It wasn't a lot compared to most serious runners, but 30 miles a week was all I wanted or could manage. I went out for my run late in the morning, after Kelly woke up. He timed me while he took care of Jamie, then went out on the same training route and tried to beat my time. I came back from my runs to find Kelly doing pushups and sit-ups on the living room floor, with Jamie right next to him doing her own versions.

After a while, his competitiveness became extremely annoying. At times I tried to run as fast as I could so he couldn't beat me, but when I was tired I ran very easy and took shortcuts instead. He would work so hard to beat my times, thinking I must be a lot faster than he was.

We actually ran pretty close to the same speed. Kelly was a little faster at short sprints, but I was a little faster from 400 meters (a quarter mile) and up. So of course Kelly decided that our speed workouts should be 10 repeats of 100-meter or 200-meter sprints. Occasionally I would persuade him to do longer efforts of quarter or half miles, but he wasn't too excited about that.

I'm sure, as a child, I ran many more miles a week while running through the streets of Port Townsend, along the waterfront and away from trouble. But I'd never *trained* like *this*. We were both growing fitter and faster, feeling positive while moving forward and seeing progress, and feeling pretty damn good about ourselves. Maybe there was a reason to run after all.

Jamie with her blankie and Bo wearing his ducky shirt

While all of that was going on, Jamie became best friends with Bo, who lived across the fence from our backyard. Bo was 3½, the same age as Jamie, and couldn't pronounce "Jamie" so called her "Me Me." He had curly reddish hair, bright blue eyes, and a smile that went from ear to ear with his little baby teeth peeking through. His favorite shirt had a plastic duck on the front that would quack when you pushed it. He wanted to wear his "ducky shirt" all the time, and he did. His mother, Lorrie, tried to coax him into wearing another shirt but he always found where she tried to hide it. Bo in his ducky shirt and Jamie toting her blankie were inseparable.

Bo was up and ready to start his day a lot earlier than Jamie, and would patiently wait for hours for her to wake up. As soon as he saw her bedroom curtains open, he would hightail it over to our yard through a loose board in the fence. Up the deck stairs leading to our kitchen door he would come, as Jamie and I were sitting down to breakfast.

Kelly would still be sleeping after his late shift at the produce company, and the toughest part of my morning was keeping Bo and Jamie quiet so they wouldn't wake him. Bo tried his best, but every once in awhile he woke Kelly up. Kelly would storm out of the bedroom yelling at Bo, "Go home and stay there until you're invited, and don't you ever wake me up again!"

Poor Bo went running home crying many times. His parents often bit their tongues when Kelly verbally attacked Bo and his older brother, Vinny, for many minor things over the years. Marty and Lorrie talked to Kelly a few times about lightening up but allowed Kelly to get away with far too much for the sake of keeping the peace and our friendship, but more importantly for Bo and Jamie. Then their dog, Bear, bit Jamie's arm after she tried to ride him and they thought Kelly would have a fit or, worse, sue them, but he was very good about it. You never could tell.

I was relieved Marty and Lorrie remained our friends despite Kelly's rude and erratic behavior. I had coffee with Lorrie in the mornings while Kelly slept and Marty was working, and a beer with them at night while the kids were playing in the backyard and Kelly was working. Other than my college roommate Kelley, they were my only real friends while we lived on Rebecca Street.

One night while we were enjoying our beers, Marty said with a chuckle, "So, Kelly decided to mow your lawn diagonally today, did he?"

Marty had caught on. Kelly mowed the lawn every five days from early spring through the fall, and never mowed it in the same pattern during the same month. He had it all worked out on his calendar: mowing back and forth from north to south one time, then west to east the next. Five days later, he would mow diagonally in one direction and then five days after that, diagonally in the other direction. In the fifth segment of the monthly rotation, he started with the outer edge, and slowly worked down the square to the center. Five days after that, he went in the opposite pattern, from the center to the outer edge. It must have been tough to be Kelly!

But he wasn't the only one entertaining our neighbors. Even though we received free produce from Kelly's workplace, I had a vegetable garden. I loved the fresh and nutrient-packed lettuce, spinach, tomatoes, beets and carrots, and enjoyed being outside working in my garden while Kelly was doing yard work and Jamie played with her toys or took care of her doll, Babes. It was nice and peaceful, all working and playing together.

Things weren't so peaceful when I pulled a carrot and found that a gopher had tunneled under an entire row, eating the carrots and leaving just the tops for me. I yelled at that gopher that day and for many weeks afterward, even though he was long gone.

Then there was Jamie, who was potty trained but hadn't yet mastered "number two." I brought her potty chair outside with us, putting it in the shade and close to the deck. I was busy in the garden when I looked up to see Jamie sitting in the potty chair, twirling her thumbs a mile a minute directly in front of her face.

"What are you doing, Jamie?"

"Shhhhhh, I'm concentwating," she whispered. Then I heard a plop.

With Kelly mowing the lawn in carefully chosen patterns on a precise schedule, Jamie following right behind him with her plastic toy lawn mower or concentwating, and me waving my gardening shovel while yelling "You little ASS!" at an invisible gopher, it must have been a sight to see. I hope it made up for Kelly's abuse.

Even though Lorrie and I took turns keeping an eye on the kids, it wasn't always enough. Bo and Jamie liked to sneak out into a wooded area next to our houses where they weren't allowed, and one of them would always end up bruised from falling out of a tree they weren't supposed to climb or scraped up from the underbrush they weren't supposed to crawl through. They didn't learn, though, until they found the hornets' nest.

I was out on our back deck the day I heard the two of them screaming and crying. Hundreds of hornets were circling them as they ran toward me as fast as their little legs could take them. I ran to them as quickly as I could. It would have been funny, like watching a comedy skit, had I not been so worried and in such a panic. Less funny were their stings. Jamie only had a few, but Bo got the worst of it with a dozen. He came over later that night with swollen eyes and big red bumps everywhere.

They never went into the woods alone again.

A few days later, I set fire to the hornets' nest.

As the year went on, we settled into a routine. In the mornings, I tended to Jamie and did what I could around the house without making too much noise. Kelly's job of loading and sometimes driving and delivering produce to local grocery stores was hard manual labor, for 40 hours a week and as much overtime as he could get. That and his new training regimen could really wear him down, and he *really* did need his sleep in the morning.

Once he was up, we did our runs and then ate a big brunch. I put Jamie down for her nap, started dinner at 2 o'clock and we ate at 3 while watching "General Hospital." Soap operas had never been my favorite shows, but even I became addicted to that one after watching it almost every weekday during those first four years with Kelly – including the time Luke and Laura had their big romance and married.

Kelly and I ate enough for eight people at dinner, especially after we started running. Our grocery bill was enormous, but I saved by making or baking almost everything. Then I packed Kelly's lunch and he was off to work at 4:30, while I did the noisy household chores that evening.

It was a long way from growing up in Port Townsend, and even further from Enumclaw. We had plenty of food, a predictable lifestyle and a nice home in which to raise a child. Being a "housewife" was harder work than it gets credit for, though it wasn't as rewarding as I had envisioned.

If only I had some control over my life. Burning that hornets' nest helped, but not for long. There is something missing.

⌐

Leading up to the next Bloomsday, Kelly and I decided to enter some small races in town. We would wake up early, eat a small breakfast and share a pot of coffee while stretching to Michael Jackson's "Thriller" album. Jamie joined in while sipping her apple juice from a coffee cup, copying every stretch we did as she danced to the music. She had the routine down.

Our first pre-Bloomsday race was a 5 miler out in the country put on by radio station KGA. I was anxious. I knew Kelly was going to try to beat me, and that if he didn't things wouldn't be pleasant. I also knew there was no way I would *let* him beat me, even to keep the peace. I didn't like the nervous energy I generated just before the race. My heart was pounding, my lungs felt constricted and I was sweating even before the gun went off.

To prevent my lungs from tightening I started the race at a relaxed pace and saw Kelly ahead of me, looking strong. The first few miles felt good and even running up the big hills didn't seem uncomfortable, so I maintained my pace. First I passed Kelly. Then I passed the woman in front of him. Then I passed all the women in front of him. A wave of shock went through me. *I am actually leading this race!* As I ran to the finish line, KGA was playing "On the Road Again," one of my favorite Willie Nelson songs. I won!

Kelly seemed thrilled for me even though I beat him. I was surprised, and happier about that than I was about winning the race. I also won a nice trophy and several gift certificates to fine restaurants as prizes. Later that night, my win was shown on the local TV news. The attention was intoxicating and the prospect for more was just enough incentive to keep me eager for more.

The next race was a Women's 5K in Riverfront Park. I took off like a bat flying from hell at the start and won by well over a minute, without being challenged, to take home presents galore. I called my prizes "presents" without thinking about it since they seemed more like gifts. I won more presents in those races than I received during my entire childhood, finally making up for all of those empty birthdays and Christmases.

The final race leading up to Bloomsday was a 4 miler, put on by a sporting good store called "Two Swabbies." The winning male and female would each receive a $200 gift certificate, along with other presents. I was still wearing the old "waffle trainer" shoes that my cross-country coach gave me in college. I needed some modern shoes that didn't cause a searing pain to shoot through my crooked toe when I ran downhill or tried to get up on my toes to run faster.

All of the best women in the Spokane area would be in the race, which was nerve-wracking, but I figured that if I didn't win the first prize of $200 I could finish second or third and still win enough for a new pair of shoes for Kelly and me with the $100 or $50 gift certificates if we bought the cheaper ones.

I noticed several women I raced against a few weeks earlier and decided to follow them, in hopes that I wouldn't develop a tight chest and experience any breathing problems while running at their pace. As the race started I remembered Mr. Brink's race instructions and tucked in behind, following the lead woman through the first three miles. With one mile to go, I took off to win, feeling that same exhilaration I did years ago from beating the showoff Jezebel. I never saw Kelly in the race, but I could hear him behind me. He was right on my heels at the finish and pleased with both of our performances.

I made good use of that $200 gift certificate, purchasing a new outfit for Jamie along with running shoes for Kelly and me. Tim Riley, the male winner, told me I'd run faster in lighter shoes and suggested a model of Nike racing flats so I bought those, too. They were the lightest, most cushiony shoes I had ever had on my feet. Wearing those racing shoes was like putting on the red velvet track spikes Mr. Royce gave me many years earlier ... I was ready to race.

Wearing new racing flats

We persuaded Mel and Laurie not only to visit us the weekend of Bloomsday 1984, but also to run the race. They were participating in fun runs in the Port Townsend area and loving it.

Lorrie planned to run Bloomsday, as well, and she and Marty joined in on our fun weekend. We all had a great time together while sharing meals and talking about our race strategy. I love that about road races; every runner, from the fastest to the slowest, has a goal, and is just as anxious and excited as an elite runner who is racing for the win. I enjoy that kind of energy. Everyone can feel the same empowerment.

The day before the race we went to the race expo in the Spokane Convention Center, where running-related companies had booths to display or sell their goods and many shoe companies had their sponsored elite athletes signing autographs. Mel came running up to Laurie and me all excited, saying, "Look, my buddy Jon Sinclair just signed my Bloomsday poster!"

Sure enough, it said "To my buddy Mel" and was signed by Jon Sinclair, whom we all thought was a nice guy and the greatest runner around, even though we had never met him. Mel tried to find some racing shorts and a singlet at the expo just like Jon's, and he did. He came out of the changing room in his new flowery short-shorts and said, "Look at my new racing unit. Do I look just like my buddy, Jon?" We laughed and had way too much fun when we were supposed to be focusing on a race.

In the early '80s, Jon Sinclair was one of the best road racers in the world. He didn't lose very often, and he won Bloomsday in 1983 after placing second for the two years before that. He was great with people, and gave interviews with a positive energy that made him popular in Spokane.

Don Kardong was an even bigger celebrity, not only for being an Olympic athlete who lived in Spokane, but for founding and promoting Bloomsday. Don looked like a runner – well over 6 feet tall, skinny and boyishly handsome. He was all over television and in the newspapers for weeks every year leading up to the race, and his sense of humor endeared him to everyone. He and Bud Nameck, my favorite sports broadcaster, would do a one-hour highlight show the night of each race, showing the elite races and then focusing on the fun along the course with the thousands of other runners. During that post-race coverage, Don would do a silly skit with his good friend, an attorney and race committee member named Steve, where they pretended to be actors thanking all the race sponsors. I always looked forward to that skit.

Every year, on the night of the race, Don and the Bloomsday committee put on a big post-race party in a huge ballroom of the host hotel for any runner who wanted to come. They showed the highlight broadcast and brought in a dance band, with good food and beer. Even if you had a bad race, you still looked forward to the party.

On race day we all woke up early to an unseasonably cold morning of wet snow. Mel put on his "Jon Sinclair racing unit" and the rest of us put on our new, nameless outfits. We were nervous yet excited at the same time, saying to each other, "Whatever happens, at least we get to go to a party tonight."

After beating the fastest area runners that spring I had a bit of pressure on me to finish Bloomsday as the first woman from Spokane. I really didn't want to let anyone down. I certainly wasn't going to beat any of the elite runners, who were some of the best in the world. Beating the best in Spokane would be tough enough.

The five of us drove downtown and parked several blocks from the start. We decided to leave our warm sweats in the car and brave the sleet and snow in just our shorts, singlets and gloves, wishing each other "good luck" as we made our way through the crowds. Some runners were serious and others were dressed in all kinds of strange outfits. It helped to have a muscular guy like Kelly leading the way through the thousands of other runners to get as close to the starting line as possible. We ended up not far behind the elite athletes.

The race had more than doubled in size since I first watched it on TV, and with 30,000 runners directly behind me I was worried about tripping and being trampled. Being so close to the front I was able to take off at race pace with Kelly right next to me. It was comforting having him there for protection, and I was relieved when everyone got off to a good start.

It's a wonder what one sees in a large road race like Bloomsday. Even though it was just above freezing, I passed a man wearing nothing but running shoes and a thong. I had to do a double take to be sure. The weather conditions might actually have been a blessing. The snow and sleet cleaned the air of pollen and dust, and my lungs didn't tighten up when I tried to push like they did in the road races earlier that spring. For the first time since high school, there were no warning signs of an asthma attack coming on and I could run all-out, up to my ability level without having to back off my pace.

I cruised along with Kelly, well ahead of the crowds and with plenty of space to run the tangents on the winding course, thoroughly enjoying the moment. It was like running with Kayla all over again. We started passing people after the first three challenging miles. When we reached Mile 5 at the bottom of Doomsday Hill I was able to pick the pace up a bit more, leaving Kelly behind as I made my way up the hill for that high-five from the big vulture.

At the top of the hill, I flew by some of the invited elite women. I looked at the clock as I passed the Mile 6 mark and did some mental arithmetic. I was shocked. My time was well under 6-minute mile pace, which encouraged me to run even faster.

I passed several more women on the homestretch, crossing the finish line in 8th place (in 42:38, a 5:40 per-mile pace) in the women's field and winning prize money for the first time. I was bewildered at first. *Did this just happen? How could I possibly do this?* Then I was jolted back into the moment by the press and congratulations from the crowd. That was much more invigorating than running from the coppers or angry hornets!

Kelly ran in a minute after me and was under 6-minute pace as well, and Lorrie, Mel and Laurie ran their goal time of 70 minutes. We were all thrilled, ready to zip home to clean up and have a good meal before going back out to the noon awards ceremony in Riverfront Park.

There, I finally met Jon Sinclair, and he was as cute as he was on television, charming and full of life. He was from Fort Collins, Colorado, and reminded me of John Denver, the "Rocky Mountain High" singer. Mel was delighted to meet him and told him about buying a racing unit to match his. I told Mel, "Maybe you should call it something other than a unit, perhaps an outfit or uniform." Jon smiled.

My finish was shocking to everyone except Anne Audain. When she saw me at the awards ceremony, for the first time since the curb, she was thrilled and began to tease me, and jokingly told others, "I was the one who found Kim – I found her sitting in the gutter!" From that day on, we became good friends and she loved to tell people that she was responsible for my running career. She was right, but I also liked to remind everyone that Anne had been sitting in that gutter right next to me.

I was called up on stage, where I was given my prize money of $800 and a beautiful gold watch from a jewelry store. I also received gifts from several businesses in the Spokane area, along with a bronze statue of a female runner for being the first female Spokane finisher. My final reward would be the celebration party later that evening after a few hours at home relaxing on the back deck sharing race stories.

Road racing was something special and I knew it was the life for me.

I met several fascinating people that night as we danced and had a few beers in the ballroom of the Davenport Hotel, including Don Kardong, his post-race TV sidekick Steve Jones, and Creigh Kelley, the lively commentator I had enjoyed as I sat in my pajamas watching the race on TV for the first time. "Your interview with Jon Sinclair inspired me to run Bloomsday," I told him. He laughed at the thought of me being inspired to run while still in my pajamas, but seemed pleased.

Everyone was happy and full of energy. They were my kind of people. From the first small race earlier in the spring, I'd felt like I belonged in the world of road racing. I knew then that I was fast enough to start racing with the best.

I became an elite runner that day.

The weekend after Bloomsday I was resting on the couch after my long run of eight miles, flipping channels on the TV, when I came across a live marathon broadcast. It was the inaugural Women's Olympic Marathon Trials, in Olympia, Washington, just two hours from Port Townsend.

I was surprised to see a road race on national television. I watched the interviews with many of the top runners, and learned about Joan Benoit. Knee surgery 17 days before running 26.2 miles trying to qualify for the Olympics! She was amazing, going for the victory even though she needed only to place in the top three to make the team. *That's a champion*, I thought, and sure enough she was. I couldn't believe that she ran 2:31 for a marathon – that's well under 6-minutes per-mile pace for over 26 miles. I decided I would like to do that sometime. Or rather, I decided I'd like to run a marathon sometime, not run under 6-minute pace in one. That was impossible.

Two weeks after Bloomsday, Kelly and Jamie came with me to Port Townsend for the Rhody Run 12K, part of the Rhododendron Festival. I was eager but also worried; it was the first time I felt I had to win a race. Port Townsend was my hometown and I wanted to make my family and old friends proud. Not only that, the first prize was a trip to Hawaii to run the Honolulu Marathon in December. I really wanted to win that prize, not so much to run the marathon but to go to Hawaii. No question, I felt I had a better chance of winning a trip to Hawaii with a road-race victory than we did by entering those football contests. However, I knew there would be elite women in the race. It wouldn't be easy.

Dr. Scheyer was the race director, and he was thrilled that I was running. He put us up in an old officers' house that had been remodeled and turned into a hotel, right on the start/finish line of the race in Fort Worden, my old stomping ground. The Fort had been through a lot of changes since I was a kid. They renovated the offices and barracks, along with the officers' quarters, which had become hotel units, visitors' centers and dormitories for dance, music and sports camps. A camping area was developed down near the beach, along the road to the lighthouse. The Fort became more popular after the movie "An Officer and A Gentleman" had been filmed in Port Townsend a few years earlier, with most of the filming taking place in Fort Worden.

There were a lot more people allowed in, and "our" bunkers were made easily accessible by developing trails and building long, steep wooden stairs to reach them. They cleaned and cleared the bunkers out to make them safe by getting rid of the weapon and gun remnants, and locked up the dangerous part of the chalk tunnels so nobody would fall into manholes or get lost. I was disappointed to find that our old play area wasn't private anymore, but pleased that I had beautiful trails to run on in that hilly and wooded area where we used to have to bushwhack our way through.

Laurie and Mel invited the whole family over to their house the night before the race for a big meal of lasagna. Kelly wasn't pleased, since Rachel was living with them, but to his credit he didn't make a big deal about it and even allowed Jamie to come along. The two girls were very shy with each other. Rachel was 9 and knew that 4-year-old Jamie was her sister, yet she didn't say anything. She seemed awkward when she came into the room, and watched us closely from afar.

When I woke up the morning of the race, I was nervous and feeling green around the gills. I drank a pot of coffee and tried to relax! After eating a bowl of oatmeal and a bagel with cream cheese, I stretched and then walked out the door to be greeted by the race volunteers setting up the start/ finish line. I walked down the stairs and started my warm up by running directly to the trails leading up to the bunkers. I'd forgotten how fresh the air was in Port Townsend. A light breeze carried the fragrance of lilacs, sea air and fresh pine that I used to wake up to in spring and summer. I'd never noticed it earlier while on our vacations, but the moment I started running again I was noticing all the subtle yet wonderful things I had missed for so many years, things I'd taken for granted. I felt so rejuvenated after running up to the bunkers, then back down on the soft trails covered in pine needles that I just knew I was going to win my hometown race.

I went back into the officers' house to put on my racing shoes, and then Kelly and I went out to do a few strides (short 20-second pickups at race pace) just before the start. When I walked out the door, it was like stepping into the past with so many townspeople around who had supported me when I ran track in high school. We reminisced for a short while, but then I had to get ready for my race. I ran down the road to limber up one last time and was surprised to find Dad there, and shocked to see who was with him: his mom, Grandma Pat; Grandma Helen and Uncle/Grandpa Harold; Aunt Jan and Uncle Ron and their kids; Stanley and Bradley; even Debbie. Mom was there to take care of all her grand-kids. Jamie was running around with her cousins in the yard of one of the old officers' houses where they were all sitting to watch the start and finish at the corner of the final straightaway. I was sweating; my heart began to race. *I can't let them down.*

In the starting area I saw Gail Kingma, an elite runner known for being kind and giving on the sidelines but tough and unforgiving during a race. I hoped she wasn't as eager for a trip to Hawaii as I was.

I headed to the front near the starting line with Kelly, while Laurie and Mel went further back into the crowd of runners. I looked up the street to see all of the kids in the family running wild and Stanley trying to control them. Mom was too busy watching us to do any babysitting after all.

I decided I had better turn my attention to my task at hand and focus. I heard somebody calling my name and I looked over to see Mr. Brink. He wished me luck and winked, just as he did during my track meets when I was apprehensive and unsure of myself. It helped settle my nerves, as it did back then.

The gun went off. Kelly and I ran side by side as I followed Gail, who took off quickly. I tried to stick with her but we were running too fast. I couldn't push beyond that effort. I had to let her go.

I went through the first mile in 5:35 as we ran out of Fort Worden and onto the streets of Port Townsend. I could see Gail on a steep uphill near Mile 2, and she looked as if she was almost a minute ahead of me. Then we hit the country roads where I used to chase Kayla years earlier, and on that familiar road I began to close on her. We started up a two-mile hill and I slowly gained on her until I was right on her shoulder.

I was finally able to give myself a breather and enjoy the memories of my childhood as I rolled along feeling smooth and powerful. But not for long, because Gail took off on a steep downhill and my crooked toe began to hurt badly. I couldn't go with her! Then I began to feel the pain from my exertion. Once I reached the bottom, my father's words came to me: "Suffering will make you my tough little Swede," and by Mile 5, I dug deep down into the hurt and caught her on another big uphill. Then it was a race.

At Mile 6, I felt a powerful surge from within and took off like there was no tomorrow. I ran past North Beach and thought about my first kiss, with Ron. I wound along the old road leading back into Fort Worden and remembered how I hobbled around on my peg leg there, along the easiest route up to the bunkers. At Mile 7 I headed onto the old Army parade field, reliving how we dodged the guards when we were sneaking into the Fort. I took a look behind me. Gail was history.

I was able to glide through the final half mile around the parade field with ease, and heard Dad and Bradley long before I reached my family on the corner. My entire family, seldom demonstrative, was cheering for me like I'd never heard or seen before. Stanley was there with a big smile, running beside me for a few steps as he shouted, "You can relax, Kimmie, you have the win sewn up!" Mom and my grandmothers were yelling, "That's our girl!" And Uncle/Grandpa Harold was the loudest of all. "GO Swede!" he roared. Debbie was cheering and Jamie stopped playing long enough to see me run by. Rachel was standing there alone, looking awkward, but she was cheering for her mother, too. I waved as I ran past, taking enormous pride in making them proud.

As I was running down the long straightaway to the finish line, I felt as if I would faint. Not from the exertion. It was from the realization of what I had just accomplished. Dr. Scheyer came up and gave me a big hug at the finish. As I walked through the finish chute, I enjoyed more praise and congratulations from Mr. Brink and other townspeople.

I turned to see Kelly running into the finish with Gail, who congratulated me and said, "I went out too fast."

I smiled. "I noticed."

I ran over to my family as quickly as I could. Bradley was fighting back tears, and I couldn't believe that Dad was still there, ready with a big hug. Usually he disappears quietly when there's a large crowd. Dad always had faith in me and said I was going to make it big in the world and I could see in his smile that maybe he thought that race was the start.

I stayed there talking with them while waiting for Laurie and Mel to turn the corner to the finish. They yelled out to ask how I did and gave me a big "thumbs up" when they heard the answer. A newspaper reporter came over and interviewed me while my family listened.

While we were walking around waiting for the awards ceremony, Rachel followed me from afar, tripping or bumping into things. Mom and Dad went home to prepare a feast for the family, every kind of seafood imaginable and comfort food like baked beans, Grandma Helen's potato salad, Grandma Pat's green Jell-O salad with cottage cheese and pineapple, enchiladas with tons of sour cream – all of my favorites. Meanwhile Mel, Laurie, Kelly and I wandered through the Rainier beer garden, drinking beer and telling our race stories as we waited for the awards ceremony. Dr. Scheyer gave out the awards, and everyone cheered and made a big fuss when I received my check for the trip. We were going to Hawaii in December!

With Jamie starting preschool in the fall, I wanted to leave the house a bit more and do something other than run, clean and bake. I planned to finish college in the near future and decided to take Don Kardong up on an offer to work in his running store, called "The Human Race," to make some extra money for tuition. After a big argument, Kelly relented. It was time to take control of my life and that was a good start.

I think I met most of the runners in Spokane while I worked at the store three days a week, for four hours each day. Our friend Mike Brady, the top male runner in Spokane, was the manager, and he gave me some tips on how to train for a marathon. Kelly and I became members of the "Bloomsday Road Runners Club." It was great meeting new people and getting together with Mike and his girlfriend, Peggy, who were also training to run the Honolulu Marathon.

Laurie and Mel were planning to vacation in Honolulu during marathon weekend. It was going to be a big crowd. Some of the other "Bloomsday Road Runners Club" members joined us on the streets of Spokane when we began training for Honolulu, and they decided to come along, as well.

My "long run" at that point was 10 miles and that seemed like enough to me, since I was plenty tired and sore after 10 miles of running on a hilly course. But, Mike Brady insisted I needed to run even farther to prepare for a marathon. We all trained together, while I became comfortable with ten-mile runs before increasing the distance.

Often, when Kelly and I finished a long run, a hard workout or a race, we would go straight to the grocery store and pick up a dozen donuts, a gallon of ice cream and whatever else looked good. Then we went home and ate it all. We assumed that was what you had to do when you ran 35 miles a week, until we watched a news story on KXLY that was part of a series meant to inspire runners to start training for Bloomsday. A well-known nutritionist was giving guidelines for a proper training diet. We were stunned. "What? That's all we're supposed to eat? That's not enough!" According to him, we were way over our calorie limit. Way over.

After my long run on Saturday mornings, I looked forward to resting on the couch watching "Scooby Doo" and the "Smurfs" cartoons with an overly enthusiastic Jamie, who made sure I didn't doze off during the "important" scenes. She owned every toy Smurf and stuffed animal, and had them lined up on the floor next to her in front of the TV while wearing her "Papa Smurf" slippers and "Smurfette" underwear.

I was enjoying my life again. Jamie was happy and Kelly wasn't as controlling or dominating after he started running well and had something to focus on other than me. Even though he still expected me to follow the daily-charted plan to the exact minute, he became less possessive. He had to, if I was going to be a prominent runner. Sharing our running, making new friends and planning our trip to Hawaii made him happy, which made life a whole lot easier.

At long last, I felt firmly settled and at peace.

One dark and gloomy afternoon in early October, I had an uneasy feeling. I paced the floor, sensing something had happened, something horrible. Around 4 o'clock I really started to worry. Kelly was already at work, and I was home alone with Jamie while she was playing with her doll, Babes. I was edgy, almost panicked. I knew I had to call my parents. I felt sick. I paced back and forth past the telephone hanging on the kitchen wall, feeling helpless while counting down the minutes, waiting to call my parents when I knew somebody would be home after 5 p.m.

I finally dialed. Debbie answered. My heart sank. "Why are you there?" I asked her. "Did something bad happen?"

Stanley had been driving home from football practice with four other boys, sitting in the middle of the back seat of his friend's car, when another car struck them while speeding through a stop sign. He was thrown through the windshield and had been flown by helicopter to the trauma center at Harborview Medical Center in Seattle with a brain injury. Mom, Dad, Laurie and Mel were with him there, waiting and hoping.

"There's nothing we can do," said Debbie, crying hysterically. "We're waiting for more news."

All I could hear was a ringing in my ears. I slid down the kitchen wall, dropping the telephone. *Maybe Debbie is on drugs. Maybe she got the whole story wrong. Maybe she is making it up, just like our father used to tell outlandish tales. Just this one time, Jehovah God, please let Debbie be on drugs.*

"I'll call you when I hear anything," Debbie said, when I managed to lift the phone up to my ear again.

After she hung up, I couldn't stop crying. *Even if Debbie is right about the crash, maybe Stanley isn't injured as badly as they think. It could be just a concussion. But what if it's worse?* I prayed. I pleaded, asking Jehovah God to please save Stanley. *If there is a Jehovah God, he won't allow my brother to die. Not another one.* He was only 14 years old.

A few hours later, Laurie called, sobbing, from the trauma center. "Kimmie, Stanley is brain dead." They were going to turn off the machines after saying goodbye to my sweet baby brother.

I felt a big rock drop into my stomach. Hornets were stinging my body. Then I went blank.

I don't remember anything that happened in the days after Stanley's death. Nothing. I do remember that I learned what hell is like. It's a place where you can never escape, you can never forget. You can't go on with life as it was. I wanted out. Everyone in my family did.

Instead of pulling together, they fell apart.

Chapter 10

Stanley died in the same exact spot as Charlie, a mile up the street from my parents' house. His last word was "Stop!" The other car went through a stop sign and crashed into them without even braking. Stanley was the only one hurt.

When I joined my family in Port Townsend, my parents didn't look the same. I didn't like what I saw in their faces. There was sadness and pain and shock, but there was something else, something worse. They looked lost.

Mom was lifeless, and Dad looked as if he had lost his reason for living. In a way, he had. Stanley was Dad's fishing buddy, his best friend, the reason he became a well-respected man. Just like me with my running, he appreciated life and his surroundings more when he was doing things he loved with someone he loved. *Now ... Stanley is gone.*

Our entire family had already experienced the shock and horror of death, and had grieved in the past, but it was fresh again and almost unbearable. When we were really brave, we tried to smile, only to break down and cry. "To lose a child is to lose a piece of yourself," Dr. Burton Grebin, a New York pediatrician, once said. My parents would never be whole again, and neither would the rest of us. We took comfort in being together, but would each have to take our own path toward accepting the loss of this special child.

Laurie was quiet, her face puffy ... her eyes swollen. She seemed distant, and had a disturbing look in her eyes. I'd seen it before, in my father when I was a little girl. It frightened me then, and it was frightening me again.

Debbie was on crack or speed, I couldn't be sure which, and trying to coax Dad and Bradley into getting high with her. Her eyes were crazed and she looked demonized, just like my troll doll with the wild hair. Debbie had changed her hair color to a beautiful, brilliant blond, which made her seem even more animated. I was not in the mood for a "dysfunctional family moment." None of us were. We were relieved when Debbie decided to use her abundance of energy productively by wallpapering my parents' bathroom and then looked for other tasks that needed doing in the house.

Bradley didn't say much, and I worried about him when he didn't say much.

I watched Uncle/Grandpa Harold. *What must be going through his mind? How can he face so many deaths? His first wife, his father, six brothers, and four grandsons/nephews ... my brothers: Timmy, Murphy, Charlie, and now little Stanley.*

Grandma Helen sat there quietly, just as she did when Charlie died. She possessed a spirit that allowed her to connect with other people without the need to speak or even look at them. We all felt the power of her silent strength.

Grandma Pat was there for Dad and the rest of us, but she looked just as lost as her son.

Aunt Jan also came over with her family. Stanley and her son Timmy had been born only a few months apart and did everything together, playing baseball or basketball or just hanging around doing what kids do. Those two came up with some colorful pranks, which sometimes attracted more attention than they expected.

One afternoon, there had been a knock on the door. Dad answered it to an outraged driver. "Do you have young boys?" he demanded to know.

"Yes," said Dad.

"There are some boys out on the main road with a cable wire," he said. "When I drove by, they took this tiny boy in a harness and slid him across the street on the cable, right in front of my car!"

"There's no way my boy would do such a thing," Dad told him.

After the agitated driver left, Dad went out to the road and found Stanley and Timmy getting ready to go again, putting little Mel in his harness back up onto the cable wire. It was attached to a telephone pole on one side of the road and ran downhill to a tree on the other side. They had rigged it all up with things handy in the garage from deer hunting and shrimping, copying a stunt pulled on them and Dad a few hours earlier. It didn't seem dangerous, just fun. It was a comforting moment for us to hear Dad tell that story on our day of mourning, and even more comforting for him to tell it.

Stanley's death took a toll on Timmy, in the days and the years afterward. He and Bradley were affected more than anyone realized. It was the end of the straw for all of us.

As for me, I wondered ... *how in the world do I go on from here? I have to for Jamie, but also for my parents, my sisters and my last remaining brother.*

I was still in hell, but had to pick myself up and get my life back in order. Stanley was like my own child, and my love for him was as strong as my love for Jamie and Rachel. Losing him was a hell I couldn't escape, yet I knew that I couldn't retreat into the twilight as I had in past traumas. I had to face my grief head on and learn to live with it to survive and go forward in my own way before I could help my family recover.

Living in Spokane, away from my family, helped me move on with life. As good as it was to be together consoling each other in the days after Stanley died, it would have been hard to be reminded every moment that he wasn't in my world anymore. I still woke up startled at times to sadness, and I knew that was something I would have to endure for the rest of my life.

Having a stable life with Kelly and Jamie helped, and I worked hard to get back into my routine. I don't know how I would have managed to deal with the emotional upheaval without Jamie and my running. Jamie was my reason for being strong, persevering and facing each day. Running gave me a sense of wellbeing and balance.

Honolulu Marathon ~ December, 1984

At Kelly's urging, I was still planning to run the Honolulu Marathon. The trip was already organized and all the arrangements made. "You can't put your life on hold," he told me, and he was right but I felt guilty about going on vacation just two months after losing Stanley.

Not only that, but even as we packed our bags and headed to the airport I knew I wasn't prepared to run a marathon. I'd managed to run 30-35 miles a week, though I never did run over 10 miles for my long run. I guess I would, soon enough.

Mom was going to babysit Jamie for the next 10 days, so we flew to Seattle first to make the exchange at the airport before boarding our flight to Honolulu. We met up with Laurie and Mel in Hawaii along with

Mel's sisters and their husbands. A few days later Mike, Peggy and several other Bloomsday Road Runner friends arrived. They all had a great time in the days before the marathon, enjoying dinners, good company and short, easy runs together. I was just going through the motions and trying to hide the fact that I felt miserable.

Then it was marathon day. The morning was humid and windy, with gusts up to 40 miles per hour along the Kalanianaole Highway, near the halfway point on the course. I had no idea how to run a marathon period, much less a marathon in those conditions.

We started in the predawn darkness, and it was just turning daylight near Mile 5 as Kelly and I began running up Diamond Head. I left Kelly soon after that, and forgot all about him as I focused on my race, running within my comfort level while taking in the paradise around me. I was moved by its beauty, awakened by the angry sea below and its enormous waves crashing onto shore, the palm trees bending and swaying as if dancing with the wind, the tropical plants waving like big colorful fans. Suddenly, I didn't feel guilty about being there. I knew Stanley was with me, and felt that he and Charlie were both in a good place and part of my experience at that moment.

I wasn't worried any longer about the windswept marathon course or the threat of torrential rains. I wasn't even worried that I'd never run farther than 10 miles. At the half marathon – three miles farther than my longest run – I saw on the roadside clock that my split was 1:24:24, and I was feeling good. Near the 20-mile mark, on the way back toward Diamond Head, I started passing people, and I still felt pretty good. I was tired, but nowhere near "The Wall" everyone told me I would hit around that point. I did notice the heat and humidity, but nothing hurt except my crooked toe and I was used to that.

I finished strong, as the 5th place woman, in 2:48:48 – running the second half in 1:24:24, the exact same time as my first half. Don told me later that running even-splits in one's first marathon was unusual and that I must have the gift of being a natural marathoner. Maybe that was it, because I certainly had no idea what I was doing.

One of my prizes was a big kiss from Rod Dixon when he handed me my award. Rod was a *very* handsome New Zealand runner who'd won the New York City Marathon a year earlier. Laurie and Mel's sisters kept taking pictures. "Kiss her again," they teased. It took several kisses to get the right shot.

A woman who finished just behind me had competed in the 1984 Olympic Marathon Trials earlier that year. "If you had run this time in a marathon before the Trials, you would have qualified to run them," she told me. It didn't take me long to decide that I would try to qualify for the next Olympic Marathon Trials, in 1988.

Laurie and Mel headed home a few days after the marathon, so we spent the rest of our vacation on Maui with Mike and Peggy, jogging slowly in the mornings to recover from the race before heading to the beach. One of our excursions was a snorkeling cruise out to Molokini, a tiny island known for its diving. On the way back, I taught several dozen curious Japanese tourists the "Montana Chug Upside Down." Well, they tried to learn it, anyway. Every time they attempted it, the beer went everywhere. They couldn't figure out how to grab the glass from the ground with their teeth and tip it in toward their chins to drink while trying to stand up at the same time – without using their hands – even after I demonstrated it fluidly several times. They finally settled for the simpler "Montana Chug," which some of them managed to master after far too many attempts. They all walked off the boat on unsteady legs, thinking I was something special.

I was grateful that Kelly persuaded me to go on the trip. It took my mind away from the sorrow and eased my grief, allowing me to escape for at least a little while. Moreover, that marathon was like having a big cry, as I came to terms with losing my baby brother and felt comforted and tranquil for the first time in a very long while.

On our way back to Spokane, we picked Jamie up at the Seattle airport. Mom looked much better. Having Jamie and her other grandchildren while we were all away kept her and Dad busy instead of being home alone thinking about Stanley.

Several months before Jamie's visit, Mom's Siamese cat had given birth to kittens and, sure enough, Jamie showed up at the airport with a fluffy white one she'd named "Punky," after her favorite TV character, Punky Brewster. Punky looked as if the other half of her was Persian, and had a tiny gray diamond on her forehead. She was in a travel carrier all ready for the flight. Kelly was not pleased, but Jamie was so excited to have a new kitten that we couldn't tell her "no."

When we were back in Spokane, Don said that with some guidance and support he felt I could become a great marathoner. He suggested I consider finding a coach and that I contact Jeff Darman, the sports marketing director for a women's athletic clothing line called Moving Comfort, to see if they would sponsor me.

Not long after my marathon, a supporter in Spokane, who wanted to remain anonymous, funded a trip to Florida in February to give me an opportunity to run in the Orange Bowl 10K, a highly competitive race in Miami. That was the perfect occasion to invite Mom and give her a chance to run in a race. I had been encouraging her to do some running over the past year. Stanley used to do the same by riding his bike alongside her and she loved it. I was pleased when she decided to join me for the vacation. She really needed a getaway after Stanley's death.

Mom had never flown on an airplane. She was so excited, looking out the window and enjoying every little experience along the way. I suddenly realized how childlike and innocent Mom was in so many ways. It was fun and a relief to see her happy, and her exuberance was a good distraction. I didn't like the enclosed space of an airplane. The first time I had planned to fly to a race, not long before, I ended up walking off the airplane and driving eight hours instead. I wasn't worried about crashing. It was my claustrophobia, being in an enclosed space and not having any control over the situation – like being locked in the closet by my sisters. A few therapy sessions helped me overcome some of the fear.

When we arrived in Miami, we rented a white LeBaron convertible. It was dark and very late, but that didn't keep us from putting the top down anyway before we headed for our hotel. I drove, and Mom was supposed to be the navigator. Big mistake. We were lost almost before we left the airport.

As we were driving through the most dangerous part of Miami, people were yelling in Spanish and flipping us off. Mom thought they were waving and saying hello. She waved back, saying, "Hello! It's nice to be here, everyone is so nice!" We had a lot of angry Cubans stirred up, and a van full of them followed us to our hotel once I figured out how to get there. We tried, but couldn't quite lose them.

Finally, we reached the hotel. I parked right in front of the entrance and told Mom to "get out – now!" We rushed inside. As soon as the security guard went out, the van took off.

"That was close," said Mom. "And here I thought they were such nice people."

The Orange Bowl 10K was run in the late afternoon. It was 85 degrees and extremely humid, and I had just come from 20-degree temperatures and snow-covered ground. Mom wasn't used to the heat either, so she decided to wear her new Honolulu running hat, a lightweight white painter's hat with mesh on the top for ventilation that we'd brought back for her from our trip. She loved that hat.

With the race loaded with Olympians, including the great Norwegian marathoner Grete Waitz, I wasn't expected to do much. It was tough from the beginning. I managed to run strong and steady, although I wasn't fast by any means. Most of the elite women had taken off like maniacs, and I didn't see any of them again until I passed several in the last mile. I finished 13th, in 35:57 (5:47 pace) and won some prize money, a nice surprise.

I was worried about Mom running in the heat and humidity, so after I finished I jogged back on the course to see if she was OK. I heard all kinds of chatter and laughter, and looked to see Mom visiting with everyone around her as she ran. She was just fine. Once Mom finished, she told everyone she met about how clever she was to cool down during her race by putting ice in her prized hat.

The race director, Basil Honikman, invited Mom and me to the elite athlete post-race dinner at our hotel that evening and we ended up sitting at the same table as Benji Durden. Benji was a legend in the marathon world. He was a 2:09 marathoner, #7 in the world in 1982 and ranked among the top 10 U.S. marathoners for six straight years. I had long admired him from afar, not only for his accomplishments but also for his quirky behavior. A few months earlier, Don had mentioned him as a possible coach, and oddly – perhaps karma had something to do with it – I was sitting at his table.

As if living and running in Atlanta in the summer wasn't enough, Benji took "heat training" to another level. He wore a cotton sweatsuit under a nylon sweatsuit, under a rubber suit – along with a PO2 high-altitude simulator that gave him very little oxygen, to really stress himself. Between all those clothes and the weight of the tank, Benji carried an extra 20 pounds on those long runs. And there I was sitting next to this eccentric man.

Benji and I launched straight into a discussion on training and his coaching philosophy. I asked him right there at the table if he

would be interested in coaching me from Boulder, where he was moving right after running the Tampa Bay 15K the following weekend. He
told me that he wasn't coaching anyone at the time, but that he was
nearing the end of his elite career and that coaching was one of the
many options he was considering for his future. Anybody who can
wear an 18-pound PO2 high-altitude simulator in the extreme heat is
capable of doing almost anything he wants to, but he agreed immediately to coach me.

Mom was so excited about having Benji and Grete Waitz at our table
that she started talking up a storm and taking pictures, telling everyone
to pose in couples, groups, toasting, holding the flowers from the table,
in front of the tropical plants – you name it – while using up an entire
roll of film. Grete was quiet and reserved but smiled kindly and was very
good about Mom's enthusiasm, while Benji rolled his eyes as he went
along with it. Then Mom decided to tell all of the elite runners about her
trick of putting ice in her hat. I was a bit embarrassed but she was quite
charming, and it was nice to see her happy and full of life again, so I went
with it, too.

The next morning, I met Benji for a post-race recovery run. On a
path just a few miles after we started, I ran through a thin wire tied
between two small trees right at shin level. The wire snapped, leaving
both of my shins gashed and bloody. I managed to jog back to the hotel,
where Benji told me I should ice my shins. He would check on me a week
later in Tampa at the Gasparilla Distance Classic 15K. I planned to join
him there after Mom and I had been invited at the Orange Bowl awards
ceremony.

Mom and I decided that we would take a road trip through the
Everglades, staying in Naples before driving up to Tampa. We had a wonderful time, with the top down on our convertible, wearing straw hats
and shorts over our swimming suits like typical tourists. Mom wanted to
stop to take photos, yet again. She asked an old Cajun man walking along
the Tamiami Trail highway to take our photo in front of a tattered forgotten sign advertising "Kelly's Boat Rides" to give to Kelly later. "Mom,
it isn't very safe out here in the middle of nowhere, talking to just any
stranger who comes along!" I warned her.

We spent five days on Naples Beach. I ran a little, even though my
shins were throbbing in pain. Whenever I had the chance I iced them,

but they still looked terrible, black and blue with deep red gashes and a huge lump on each one.

After my runs we bought sandwiches and drinks and spent the day on the beach. Mom had never seen a pelican before. "Kimmie, take a picture of me next to one of these prehistoric-looking creatures," she would say. They seemed to be everywhere. So were the seagulls. I was once again posing for Mom when a big flock of them came soaring down from the sky, directly toward me and the sandwich in my hand. They were so aggressive and coming toward me so fast that I tossed my sandwich at them before they nailed me. Mom got a great photo.

We arrived in Tampa the night before the race. I woke up early the next morning and went through my usual pre-race routine of drinking a pot of coffee, eating a bowl of oatmeal and a bagel with cream cheese, then stretching lightly and relaxing for an hour. A 15K was a little long for Mom, so she decided to sleep in.

My shins *really* hurt, but I decided to run anyway. At the starting line, I recognized many of the elite runners from photos in *Runner's World* and *Running Times* magazines. Again, it was a sultry morning. I eased into the race hoping to finish without incident and that's just what I did, except for it being the most miserable race ever. My shins were throbbing, I was hot, even my crooked toe ached from the start. I ran 52:59 (5:41 pace), respectable but not fast enough to break into the top 10, or even close.

I was relieved to have that race over. I walked away ready to train properly. Lesson learned, I should focus more and not have such an entertaining week leading up to an important race. No more spending five days on the beach in the hot sun and having one too many cocktails with Mom during dinner. And most importantly, to never run in a race when I am injured.

It wasn't until years later that I learned how badly injured I really was, when an X-ray after another incident showed the wire I hit had sliced halfway through the tibia. I had run a 9.3-mile race, and then continued to train, on two partially severed shinbones. Eating all of that tuna with the bones in it must have protected me more than I thought. My shins healed up just fine.

At the Gasparilla awards ceremony, I met Benji's fiancée, Amie Cotter. They were packed up and ready to move to Boulder. Amie was adorable, caring and good-natured, with a happy face. She was the perfect match for Benji, who was matter-of-fact and masked his kindness beneath a gruff exterior. He looked like Zonker in the Doonesbury comic strip and reminded me of a hippie professor, bearded and analytical. He would often be figuring out a Rubick's Cube while conversation went on around him, going hmmmmm, hmmmmm as he concentrated, and you'd think he wasn't paying any attention until suddenly he would pipe up with exactly the right response or perfect observation. He had been listening all along.

I had learned from many experiences in my life's journey, and that journey led me to Benji. I had found my running mentor.

Benji started working with me right away, in March 1985. He explained that we were going to approach my marathon career by taking small steps, growing stronger in a progressive manner over the years. "No shortcuts," he said. "We want to slowly add mileage and intensity. That way, you'll be very durable and without injury, and as a result have a long career."

That was just what I needed, some guidance from somebody I trusted and respected. He had plenty to work with because I was only running 30-35 miles a week. A lot of recreational runners do more than that. He planned my workouts and coached me over the telephone a few times a week. I was shocked when he instructed me to start running 4-miles for a second run three days a week. I had never done such a thing and it was overwhelming even to consider running twice in one day, but Benji explained that I needed to bring my mileage up to 50 miles a week before my next marathon. We had decided on the Twin Cities Marathon that October.

Knowing I would soon be running more mileage, only that one time did I complain to the doctor about my crooked toe. He told me that the bone in the toe was deformed. "You compensated for that crooked toe from the moment you started walking, and later, as you developed into a runner. We could take the bone out, but that may cause problems with your balance ... your forceful toe push-off, and possibly change your walking and running gait." That ended anymore complaining.

I adapted to Benji's training right away. The weekly plan was:

Monday: 0-4 miles slow

Tuesday: AM – Hills or speed session: 4 miles of easy running over hilly terrain, then 6 to 8 (half mile) hills at race effort, jogging down the hill for recovery, then 4 miles of easy running to finish up. That totaled 11-12 miles of running. Later in the year, closer to racing season, the hill workout was alternated with a track session every other week, usually 6 miles of short speed efforts: ¼ miles up to miles at race effort, with a ¼ mile jog between efforts to fully recover before going again.
    PM: 4-mile second run

Wednesday: 0-4 miles easy

Thursday: AM – Long run starting at 15 miles, slowly adding miles every other week until reaching 25 miles, which came four weeks before my marathon. We usually incorporated 3-minute pickups at race pace every 10 minutes into the middle hour of that run.
    PM: 4-mile second run

Friday: 0-4 miles easy

Saturday or Sunday: A race, which I would use as part of my training rather than rest up for, or a "tempo run" of 4 miles at a strong and steady pace, less intense than a race. Including a 3-mile warm up and cool down.
    PM: 4 mile-second run

The other day was a day off.

I had a recovery day (0-4 miles, my choice) between each hard workout day, to ensure recovery and reduce the risk of injury. I looked forward to my recovery days and called them wimp days. That was definitely an extreme hard/extreme easy program, and one that I would excel at from the very beginning. The training seemed overwhelming at times, but I trusted Benji and had no doubts. I just did it.
    Only once did I say "no" to Benji. He wanted me to learn to deal with the mental and physical stress of running in the heat the way he did,

and instructed me to do a run wearing a heavy cotton sweatsuit, under a nylon sweatsuit, under a rubber or Gortex sweatsuit. At least the PO2 high-altitude simulator wasn't in his plans. I did as he said for about 20 minutes, and then ... claustrophobia struck. I frantically pulled off all of the hot, heavy layers in a panic, ditching them in a bush as I went on my merry way running in a jog bra and shorts along the beautiful trails in Spokane Riverside State Park for the rest of my 20-mile run, in 90 degrees. Benji attempted to persuade me to try again, but finally gave up.

Kelly tried to keep up with the training but with such a demanding job he struggled with the hard days and especially the second runs. I adapted well, however, as we slowly and progressively added to the volume of training.

Leading up to the marathon, I used a few shorter "practice" races as steppingstones toward my goal. The races were part of the training, so rather than rest for them I raced on tired legs to allow my body and mind to feel the same fatigue I would face in the latter stages of a marathon. It wasn't pleasant, but the mental toughness was as important as the physical, and needed to be trained just the same.

That spring I ran Bloomsday in 43:25, thirty-five seconds slower than the previous year. I had to "let it go" when I finished behind women I should have beaten, and walked away with a strong belief that it would pay off in the important race: the marathon.

One woman who was beating me consistently the past two years was Regina Joyce, an Irish runner who had won Bloomsday in 1984 and beat me by three minutes that year (1985). Miraculously, two weeks later I beat her in the Rhody Run. My hometown race was always magical, with my entire family there to support me. I knew I would make them happy by winning, which was all the incentive I needed.

Running is contagious. That year Mom, Kelly, Laurie, Mel and Mel's sister, Debbie, ran the race, along with Dad's fishing buddy, Jim Rhondo and his wife, Pam. Pam was Laurie's best friend, the one who helped pierce our ears years earlier. With a younger generation in higher positions as Elders, restrictions were easing and many of our Jehovah's Witness friends were allowed to run in the race without having to deal with the guilt trip the older Elders put upon them for participating in a worldly event.

Even with my family there in full force, running or cheering us on, it wasn't the same without my precious Stanley.

While staying with my parents for a few days after the race, I could see they were sad and distressed. Dad seemed to have hit bottom just before our visit, but by the time we arrived he had quit drinking and partying and was more solemn than I'd ever seen him. I wondered how low he had fallen in his grief before beginning to pick himself up. Mom, on the other hand, was on some kind of high, and I could tell that Dad was concerned. She was very animated and drinking excessively.

We spent almost every day at Fort Worden Beach and running on the trails near the bunkers above. One morning when Mom told everyone that she was going out for a run, Jamie said, "You don't wun, Gwamma ... my mom wuns. You jog." Everyone laughed. Jamie knew what it took to be a "runner," and in her mind it was more than moving at "Grandma pace."

Jamie on the beach with the Fort Worden dock behind her

Jamie and me at Fort Worden with Chetzemoka Park in the background

While we were down at the beach with Laurie and Bradley and their families, Jamie became a drama queen, feeding off the attention she attracted from everyone. Wearing her orange water wings and Smurfette swimming suit, she frantically ran down to the beach looking for her 10 babies. Laurie asked, "What babies?" Jamie replied, "I have 10 babies and they awe gone!"

I was horrified. I flashed back 18 years to the times my father would run from window to window, peeking out and screaming at Mom, "Call the police! People are throwing rocks at the house and breaking windows!" Then the imaginary people would suddenly become his friends. "Cook up some hamburgers, they're getting hungry!" he would say cheerfully.

When Mom said, "There's nobody there," he would take his gun out of the closet, walk out into the field and then fire. Mom couldn't be sure if he'd killed himself, or maybe somebody else. He was so intent, and so sure those people were there, just like Jamie was at that very moment.

I was thankful when Jamie finally explained that she was looking for her "pretend babies." She knew they were pretend.

Jamie managed to keep her "pretend babies" around for well over a year. She would run all over the place while taking care of the babies, moving them from place to place and away from harm. She attracted a lot of attention and it kept her busy, but I was relieved when those "pretend babies" disappeared forever.

I left Port Townsend with an uneasy feeling about the state Mom and Laurie were in. They seemed OK during our visit but I sensed a lot of dysfunction behind the scenes. I could read Laurie and Mom very well. They were both too euphoric and overly enthusiastic. Dad was concerned for a reason.

Debbie wasn't there, which was an even bigger concern. *What is she up to?*

~

I was surprised at how much I raced in 1985, which only made me tougher. I learned the skill of running hard on tired legs. For the most part I was consistent and able to run strong, and even set a few personal bests. I made several thousand dollars running in 10 of the big races around the country, while using the local races (14 in all) as fast training runs. It worked well and I saw a big improvement in my racing toward the end of summer and into the fall.

After running another breakthrough race in Portland at the Cascade Run Off 15K – a personal best of 52:01 (5:34 pace) – I decided to take Don's advice and contact Jeff Darman to see if I could get some kind of sponsorship from Moving Comfort, the popular and stylish women's athletic-wear company. Jeff agreed to take me on as a sponsored athlete, giving me free clothing and a small stipend for expenses and travel money, along with a bonus structure based on performance in key races and media exposure. It was a fair agreement, especially because I really hadn't accomplished much other than placing in the top 10 in some major road races.

I signed on with Moving Comfort in August, just before making a big improvement in my 10K time in high-level races. I managed to bring my time down under 34 minutes in winning the Seafair 10K in Seattle, running a personal best of 33:26. Several weeks later I placed second in the Nordstrom 10K in Portland, following Australian star Lisa Martin the entire race and finishing a few seconds behind her, in 33:28 (5:23 pace).

My mileage was up to 50-60 miles a week. Things were starting to come together just in time for my first big marathon.

In the fall, four weeks before the marathon, my attention was diverted when Jamie started kindergarten. It was so stressful that I let her take her cat, Punky, to school for "show and tell" to ease her fear and awkwardness. It was a disaster. Punky ended up running in circles around the classroom while the kids laughed and chased her until the teacher managed some order. Meanwhile, Punky sat quietly in a corner waiting for the chase to begin again. That went on for the entire three hours. The class didn't accomplish much that morning. Jamie felt more confident after receiving extra attention from her classmates, but Punky came home terrified and wouldn't leave the house for days.

Kelly did a lot of my track workouts with me on the Ferris High School track, which was only half of a mile from home. Jamie always came along with her plastic shovel and bucket to play in the sand of the long-jump pit, and would time us with her plastic stopwatch by calling numbers as we ran by. The numbers were random, of course, but she had the right idea. The Ferris track coach would recognize us during the workouts and smile as he watched us in action. It was definitely a family effort, especially the time I allowed Jamie to bring Punky along, which was another disaster, although I managed my best sprint session of all time while chasing the cat around that track, over the pole-vault pit, across the grass, over and under the bleachers and finally into the long-jump pit. There, Punky decided to take a rest with Jamie, who was laughing and enjoying the show. After Punky's performance in school, I should have known better. She was so much like a dog that sometimes we forgot she was a cat.

Jamie wasn't the only one who was stressed, as I tried to juggle a heavy load of training with taking care of my family in the month leading up to the marathon. I needed to start focusing. Most of my competitors didn't have families yet, and most also had husbands who gave up a lot to support their careers. Everything revolved around the athlete. After all, that's how elite athletes train and perform at their best. I couldn't imagine putting my family's lives on hold all year to pursue my training and racing, but I had to get into the right mindset and become "race ready" in the three or four weeks before my important races. Perhaps this was why most of the women I ran against started their families after their competitive years.

My last long run was 25 miles – my first three-hour run ever – followed by a 4-mile second run later in the afternoon. I was having a hard time dealing with the thought of it, but once I got out there it seemed effortless. The 3-minute pickups Benji incorporated into the middle hour of the run helped make the time go fast and took my mind off the challenge of the distance. Once that run was over and done, I felt ready.

I left Jamie and Kelly (and Punky) home and did the critical track workouts the few weeks leading up to my marathon alone. I enjoyed that ever-so-needed quiet time to myself, and that was the only time I could get it. My final speed session went well – 8x ½ mile (2 laps) at 10K race effort (5:20 pace), followed by a full recovery (a ¼ mile jog – one lap) – and then finishing with 4x 200 (half of a lap) in 30-33 seconds. That was my typical speed session 10 days before major races.

I was surprised when Benji didn't plan a taper for me. During the week leading into a marathon, most runners back off the mileage so they can arrive at the starting line totally rested. I backed off a little, but still ran over 50 miles the week before Twin Cities, to stay in my routine as much as possible. As it turns out, I felt it *was* resting because I didn't have to do second runs that week, but others thought it was too much. I had complete trust in Benji and that was all that mattered.

Twin Cities Marathon ~ October, 1985

Kelly and I flew to Minneapolis/St. Paul on the Thursday before the race, along with Mike Brady who was also planning to compete in the marathon.

We waited patiently for Sunday to arrive. I was an invited runner and had to attend a few press conferences, but I didn't have to be up on stage as one of the favorites. Nobody paid any attention to me, and I certainly wasn't a threat. I was just a 2:48 marathoner, and it had been difficult even persuading Jack Moran, the race director, to give me a free hotel room and a promise to reimburse me for my plane ticket if I placed in the top 10. I'm sure he invited me only as a favor to Don and Jeff.

I'd trained day in and day out for seven solid months, and was ready to see if all that effort would pay off on race day. I had beaten many of the other invited women in short races over the summer, but I hadn't proven myself over the marathon distance.

Most of the top American women were competing that year in preparation for the U.S. Championship Marathon, which would be held on the same course the following year. There, the top three athletes would earn a berth on the U.S. team for the 1987 World Championships in Rome. The women's field was packed, not just with American runners here for the "dress rehearsal" but with many foreign athletes, as well. Boston Marathon winner Kim Merritt and 1984 Olympian Gabriela Andersen were among the women who would be on the starting line.

The morning of the marathon was crisp, clear and cold – 25 degrees, with no wind. Since I had previewed the course, I knew what to expect. The race would start on the city streets in Minneapolis and then wind around lakes and along the river into St Paul. There were small climbs throughout, but at 19 miles the course became a gradual, and sometimes not-so-gradual, 6-mile climb to the St. Paul Cathedral before the final mile descent to the State Capitol. It was a challenging yet fair course that would allow for a fast time. Benji and I talked about race strategy and came up with a conservative plan to start slowly and feel as if I was holding back.

Most of the top women were racing all-out from the gun. My plan was to run well within my comfort zone for the first 10 miles, no matter what, and I did. At 10 miles, I was in 20th place, running at just over 6-minute pace. Continuing at that pace for 16 more miles seemed overwhelming, but I quickly put the thought out of my mind and carried on. I was comfortable, my breathing was good and I had no worries about any asthma problems. I went through the halfway point feeling strong, enjoying the beauty of the autumn leaves and the many lakes and parks surrounding the beautiful course. When the sun came out, it warmed the freezing morning to a comfortable 50 degrees. As it hit the colorful leaves, the reflection was almost blinding.

Because of road construction and a rising river, we were faced with a detour. Instead of crossing a bridge, there was an out-and-back portion that gave me a glimpse of everyone returning as I was heading out. Most of my competition looked tired and not very pleasant at all. I was far behind the lead women and decided that I might be relaxing and holding back too much, even more than Benji suggested. Seeing the other women struggling encouraged me to pick it up a little.

Once I hit the turnaround at 19 miles, I came back fast, weaving through so many women that I lost count. American athletes, foreign athletes, I just sailed by them while heading up the hills toward the cathedral. I looked a long way up the course and saw a press vehicle and a cyclist. *They must be with the lead woman.* I squinted for a closer look. There she was, and I didn't see any other women between us. *I'm in second place!*

That encouraged me even more. I started running faster. Once again, I never hit "The Wall" that everyone continued to tell me about. I was executing our race plan perfectly. I drew closer and closer as we approached the finish line, but the other woman crossed it first, 12 seconds in front of me.

Janice Ettle, the nicest competitor I had yet to meet in my running career, won the race. She was from Minnesota, and the crowd was ecstatic over the hometown victory. I was happy for her, and thrilled with my second place. I shocked myself by running under 6-minute pace, 2:35:59. Janice, who had finished 5th in the 1984 Olympic Trials, ran 2:35:47. At that moment, I knew I was a marathoner. More importantly, I knew I could run faster.

I had faith in Benji, I had faith in the plan, and I had faith in myself.

I made some decent money for my second-place finish – $12,000, plus the Moving Comfort performance bonuses – besides winning several nice presents. I never dreamed I could win so much money just for running. I was ecstatic to see that I was rewarded tenfold for what I did best.

Everyone was overjoyed after the shock wore off. As for me, I was beaming with pride. I had lopped 13 minutes off my marathon time in 10 months. Still, I wasn't satisfied with my performance. Being satisfied leads to being less motivated, less likely to continue to strive. I went home full of high spirits, recharged and ready to train harder with more confidence and experience to tackle the marathon world. I wanted to reach a higher level.

I walked into the professional world of road racing at the right time. Prize money was in full force because of a lot of planning, energy and work on the part of key figures in the running world. Don Kardong, Benji Durden, Jon Sinclair, Anne Audain, Chuck Galford, Billy Rodgers, Greg Meyer, Herb Lindsey and Lorraine Moller, to name a few, banded together working toward a circuit of professional races where runners could accept money openly, based on performance, with no consequence of losing their "amateur" status and being banned from the Olympic or World Championships teams. The ARRA – Association of Road Racing Athletes – was born.

In 1981, athletes at the Cascade Run Off openly accepted prize money, which jeopardized them and any athletes who competed against them at other races with being banned from running TAC events. It was called the "contamination" rule. Eventually the ARRA and The Athletics Congress (TAC, the governing body of track and field and distance running in the U.S.) reached a compromise: prize money could be openly accepted if it were put into a TAC TRUST account in the athlete's name and be used for living and training expenses. Of course, that meant it could be used for almost anything.

After Twin Cities, I asked a good friend and fellow runner from Spokane, John Woodhead, to form my TAC TRUST. John was a brilliant financial broker, and started investing my prize money wisely while it was sitting in my trust.

Then I took four weeks off from running. Benji insisted it was best to take a complete break from running and my routine to give my body a total rest. "You should even try to gain a few pounds," he told me. He was a bit surprised when I agreed with him. Little did he know at the time, I thoroughly enjoyed "de-training." After taking off my four weeks, I eased back into some easy enjoyable running, with no training structure or immediate plans to race through the remainder of the year. The winters in Spokane were challenging, with snow often on the ground from November to March, so that was a good time to take my breaks.

My family went through a lot of changes in 1985. Jamie turned 5 in October and was becoming even more aware of things. She became very shy when she started kindergarten and was still struggling. That surprised me, since she had always received a lot of positive attention, but in school she turned bright red and didn't say a word, just like I did in school. I'm sure her cheeks felt like they were on fire. Maybe it's hereditary. I knew just what she was going through. It was torture coaxing her into going to school, and once we were there I felt terrible leaving her for half the day. It took Jamie several years to find a way out of that uncomfortable and awkward stage. Thankfully, she didn't whistle from the spaces between her teeth.

My "Whistling 33" story helped her through that time and made her realize we all deal with insecurity and self-consciousness. She loved that story and asked, "Mommy, would you tew me about when you whistewed and wewe scawed of youw teachew" almost every night when I put her to bed. Maybe talking like Elmer Fudd was as bad as whistling, poor thing.

That winter, after I recovered from Twin Cities, a group of us entered some "All Comers" indoor track meets at a local college, which are technically open to anyone, to improve my speed in the shorter events. There wasn't much competition from women, leaving only Kelly to compete against in the 800 meters (half mile), the mile and 3000 meters. We had a team called the "Silver Bullets." One of our running buddies, Mike Sells, worked for Coors and had silver singlets and bandanas made up for all of us. Moving Comfort probably wouldn't have been happy with me had they known. I've always wondered if Mike Sells was my anonymous benefactor for the Florida racing trip that helped launch my career.

In one of the 800-meter races, Kelly ran 2:07 and I ran 2:06, my fastest 800 so far, excluding my race with Charlie on the high school dirt track that we unfortunately didn't time. Kelly also ran a 4:54 mile and a 56-second 400 meters indoors. It was amazing how much natural talent he had, although he began to feel the wear and tear on his body. He worked hard on his night shift and then tried to keep up with the training schedule, which he managed, but it was draining him. During our first few years of racing, Kelly and I ran close to the same time in every race. In the beginning he beat me in several 5Ks and was quite proud. Toward the end I was beginning to pull away from him, getting faster and stronger, especially in the longer events.

Kelly decided to join me in Florida for the 1986 Orange Bowl 10K, along with the Gasparilla Distance Classic 15K, in February. I was an invited athlete in both races that time, and they shared in covering my travel and lodging expenses. Benji's training program became more demanding after he increased my weekly mileage from 55-60 up to 60-65. My second runs went from 4 miles to 5 miles (three days a week, after my long run and hard workouts), which was mentally overwhelming during the dark dreary winter nights.

Running those indoor meets, along with long, slow mileage in the ice and snow was our training before heading south. Kelly and I traveled to Florida a few days before the Orange Bowl 10K. That year it would be staged on a beautiful course along Biscayne Bay in the evening. The field was packed with the best runners in the world. The Florida races were hugely popular because they were the only competitive races on the prize-money circuit that time of year anywhere in the world, bringing the foreigners to the U.S. in full force to start their season.

Kelly and I took off together, running an even pace while trying to breathe in the warm and heavy air on a humid and windy evening. I hadn't had enough time to adapt. Immediately, asthma gripped my lungs. My chest was heavy and didn't want to expand, and I wheezed as I tried to force the air through. The sudden fatigue from the effort turned my legs to lead. I did what I always did, backed off just enough to release the grip and keep my breathing under control.

As usual, I began passing many of my competitors toward the end, but it wasn't because I was picking it up and running strong to the finish as in past races. It was because they were slowing down. Kelly ran on my heels. I finished 10th in 35:30, my comfort pace of 5:40, and as always, Kelly was right behind in 35:35. Not a great race, but I was grateful to have the first race of the year under my belt, and it was a little faster than the previous year.

Kelly wanted to see where Mom and I had stayed, so we vacationed in Naples for a week before heading up to Tampa for the 15K. I didn't enjoy the vacation as much as I had with Mom, which was probably a good thing before an important race.

As expected, it was oppressively hot the morning of Gasparilla. I was hoping for a better performance after my mediocre race a week earlier, and was eager to get out there and race. I ran hard yet in control, and didn't develop any breathing distress as long as I didn't try to speed up. The need to stay consistent brought me into the finish line 10th in 52:01, a 5:34 pace. It was a big improvement, much easier than the 10K a week earlier and certainly easier than the year before when I had to deal with my throbbing shins. Kelly was 2 minutes behind me and really struggled in the heat and humidity. We were ready to go home to Jamie and Punky – and Mom who stayed with them while we were away.

Through experience I had learned that Benji's marathon plan worked for me. I continued to make progress and didn't get discouraged when I didn't race the shorter distances as well as I should. I had total faith in my ability to run a fast marathon in the fall at Twin Cities, which would be the 1986 U.S. Championships. I had learned how to race on that course a year earlier and all I had to do was get through the racing season, which promised to be adventurous and rewarding. The only problem was, I was absolutely miserable in my marriage. Kelly's dominating behavior was taking its toll. He would explode in anger if something didn't go his way. Perhaps he was feeling threatened by my success as a marathoner – or that he couldn't keep up with the training anymore – and the fact that he didn't have total control.

When I started dragging in many of my workouts and showing fatigue during my spring races, Benji asked, "What's going on?"

"It's a lot like growing up in a Jehovah's Witness family, where I'm told what to do, with strict rules and regulations," I explained. "Kelly's the father figure, and I'm reverting back to being a child. I despise this feeling and I don't want to live like this anymore." Sneaking out my bedroom window wouldn't be enough *this* time.

It wasn't the first time Benji had heard that. He and Amie had been good listeners for a while, but he could see that it had reached the breaking point. "You need to do something one way or the other," he said. "Talk to Kelly, and if that doesn't work you have to decide whether to continue or get out of the marriage. Living like this is more stressful than intense training. You need to make a decision and then go through with it," he insisted, but added, "It might be better to wait until after the marathon."

I really needed to hear that. I knew all along, but I wanted and needed some support. It would be tough from here on out.

Soon after, I decided to talk to Kelly. He became defensive, yelled and then left without hearing me out. A few days later when Jamie was in school, I told him, "We need to talk now or I'm going to leave without trying to work things out." He listened and agreed to make some changes, but then went right back to his old ways.

I had been anticipating an opportune time to leave Kelly ever since he took control of my life and forbade me to have any contact with Rachel. My brothers' deaths taught me how short and precious life is, and that was no way to live. I craved happiness and a better quality of life for Jamie's sake as well as mine. Kelly would be happier, too, if he found a woman who enjoyed having a man in charge. He certainly was attentive, and some woman would love that.

I told Kelly clearly and straightforwardly, "I am going to file for divorce." After a long and draining discussion, he agreed. I was shocked. *This isn't like him at all.*

"We should wait until after the marathon," he said, and then started sleeping downstairs while I stayed upstairs with Jamie. That would be our separation for the time being, and it seemed to work. He was fine, as if nothing had changed. Still, something didn't seem right.

Just a few weeks after our "separation" I returned home from a race in Washington, D.C., to find that Kelly had moved back upstairs. I had to go through the "long and draining talk" again. He looked puzzled and said, "Whaaat? Whaat do you mean? Whaaat divorce?"

That pattern continued between one draining talk after another. His mood kept swinging from explosive to meek and sorrowful. It recalled some of my father's erratic behavior. I was frightened, then frustrated and later became angry. He didn't mention our separation to anybody. *I'm not feeling very good about this.*

Over the next few months, Kelly's temper grew wilder, his fuse shorter, his actions unpredictable.

In May, it was time to run Bloomsday. People expected a lot from me that year, but it wasn't their pressure that got to me. I had enough of that at home, and was mentally drained. I went into the race tired, I raced tired and I looked tired. It was a struggle to place 13th in my hometown race.

Benji and Amie came to Spokane to run Bloomsday, and after the race we had a talk. "I think Kelly's going to blow a fuse," I told them. "His inner thermostat is set a few notches too high." Amie smiled, but Benji didn't find it very amusing.

"You're going to have to pick yourself up out of this slump and get fired up about the marathon," said Benji in a strong decisive voice. "Put all of this wasted energy and frustration toward your training and racing. You need to pull things together and focus on Twin Cities. This is the most important race of your life."

I ran some good races after my talk with Benji and Amie. I found that going to races was a way to escape, for a little while anyway. The Cascade Run Off was one race in particular where I could tune out and put my worries aside. As a result, I had a decent performance – 52:03, close to my 15K personal best – even with Kelly there.

At the post-race party I met Damien Koch, a top masters runner (age 40 and over) who was dating one of my competitors, Maureen Custy. "Were you the one who passed me wearing a Speedo?" I asked.

"Yes," he said with a laugh, "I was wearing Maureen's track uniform, the bun huggers."

"You're never going to live this down," I warned him after we all stopped laughing.

Damien, a charismatic man who looked and acted like a skinny Chevy Chase and was always the life of the party, enjoyed a few beers with Kelly and found him amusing as most people did when Kelly was relaxed and things were going his way. He and Kelly talked for hours about training, and I mostly watched and listened to them carry on an entertaining conversation. I had never seen Kelly like that, or enjoy himself as much as he did that night. I learned that Damien was a coach for the women's track team at Colorado State University in Fort Collins and coached Jon Sinclair and Libbie Hickman, among others, over the years. He was giving Kelly all kinds of racing tips on how to beat me.

After his visit with Damian in Portland, Kelly's demeanor changed – again. He became docile, and even though I was on "Red Alert" at all times, his temporary mild state was vaguely peaceful, leading to a summer of productive training.

Late that summer, I ran my first sub 33-minute 10K, a 32:49 with an overly stressed mind and a highly trained body. After that, I knew I would be ready to tackle the Twin Cities Marathon.

My contract with Moving Comfort was up and after a good solid racing season in which I showed steady progress, I signed with Nike. I talked to Jeff about my potential agreement with Nike, which was $3000 a year with all of the equipment and shoes I needed along with a great bonus structure: money for placing in the top 10 in major road races, a bonus plan for U.S. and World Championship performances, and for placing in *Track & Field News* magazine's year-end athlete rankings. The bonus structure was attractive. Jeff told me, "With the limited amount of money Moving Comfort has for sponsorship, I can't match that offer. You should go for it, Kim." I hated to leave the Moving Comfort team and Jeff. He was so good to me at the beginning of my marathon career and became a dear friend.

Along with all of the other changes going on in my life, Don sold his running store to Curt Kinghorn. Curt was like a big brother. I could tell him anything. Furthermore, he was just like Chuck, always wanting the best for me. During my three workdays a week, Curt told me I could come in anytime between 11 a.m. and noon and leave before dark on the days when I had a second run scheduled. That was pretty early, as fall was in full force and the days were growing shorter. Curt would take care of the customers, suggesting I answer the phone and visit with all the runners who stopped in to say hello. He actually did my work for me, especially when I came in looking tired, as the marathon grew closer.

Curt and I talked for hours about my upcoming marathon while enjoying an extra large "Uncle Sal's Spectacular." That pizza had everything on it: Italian and summer sausage, pepperoni, olives, onions, garlic, tomatoes and peppers. After our pizza, it was time for our cinnamon rolls from "Cinnabon" a few doors away. Of course we each needed to have our own. I burned off all those calories with no problem. Curt was putting on weight, though.

When discussing strategy for Twin Cities, Curt and Benji kept reminding me, "You need to keep third place in sight at all times. You can't sit back and allow everyone to get away from you. If you don't place in the top three, you don't go to the World Championships." I knew they were right, but asked, "What about my asthma problem? If the women take off too fast at the start, I'll be in huge trouble." Benji assured me that I was much fitter and faster than all of them.

When I reminded Benji that I hadn't improved much during the year in my shorter races, he laughed. "You raced on tired legs. You could start out at your 10K race pace in the marathon and be fine. The marathon won't feel any harder than your 10Ks. With a little rest and some speed sessions, you'll be ready for a great marathon."

Curt and Benji told me to ignore anything stressful at home because it would only drain my energy. I had my attorney working on the divorce and planned to move out of the house once I returned from Minneapolis/St. Paul. There was nothing more I could do at the moment.

Just weeks before the marathon, I was feeling optimistic about the upcoming race and so looking forward to escaping my life with Kelly that I started packing a few boxes.

"What's going on?" Kelly asked when he walked in.

"I'm getting things ready for my move."

"Whaat do you mean? Whaaat divorce? Whaaat are you talking about?"

I was not up to another "long and draining" discussion and was tired of being patient. Both hands shot up in front of me, palms inward, the way they do when I'm exasperated. "You have got to be kidding me," I said, speaking slowly. "I. Am. Divorcing. You. I'm leaving right after the marathon. My attorney is preparing the papers, so please accept this and try to move on."

This is ridiculous! I felt sorry for him, but I'd told him five times already. He went storming out of the house.

Jamie was next door playing with Bo all the while, but it was dinnertime and Kelly had been gone for quite some time. I went over and visited with Lorrie before bringing Jamie home and giving her a bath. Still no Kelly. After dinner, Jamie and I were reading her favorite book, "Bronty the Dinosaur," when Kelly walked in. I couldn't tell at first that he was drunk, because he had a way of speaking that made it difficult to tell what kind of mood or condition he was in. He walked in with a smile, saying hello to Jamie and patting her on the head. As he was walking into the living room, he fell butt first right into a big potted plant. At first Jamie and I were startled, but when he tried to pull himself out of the planter it stuck on his butt. He fell back again. He kept trying to get up, and kept falling back in. Jamie and I were hysterical. I desperately wanted to stop laughing, but I was so nervous, I just couldn't control it.

Kelly didn't think it was funny. By the time he'd hoisted himself out of the planter, he was in a rage. Then there was a long silence as he disappeared into the basement while Jamie and I went into my bedroom to finish our reading.

When Kelly came back upstairs, he began hitting his head against the bedroom wall so hard that his eyes were rolling back into his head. "Jamie, look what your mother is making me do," he kept saying as he banged his head against the wall, harder and harder.

I was sitting on the bed with Jamie crying in my arms, her little body shaking and shivering in fear. She would be 6 in a few weeks and was old enough to understand the danger and horror of her father's actions. It broke my heart. I'd always tried to protect her from any kind of dysfunction. I didn't want her to have to experience what I did as a child.

I'd learned from childhood to never, ever react to somebody in that state of mind. I stayed calm and tried to keep the situation as light as possible, for Jamie's sake. In a strong voice, I said, "Come on, Kelly, nobody's making you do this. This is your choice and you need to stop."

After a few more attempts to provoke me, he stopped. When he left the room, I ran out the back door to see if Marty was home. He wasn't. I called another neighbor, Tom, and asked him to come help. I went back into the bedroom, thinking the worst of it was over.

Kelly came in with his hunting rifle. It was loaded. A wave of terror rushed over me. Jamie screamed and ran into my arms, sobbing and trembling. I was horrified, not so much at Kelly but because I was the cause of his meltdown. I felt guilty that I'd driven him to do something so dramatic that it could lead to a murder/suicide. My baby could die because of the actions of the two people who loved her most.

"Please, Kelly, you need to think about this in a sane manner," I said, trying to keep my voice even. "I know you're upset. I'm to blame. We can talk about this."

Jamie was crying. Kelly started crying. But I couldn't cry. I was too angry. Kelly put his rifle down and tried to hug Jamie. She was afraid, but went to him. Tom walked in the door just as Kelly put the rifle down.

Tom took Kelly into the kitchen and talked to him for hours. Thank God for Tom Iredale. Tom invited Jamie and me to move in with him, but I stayed. I kept thinking about the marathon and uprooting Jamie so suddenly. I remembered how that felt when I was her age.

Kelly moved back downstairs, and Tom, Marty and Lorrie checked in often to be sure Jamie and I were OK. Kelly said he was terribly sorry and promised he wouldn't drink while we were still living there. He seemed to have learned from that emotional outburst, and I trusted that he had. Our divorce was the most traumatic thing Kelly had been forced to face in his life, and the alcohol made it worse. I'd been in the midst of trauma since I was a little girl, so I could understand why he did what he did. But I didn't accept it.

Shortly after that, I had to run the biggest and most important marathon of my life. I was careful, making sure Kelly wasn't drinking or out of control, and I was ready to flee with Jamie the moment there was cause for alarm. All the while, I tried to focus. I had no idea what I could do in the Twin Cities, but I was going. I knew I was prepared and as always ... I was hoping for the best.

All I had was hope. No one had ever taken that away from me, and neither could Kelly.

Chapter 11

The week before the Twin Cities Marathon, I went through my pre-marathon routine. It worked so well in 1985 that there was never a need to change it.

Sunday: 17 easy miles, to start a depletion process. After that run, I would eat mostly protein and fat to starve my system of glycogen – carbohydrate stored in the liver and muscles and used for fuel during exercise. That was fine with me, because I love steak, burgers, chicken, fish, eggs and nuts, which are the main ingredients of the depletion diet. I also ate a lot of vegetables and salads, which are low in carbohydrates. I would eat just enough carbohydrates to keep me sane. That was my diet through Wednesday afternoon.

Monday: 4 mile run

Tuesday: 7 mile run, which included a one-mile time trial at 4:40.

Wednesday: 13 miles very slow around noon to ensure that depletion was total before beginning my carbohydrate loading, which would allow my system to start hoarding glycogen/carbohydrates because it was starving for them. Before and during that run, I was irritable, lightheaded and forgetful. Running was a huge challenge with so little glycogen to burn for fuel. After the run I ate everything I'd been craving during those three days of depletion, and then some. I'm sure I did most of my carbohydrate loading in the first hour. I was beside myself, eating everything in sight. I ate as many healthy, and some not-so-healthy, carbohydrates as I wanted: potatoes, pasta, rice, cereal, pancakes, breads and many desserts. Chocolate cake with chocolate frosting, along with a big glass of skim milk, was my favorite. I also ate a few vegetables, many fruits and a small amount of fish, steak or chicken for protein.

Thursday: Off

Friday: 4 miles easy

Saturday: 4 miles easy with 4x 20-second strides at marathon pace

Sunday: The marathon

Kelly was quiet during that week and I wasn't sure what was going through his mind. He stayed out of the way before heading to work in the late afternoon and gave me some peace. I've always needed my quiet time, long before my life with Kelly – it's almost like meditation, and was especially important to me before a big race or during times of stress. At that moment, I was dealing with both.

Poor Jamie was stressed, too. Not just from the gun encounter, but from starting first grade. Now she had to be in school all day. She asked me every night before bed, "Would you tew me some mow stowies about when you didn't wike youwsef when you wewe gwowing up?" She liked the story about when I spanked the little Jehovah's Witness girls after they made fun of my family's funny haircuts and our dad being crazy, but her favorite was my orange face covered in brick powder on Picture Day. My stories seemed to make her feel much better about herself. Plus, she enjoyed our quality time together while I sat in bed with her visiting.

The day before I was to leave for the marathon, Mom set out to drive the seven hours from Port Townsend to Spokane to take care of Jamie while I was away. Just 90 minutes out of Spokane, in Moses Lake, she managed to crash into the wall of an underpass on I-90. Mom was trying to get her life back in order and seemed to be doing much better, and I thought a chance to get away from Port Townsend would help her. The crash certainly wasn't what I had in mind.

Kelly drove to Moses Lake to pick Mom up and bring her to Spokane. She was a little bruised and beat up, but seemed fine and reassured me that she could take good care of Jamie. I knew she was OK when she started joking around about the accident. She told me that when the police officer helped her out of the car, she had been in shock and couldn't answer when he asked, "Is there anybody else in there?" When he leaned through the window into the back seat to check for himself, he put his hand directly into a spilled container of oysters that Mom was bringing for us.

"It was awful, Kimmie," she said. "He screamed like a girl when he jumped back from the car. He thought he put his hand into somebody's guts or brains."

Kelly was excited about going to Minneapolis/St. Paul again, and as much as I wished he would stay home to be sure Mom was OK with Jamie, I couldn't take that excursion away from him. Kelly was my closest friend on his good days, and I would rather deal with the distraction of him being there than cause him more sadness and disappointment.

Twin Cities Marathon ~ October, 1986

On Thursday, we left for the Twin Cities, along with Don and Mike Brady, who also planned to run. It was good to have them along as a distraction because I was worried about a lot of things. Leaving Mom and Jamie in Spokane, hoping Mom was OK and not hurt too badly. The man I was about to divorce was staying in my hotel room. It would be my first big race as a Nike athlete and I wanted to run well enough to justify the decision of Keith Peters, the Nike promotions coordinator, to take a chance on me. What's more, I was concerned about wearing new racing shoes. There was so much stress around me that I had to sit back and mentally push it away. Perhaps I became mentally tough and able to handle stress from dealing with so much craziness as a child. Surprisingly, I managed to focus, relax and wait patiently for marathon morning.

I attended a press conference on Friday and spoke with a few reporters, but the only one who seemed to take me seriously was Kathrine Switzer, the first woman to officially run the Boston Marathon back in 1967. She and Frank Shorter, an Olympic gold medalist, would be the commentators for the live marathon coverage on ESPN on marathon morning.

The main topic at the Friday press conference among the athletes and media was "How are you going to run in these conditions?" The race day forecast was for subfreezing temperatures with snow and wind. As for competitors, the media spotlight was on Nancy Ditz, the #4-ranked runner in the U.S. who was being coached by Rod Dixon. I wondered if he remembered kissing me at the awards ceremony in Honolulu while my family took so many pictures. Most of the media seemed to think my second place the year before was a fluke, so no one asked me much of anything, which worked to my advantage. It's tough to be in the spotlight, the stress alone can drain a person.

Over a relaxing dinner that night, I told Kelly, Don and Mike my plan for dealing with the freezing temperatures and snow. "I'm wearing my shorts and singlet, and no hat," I announced. "I'll wear gloves and my new invention – long tube socks on my arms, with the foot cut out to make an opening. This way I can take them off if I need to but keep my gloves on." It would be much better, I was sure, than wearing a long sleeved T-shirt and having to pull it off later once I started to warm up in the race. "Besides," I added, "Wearing white tube socks on my arms along with my white gloves will make it appear as if I'm wearing long, elegant evening gloves." We all laughed.

Mike said he was wearing just the bare necessities, as well. "We're used to running in this weather," he reminded me.

My outfit was figured out and ready. Most of my competitors were going back and forth that night on what to wear and all the "what ifs" about the weather, but I had no second thoughts. I went to bed so exhausted from the turmoil of the past several weeks that I slept better than I had all year, even with Kelly in the bed next to me.

I woke up Sunday at 4 a.m. and enjoyed a pot of coffee with cream and maple syrup, a bagel with cream cheese, a big bowl of oatmeal and a banana. I was ready.

The U.S. Championship races started in the early morning hours, well before the citizens' race, with the elite U.S. men starting several minutes before the women's race. I walked out of the hotel lobby and directly to the staging area a few blocks away, where we could stay in a warm building until braving the miserable conditions to run to the starting line. I stayed in that building until the last possible moment, then headed out in my shiny royal blue uniform and "elegant evening glove" look.

All of the women in the race respected my accomplishments over the past year and knew that I paced myself well, and from what I could tell all but Nancy Ditz were keying their races on my race strategy. I had beaten most of them at shorter distances; however, the marathon is a totally different type of event. Experience is the key to a successful marathon, and a positive experience really helps. Most of the other women had run more than two marathons, but I'd had a positive experience in both of mine.

As the men started their race, I noticed that some of them were wearing heavy uniforms. Jon Sinclair had a long-sleeved thermal top under his singlet and warm tights under his brightly flowered "Mel's racing unit" running shorts. He also wore a warm winter hat and warm gloves. I could barely recognize him. Suddenly ... I was a bit concerned about my scantily clothed body. Those long elegant evening gloves weren't going to keep me *that* warm!

It was windy and just above freezing as we started out onto the dark streets of Minneapolis, with snow occasionally turning to rain. Nancy Ditz took off right away, while I stayed in my comfort pace. The pack of women stayed with me. We were by ourselves, with the elite men well ahead of us and the men who run with us in most marathons starting later, in the citizens' race. We ran together, flowing along under the darkened skies, our colorful uniforms glowing like beacons.

At 5 miles, Nancy was running along with the press vehicle, only 100 meters in front of us. She wasn't running any faster than we were, but she had the road to herself and could negotiate the tangents and dodge the puddles and slippery autumn leaves instead of fighting for space and bumping into a pack of nine other women all battling for the same pathway. At 6 miles, even though we were running at a 2:34 marathon pace, I decided I was running slower than my comfort level. I sensed that I needed to listen to my body and run off of perceived effort, regardless of what that might bring. With clean, fresh air from the snow and rain clearing out any pollens, dust or pollution, I was breathing as well as my competitors with no worry of having an asthma problem.

I ran right up on Nancy and then hesitated. We glanced at each other as we ran stride for stride, nudging, elbowing and clipping one another in an attempt to control the pace as we avoided the puddles. She lengthened her stride as I lengthened mine. She seemed to have a bit of an attitude. *Hmmm.* I immediately passed her. As I was hugging the corner around the next turn I almost tripped over something. I turned back to see Rod Dixon, her coach, kneeling on the side of the road. *What the ... he's analyzing my stride!* He got up and ran with Nancy for a short time. After his feedback, she let me slip away, possibly because she knew it was cold and slippery and that I would have to brave the wind alone. She seemed content to stay in second place, believing she had the best chance of winning the race because she was more experienced and I hadn't run faster than 2:35:59.

It was only misting as I ran alone in total silence. It was like running in Port Townsend as a child in the winter, and the golden and apple-red leaves blowing all around me in the blustery winds made it seem like a comforting dream. The entire race was damp and oddly nostalgic, bringing back fond memories of running freely on the beach and country roads. I was in my own private place.

As I approached 15 miles I went through an aid station and scooped up some Vaseline, putting it on my hamstrings without breaking stride, for no other reason than some of my competitors having talked about rubbing it on their arms and legs before the start of the marathon as insulation and to repel the splashing water. I pressed forward, growing stronger. I was on pace for a 2:33 marathon. After crossing the bridge at mile 19 the hills started, all the way to mile 25. I remembered them from the year before, but unlike the previous year, I had nobody to focus on or pass. Only the press truck was in front of me, with Keith Peters on it watching his new Nike athlete streaming along.

With my bright and shiny uniform, my hair held back in a sparkling-silver ponytail holder, and my brand-new showy racing flats, I looked and felt like the flashy Jezebel from the Bible story Mom read to us many years before. The crowd, bundled up in winter coats, cheered for me as I ran by, flowing along just like Jezebel. I can remember imagining the same euphoria during story time. It's strange how a childhood dream often comes true in some form or another.

At Mile 23, on a big climb, I finally threw off my elegant evening gloves. Big mistake! My forearms and hands were cold and numb by Mile 24. I knew that I was almost finished, so I put that discomfort, along with my throbbing and numb crooked toe, out of my mind. I cruised past the cathedral and down toward a huge crowd along the finish line.

I was living a dream, literally. A week before the race, I had a dream of winning that marathon: first a vague sensation of the comforting, nostalgic early miles; then a vivid scene of running down into the straightaway and seeing those exact faces in the cheering crowds as I was running alone and feeling invincible.

Yes, I have to say the prize money was on my mind. It was an amount I would never have thought possible to earn all at once, an amount that would give me a kind of freedom I had never known.

I crossed the finish line in 2:32:32 (5:49 pace). I was over the moon! Two minutes later, Nancy Ditz finished second (2:34:49). When Connie Prince (2:35:25) came in third, we had our World Championships team.

Once I was crowned with the winner's wreath and saw my support crew celebrating exactly as I had envisioned in my dream, I felt like a champion. Don was pumping his fists, Keith Peters was rushing to hug me and Kelly was shouting, "All right, Kimmie!" Mike Brady ran an excellent race, 2:15:39, placing eighth and winning some decent prize money. Another friend and training partner, Dick Leland, placed just behind Mike in 10th place, winning some prize money and running a personal best of 2:16:41. They were there behind the crowd, wrapped in mylar blankets and waiting to greet me, as enthusiastic about my win as their own performances.

I was so cold that my lips were as blue as my uniform, but I was elated. I had just made my first World Championships team!

It didn't take long to get through the press conference, drug testing and more interviews, and then I was off to my post-race meal: a big bacon cheeseburger, a large order of fries and a chocolate milkshake. It wasn't enough, so I ordered another round of everything. Chuck would have been proud.

I won $25,000 in prize money, another $10,000 for making the World Championships team, plus bonus money from Nike for making the team and for winning a major marathon. Later, I received another bonus for being ranked the #1 marathoner in the U.S. for 1986 on the basis of winning that race. I finally believed what everyone had been telling me. All of that hard work really did pay off.

Later that night, I left Kelly in the room and had a few beers at the hotel bar with my four favorite post-race people, Don, Jeff, Keith and Chuck Galford, the Cascade Run Off race director. They were funny, intelligent friends who could always bring out my big belly laugh and they treated me like a queen. We toasted my race and many other things, while laughing and joking for hours. Only then was my triumphant day complete.

I couldn't sleep that night. There was too much adrenaline flowing through my system, my muscles felt achy and my crooked toe was pulsating with searing pain from twisting too much on the slippery roads. My mind was racing all night about my great accomplishment, but my main concern was my immediate future; especially, how the next few weeks would play out in my "other" life. The marathon victory was an escape to fairyland. Unfortunately, in a few hours, I had to go home and deal with reality.

When Kelly, Mike and I arrived back in Spokane on Monday afternoon, we were greeted by a message in big, bold letters on the airport welcome screen that read, "Congratulations Kim, Spokane is proud." I was honored, and took great pride in making them proud. Farther down the walkway, friends and all of Mike's family were there to greet us. Curt Kinghorn seemed to be the proudest of all.

I went home to find Jamie and Mom happier than big clams. They had watched the entire marathon live on ESPN starting at 5 a.m. and, much to their delight, I was in the spotlight, although throughout the broadcast the announcers were saying I was from Seattle. Kathrine Switzer not only corrected them but mentioned how elegant I looked while running down the street alone, in the darkened skies in beautifully color-coordinated attire, wearing long "evening gloves."

Mom was my buffer for those first few days back in Spokane. I felt safer with her there and I was sad to see her leave. Kelly had asked Mom to stay a few extra days so she could join him for a Bible study with Connie. He had decided to become a Jehovah's Witness in a desperate attempt to keep me from leaving him. Mom stayed for one Bible study, while I was packing up. She and Connie thought I should stay with him, now that he was planning to become a dedicated Jehovah's Witness. *Right!* His mother would have had a fit. He managed to sway Mom to his side, but his trick didn't work with me.

Aside from all of that, I was very sympathetic toward Kelly, he was only 26, and was sure to mature and become less demanding. I married Kelly for a reason. He could be a good man, but sometimes desperation causes one to do outrageous things. I certainly wasn't perfect and may have contributed to our problems more than I realized. I began to feel remorse.

In late October, two weeks after the marathon, it was time to move out of the house. Jamie was crying and begging me to stay with her dad. I felt so badly for her. "You'll understand someday," I told her. "This is tough on both of us."

"Whaaat?" said Kelly. "Why are you moving out?"

Kelly had gone along with everything up until then, hoping I would change my mind. He couldn't deny any longer that I was leaving and I couldn't deny any longer that he was going to fight me every step of the way – which he did, after calling off his Bible studies. He went to a lawyer the minute he realized I was really leaving, wanting full custody of Jamie and the house, along with all of our family savings and possessions. Eventually, his attorney told him that he had better settle down and work things out properly. I would have custody of Jamie and keep my Twin Cities earnings. He would have visitation on the weekends, but he kept the house, everything in it and whatever else we owned together. Kelly had to pay child support, choosing to put it into a savings account for Jamie every month to go toward her college education instead of, as he said, "giving" it to me. I agreed, only to be sure that part of Jamie's life would be secure.

Since I hadn't yet received any prize money or bonuses from winning the marathon, I had nothing when I drove away from that house except for Jamie and my sewing machine. Nonetheless, I was happier at that moment than I was when I won the marathon. I finally had control over my life.

⌒

Jamie and I moved into a two-bedroom apartment on the South Hill, near Kelly's parents and not far from our old house. I wanted to keep Jamie in the same school and near her father and grandparents to keep some stability in her life. She still hated going to school, but was feeling a little better after she made one special friend named Barbie.

I made good use of that sewing machine right away, making two big pillows the size of Jamie and me to use as furniture. That's all we had for months until I ran a few road races and won enough prize money to buy Jamie a bed and dresser, along with a television and futon. As I ran more races and won more prize money, we slowly filled the apartment with the bare necessities.

My first plan was to find a backup job, just in case the running didn't work out. Whitworth College had a position available working with athletes on their diets and eating behaviors. I could also finish school while working there. They agreed to hold the job until fall 1987, allowing me the chance to first see if I could make enough money as a professional athlete to support us.

Meanwhile, I continued working part time in the running store and, after taking a month off, began running again. After setting a personal best on such a cold day in the Twin Cities, I was really beat up that first week. I felt out of sync and awkward, and things hurt. Many things hurt. I plodded through easy, short runs until my body quit rebelling, and then, after the holidays, began the Benji training program once again. It was time to train for the 1987 World Championships.

I started doing one run a week with Mike, Don and their friend Steve Jones, an attorney who worked downtown in the Paulsen Center, the same building as the Bloomsday office. Steve was Don's roommate when they went to Stanford 20 years earlier. They were still good friends – Steve was the sidekick during Don's skits for the Bloomsday coverage. Dick Leland and Rob Greer, who were also attorneys at his firm, joined us as well. We would all meet after work almost every Monday night at the Paulsen Center.

I was in awe of that building. August Paulsen came to Spokane from Denmark in 1892, and three years later invested $500 in the Hercules mine, in the Coeur d'Alene mining district. In 1901, Hercules struck a rich vein that made Paulsen one of the wealthiest men in Spokane. In 1908, he had a well-known architectural firm design the best 11-story office building that money could buy, which became the Paulsen Building. It used an early form of high-rise construction, making it architecturally significant and allowing it to be the tallest building in the city at that time.

About 20 years later, the Paulsen Medical and Dental Building was built next door, and the two buildings together became known as the Paulsen Center, one of the most prominent features of the Spokane skyline. Old Mrs. Paulsen, August's daughter, lived in the penthouse just above Steve's law firm, which occupied the entire 14th floor. The Bloomsday race starts in front of the building.

I felt a connection to the Paulsen Center for some reason. It may have been its charm, history and solidity that gave me a sense of feeling welcome and secure. Or maybe it was my need for something solid in my life, my desire for stability. I enjoyed looking down on it from the South Hill, especially on my second runs during the holiday season, when Mrs. Paulsen decorated the big tree on the top of the building with colorful lights. Looking forward to that view as I ran on Overbluff Drive lured me out the door for those late runs. The Monday runs were my only hard workout each week during the winter because of the snow and ice. I didn't know what a "snow floor" was until I started running in Spokane. The snow becomes so packed that it's like running on hard dirt. It wasn't very slippery unless we hit an icy patch, which was usually when we least expected it. We ran a very hilly 10-mile loop, the Thorpe Road loop. If that was too icy, we ran a flat 10-mile loop near Gonzaga University that they called "The Dog with No Bark" run. I realized how it got its name when we ran past a house with a big, ferocious dog in the front yard, its teeth showing, struggling to bark with only air coming out. The guys laughed every time we ran past him, as if it were the first time they ever saw it. I felt sorry for the dog, but it *was* humorous.

The boys were all faster than me and I had to really work to keep up with them. Benji added a workout into our weekly run, usually eight 3-minute efforts at 10K race pace followed by 2 minutes easy. The guys were happy to do that with me, making me work hard while trying to negotiate any icy areas along the way.

Benji suggested I wear a heart-rate monitor while running up Thorpe Road with the guys. He instructed me to get my heart rate up to 180 beats per minute during the 3-minute efforts, since I was planning to do a few winter races in Florida and that would be my only speed training leading up to them. He felt that 180 would be about right for my age and fitness level.

After warming up, we started running up Thorpe Road for our first 3-minute effort. We ran harder and harder in the pitch dark, waiting for my heart-rate monitor to start beeping, which it was supposed to do when I hit my target of 180. We kept pushing, harder and harder, until we were running all-out. "When is that f...ing thing going to beep?" Don cried out. It never did. We ran ourselves into the ground, exhausted.

I really enjoyed running with the guys, especially when Staffan moved to town. Staffan, who was from Sweden, had just finished graduate school in Arkansas and moved to Spokane to work as a physical therapist. He looked like most Swedes – tall, blue-eyed and fair – but he stood out for his Swedish/Arkansas accent. Our group enjoyed teasing each other and always came up with some joke about somebody. We teased Staffan about that accent, and for wearing long tube socks during our runs, a different pair with a different color stripe for every day of the week. On one cold and rainy run, I looked at Staffan and said, "In the United States, serious runners don't wear tube socks." That's all it took.

Staffan was off like a rocket and we ran the fastest Thorpe Road loop of the year.

Staffan was faster than the rest of us and always pushed the pace. I couldn't keep up with him when he and the guys started racing but I tried, which was good for me considering that when I ran alone the rest of the week I always stayed in my comfort zone.

Even though I enjoyed the guys, I also loved my time running alone. I was outside enjoying my freedom and the beautiful Spokane area: the river flowing through downtown and Riverfront Park; the vast and golden wheat fields in the countryside; Mt. Spokane off in the distance, snow-capped in the winter and early spring; the River Road with camp-grounds along the way, leading to the State Park with miles and miles of trails lined with wildflowers and Ponderosa pine. I could run through that paradise for hours at a time.

The boys prepared me well for my winter races in Florida, where I won enough prize money to support Jamie and me. Soon after that I was awarded my prize money from Twin Cities, which went into my TAC TRUST account. That was my security.

I also received a $10,000 stipend from TAC for making the World Championships team, which included seeing Dr. David Martin, one of the world's top exercise physiologists, for testing in his lab down in Atlanta. The top three men and women in the Twin Cities Marathon were to see him at least twice before the World Championships, so he could monitor our fitness levels, as well as test us to measure our strengths and weaknesses. Then he would give us guideline training-paces for our easy runs, tempo runs and speed sessions, along with specific heart rates and workouts to help us reach our optimal race performances. Dr. Dave also took blood samples to monitor our iron levels and any specific imbal-ances we may have before giving us an overall evaluation, sitting down with each athlete and explaining everything in layman's terms.

During a stress test – an all-out performance on a treadmill to dis-cover what my aerobic capacity (VO2 Max) was – Dr. Dave started me at a comfortable effort and then increased the speed and incline until I could barely hit the red "panic button" to stop the treadmill when I couldn't run any longer. During the test I wore headgear with a breath-ing tube secured to my mouth, to monitor my airflow readings, and I was given a blood test immediately afterward. "Did you grow up in a home with secondhand smoke?" he asked after my first stress test.

"From the day I was born."

He scratched his head. "Do you know that you have a breathing situation?"

I said, "Yes ... I have asthma." He looked relieved, because he didn't want to give me any bad news. He worked with me on different ways of dealing with it other than slowing down during a race. Dave warned me about training or racing on days with high pollen or pollution levels, suggesting that on bad days I train on a treadmill with an air purifier in the room. The testing was extensive and extremely stressful. I knew he would challenge me during the VO2 Max tests to the point of exhaustion, but the outcome was well worth the effort.

Of course, the asthma never goes away. The fitter and less stressed I am, the better I'm able to deal with it and the less it interrupts my racing and training. I just have to be fitter than other runners and be cautious when running above my anaerobic threshold, or else! Perhaps that was why I always paced myself, even when I was a child. I learned a valuable lesson after my first serious asthma attack, when I was trying to sprint home from Fort Worden in time for dinner and the town's milkman, Mr. O'Meara, rescued me.

During the testing, I also learned that my iron level is very high for a woman, close to 16 for my hemoglobin level and 45 for my hematocrit when I'm healthy. There are many men who don't have levels that high.

Dr. Dave and I theorized that my body reacts as if I am always at a high altitude – sleeping, living and training there. My heart has to work harder as well, along with everything else, to function with less oxygen. This may have made me the physically strong athlete I am today. With a resting heart rate of 29-31 beats per minute, my working heart rate is low, as Don found out when we ran up Thorpe Road. I can't get my heart rate above 173 no matter how hard I try.

This also may be the reason I can eat so much, and why I don't tire or hit "The Wall" in the final stages of a marathon like most athletes. Maybe asthma has helped me almost as often as it's hindered me, and has been as much a gift as a disability.

―――

During that same winter, I became infatuated with Steve, a charming and handsome man. He looked like Pernell Roberts, who played Adam Cartwright, the oldest son on the television show "Bonanza," only with a mustache. His blue eyes were striking and he was confident, comfortable in his skin, walking and talking in a nonchalant manner as if he were in charge of everything. Like most runners he was fairly thin, and he had a kind and soft-spoken way about him. I noticed his soft and mani-cured hands while shaking his hand the first time I met him. He and Don are about 10 years older than me, as are Keith Peters, Jeff Darman and Chuck Galford. I preferred to be around the older men, enjoying their humor and logic.

Before winter set in, Steve showed me more of the trail system around Spokane, along the River Road, into Riverside State Park and on the rugged trails farther into the forest where I had never ventured alone. He was extremely attentive and I started seeing him more. When I was working he would often come into the running store around noon, since his office was on the same skywalk system as the store and the restau-rants he frequented for lunch.

Earlier in the fall, Steve had met Jamie at a small town race where she was helping hand out T-shirts and asking, "Do you want to be mawked?" She was marking the finishers' race numbers with a felt pen when they came to pick up their T-shirts. Jamie liked Steve immediately, so much so that she asked him for his telephone numbers both at his office and at home. Smart girl.

Steve was engaged to a beautiful woman who had a daughter Jamie's age. They were in the middle of planning their wedding and everything was set. Therefore, I was very surprised when he asked me if I would start dating him if he called it off with his fiancée. I had my reservations. Even so, I said yes immediately. Perhaps I should have taken some time to think it through.

Steve was romantic. Some would say he was a flirt. To me, it just seemed as if he appreciated women. He was the best looking 39-year-old bachelor I had ever met. He was kind and gave all women "a look," along with the words that made them feel special. Many women, even younger girls, had crushes on him. Even Jamie liked his caring energy. I wasn't so sure about that "look" he gave most women, but assumed that because he'd been a bachelor all his life that it was just his way. Just in case, I put that wall up.

Now that Jamie had Steve's number, she called him at his office. Still unable to pronounce most of her L's or R's, even at age 6, she would begin, "Hewow, can I pwease speak to Steve?" When she got him on the phone she would invite him over for dinner, telling him we were preparing liver and onions. *Of all things, liver and onions.* Not many people like liver, but I love it and once a week made Mom's "Chinese Liver" recipe, with a blend of spices, soy sauce and green onions. I practiced cooking liver and onions until it was close to perfect.

Steve must have really liked us because he came over for every invitation. Sometimes it was only an hour before dinnertime when Jamie would announce, "I just invited Steve ovew fow wivew and onions," and then I had to scramble. Jamie had her three "Pound Puppies" join us, with their own plates, glasses and silverware. Steve was good about it and went along with her pretend dinner party. He sent me romantic cards in the mail and took me, and sometimes Jamie, to nice dinners. We went to many extravagant parties and events together. Things were moving fast and we began spending all of our free time together.

Toward the end of February, Steve asked, "When should we get married?"

What? This is so sudden! I had been captivated from the beginning. Steve was kind, appreciative and attentive, but as much as I wanted to, I didn't answer him. That wasn't the time to jump back into a relationship. My divorce was final only a few weeks earlier and, more importantly, I had Jamie's needs to tend to.

Throughout that adjustment period, I was trying to find a balance in my life. I hadn't developed a solid routine since moving into the apartment, and there were a lot of conflicting demands on my time. I wanted to be home when Jamie came home from school, but there was no one to babysit her while I ran. Plus, I was still working at the running store and I was in a new relationship that was taking up a lot of my time when I should have been focusing on training for the World Championship Marathon that August. There was no place to retreat: no beach, no clover patch, no plum tree with dandelions growing wild all around. There wasn't even a hornets' nest to burn up.

By early spring, I managed to establish some order and steer my routine on the right course, finding the control I needed to start serious training. I had to. It was my only chance in the running world.

Jamie was my first priority. I took her to school in the mornings, did my run and then went to work at the store three days a week. That was simple enough, but then I had to figure out a way to fit in a second run after Jamie came home. I bought her a bike, a prissy pink banana-seat model like Rene's years before. It had the pink and white streamers coming from the handlebars and love flowers all over the seat, the whole works.

As I ran through the neighborhood, Jamie would ride beside me careful to watch for cars, saying every time we went through an intersection, "No caws" as she looked to the left and "No caws" as she looked to the right. But whenever we had to climb a hill she would pedal as hard as she could and then run out of steam in the middle, starting to cry and begging, "Hewp me, Mom. I can't make it, pwease hewp." I had to push her up every single incline. She could make it up those hills just fine when riding with her friends. Maybe she was testing me to see what was more important – my run, or her?

I was worried about Jamie. She was having tantrums at the worst possible times, acting out and doing things to test me to see just how much she could get away with. One afternoon, I took her clothes shopping at the Nordstrom department store, hoping a new outfit would help her feel better about herself and more excited about going to school.

We found some Guess jeans with tapered legs and zippers at the ankles. She needed those zippers to get the jeans over her big, long feet. She looked adorable in her slim jeans, her new pink blouse – shoulder pads and all – covered in tigers, zebras and giraffes. With her hair pulled to the side in a bright pink scrunchy, she looked like Stephanie on "Full House," one of her favorite TV shows.

Later that afternoon, when I was preparing dinner, Jamie came walking out of her bedroom wearing her new outfit. I noticed a gold chain with a large gold elephant pendant, which looked great with the "safari theme" blouse.

"Where did you get that, Jamie?"

"At the stowe," she answered. Her voice was as calm and relaxed as could be, but her face was turning bright red.

"Did you buy it?"

"Not weawy."

"Hmmm, if you didn't buy it, then you must have taken it."

"Pwobabwy."

I had never talked to Jamie about stealing because she had never shown the desire to take anything that didn't belong to her. I thought for a minute and then tried to keep my voice as emotionless as I could.

"You know that you stole that necklace, don't you?"

"Yes I know, but I just weawy wanted it, mow than anything."

"We're going back to Nordstrom to return that necklace, right now," I said sternly.

"Oh, pwease no," she said, in tears. "I will nevew steaw again, I pwomise but pwease, I don't want them to see me. I'm embawwassed."

I grabbed her hand and we headed out the door. "You need to return this necklace and face some music." Jamie was still crying. "No! Pwease, I don't want to see the music." She suggested that she could just put the necklace back and nobody would notice.

I marched her into Nordstrom and up to the counter, where I said to the saleslady, "My daughter Jamie has something to tell you."

The woman looked at Jamie in her new outfit, standing there staring down clumsily at her brand-new aerobic high tops with the necklace in her hand. Her face was on fire and she could barely speak. "I stowe this neckwace," she said in a voice so faint we could hardly hear her. "I'm sowwy."

The saleswoman was neither sympathetic nor pleased. She took the necklace from Jamie and glared at her. "You should be ashamed of your-self," is all she said.

Jamie looked up at me as we were leaving the store. "I'm gwad that's ovew," she said.

"Me, too."

That night, I was sitting with Jamie on her bed for our nightly visit when she started crying. "Awe you ashamed of me?"

I told her I was disappointed, but not ashamed. "You made a mistake and hopefully have learned from it," I told her. "Have you?"

"Yes, I wiw nevew steaw again evew. But I don't wike mysewf and I'm ashamed."

"We all make mistakes," I reassured her, and went on to tell her about stealing from Aldrich's when I was a little girl and how Mom marched me down to the police station and then on to Aldrich's to tell the police and Old Man Aldrich that I was a bad thief. Jamie loved the story and even laughed about some of the things I did before, during and after I was caught stealing. Jamie felt so much better knowing the person she loved and admired the most could make mistakes and feel awkward, too.

Every week Jamie and I went grocery shopping at Rosauers Supermarket. One time, Jamie was bored and ran off to the toy aisle, coming back with a stuffed animal. It was nothing special, just a small, light brown stuffed dog. "Mommy, I need this, can I have it pwease?" I told her, "No, you don't need another stuffed animal right now." I wanted her to value what she had, just like we did when Chuck took us shopping in Port Angeles and bought us toys years before. We appreciated his kindness, as well, along with those burgers, fries and milkshakes.

Jamie cried and carried on, with people walking by looking disgusted to see a spoiled little girl lying on the filthy floor screaming and kicking. I took her hand and walked right out of the store, leaving the full grocery basket behind. "OK, OK, I don't need the dog, I pwomise, I wiw be good." So we finished our shopping and went home.

Months later while we were doing our regular shopping, Jamie disappeared for a few minutes before coming back with the same stuffed dog. "Mommy, pwease can I have it now? Pwease?" I said no, and she dashed away.

Why in the world would that stuffed dog still be here after so long? I followed her to see what she was up to. She quickly went to the toy section and put the stuffed dog back in hiding behind all of the other toys, and then behind a board on the shelf for the next trip. She never begged for it again, happy just to have 30 minutes with it during every shopping trip. Until ... one shopping day, it just suddenly disappeared. Jamie came to me frantic and crying.

"What's wrong, Jamie?"

Not wanting to get into trouble over the dog issue again, she answered, "Nothing."

Later, as I was putting Jamie to bed and we were saying goodnight to her many stuffed animals, I climbed up on the top bunk with her as I did every night to read "Bronty the Dinosaur." She had it memorized by then and read it to me. When we finished reading I handed her the stuffed dog from Rosauers.

"Fhank you so much! It's the best pweasant evew," she exclaimed, hugging the dog and me. She named her new stuffed animal Chablis. I had a glass of Chablis almost every night while preparing and eating dinner, and I guess she was paying attention.

Jamie slept with Chablis every night. The poor dog's ear was rubbed off from the many nights she fingered the satiny part of it as she sucked her thumb while falling asleep. She certainly appreciated that dog.

It was a bad winter, even into the early spring. After my winter races I took Mom, Jamie and Rachel to Hawaii during spring break to spend time with them and do some decent training in the warm weather. That would be a legitimate training expense, and I could take the vacation money out of my TAC TRUST account without a problem.

Mom went up and down for a long time after losing Stanley, and she was struggling again. She needed a break. I wanted to be closer to Rachel since I was able to openly spend time with her, and Jamie deserved a getaway after everything she had been through dealing with the divorce.

More importantly, I wanted Jamie and Rachel to spend some time together, giving them a chance to grow closer. I finally told Jamie that she had a sister when she kept asking me for one after we first moved into the apartment. It seemed like the perfect time. "I'm so happy Wachew's my sistew!" she said, beaming. I bought her the popular doll "Kid Sister" but her reaction to that was less enthusiastic. "Oh Bwothew, she's not weal."

Jamie and I flew to Seattle and met Mom and Rachel there before we all went on to Oahu. About four hours into our flight I noticed several red bumps on Jamie's face and arms; even her skinny little legs had a few bumps. By the time we landed she had bumps everywhere. To make matters worse, Mom's back had gone out and she could barely walk off of the plane.

Before we could enjoy the beach and shopping near our hotel, we called the hotel doctor to come to our room. Mom had a severe back spasm and couldn't move from her bed, so he gave her a muscle relaxant. Jamie was prescribed Benadryl for her chicken pox. That was how we started our vacation.

For the first few days, I went running early each morning and then Rachel and I went shopping for snacks and played nurse. Mom started feeling better after a couple of days, and once Jamie's chicken pox scabbed over we could all go out as long as we covered Jamie with a baggy T-shirt and long shorts. Then we could shop, go to the beach, go out for nice dinners and watch movies while snacking and visiting in bed late at night. It turned into the perfect vacation after a very rough start.

I had to take advantage of the nice weather and get a long run in on Thursday morning. I left early, telling Mom and the girls, "Have a big breakfast and then meet me at the beach around 10:30 with snacks," and off I went for a three-hour run of 25 miles. I ran over Diamond Head, which brought back fond memories of my first marathon, and headed down the highway into a residential area. Several times I noticed a beige car. It was nothing unusual, just one driver who seemed to be driving through the same area. But my senses told me to beware.

Two hours into the run, I started feeling hot and dehydrated so headed over to an elementary school for a drink of water. As I was running down a sidewalk toward the school, I saw the same beige car parked along the sidewalk. Just as I was ready to pass by, I noticed the driver had moved to the passenger side closest to the sidewalk. The car door was slightly ajar. *Danger!*

I darted away just in time. As I quickly turned back, the car door flew open. The man's hand came out to grab me, and I saw a knife in his other hand. I ran to the school. It was closed!

I hightailed it out of there, bolting up and over Diamond Head and straight to the beach. I could have been mistaken for Lindsay Wagner playing "The Bionic Woman" during one of her fast-forward scenes.

After finding Mom and the girls I immediately called the police, who told me there were several women missing in the area and that bodies had been found. I described the car. "You're very lucky you escaped," the policeman told me. "Be careful when you're out there running alone. Better yet, take somebody with you next time." I ran in busier areas after that, and knew to always trust my instincts from there on out.

Two days later, all four of us decided to run the Cane Dwellers Sugar Cane 10K (6.2 miles). The course was near the Navy base where my Aunt/Cousin Billie Anne was stationed, and afterward we would spend the rest of the day on "her" beach in the Navy yard, where the waves were dramatic and the sand was deserted and even more beautiful than Waikiki Beach.

The morning was hot and humid. Nevertheless, I was planning to run the race hard as part of my training and try to win. Mom, the girls and I drove to the race start and I told them, "Run and walk. Don't hurt yourselves. I'll see you all at the finish." I gave them all a kiss and told Jamie, "You be sure to stay with Grandma and walk a lot. This is a long distance for a 6-year-old." Her reply, "Oh Bwothew, I know how to wun a wace, and I wiw be 7 this yeaw."

We could see nothing but rows and rows of sugar cane as we ran through the mist of the early morning humidity. After winning, I waited at the finish line and soon Rachel came running in strong and looking great. Then the two of us waited and waited, and Mom came in, smiling and waving to the crowd. Then we waited and waited and waited, so I assumed Jamie had fallen behind Mom from the very beginning. Eventually, Mom quit chatting with other runners long enough to tell me, "You know, Jamie took off right behind you and the leaders. I passed her around 4 miles and she was walking."

I immediately ran back on the course to find Jamie. She'd stopped 4 miles into the race, and I found her sitting on a rock and crying. "Hewp, I can't move my wegs," she told me. I carried her to the 6-mile mark, where I told her to finish the rest on her own. She went sprinting in, with everyone clapping as if she were the winner as she smiled shyly and waved.

The best part was, we all won medals. Mom and the girls placed in their age groups. Jamie may have been last in the race but she was the only runner in her age group! They were so pleased with themselves, and that made the trip for me. "Three generations of medal winners in the same race! I'm so proud of us," I told them as we walked away wearing our medals.

The last night of our vacation, Billie Anne came into Waikiki to have dinner with us. After our meal, I left her and Mom to enjoy their drinks while I took the girls back to the hotel to order snacks from room service. We put on our pajamas, hopped into bed, then watched scary pay-per-view movies and talked late into the night. The girls wanted to hear stories about my childhood, so I told them about the many times I played on the beach in Port Townsend with my siblings and friends. Jamie would chime in, "Tew Wachew about youw fwiend sitting on the jewwyfish and when you jumped off the high dock to save youw fwiend's dog, Pwecious." She had many of my stories memorized, and it was especially nice to have Rachel enjoy them as she laughed along with Jamie and me.

Rachel kept trying to teach Jamie to say her name properly. "Jamie, say Rachel and pronounce it very slowly, using your R and L."

"Waaaacheeeeeew," Jamie would say, very slowly.

I talked to Rachel about giving her up when she was just a baby, telling her about all of the cute things she did and how I loved her then, but even more as time went on. Jamie listened, adding her two cents, but fell asleep early from taking her final dose of Benadryl while Rachel and I enjoyed our alone time together.

After partying and having too much fun, Mom and Billie Anne came in very early the next morning. Apparently they'd decided it was too late for Billie Anne to go back to the base. Mom went directly to bed and Billie Anne crawled into Rachel's rollaway bed with her, and then started throwing up. Rachel bolted into bed with Jamie and me, whispering, "That is disgusting. I will never do that, ever!" Jamie whispered, "Me eithew, Wachew."

Then Rachel delivered a broadside. "Laurie is acting like Billie Anne now. She comes home late at night and acts crazy. Sometimes she yells for no reason." I found out that Laurie was threatening Mel and scaring her kids, changing from the good Laurie to the bad Laurie when they least expected it. I knew that behavior so very well. I had a hard time going back to sleep, worrying about what was going on in their household, about their boys, and about Rachel.

When we woke up late the next morning, Aunt/Cousin Billie Anne was groaning about her headache and how miserable she felt. We all laughed when Jamie said, "That's youw own fault, Biwie Anne. You shouldn't dwink like that!"

"You're right," agreed Billie Anne. "I'm getting too old for this."

After Billie Anne left, Rachel rushed over to get her favorite pillow only to find that Billie Anne had thrown up all over it. "That is so not right," she said, her lip curled with disgust. We laughed again, even though her pillow was ruined. Laughing for our family was more than an outward display of amusement. It was the most soothing music in our world, giving us a distance to cope with things and move on, easing our tensions and distress and helping our family through many disappointing times. That was certainly one of them.

Several years after our visit, Billie Anne died from a heroin overdose. It was a shock to all of us, especially poor Uncle/Grandpa Harold. His first wife – Billie Anne's mother – had committed suicide, as did six of his brothers. Four nephews/grandsons died. And then his youngest daughter had died so needlessly. Yet he still stayed strong for Grandma Helen and for the rest of us. He was sad, and he could be distant, but he was still the strongest man I've ever known. I wish my dad could have been that strong.

Chapter 12

It was only April, but 1987 was shaping up to be a very long year. Already it seemed more like December. I was worried about Rachel and the boys and whatever was going on with Laurie. I'd been to Hawaii, to Atlanta to see Dr. Dave, and twice to Florida to race. My divorce was final in February and already I was in a relationship with someone who wanted to marry me. It sounds great and mostly it was, but I needed to be on a schedule, my schedule, with everything in order so that I could focus. That was how I survived, and it wasn't happening. *I need to deal with this now.*

I called Laurie to find out what was going on.

"Kimmie, I'm so glad you called," she said. "Mel and I are going through a rough time and I'm going to be disassociated from the congregation. You don't know what I've been through. It feels like everyone is against me."

"What have you done?" I asked her. "I'm worried. Why do you sound so desperate?"

It turns out she'd made some bad choices during a vulnerable time in her life. "They're watching me," she said. "I'm being followed. I need to get away from my life, away from the Jehovah's Witnesses."

Then she asked, "Would you take Rachel?"

I'm going to get my daughter back.

After so many years of self-torment and regret for giving Rachel up when she was a baby, I was overjoyed that I would have my daughter with me again. But the elation had a price: I was distraught that Laurie was on a downward spiral, and her family along with her.

"Is there anything I can do for you to help?" I asked her.

"You just need to take Rachel after I give her the news."

Soon afterward, I talked to Mom. "Laurie is into drugs," she said. "We think she's either bipolar or schizophrenic and acting just like your father did." Mom went on to say that Laurie was dragging Mel down with her, and that the boys, only 8, 10 and 13 years old, were rebelling by drinking and skateboarding downtown at all hours of the night.

"Mom, that's terrible!" Then I asked, "How's Rachel handling all of this?"

"She's OK, staying with us or her Jehovah's Witness friends when things are bad at home." I was relieved that she was being cared for.

I had no idea what Rachel was going to think or how she was going to feel. The poor thing had been passed around from family to family since she was a baby. For a long time, she had felt happy and secure with Laurie. But again, she was about to experience the turmoil of a family falling apart and her life would be disrupted once more.

Rachel needed some balance in her life. So did I. We would find it together.

So began a regular routine. Jamie spent one weekend night a week at her dad's while I continued my "Benji marathon program." I quit working at the store in order to put more energy into training, along with the other things needed to excel at my sport: eating more vitamin-enriched and wholesome foods, staying away from the Uncle Sal's Spectacular Pizza and those Cinnabon rolls Curt and I enjoyed so much, taking a nap in the middle of the day. I started doing a second run in the afternoons three days a week and lifting weights on the other afternoons, all before Jamie came home from school. It was working. It had to. I wanted Rachel back, in the kind of safe, sound and balanced environment where she belonged.

Staffan started giving me massages on a regular basis, which really helped my recovery. Staffan isn't one to go easy on a person; he digs into the muscle and gets the job done, and seemed surprised that I didn't scream or squirm around on the table when he dug into my calves like all of my "tough" training partners did. He asked me in his Swedish/Arkansas accent, "Do you feel pain ... do you feel anything?" When I didn't object, he would dig deeper.

I continued to train with the boys off and on. Don, Steve, Staffan, Mike, Rob Greer, Dick Leland, and later with two more of their training buddies, Steve Kiesel and Mike Hadway. We called him Mike "Hardway" because that's how he trained – the hard way. Having Steve Kiesel there worked to my advantage because he ran with me while the rest of the gang was up front pressing the pace.

During late spring into early summer I started alternating my weekly track workout with speed sessions around Corbin Park. Many years ago, Corbin Park was a horseracing track. Now it's a small neighborhood road, flat with smooth asphalt that circles a park shaded by pine trees, with no intersections and little traffic. The "Corbin straights" were over a quarter-mile long; we ran them fast and then jogged the turns, which were close to an eighth of a mile. We did that for several laps, and of course it was "all out" with the guys. As the season went on, Benji wanted me to do longer intervals and the boys followed suit, so we did full Corbin laps of close to a mile and then jogged the short turn before hitting it again.

I was in the best shape of my life leading up to the 1987 World Championships.

Things were falling into place. My life was in order – I was fit and prepared to race well – Jamie was happy and settled into her new life. At long last ... I was ready for my 12-year-old daughter to join me.

Rachel

In early summer, I had to get a passport and plan my trip to Rome with the U.S. team. Steve decided he wanted to go with me. He was becoming chummy with the Nike group once he started to travel with me to most of my races, and during a trip to D.C. nonchalantly asked them to take care of his travel. They offered to pay for his trip instead of giving me my bonus for making the team.

I finally accepted Steve's proposal of marriage. I knew Rachel would be with me once again and that clinched the deal. Rachel and Jamie needed the security a family provides and, what's more, I really loved Steve. He was the perfect man, in my eyes. We became engaged in May and planned to marry in early October. Steve would get his wish to marry before he turned 40 in November.

Our plan was to look for a house in the historical part of the South Hill, near the many parks and on the cliff just above downtown, close to Steve's office and where I could look down on his magnificent historical building. There is something magical about the stability I feel when looking down on the Paulsen Center and the energy within. It's the same sensation I have when hearing a train traveling down the tracks in the middle of the night, whistling to let everyone know there is always something going on in life. It will always be there.

This is exactly what Rachel needs from us.

Things were moving fast, and I began to wonder if they were moving too fast. I asked Steve, "How do you feel about Rachel and me being reunited? Do you think I should spend a few months adjusting with the girls before marrying so soon?"

"I'm thrilled about Rachel! We'll adopt her right away," he said proudly.

"Hmmm, I wonder how she'll feel about that?"

"We should find a house and be well-established before taking Rachel into our lives. She needs family structure," Steve told me. He had always wanted to be married and have a family life. He was going to get it all at once.

Steve and I, with Jamie sitting eagerly in the back seat, searched on the weekends. At first we would just drive by and look at the houses with for-sale signs. Jamie really got into it during our drives, calling out, "Thew's a house on saew!" Through the summer, we had a good time looking and searching until we found the perfect house.

It sat on top of the hill on 15th street, 15 blocks from the Paulsen Center. There was a long sidewalk leading up the steep hill to the house, winding around a gigantic boulder in the front yard. A long set of steps led to a big front porch with large pillars and overhead beams. We walked through the front door into a small entry, then through another door into the large living room with the original woodwork and wooden floors, which had a bordered inlay of darker wood. The west wall was mostly fireplace, with two small windows on each side. The north wall had a wooden archway at the stairway leading upstairs. It was an open frame-work of lattice made of wood designed to hide the staircase.

Next to the stairway was a door to a small room we called the "red room," a study that had a deep red carpet and a fireplace with dark green tile. The walls were covered in bookcases with darker woodwork, and the west wall was one big window. There was another small door leading out to a hallway and a small bathroom before entering into the kitchen and the back way to the staircase. The kitchen was huge, with more cooking space than I dreamed possible. The north side of the kitchen had a sliding glass door going out to an upper deck with steps leading down to a larger lower deck, then a few steps down to the backyard and a walkway to the garage.

There was another archway from the living room to the east side of the house with several built-in bookcases on each side, entering into a dining room with big windows all along the south and east sides of the room, looking out onto the front porch and into the dining room of two extremely curious older neighbor ladies. The north wall was a built-in china cabinet with a doorway and another entrance into the kitchen. The house was full of more beautiful woodwork than I had ever seen in one house.

The upstairs had two gigantic bedrooms with a walk-in closet in each room, two smaller bedrooms and one full bathroom. The best part was the laundry chute, which started in the upstairs hallway, included another opening at the top of the basement stairs and ended in a claw-foot tub in the basement.

We decided that we would remodel the attic space, which was the size of a small basketball court, into a master bedroom suite. We already had a plan: A sitting room at the top of the stairs with French doors leading into a large bedroom, and more French doors leading into a marble bathroom with a pedestal sink, oversized claw-foot bathtub and a walk-in shower. The north wall would have all windows looking down onto the backyard and deck. There would even be a French door leading into a walk-in closet, where we would keep the small attic window that over-looked our walkway to the front porch.

I had just walked into my dream house.

Other than house hunting, I put my energy into training over the summer and raced sparingly. The few I ran were successful, however, and I was making headway while getting faster, more confident and more comfortable with my racing. I kept reminding myself that confidence is the key to success. I was running most of my races at 5:20-5:25 pace with ease. I had the pacing down, I was aware of my asthma warning signs and I worked with it, never taking myself over that danger threshold.

Before I knew it, it was time to go to training camp in Germany for 10 days before heading to Rome for the World Championships. Jamie would go to Port Townsend to stay with Mom and Dad. Earlier in the year, Cathie Twomey and I had decided to room together. Cathie was the alternate marathoner and would be coming on the trip because Connie Prince had a stress fracture and was in doubt for the race. Cathie was funny, smart and extremely confident, which made her easy and fun to tease. She could take it and give it right back.

I had never been overseas and was looking forward to a new adventure, but was also apprehensive about running the marathon. All I had to do was race like I did throughout the year and I would medal, or so a lot of people were predicting.

I enjoyed training camp in Stuttgart, where the team was put up in a decent hotel near a park and a track with training facilities. I spent most of my time with Cathie and two track runners, Leslie Seymour and Lynn Jennings. Leslie, a 3000-meter runner, was a petite redhead, funny and fiery, who reminded me of my good friend Sarah Level. Lynn was one of the top 10K runners in the U.S.

Right away I realized that Lynn was one of the most professional, confident and focused runners out there. I was told that she was arrogant and didn't have a lot of respect for road racers, making comments even during press conferences that the roads were inferior to the track. After getting to know her, I figured out that she was one to say what was on her mind even if it riled her competitors and took their focus away from the task at hand – perhaps that was her plan. Lynn would smile and say something tongue-in-cheek, which I found quite amusing.

Lynn was purely a track racer, running road races only to prepare and to make some extra money along the way just as I did when training for a marathon. We understood each other right away and hit it off immediately. She had short brown hair and a strong physique, and looked fierce during competition with her stern expression. But she had very kind brown eyes and a sweet voice, and off the track and away from competition she laughed a lot and had a great sense of humor. Not too many of our competitors saw that side of Lynn.

We did our runs, ate our meals together in the hotel restaurant, and enjoyed castle tours and sightseeing. When we weren't busy training or touring, the four of us would go to a pub for a good, heavy German beer. Other times, we sat around in our rooms, played cards with the men's team and enjoyed time just talking, laughing and getting to know each other.

One sultry afternoon, the four of us went to a park near our hotel where the Germans enjoyed their nude sunbathing. I persuaded Cathie and Leslie to join me and take off their bikini tops. Lynn laughed and said, "No way," just before several male distance runners came walking by, looking shocked to see us joining the Germans.

On our last night in Stuttgart before heading to Rome, the Germans gave us a big party. Everyone drank a little beer and ate a lot of good, solid German food: spaetzle, sauerbraten, pumpernickel bread and potato dumplings filled with everything you could imagine! I was in heaven, since the marathon was only a few days away and I was just starting my carbohydrate loading. As most teams do, we bonded by spending those days together and I was having the time of my life.

The U.S. team flew to Rome and then went through the process of checking into the hotel that was being used as an athletes' village. At check in, we received credentials that we had to wear at all times and show whenever we passed through the gate surrounding the hotel or stepped into the elevator to the athletes' quarters.

What really shocked me was that, before I could compete, I had to have a "femininity" test to prove I was a woman. A nun rudely scraped the inside of my cheek several times with a cotton swab to get the DNA.

Once we passed the test, we were given a photo I.D., stamped by the nun and a doctor. No woman could compete without presenting the I.D.

At the athletes' village, I was a bit concerned when I saw armed Italian guards at every entrance, as well as near the elevators and in the hallways. Our rooms were like tiny dorm rooms, with mattresses on the floor and shared bathrooms down the hall. However, the pool was nice, and they served decent food in the restaurant.

I wasn't going to be spending much time there anyway. Steve arrived the afternoon before my race – with a bad cold! I didn't need to be around someone so contagious, so kept my distance until I ran. After the race, we were planning to stay together in Steve's hotel for a few days to watch some of the other events before taking a train to Florence for a side trip. Even though it wasn't fancy, I wasn't looking forward to leaving the athletes' village and missing out on an invaluable experience with fellow athletes. I was 29, though I felt like I did back in high school when I wasn't allowed to attend any worldly functions. That was the first time I had felt alive and free since I'd married Kelly seven years earlier.

World Championships, Rome, Italy ~ August, 1987

I was rested, I was carbo-loaded and, most importantly, I was fit. Having the marathon on the first day of the 10-day World Championships was an added bonus, because afterward I could relax and enjoy the rest of my first trip overseas without any pressure.

The race started in the early evening. I was prepared for the moderate heat and humidity, so that wasn't a worry, and I mostly succeeded in staying calm and relaxed, taking it all in as I waited for my race to begin. Once it did, I settled into a good position just off the back of the lead pack and stayed there to negotiate the many turns on the narrow cobblestone streets. I felt smooth, strong and powerful while biding my time.

For the first few miles, the cobblestones had been smoothed over by traffic and weren't much of a problem, but once we started a big loop through St. Peter's Square, where traffic wasn't allowed, it was like running on small boulders. Because of my running style – on the balls of my feet with a forceful push-off from my toes – I was having problems. To avoid having to push off on top of my crooked toe, I have an exaggerated twist to my right foot, but ... *on these damn ass cobblestones, my balancing act isn't working.* Every time I pushed off, my right forefoot would slip off the stone and twist into the cracks.

The rough loop was less than a mile. *Keep going ... it's not far ... don't waste energy worrying ... keep going ... keep going.*

Suddenly, my right foot twisted hard into a crack, and I felt a pinch as my shoe wedged itself between two cobblestones before a stabbing pain shot through my ankle. I tried to yank my shoe out of the crack. I was stuck. I pulled my foot out of the shoe and leaned over, trying to pry the shoe out. It wouldn't budge. By then my ankle was in searing pain.

After just 3 miles, my race was over.

I had tears in my eyes, but I don't like people feeling sorry for me or knowing how vulnerable I really am so I held them back. That was my first big racing disappointment, and I didn't know how to react. I sat down right there next to my shoe and stared at St. Peter's Basilica as the sun was setting. It was the most brilliant sight I had ever seen. I thought about its history and the many significant things that had happened in that very spot over the centuries. Sitting there in the grandeur of St. Peter's Square, my problem at the moment didn't seem so big or terrible. Suddenly, I was OK with the situation.

It was out of my control. I didn't make any mistakes in the race. I was properly prepared. I had a faster marathon time than the woman who ended up winning the bronze medal, and had been running faster than she had all year. I knew I would have medaled if my shoe had stayed on. It didn't. Life goes on. There are times to be hard on yourself, but that wasn't one of them.

If I learned one thing that day, it's that the marathon is like life: *no matter how well prepared you are, there is always something unexpected around the next corner.*

I never did get the shoe out of the cobblestones. It may still be there. I got up and hobbled away on one bare foot.

The team doctor who looked at my ankle said it was so badly sprained that he was surprised I didn't break it. "It would have snapped on most athletes with such small ankle bones," he said. Once again, tuna with the bones in it saved the day.

After they taped up my ankle so I wouldn't do too much damage while hobbling around the city, I enjoyed the rest of my time in Italy. Steve and I watched some of the track events, including Lynn's sixth-place finish at 10,000 meters, and then did the usual sights one sees in Rome: museums, the Coliseum and – even though I'd already had an up-close and personal visit – St. Peter's Square.

A few days later we took the train to Florence, eating at the fabulous restaurants and enjoying the sights. Mostly enjoying them, anyway. Steve persuaded me to go on a tour of one lovely historical church even though I was concerned about the dusty, enclosed space. We climbed up a small, dark and narrow staircase that wound around and around, getting smaller and smaller, until we reached the top. Claustrophobia hit big time! I was so ready to get out of there that I hobbled down as quickly as my sprained ankle would allow. I had to use my inhaler halfway down and felt queasy the rest of the day.

We returned to Rome after a couple of days, and toward the end of our stay we went to an elegant Nike party in a mansion in the hills, with an incredible view of the city. The event called for formal attire. Steve appeared exceptionally handsome wearing a light-blue silk shirt that brought out his bright blue eyes. I had to scramble for an outfit, and managed to make my pink, cotton tank-topped dress stylish by adding a white belt and sandals. Everyone was served champagne and every type of the most wonderful Italian food you could imagine. Nike knew how to throw a party.

Soon after, I was pleased to learn that Nike felt I had potential despite my disappointing race in Rome. They signed me on for two more years with the same bonus structure, but they tripled my base salary.

It was early September when I returned home to prepare for my next adventures in life – not only getting married, but also being reunited with my daughter.

I needed to recuperate and obtain therapy for my sprained ankle. Staffan teased me ("How in the world could you go all the way to Rome and sprain your ankle in the first 5K of a World Championship Marathon?") but with his help the ankle healed miraculously and I managed to do a few easy runs in September to maintain some fitness.

Meanwhile, we may have found our dream house on the South Hill but we didn't have enough money for a down payment. Steve already had a mortgage on a small house he lived in on the north side of town. It needed some work, was too small for a family of four and wasn't likely to sell immediately. We couldn't get a loan for the new house without a decent down payment.

I had no choice. I had to run the Twin Cities Marathon the first weekend in October and win enough prize money for that down payment. It was only six weeks after the Rome fiasco. I wasn't race ready, but I was fit, my ankle was healing nicely and I could tolerate the pain from the bit of tendonitis that lingered. I didn't need to win as long as I placed at least second, worth enough prize money to move my growing family into our new home.

I hadn't trained much, but I was hoping for the best.

Twin Cities Marathon ~ October, 1987

It was a perfect morning for a marathon – sunny, cool and no wind. I took off running with the leader, a tiny Frenchwoman named Silvie Bornet. She was running the race of her life. I knew I couldn't stay up on my toes, pushing off forcefully and stressing my ankle, so I backed off and let her go. I could continue running strong, just not fast. I was cruising along at a solid pace, not putting too much pressure on my ankle, and actually enjoying my run until the 25-mile mark when Gail Kingma passed me at the top of the hill by the ever-so-familiar St. Paul's Cathedral. I took off like there was no tomorrow. Third place wasn't going to be enough for a down payment!

A half mile later, I passed Gail like she was standing in cement. As I was flying down the final straightaway, Steve yelled, "It's OK, you can slow down now! You have second place!" I threw my hands in the air as I went by him, as if to say, "I can't!" My legs had a mind of their own.

My ankle was sore but my job was done.

The following week, Steve and I were married in his older brother David's house in the Seattle University district. Almost all of Steve's immediate family – two brothers and two sisters – lived in the Seattle area, and David had plenty of room since it was going to be a small wedding with just family.

Steve's siblings are gentle people with dark hair and kind eyes, highly educated and focused on family values. They were all health-oriented, earthy and into environmental issues early on, going green well before most people. His father, Harlan, was a Methodist minister and planned to marry us. A round, jolly man, he always seemed to be humming, and his sweet demeanor brightened up a room. He was the backbone of the family and adored by his wife, Sally, and all of his kids and grandchildren. Sally was supportive of Harlan and her kids. She and Harlan weren't runners by any means, but they traveled around Washington State to cheer for their children when they all ran races. I soon found out the Jones family was extremely close and spent time together at birthdays, holidays and any other special occasion.

My family lived close to Seattle, so the wedding was convenient for everyone. The only one from my family not to show up was Debbie, even though she lived just 20 miles away.

Jamie and Rachel stood with Steve and me during the short ceremony. My two bridesmaids: Jamie standing up there in front of everyone acting goofy while Rachel looked embarrassed and concerned that her life was about to change that very day. After the wedding, she would leave Laurie's family and come back to Spokane with us. Poor Rachel. She didn't know what to expect in her new home, and she didn't know Steve at all.

Laurie was on her best behavior, helpful though anxious, while working hard to keep herself under control for all our sakes. She was fighting two distinct personalities, the good Laurie and the *very* bad Laurie. She was torn about her decision to give Rachel away, but her life was becoming more and more unraveled. Laurie had changed dramatically over the past year. Not only was she taking cocaine, but also drinking too much and playing hard. She would swing from being wild and out of control to being the perfect mother and wife. We all saw that bipolar behavior in our family members over the years, and we always knew it was in Laurie. Stanley's death made her snap. As a result, she was becoming self-destructive and ruining the lives of the ones she loved the most. Mel couldn't look me in the eye, nor did he flash his wonderful smile easily. Their boys were fighting back tears, not just because they were about to lose their sister, but also because they were about to lose their life as they knew it. They were such sweet, kind boys. My heart ached for all of them.

As Dad gave me away during the ceremony I thought about what a wonderful man he is. I was appreciating him more and more as time went on. Mom was happy, as she always is when our family gets together. Bradley was there with his wife, Sherri, and their three kids – Little Brad, Ashley and Chaz. When my brother Charlie was alive, Bradley called him "Chaz," so that's what he named his son. Chaz even had Charlie's red wavy hair. They were sweet kids with big hearts and good manners, except that Chaz had picked up a few swear words. Even at the age of 2, he liked getting a reaction out of people. He managed to get a big reaction out of the proper Jones family.

It was a nice wedding. Even so, I was relieved to have it over. I was a happy bride, but I never get all joyful and effusive. Plus, there had been a lot going on. It was time to settle in and put things in order again.

With Jamie, slipping through the Ferris track gate for a workout ~ 1987

With all four of us in our small apartment, it was tight quarters for a month before moving into the new house. Jamie and Rachel quickly started fighting, so I knew they were adjusting and getting comfortable with each other. I enrolled Rachel at Sacajawea Middle School and hoped she would fit right in.

Once we moved into the house, Jamie and Rachel picked out the bedrooms they wanted. Jamie made a sign and taped it on her bedroom door. It read, "No Fahtews awowed." She was still spelling things the way she pronounced them. Steve asked, "What does that say?" Rachel translated, "No farters allowed." She and Jamie laughed, but Steve was angry, saying, "We don't use that kind of language in this household!" It was not a good way to win Rachel over.

Rachel was beautiful – tall and blond, with extremely long legs, knocked knees and the turned-up nose that we share. She may have looked sweet, but that adorable exterior belied a remarkable inner toughness and fearlessness. She was a strong, stubborn little girl with a wary look who always seemed to be figuring people out. She never trusted people easily ... just like her mother.

Unlike most girls, Rachel didn't like looking pretty and dressing up. She'd rather be a tomboy and go out and do things, sometimes things she shouldn't be doing. She liked having control over her life, and would rebel when she felt there was an imbalance of power involving anybody she cared for. When somebody did her wrong, look out. If they did Jamie or me wrong, they really needed to look out!

The sisters looked a lot alike, but Jamie had a perm that she just loved. When she turned her head quickly, the curls would fly around but they stuck up in places so much that we had to water them down. Unlike Rachel, Jamie liked to look pretty, but she just didn't like taking the time to make that happen. She brushed over the top of her perm, leaving the hair underneath tangled and ratted until it was so matted there was no way to comb through it. I took her in for a haircut and the hairdresser looked appalled and gave up. I took Jamie home, dumped a ton of conditioner on her head to try to soften the mess, and then began gently rescuing as many strands of hair as I could before cutting out the rat's nest. It ended up looking pretty good, from a distance.

Even though Rachel, the tomboy, rarely wore dresses, she liked to be stylish in jeans, sneakers and nice shirts or T-shirts. Jamie tried to be stylish, too, and came up with the most hideous outfits. Once she strutted downstairs with three ponytails in three big scrunchies in three different colors, my half tights that were baggy on her skinny legs and came down to her shins, an oversized dress shirt and bright-pink high-top aerobic shoes on her long feet. Steve and I tried not to laugh, but Rachel couldn't help herself. Jamie was mad, saying, "What's wong wid dis?" That only made Rachel laugh harder, but I thought she was adorable. She thought she looked great and went to school dressed like that many times. Poor Jamie. It took a few years before she figured it out.

Steve, on the other hand, dressed in a suit and tie almost every day before going to the office, appearing so distinguished. It was as if he became the father of "The Brady Bunch." His bright pink running shorts with the black polka dots were another matter. He had them specially made and wore them whenever he could, adding a matching singlet on important occasions. The girls didn't want to be seen near him when he wore that getup.

I knew Steve must have loved us all very much to be so patient and caring with my two lovely, yet demanding and sometimes misbehaving girls. He tried very hard to make Rachel feel welcome and special, and Jamie smart and important. They were a treat, but they could be a big challenge.

Steve was the one who worked with them on their homework. Rachel always seemed to get upset and yell at him when she couldn't understand her math problems, while Jamie was always trying to look smarter than she was and smarter than Steve, as well. When he would try to subtly correct her on something, she would protest loudly, "I know, I know, I was just going to tew you dat." That was better than Rachel yelling, "I hate homework! Why do I have to do this? I want to tear it up!" Steve stayed calm. "I'm trying to help you understand so you can figure this out and not get so frustrated," he would say quietly. "Once you finish you can go watch your television shows."

Fortunately, Rachel and Jamie enjoyed the same television shows. There was enough fighting going on without arguments about that.

Just like Debbie and me when we were young, Rachel and Jamie loved each other and were close but fought a lot. One of the things they fought for was my attention. To look like the good daughter, Jamie often "told" on Rachel. She really knew how to push her buttons, and could be obnoxious about it, but Rachel knew just what to say to Jamie to make her angry and act out just as I was about to walk into the room. I caught onto it all right away and really tried to keep things fair, giving them both equal time and attention. It just never seemed to be equal in their eyes.

Because Rachel and I were so much alike and only 16 years apart, I was more like her older sister than her mother, making for a wonderful mother-daughter relationship. Even back then, however, I felt there were times I should have disciplined her more.

One of the many times I caught Rachel smoking in her room, she seemed shocked. "Mom, how do you always know I'm smoking?" I told her that I had a good sense of smell, especially for cigarette smoke, and that I could smell it all the way from the basement. "Besides," I said, "you smell like an ashtray after a good smoke! Why do you do it? It's such a nasty habit."

"You know how it is to fit in. All of my new friends smoke."

"Yes, but you're smarter than they are and now it seems, since you're hiding in your bedroom, smoking alone, that you're addicted!"

"I can stop anytime I want," Rachel said. "I'm in control of everything I do."

"OK," I said. "Then stop *now*."

She looked down, ashamed. I hugged her. "You are definitely the boss of yourself but really, try to toe the line. Smoking is so bad for you. Besides the smoking, you need to treat Steve with some respect and Jamie with a little more patience. Work with me here."

"What's 'toe the line'?" she asked.

"Follow the rules!" I said sternly.

A week later, Jamie came running downstairs as I was preparing dinner.

"Mom, I have to tew you something! You can't tew Wachew I told you, pwease! Wachew is on the woof outside her bedwoom, smoking."

I ran upstairs as fast as I could to get her off that slippery roof, which was two stories up and dangerously peaked. I hurried into her room and to the window, leaning out into the rain to say, "Rachel, get back inside right now!" just as she slipped and bounced from one peaked roof to the other on her way to the ground. Worried sick, Jamie and I rushed down the stairs and outside to find Rachel sitting in the bushes with cigarette still in hand!

Smoking on the roof was typical of the trouble my thirteen-year-old daughter got into – staying out too late, skipping school and talking back to Steve. She was always sorry, saying, "Mom, I will try to be good."

It wasn't easy. One of the many weekends she was restricted to the house, again for smoking at school, she and Steve had a fight. As much as Steve loved Rachel and Jamie, he wasn't used to sensitive young girls and would often say things they took as demeaning, and that's what set things off that night. With her low self-esteem, Rachel was easily offended and took everything personally. She decided to go to bed early.

I knew she was sulking, and went up to her room to talk. From the hallway light I could just make out her cute turned-up nose and beautiful blond hair on the pillow in the dark. I knew it was too early for her to be asleep, so I sat down on her bed.

"I'm sorry about your restriction and know how miserable you must be. Once you and Steve get to know each other, you'll understand him and know he means well and wants what's best for you." I went on for several minutes, and began caressing her hair as I talked. It felt funny. I touched her turned-up nose. It was huge and hard, like plastic! I screamed.

When I flipped on the bedroom light, I found Miss Piggy on Rachel's pillow, with more pillows stuffed into the bed as her body. Her plastic head was the same size and shape as Rachel's and for the first time, I realized how much Rachel and Miss Piggy looked alike. I had to laugh. My daughter was good at covering her tracks!

The look on Rachel's face when she came sneaking back into the house late that night as I sat on her bed with Miss Piggy was priceless. It was hard, but I held back my smile. Rachel knew she was in serious trouble.

The first thing she said was, "Mom, I'm so sorry. I never want to make you worry or sad." To hear the concern in her voice made me realize how special Rachel was, and how much she loved me. She was worried more about me than whatever punishment awaited her.

Rachel was a good girl, but she was rebelling against so many things. I'm sure some of it was about me giving her up for an early adoption, although she would never say such a thing to anybody. It was also about the Jehovah's Witness couple that adopted her and then divorced, tearing her world apart, before passing her on to Laurie and Mel. And she was rebelling against Laurie and Mel for giving her away – she had been so happy there, before having to experience another horrible family breakup.

After so many years she was finally reunited with her mom and sister, but didn't want Steve to be a part of our family. Rachel never warmed up to Steve as much as she should have after he scolded her for saying "farters." She could read people, and developed an opinion of Steve early on. She grew to love him, yet didn't give him the respect he deserved. Many times after being disciplined by him she told me, "It would be a perfect life if it were just the three us: you, Jamie and me. No man."

Jamie felt it would be perfect with just the *two* of us. Many times she sat on the toilet seat as I tried to relax in my bubble bath, telling me, "Wemembew when it was just you and me in the apawtment togethew? I miss ouw alone time. I wish it was just you and me, no Wachew or Steve."

I knew they were trying their best to cope with the changes. So was I, suddenly living with two more people, two people who weren't as tidy as Jamie and me and didn't care if things were out of place or there was a crumb on the floor.

Jamie noticed the attention Rachel received when she got into trouble, and decided to act up whenever Rachel did. That made Rachel laugh. I had to smile myself, seeing Jamie try so hard to outdo her sister in being bad, especially because she was such a "goody two shoes." To Jamie, it didn't matter whether it was positive or negative. Attention was attention.

One time, it wasn't so funny. Jamie had been sent up to her room for talking back to me, but soon came halfway down the stairs yelling, "Mom, I need to come out of my woom." I told her, "No, you go back upstairs and think about why you were sent up there. When you figure it out you can come down and we can talk about it."

She disappeared for a while and then came back with a sharpened pencil. "Wook, wook what you awe making me do!" she said dramatically, with both hands holding the pencil above her head and stabbing it toward her face. She kept saying, "You awe the cause of this. You awe the weason I'm so unhappy."

At first I was horrified, knowing she was reliving the time that her father hit his head against the wall over and over before threatening us with the rifle. She was even saying the same things. I reacted to her just as I had reacted to Kelly, calmly and without emotion.

Instead of panicking and giving her the feedback and response she expected, I asked, "Jamie, what is that going to prove? That's just a little pencil but if you poke yourself, it's going to hurt really badly. You would never want to harm yourself. You're too precious and we both know you like yourself."

I walked away. She sat there for a while and then put the pencil down.

The following week in the Nordstrom department store, I found the perfect outfit for her – a fleece turquoise sweatshirt and a matching fleece skirt with "I Like Myself" written in bright pink lettering on both.

~

Winter came hard that year, and we had a few miserable snowstorms that dropped several feet of snow at a time. On one of those wicked winter nights, Steve was out at a Bloomsday board meeting and Rachel was at a friend's house. I was watching the news with Jamie by my side when the meteorologist came on with a warning, telling everyone with pets to bring them inside. The wind chill was dropping so low that pets wouldn't survive outside for even a few hours that night. Hearing the news, Jamie panicked.

"Mom, Punky's outside! Dad is at wowk. He doesn't bwing her in the house anymow and she's been outside since you weft!"

I felt sick. *I should have taken her with us!* I'd always wanted Punky, only Kelly and I agreed that she was well adjusted and had her territorial boundaries set where she'd lived for most of her life. It wouldn't have been right to move her to an apartment. I assumed he was taking good care of her. But that night, she was in danger.

Jumping out of my chair, I told Jamie, "Bundle up. We're going Punky hunting."

I grabbed my inhaler in case the cold air sparked an asthma attack. Wearing all of our winter attire and barely able to see out of the windshield through the snow, we drove to Kelly's. When we arrived it was pitch dark and so cold it hurt my lungs to take a breath. We went to the front door calling for Punky, and then the backyard. I even went over to Marty and Lorrie's to see if they might know where she was or had taken her in, but they weren't home.

By then, Jamie was freezing. The reflection off the snow offered a little light in the backyard, but with Punky the same color as the snow I wouldn't have been able to find her if she were lying right in front of me. I asked Jamie, "Where do you think Punky would go?" Jamie replied, "She is always undew the deck in a big giant doghouse."

"Jamie, how long has this been going on? Has Punky been outside every night?"

"Yes, but Dad said she is fine undew the deck in an insuwated doghouse."

"What!?"

"Dad doesn't feed her anymow eithew. I sneak Punky food when he's asweep."

The bottom of the deck was well above my head, but the doghouse was way back against the main house and I had to find my way to it with tons of snow piled up. It was so dark I had to feel my way to the so-called "insulated" doghouse. Once I found it, I got down on my hands and knees and put my head inside.

"Punky, are you there?"

I heard a faint purr and I went in farther, blindly feeling my way toward the back as my hand kept touching one bird carcass after another and several frozen furry things. Then I knew how my poor Punky survived for the past year! I was horrified to think of what else I might touch. I was over halfway into the doghouse before I felt a very cold nose rub against my hand. Punky came forward, barely able to purr, yet trying hard to be strong and brave. When she crawled close enough to my hand that I could reach her, I pulled her out of there and rushed her to the warm car and into Jamie's lap.

With her beautiful green eyes, long snow-white hair and tiny gray mark on her forehead, Punky looked prissy. She even walked prissy. But Punky was a fighter.

When we brought Punky into her new home, I held her close, right next to the steam radiator, while sitting on the living room floor. I told Jamie to heat up a small bowl of milk in the microwave, but not too hot. Punky's eyes were constantly tearing up and her little heart was barely beating. She was so loving that she was purring and wasting energy.

After several attempts to get her going, Punky started drinking her milk. Once she drank the entire bowl, she sat on my lap and purred louder. Jamie fixed her some snacks. Since we didn't have any normal cat food, we fed Punky some warmed-up mashed potatoes and small pieces of chicken. It took a long while, because we kept taking the food away from her to slow her down. I didn't want her to eat too fast, remembering what happened to me the time we were starving and Mom marched us to our distant neighbor's house miles from our home years ago, where I ate the sandwiches way too fast and they almost came back up and gave me a terrible stomach ache. I didn't want her to pop like Blondie, either.

And that's how our new life together started out. It certainly wasn't boring, and it wasn't the daily life of most elite marathoners.

I had taken October, November and most of December off from running to establish our new life together, but I knew it was time to start training like I had never trained before. The next year, 1988, was an Olympic year, and the U.S. Women's Olympic Marathon Trials were set for the first weekend of May, in Pittsburgh. It was time to return to the Benji training program. Given all of the chaos surrounding me that year, I needed Benji more than ever.

Chapter 13

On New Year's Day, I started back into full training. Some athletes find taking a total timeout more difficult than the training itself, but I found starting from scratch, unfit and totally de-trained quite gratifying. I knew I would lose my fitness, so it took a lot of discipline to stop running; nevertheless, my trust in Benji and in my own experience meant that I knew I'd become a better athlete for it.

I thrived on the challenge of hard work and the mental toughness of facing the cold and dreary winter mornings, fully aware that I wasn't going to cruise through a workout. Soon, I would begin to see progress with every week as my fitness moved to a higher level. That season, as usual, I did my base training alone, miles and miles of easy running out in the country with nothing but whitened wheat fields and an occasional hawk soaring overhead to keep me company.

We didn't have many snowstorms after we rescued Punky that night in late December, and the mild weather in January and February meant we didn't have to deal with a snow floor or much ice. That made for more productive training. I went to my late winter and early spring races strong, mentally fresh and eager to push myself hard. I ran personal bests at the Orlando Red Lobster 10K in 32 minutes and a week later at the Tampa Bay Gasparilla 15K in 50:09, going through the 10K mark in 32:08 (5:10 pace). It seemed so easy. I knew my body was rewarding me for the long rest in November and December.

Once the snow melted in early spring, I joined Don and the boys out on the River Road and along the Riverside State Park trails for their Sunday long runs of 13-15 miles. For me, it was a "short" long run of a hard effort at their pace. Even then, I would have to tease – or pimp, as they called it – Staffan or Hardway to speed up enough to give me the long tempo effort I needed. "Why are you guys running so slow? We're crawling here!" With that, sometimes it turned into a race effort.

Every other week, I did my speed sessions on the track with Don. He helped me work on running consistent half miles at race effort, then running four extremely fast 200's (half of a lap) in 29-31 seconds on very tired legs and jogging a 200 after each for recovery, which is how we ended every workout. Once I put my spikes on before the 200's, after running 8 x half-mile efforts. Boy, did Don look worried! But he pulled me along, running in Lane 2, through 28-29 second 200's.

During one morning workout we did 20 x 200 in 29-32 seconds, with an easy 200 jog after each. The next day Don dropped something off at the house for Steve and asked me, "How do you feel after those 200's yesterday?"

"I don't feel too bad. I seem to have recovered and loosened up after my second run last night," I told him.

He shook his head. "I went home and rested all day, and this morning I feel like I was hit by a semi-truck." Then he hobbled down the long walkway to his car as I stood there and smiled at my dedicated training partner, always there to help me through a workout when I needed it most. By the time the Olympic Trials came around, I would be in the best shape of my life, and Don would be in pretty good shape himself.

Don and the boys taught me a lot, including why *not* to race in a workout – they all ended up injuring each other – and the meaning of "Orb." After a brutal workout, we were jogging an easy 3 miles for a cool down when Don said, "I'm Orbbing."

"What's that?" I asked.

"It's when you can barely move, you break out in a cold sweat and your body needs sugar immediately or you're going to pass out," he replied faintly. "It's a lot better than the 'Golden Orb.' That's when you start seeing spots before your eyes and everything is magnified."

Soon after that, I began to experience the power of the Golden Orb for myself. The first time one hit me, I was on a second run after finishing 25 miles only three hours earlier. I stumbled after trying to run through it. Miraculously, I saw a Milk Dud on the road directly in front of me. Sugar! I examined it to be sure it was truly a Milk Dud before desperately putting it into my mouth. I could hardly believe I did such an unsanitary thing, but it brought me right out of that damn Golden Orb, allowing me to continue.

My weekly mileage was up to 70 miles and I didn't miss a beat to the drummer. The boys pulled me along on the 13-15 mile tempo efforts on Sundays, which I followed with a 5-mile second run. Don sacrificed himself to push me hard in my speed session on Tuesdays, which I also followed with a second run. I did my long run of 20-26 miles over hilly terrain on Thursdays alone, again with a second run later. Between those hard days, I enjoyed my wimp days, running as slow as I could go at times.

Despite my training schedule, I wanted Rachel and Jamie to have a perfect family life. I went grocery shopping, cooked nutritious meals, baked, kept the house up and tried to do most of my training while they were in school. That meant there were times when I only had two hours to eat a big lunch and take a quick nap between my 26-mile long run and 5-mile afternoon run on Thursdays, sometimes covering over 30 miles within 5½ hours. I tried to plan most of the challenging or tiring activities with Rachel and Jamie for my wimp days of short easy runs and weightlifting, making sure to spend equal time with each one so no fights would break out. If the training didn't toughen me up, my tight schedule did.

We had a housecleaner named Ruby, which should have helped me out. Ruby, however, was a treat. She had cleaned Steve's small house on the north side of town for several years, and we kept her to clean one day a week when we moved into the big house. Other than her glass eye, Ruby looked and talked like the maid on the TV series "Hazel," round and sometimes jolly, but she was no "Hazel" when it came to keeping house.

Ruby did whatever she wanted with the housecleaning. Sometimes she would iron just the arms of Steve's shirts, and other times just the front and back. I guess it depended on her mood as she watched her soap operas. I think she gave the carpets a quick vacuum every once in a while, and I'm not sure but maybe she did some dusting now and then. I didn't have the heart to fire her so I ended up cleaning everything she missed, which was pretty much the entire house. To get out of the serious housecleaning, Ruby did the laundry, but she would toss Rachel's brightly colored shirts in with her white jeans and the rest of our clothes, ruining everything.

Rachel had other issues with her. "Ruby snoops through my bedroom. I don't want her in there, ever!"

"I don't think Ruby would go through your things," I told her.

The next time Ruby cleaned, she came to Steve and me holding a joint she'd found in Rachel's "secret" box. Poor Rachel got into trouble many times because of Ruby. Not only did she create more work than she actually did, she was snooping through *everything*. We finally had to let her go after several painful years of trial and mostly error.

One quiet night, I took advantage of an empty house to go to bed early. Rachel was sleeping over at a friend's, Jamie was staying with her dad and Steve was away for the weekend hunting with a friend in Montana. About 10 p.m., the doorbell woke me. When I flipped on the porch light, I could see Rachel standing there. With a policeman.

"Is this your daughter?"

"Yes," I replied, glancing at Rachel suspiciously.

"She was running all over the South Hill with a bunch of hoodlums, toilet-papering and egging houses and then running from the police, calling them names while they chased her all around Manito Park and the neighborhood."

Rachel was staring at the ground defiantly, but I could see that her cheeks were bright red and smudged with dirt. Her hair was a mess. One of her shoes was missing.

"I'll be sure to take care of this," I assured him. "Thank you for bringing her home."

The officer told Rachel, "You and your friend Nicole seem to be good kids and have nice families. You shouldn't be running around with those kids. They're trouble."

After the policeman said goodnight and left, Rachel tried not to smile as she slowly looked up. When she was in an awkward situation or under pressure, she tended to laugh. That sounds familiar. After some nervous laughter she said, "It was so much fun, Mom! The police were chasing us and they couldn't catch me. I was so fast! I think I could be a great runner like you. They almost caught Nicole so I threw my shoe at them and then they chased me around the park. It was so exciting and I felt *so* powerful!"

That sounds familiar, too. I told her my stories of being a thief and throwing rocks and breaking windows only to be chased by coppers, and how becoming a runner gave me that same adrenaline rush and feeling of invincibility.

"Now," I said, "It's time to join a sport."

Rachel chose soccer and softball, saying, "Mom, I don't want to be a runner." I told her I understood. In track and cross country you may be on a team, but you're out there as an individual in your event and success or failure is all on your shoulders.

"I'm not that brave," Rachel said, looking at the floor. "I know I would fail."

"Rachel, everyone fails. People learn from failure and do better next time. The most successful people are the ones brave enough to face it."

By early spring the girls were heavily into sports, softball for Rachel and track for Jamie. They were standout athletes. It was tough transporting them to and from their practices, and attending the middle-school softball games and the elementary-school track meets, but I was always there on the sidelines. Luckily, their events never coincided. Steve was just as supportive, always there through thick and thin to drive them where they needed to go and watch their games and track meets.

Later that spring, as I was getting a handle on everything, Laurie decided to visit Spokane. She never told me she was coming, which was bizarre. I didn't find out she was in town until Jamie came home from a weekend visit at her dad's and told us that Laurie was staying there. *With Kelly?* That was even more bizarre. I didn't want to know anything about it and didn't ask any questions, but Rachel did.

"So, where did Laurie sleep?"

"She swept in Dad's watew bed with him. I hewd them sweeping in thew."

Laurie called me from Kelly's, asking if she could visit the girls and me. She wanted to come over in the afternoon when Steve was at work. Laurie didn't like Steve because she was intimidated and couldn't be herself around him. Before Steve left that morning he told me to call him immediately if I felt threatened by Laurie in any way. Steve had reason to worry, after hearing that Laurie had recently become verbally abusive, even threatening to harm people.

"Whatever you do, don't give her any alcohol," warned Steve as he walked out the door.

"I'm hoping for the best," I said, as always.

I was sick all morning wondering what to expect. A few hours before the girls were due home from school, and much earlier than I expected, the doorbell rang. Laurie came in and hugged me. "Kimmie, I've missed you so much."

Then she pushed me away, her dark eyes narrowing as she hunched toward me ever so lightly. She smiled wickedly. "You know I have always wanted to pour gasoline all over you and light you on fire."

"You need to leave if you're going to be like this," I told her. "I don't want the girls seeing you this way."

"I'm just kidding you. I wanted to see those blue eyes light up. Come on, I'm joking."

From as far back as I can remember, Laurie was always trying to get a reaction out of me: making sure I knew that I'd eaten my cow Blondie, telling us our dad was comatose, all of those mean tricks she pulled on us when we were younger. I think she learned that from our father. Dad was a victim of illness and the circumstances he grew up in. So was Laurie, and she was turning out to be a lot like Dad.

We sat at the kitchen table, talking about old times. She seemed to be back to normal again. I didn't like "the evil" Laurie, but she was my sister and I loved her. It was sad to see her veer back and forth from nice, to evil, to nice again, right before my eyes. Then she demanded some wine. I thought about Steve's warning and I knew I shouldn't, but I said OK without hesitation. I was more afraid of what would happen if I said no. I poured us both a big, solid glass of Chablis – I needed one – and counted down the minutes to when the girls would be home, hoping Laurie would leave before they got there.

The girls walked into the kitchen, and Laurie went back to her evil self, telling me embellished stories about Mom – how she was coming home drunk, being put in jail for a DUI and making other bad choices. There was no time to stop her as she rushed on, telling me sexual things about herself. She even told the girls about wanting to light me on fire.

Then, in a demonized voice she said, "So, Rachel. Who is your mother? Is it *her* or is it *me*?"

Rachel didn't say a thing. The look on the girls' faces said it all – they were angry with Laurie and afraid for me. Rachel ran up to her room, but came down soon after to make sure I was OK. Laurie didn't leave until she saw Steve pulling into the garage. We looked so relieved that Steve could immediately tell something was wrong and asked what happened.

"Why did you give her alcohol?" he asked. "You know that makes her worse."

Jamie answered for me. "Steve, Mom had to, othewwise Aunt Wowie would have lit her on fiew." Rachel and I laughed our nervous laugh. It was better than not laughing at all.

~

As May approached and the day of the Olympic Trials drew near, I was as fit as I could possibly be. With a few more workouts with Don by my side, I would be ready for a marathon performance that would surely make me an Olympian. However, there was one family member who wasn't so fit, and continued to de-train.

Over the winter the sleek fighter and hunter who survived in the harsh outdoors for so long had grown fat. Punky would venture out to use the garden as her litter box but dart right back inside to watch the squirrels and birds from the window. She couldn't even jump up on the couch without putting a lot of effort into it. After starving for so long while struggling to stay alive, then being rescued and eating tons of gourmet cat food for months, Punky had followed the plan for depletion and carbo-loading, but there was one problem: when I did it, I ran a marathon a few days later. Living the high life, with no exercise, Punky didn't burn those carbohydrates. She just loaded up. We had to give her expanding bottom a little shove to get her outside for a few minutes to take care of business.

Punky lazing around the house all day was *not* good for my asthma, especially in the springtime when I was dealing with all kinds of pollens. However, Punky adored me and would sit near the radiator in the living room while I relaxed with my feet up in "Big Red," my leather recliner, while reading or watching reruns of "Little House on the Prairie," "The Waltons," or "Bonanza" between my training runs and the time the girls came home from school. She sat there looking eager and so ready for special attention that I couldn't help myself. All I had to do was pat my leg and she would jump – well, hoist herself – up immediately. She would circle my lap and knead my legs softly with her claws just catching in the soft fabric of the blanket covering me, then edge closer and closer to my face until her paws were on my shoulders and her face was nuzzled into my neck, where she lay contently, purring and purring.

Punky also liked to curl up on Jamie when she did her homework while lying on her stomach on the floor in the Red Room. The cat would climb on and cuddle into the small curve of her lower back, and Jamie would say almost every time, "Mom, Punky needs to woose some weight. She's going to bweak my back."

I decided that since it was an exceptionally warm spring, Punky needed to spend some time outside for her own good, not to mention Jamie's and mine.

The first day we put her outside and closed the sliding glass door behind her, she turned around immediately and started pawing and scratching, her fat stomach all white and fluffy rubbing against the door as she tried to claw her way back in. We were laughing at how cute she looked when Buffy the neighbor dog came charging over. Punky took off into an abandoned lot behind our house and disappeared.

We searched all afternoon and into the evening, with Jamie crying. No luck. We searched every day. We passed out photos of Punky and offered a reward. No Punky. Every day, Jamie put out a can of tuna in the abandoned lot. Later she would find the can empty and come back with it saying, "Punky is thewe, Mom, she's eating her food." I was sure the cats in the neighborhood were appreciating that tuna every day.

A week went by. My hope of ever seeing Punky again had faded but Jamie's was still very much alive. She begged me to sleep outside in our backyard next to the abandoned lot, so sure that Punky would come to us. "I just know she's out thewe, I just know it!" Even though I should have been resting after my last 30+ mile workout day, only three weeks before my ever-so-important marathon, we brought out our sleeping bags along with some snacks and laid there hoping for Punky to return. We talked about the stars, told stories and waited. No Punky. Finally, we fell asleep.

I woke up to a loud purring. Punky was lying next to Jamie, rubbing her head against Jamie's cheek. Our Punky was home.

But by then, that cat wouldn't step foot outside. She hid down in the basement catching bugs and occasionally a few mice, bringing them up to the top of the stairs for us to admire. We had to put a litter box down there. Whenever we tried to catch her, she would jump up the rock wall and into the rafters, where she became covered in soot. Her white fur turned gray prowling around and hunting in the dark and dirty dungeon that became her domain.

At least my problem was solved. Cat dander was not an issue in the few weeks leading up to the Trials.

The Olympic Trials Marathon and Bloomsday both fell on May 1, which made the month of April stressful in our household. Steve was on the Bloomsday board and busy preparing for the big race. The bulk of my training was in, so for the next few weeks it was time to rest a little and sharpen, doing some faster running, with more intensity and less volume. That was good, but I was experiencing some asthma symptoms, feeling lethargic and sluggish as if I were training at 8,000 feet. I was sleeping and eating well, however, and it seemed I had a handle on it.

Until the week before the race, that is. I was on my depletion diet and very edgy. I was also about to turn 30, which didn't help matters. As he did every year, Steve's brother David stayed with us for the 10 days leading up to Bloomsday, using his vacation to help with the race before running it. With everything Steve and David had to do, I was in charge of the girls and their homework – a very scary place to be! Rachel was her usual self, upset and angry as she struggled to grasp her algebra problems. Jamie was *her* usual self, smarter than me and the rest of the world. "I know what to do, just weave me awone," she said as she did her work incorrectly instead of feeling inadequate by admitting she didn't know how to solve a problem. It was tough and I admired Steve more than ever for his patience with the girls.

Steve and David were out working on Bloomsday runner packets when the junior-high principal called wanting to meet with me about Rachel. That was the last thing I needed, to be in a school during a flu outbreak with the Olympic Trials less than a week away. I decided to wear gloves, knowing I would have to shake hands and touch germy things while I was there.

"Rachel has an attitude," the principal said when I was seated in his office. "She won't obey the rules and has no respect for her science teacher, Mr. Smith. She won't give him the time of day when he asks her a question." I listened patiently and assured the principal I would talk to Rachel and sort it out.

Before going home I went into Mr. Smith's room to talk with him and right away I could see the problem. The man had a large chip on his shoulder. "Girls don't understand science and have a hard time understanding the concept," he told me, after barely a hello. "They should just listen and try to get a passing grade. They don't have the brain network of a man when it comes to the study of science."

"No wonder Rachel doesn't want to try in this class," I told him bluntly. "I don't blame her. You've defeated every girl in your classroom with that attitude."

I went home and talked with Rachel right away, at least after scrubbing my hands and arms and then gargling with Listerine. Rachel said in her defiant voice, "Mom, I hate Mr. Smith. He's an Ass."

"I know Rachel, he is an Ass of all Asses, but you need to work hard, get through the class and later you'll enjoy science when you have a good teacher."

"OK," she said, "but I will hate it."

The very next day, Jamie's school principal called, wanting to talk to me about her behavior. *Unbelievable!* Once again I had to put those gloves on and go to yet another school and face more germs, to talk about Jamie writing a nasty note to her teacher, using swear words and spelling them wrong. *Hmmm. Was this just a coincidence, one day after Rachel received special attention and only four days before an important marathon?*

"What was that all about?" I asked Jamie, who was eagerly waiting at home.

"I just wanted to write Mrs. Cwemens a note. I didn't know what those wowds meant," was all she had to say for herself.

It didn't help that Steve was entertaining in the evenings and had invited several elite Bloomsday runners to stay at our home the week before the race, then asked some runners over for a home-cooked lasagna dinner on Thursday night. Home-cooked by me, the night before I was to fly out for the marathon.

After all of that, I was exhausted. Everything caught up to me – not just everything from the last few days or even months – everything from the past few years. "We can't entertain house guests this week. You're too busy with Bloomsday preparations and I'm under far too much stress," I told him.

He looked stunned. "I already invited them."

I compromised. "I'll cook the lasagna dinner, but you'll need to find another place for them to stay."

I was furious with him for being so nonchalant about such a significant and consequential marathon. He was being kind and hospitable to his friends, yet didn't consider how much it was taking away from my focus and energy reserve.

When I tried to explain, he walked away. He didn't seem to understand my situation. Maybe no one can, unless you've been in it. Some people think elite athletes are pompous and spoiled – and believe me, some are – but most of us just need some time to take care of ourselves, letting others take on our responsibilities even if it's just for a few days before an important race. I can train my body to be strong, go fast and handle the stresses needed to win a marathon, but I can't perform to my potential unless my energy level, thoughts, emotions and goals are in balance.

Olympic Marathon Trials, Pittsburgh ~ May, 1988

I traveled to Pittsburgh on Friday. Steve planned to join me Saturday, after helping with Bloomsday for as long as possible. When I arrived, it was late and as soon as I checked into my room I went down to find something to eat. Even though the last restaurant in the hotel had just closed, a cook kindly agreed to make me something – a grilled cheese sandwich and French fries. It wasn't what I would choose to eat two nights before a marathon, but I was starving.

Just then, who came walking through the restaurant but Mary Level. The Mary Level who chased us around her swing set naked with her little sister Pippi when we were all so young. The little girl who made me good-luck charms before every high school track meet and told me she wanted to be just like me when she grew older.

I was pleasantly surprised when she told me she was there to run in the Trials. I knew she had been a high school track star in Port Townsend in the same events that I ran. But I had no idea she had come so far in her running.

It was so good to see her. She sat with me while I ate, surprised at my "choice" of a grilled cheese sandwich and fries. We talked and laughed about old times and caught up on our lives. Mary had been following my career from her home in Florida, where she was married and had become one of the top runners in the state. We laughed when I asked her, "My little follower followed me to the Olympic Trials. Do you have any good-luck charms for me?"

Pittsburgh's weather in late spring can be many different things. Unfortunately for us, the weather had been warm enough the few weeks leading up to the Trials that everything seemed to be blooming at once, and the air was loaded with pollen. The course was challenging – downhill for the first 5 miles, some climbing in the middle section with several big hills thrown in, then downhill again for the final 5 miles. I was ready for all of that, especially the hilly section.

To compete in the Trials, marathoners had to run a qualifying time of 2:50 or under. Unfortunately for me, the Women's Long Distance Running Committee decided to make a change for 1988. Anybody running 33 minutes or better for a 10K, or faster than 1:16 for the half marathon, would qualify even if they had "never" run a marathon. Therefore, between the fast 10K runners with no marathon experience and the downhill start, the race was almost guaranteed to go out fast.

It did. The track runners took off at the gun with Sylvia Mosqueda leading the way, like a bat flying from hell. Sylvia was known for taking off way too fast and then dropping out after it caught up to her later in the race. That was dangerous for me, or for any marathoner – we had to be disciplined enough to follow our own race plans and not get carried away.

My plan was to keep third place in sight and not allow the lead pack to get more than a minute ahead of me. Benji and I thought that would be safe, since I was stronger and faster than most runners in the final stages of a marathon, and surely no one would go out with Sylvia.

But some runners did go out with Sylvia, and from the beginning we were running way too fast for a marathon. I felt some tightness in my chest and my breathing wasn't right. I kept running and hoping for the best, but "the best" didn't happen. The worst did. I started having a mild asthma attack, that dreaded grip growing tighter and tighter, like a vise clamped around my lungs, and I had to stop at the aid station near the 5-mile mark or I would have the devil to pay.

I had my inhaler with me and used it once, inhaled deeply and exhaled forcefully, drank a big glass of water and some Gatorade, then used it again. After several minutes of breathing exercises to work out the tightness and cramping in my diaphragm – I'd learned a few tricks over the years since my sisters were no longer around to perform their special CPR – I was able to jump back into the race.

I was in last place. At least I think I was – I saw no one on the course behind me. Last place! *This* is a nightmare all runners have at one time or another. I was living it, in the Olympic Trials, of all places.

Easing into a 5:45 pace and running strong and steady, I was passing people to my right and to my left. Just before the halfway point somebody from the crowd told me I was in 24ᵗʰplace. I'd passed well over 100 people! *I should have started at this pace. Damn!*

I felt hot, and I especially needed to stay hydrated after my asthma attack. I was watching for the next fluid table, where we each had our special drink bottles labeled with our race number. Most elite runners have special drinks that they know work well for them in a race. Everyone drinks something different so getting the correct bottle at those special tables was important. As I approached, a runner was knocking bottles off the table left and right – mine included – as she carelessly searched for her bottle as she ran.

"Excuse me," I said as I tried to pass inside to grab some plain water at the next table.

She still wouldn't move away, so I did what came naturally. With both arms in the air and hands out, I called her an "Ass." She didn't respond as she continued to knock the bottles off the table, something that could get her disqualified.

"Ass, Ass, Ass," I called her, emphasizing my gesturing hands with each "Ass." Without even turning her head to acknowledge me, she said loudly and harshly, "F...k you."

By then I was so angry it didn't matter that I'd missed my replacement drink. I was so fired up it felt like I had an infusion of glycogen, a burst of adrenaline as if dozens of hornets and coppers were after me.

At that point, somebody in the crowd told me I was in 20ᵗʰ place, four minutes behind the leaders. The next thing I knew, I was powering up the hills and began passing runners who were once in the lead pack. By Mile 20, I was in sixth place. In the final descent, I was inching closer and closer to the leaders – I could see them!

I ran out of road, finishing fifth. Amazingly, my time of 2:32:16 was a personal best, but a personal best wasn't what I was after that day. I was two minutes too slow, two minutes too late and two places from making the Olympic team.

I walked away calmly. But I was devastated.

If an athlete doesn't perform well or we don't meet the expectations of others, competition can be tough. Our humiliation is seen by everyone. I don't like being pitied so I hid my shame by showing very little emotional response. When the race director asked later how I was doing. I answered stoically, "I'm OK. I'm disappointed, but I'll get over it."

When he asked what happened out there, I told him about the woman who knocked over the bottles at the aid station. "She just kept running straight ahead, ignoring me," I said, still exasperated.

"That would be Jane Welzel," he said. "She was in a terrible car accident and can't turn her head easily. It's a miracle she was able to come back and qualify to run here."

Jane had fractured nine vertebrae three years earlier when she was in a car that rolled down an embankment. She spent two months in traction and six weeks in a body cast. She wasn't expecting anyone to come up behind her at the aid station since she was getting faster as the race went on and thought all of the faster runners were well ahead of her. She ran a great race, finishing 13th. I felt terrible, especially after all she'd been through, and there I was calling her an ass! I didn't know how to apologize. Instead, I sent her a Christmas card every year after that to let her know I was sorry.

Margaret Groos, Nancy Ditz and Cathy O'Brien finished the Trials 1-2-3 and were going to the Olympics. Poor Lisa Wiedenbach placed fourth, just as she did in 1984, once again missing the team by one place. She might have been the only runner that day more disappointed than me.

Steve and I came home Monday afternoon. I was sore, exhausted and feeling sorry for myself, but as soon as I walked in the door I could see I had some work to do. Jamie felt so badly for me that she was in tears, and hugged me tight. "I'm so sowwy, Mom. I know you must be sad."

Then Rachel, her head down, slowly came up to me. "Mom, is it my fault that you didn't make the Olympic team? Did I ruin your race? I've been really bad."

I had to cheer them up. "It would take a lot more than that. I ran a personal best. I didn't race badly, I just didn't run fast enough and there were four women faster than me yesterday."

"So you're happy?" Rachel asked.

I told her I was as happy as I could be. "There will be another Olympic Trials in four years. I'll be faster and much stronger with four more years of training under my belt. I'll be in my prime by then."

They seemed to feel better, but I didn't. I was heartbroken. Still, I knew I couldn't beat myself up over a race, especially in front of the girls.

I recovered so quickly from the marathon that I started racing again right away. Just two weeks later I impressed even myself, by winning the Rhody Run for the fifth time, running faster than I expected and beating several elite runners. A good win back in Port Townsend was just what I needed to regroup from my Olympic Trials failure.

From there I went directly to Boulder, Colorado for the Bolder Boulder 10K the following week. Rosa Mota, the Portuguese marathon phenomenon, took off from the gunshot on a hot and windy day. I chose to stay with a pack of women. Once we started running into a headwind just after two miles, the women took their positions in single file directly behind me while I was trying to catch Rosa, who was faltering. Nobody worked with me. They were all running a smart race, forcing me to do all the work into the headwind.

Because Rosa was running all by herself, the press truck had come back to our pack, where the "real" race was, and I was trying to get as close to it as possible in order to draft off of it. I was disappointed when it speeded up to give us more room. I wanted to yell to them, "You're fine, stay close!"

Whenever I slowed, the pack behind me slowed. I was almost walking in a few places, trying to get somebody to help out with the lead. We were running a slow, 7-minute mile pace at times. Rosa was getting away – there was no chance of catching her after all that. Since nobody was going to help, I was stuck in the lead unless I chose to walk, so I put my head down and pressed on.

Actually, I did get some accidental help. Glenn Latimer, a British coach/agent and commentator, was on the truck, reporting the race on live TV, and had no idea that his voice was traveling straight toward me in the wind. The camera was on me when he said, "Kim Jones looks flushed, her arms and legs are turning red." I looked down at my arms and legs to see. "She must be tiring, she's shortened her stride." I thought, *yes I am feeling a bit tired and my stride is short.* I lengthened my stride. Then he announced that Judy Chamberlin was moving up on my right shoulder. I turned to my right.

By then the viewers were figuring out that I could hear everything he said, but poor Glenn had no idea. As we ran up to the stadium I heard him say, "There are six women right behind Kim and it looks like they're going to make their move just before they enter the stadium to pass her in the final quarter mile!" The press truck took off to see Rosa finish, but I turned into the stadium well-prepared thanks to Glenn. Just as Judy and the others were ready to pass me, I started sprinting and out-kicked them to finish second.

It was a double prize money day – for finishing second overall and for being the first American. Later that afternoon, Steve went to an art studio and spent all of it on a painting by a Belgian artist, the husband of one of my competitors. I didn't like the painting at all and couldn't believe he would spend thousands of dollars on it. The artist knew I wasn't pleased and gave me a deal on a wonderful painting called "From The Inside Looking Out," selling it to me for just $500.

Steve had to have his painting shipped home. It was quite large, close to 5 feet x 5 feet. Rachel described it as "puke olive," a pale olive-green canvas with a drab yellowed newspaper painted as if taped onto it, with a plant in the middle of the newspaper, as if somebody was repotting a plant. The only real color was in the tiny half-naked women in different poses painted at each corner.

Steve was so proud of that painting. He hung it in the dining room where everyone could see it. I walked into the room while Rachel and Jamie were looking at it for the first time, their hands on their hips and heads turning from side to side. Rachel: "I don't see what Steve sees in this." Jamie: "What's so gweat about dis?" Steve showed it to everybody who walked into the house, and invited Don's wife, Bridgid, over to see it. An art teacher, Bridgid said a few things like "this is interesting, art is interpreted differently by everyone, it's not something I would choose but it has some interesting aspects."

I might not have minded Steve splurging on the painting if he would have discussed it with me first. Maybe I would have even liked it, at least a little.

My hectic spring wasn't quite over. Soon afterward, Nike wanted me to do a photo shoot for a two-page centerfold magazine ad to help kick off the Nike Zoom series. I traveled to Palm Desert to meet up with the photographer and his staff, along with the Nike promotional crew. The shoot was out in the desert at midday in 120 degrees to capture the waves of heat coming off the sand. Tantalizing mountains off in the distance formed the backdrop – pale purple with a hue of pink, against a pristine dark-blue sky. A jeep would drive across the same stretch of sand where I was running, kicking up dust to put the final touch on the photo.

We had planned for a four-day shoot. All I had to do was run in the desert using good form. However, I wasn't too pleased at the thought of being out in the heat for so long wearing heavy shoes and socks, running tights and a tank top, all in the new bright aqua and pink Nike colors for the upcoming year.

Once we were out there, surprisingly, it only took us a few hours. The photographer knew immediately that he had exactly what he wanted. Our job was done. Then we had 3½ days to enjoy fine cuisine and do some running in the desert. We went to batting cages, drove bumper cars, played miniature golf, and hung out by the pool enjoying Coronas and good company. That was a mini vacation – the time out from real life I desperately needed when things began to catch up to me – and I went home ready to tackle the rest of the year.

The advertisement turned out great. In the bottom right corner of the photo, I am running amid this beautiful scenery. Just behind me is a cloud of dust, as if I'm kicking it up with my Nike Zoom shoes. Everyone was pleased with the advertisement, and it turned up in *Cosmopolitan*, *Glamour*, *Shape* and many other magazines. It was a hit.

I ran a few more races that summer and then began to train for the Chicago Marathon. In late September, I ran the Philadelphia Half Marathon as a tune-up race, placing second in a personal best of 1:11 (5:25 pace). Later that evening, Race Director Tony DeSabato and Glenn Latimer invited me out to dinner along with some of their friends. We laughed about the Boulder press truck incident, and Glenn introduced me to Mark Plaatjes, one of the athletes he coached and represented. Mark is a sweet, caring South African runner with a gentle accent. At 5'7" and 117 pounds, the same size as me, he was smaller than most elite men at the time, yet talked fast and loudly in sharing his many strong opinions. That made him even more adorable, as far as I was concerned.

I admired Mark. He was born in South Africa under apartheid and unable to compete outside his country because of the sanctions at the time. He had recently sought political asylum in the United States, partly so that he could compete around the world but also because he didn't want his daughter to grow up in a country where she felt inferior.

That night, Glenn also introduced me to the "other" Steve Jones, the former marathon world-record holder from Wales. A kind and proper gentleman, Steve had the dry wit of the Brits that I found amusing. Steve started calling me "Mrs. Jones" and I began addressing him as "Mr. Jones."

I knew I had met some special people that weekend.

Two weeks later and just five days before the Chicago Marathon, I took the girls to our new dentist, Mark Walters, whose nickname was Moto. A dear friend of Steve's, Moto was like a brother to him, taking more time and effort than most dentists and having the patience to work with *our* family. Jamie was being fitted for yet another retainer. She was losing them left and right. Rachel was getting prep work done for braces again. The first time Moto started the process, Rachel pulled everything out with wire cutters and pliers before he could finish the job. She was back to face some serious music.

That visit was going to take a while, so I checked in the girls and went for a four-mile run from the office. As I strode along, feeling great from the rest leading up to the marathon, I smashed directly into a parking sign, right at face level.

The next thing I knew I was trying to get up off the ground, but my legs weren't functioning. I tried again and again until finally I grabbed hold of the pole that held up the sign and pulled myself up; only to have my Jell-O legs give out. I slid back down to the ground.

A woman drove up and asked if I was OK. I told her I didn't know. She helped me up.

"Can I drive you someplace?"

"I don't know. I don't know where to go."

I didn't even know my name; only that I'd left for a run from a dentist's office. After she helped me into her car, I started gathering my thoughts and reassembling small pieces of my memory.

"The dentist's office is by a Rosauers store and on a busy street, but I don't remember the dentist's name."

After a surprisingly short search, she found Moto's office and I thanked her after she helped me up the stairs. Moto called Steve to pick us up. Steve took me directly to Dr. Wigert, who checked me out and seemed quite concerned when he told me, "You have a concussion and need to be extremely careful for the next several days!"

My memory continued to improve as the day went on, but I had the worst headache of my life for the rest of that week – right up to the start of the Chicago Marathon.

Dr. Wigert had warned me that I shouldn't run the marathon if I was still dizzy or having problems with my coordination. I really wanted to go because Benji and Amie were planning to be there, and I felt obligated to run. I was set to receive my first appearance fee ever: $10,000 just for showing up at the starting line, taking part in the press conference and doing a few interviews.

Just before I left for Chicago, Staffan gave me a massage and he just couldn't help himself. "Why in the world would you give yourself a concussion just before a marathon?" Thank goodness for laughter. Once again it eased my disappointment and embarrassment.

Chicago Marathon ~ October, 1988

Once we arrived in Chicago, the special treatment and many welcome presents I received from the race organizers took my mind off of my stupid accident. It also helped that Benji was there for support, while Amie and Steve planned to run, making it seem more like a group effort.

When Benji noticed that my eyes were red and swollen, and after I complained, "My eyes are killing me in the sunlight with this damn ass concussion," he generously offered me his bright red Oakley sunglasses. They weren't the kind of Oakley sunglasses runners wear now. They were more like ski goggles that covered most of my face. That was before every athlete and their mother tried to get a contract with Oakley; except for Benji and Amie, runners didn't wear sunglasses back then. Everyone teased me, "So, you think you're a movie star now, do you?" I really needed those glasses, so I tried to ignore them. I almost forgot about the 26.2 miles ahead of me until the gun went off.

I started out feeling as if I was running in a fog and I finished in that same fog. It didn't seem like I was even in a race. I felt detached, confused, with no thought to what I was doing and no desire. I had no idea how I managed to finish fifth, in 2:32:03 – a personal best by 13 seconds.

There was an added bonus. A few months after Chicago, a photo ran in *Track & Field News* magazine of me wearing Benji's Oakley sunglasses. Later, there was an exceptional photo of me wearing a sleeker pair of sunglasses, half in the sun and half in the shadows, in *Runner's World*. The caption read, "Jones has it made in the shade."

Soon I signed a contract with Oakley that included a stipend and bonus money. Shortly afterward, they began to design smaller and sleeker sunglasses for runners. Oakley sent sunglasses to everyone in my family and in Steve's. Everyone was set, all 20 of us. Most of the runners who taunted me in Chicago started wearing sunglasses soon after. Some say I started the trend, but that's not true. Benji did.

My 1988 season was over after Chicago. It had been a long, disappointing and draining year. Despite managing to run two 2:32 marathons with some decent races in between, I knew I was fitter and better than my race results, and I was deeply disappointed for failing to make the Olympic team.

I was ready to take a mental break and looked forward to the holidays.

That fall Rachel rescued a Tabby cat from a box left on the corner. Burt was more of a tomcat, preferring to live outside and hunt. He even stood up to the raccoons that came around the yard. Shortly after his arrival, Punky appeared from the basement. I think she was envious as she peeked out from her dungeon to watch Burt in action. When she emerged, Punky decided it was time to go outside again and before long, just in time for the holidays, she became the beautiful lean cat we remembered.

By then Staffan had become a member of the family. He saw us in action through the good and the bad. I think we amused him. Sometimes we shocked him, I'm sure, but he kept coming back for more. He enjoyed having a family away from his home in Sweden.

We tried to be a normal functioning family, almost always having a proper dinner at the table with a full dinner setting. We even took turns saying the prayer before we ate. Rachel usually mumbled through her prayer, "Dear Jehovah God, thanks, in Jesus name Amen." Jamie was a little more into it, "Deaw Jehovah God please be with those who need youw help. In Jesus name Amen." If she was in a good mood after having a good day and liking herself, she would add, "Thank you for the twees and animals." At age 8 she was still talking like Elmer Fudd when it came to most of her R's, but her L's were getting better.

We weren't churchgoers, and I never studied the Jehovah's Witness religion again after divorcing Kelly, but the religion was embedded into all three of us. Rachel was raised a Jehovah's Witness and Mom convinced

Jamie that she was one, taking her to the Kingdom Hall when she visited and making sure she knew God's word. Poor Steve. If he didn't start his prayer off by saying "Dear Jehovah God," the girls would scold him right there.

Punky loved Staffan. He always sat on the floor when we were watching movies or visiting and relaxing, and Punky delighted in sitting on his lap for the extra attention he gave her. Jamie and Rachel adored him, as well, and enjoyed his attention as much as Punky did. They were always trying to show off for him, overdoing it once in awhile. Sometimes a fight broke out. They became out of control just for Staffan.

Staffan often spent holidays with us, and that year we had a nice Thanksgiving together until the end of the day turned a bit dramatic. I couldn't get enough to eat, so I ate. And ate. I continued to eat until I was rolling on the floor in agony. "I need to go to the hospital. I'm going to pop!"

At first everyone laughed, but then I started crying and my stomach was distended beyond belief. I told Steve, "I mean it. I'm going to pop just like Blondie did!" He took me to the minor emergency room.

"Why do you do that?" asked Steve, more concerned than exasperated, since that wasn't the first time.

"I just can't help myself," I told him. "After living on food rations, or no food at all early in life, I feel the need to eat everything in front of me, and now I have a hard time walking away from the dinner table. There's all this food in front of me, and I wonder, what if there isn't any tomorrow?"

"This explains a lot," he said, chuckling. "You're not like most elite female marathoners, some who eat very little and a few who don't eat at all."

"I know, I eat plenty, and I especially need to eat things I'm not supposed to, when I'm not supposed to." Then I asked in alarm, "Do you think I have an eating disorder?"

He smiled, "No, you just need to learn to back off."

Later that night the girls asked, "Who is Blondie? How did she pop?" I told them the story while we were lying in my bed together. Rachel said that was her favorite story so far. "You awe a lot like Blondie, Mom," said Jamie.

One of Steve's favorite Christmas activities was to go out with his brother Evan's family to cut down a Christmas tree. Steve wanted the girls to enjoy the adventure, too, so he took them along, deep into the woods. Rachel didn't like that activity very much. "Why can't we just buy a Christmas tree like most human beings?" Jamie laughed. Steve didn't think it was funny. The poor guy was trying so hard to win Rachel and Jamie over with wholesome, family-oriented endeavors.

Just after they brought the tree home and set it up, Punky and I were in the kitchen when we heard the girls screaming. I rushed into the living room, with Punky in tow, to find them standing on the sofa. A small mouse had come running out from the Christmas tree and was darting all around the living room. I jumped up with them.

Punky took charge. She chased the mouse around and then stepped on its tail, batted it around with her other paw, let it go for a while and then did it all again as she played it to death. Staffan walked in during all of the commotion and helped us cheer Punky on. She finally grabbed it with her mouth and headed to the door, where Rachel let her out. She ate it!

After dinner that night we didn't want Punky near us, not even her buddy Staffan. She was strutting around so proud of accomplishing such an important task, and didn't understand ... we didn't want mouse germs!

It was a sad Christmas for Jamie because Rachel decided to enlighten her regarding Santa Claus, not only telling her he doesn't exist but proving to her that Steve and I had been deceiving her. On Christmas Eve, they sat hiding on the stairway, peeking through the wooden lattice to watch us put their presents under the tree, then eat the cookies and drink the milk that Jamie had left out for Santa.

Jamie was destroyed. That was the first time I was really disappointed in Rachel, and I told her so. "Mom, I was just trying to educate her."

I gave her a harsh look. "Hmmm," then I walked away. Everyone knew that if they got "Hmmm" or I became quiet, they were in trouble.

We spent several holidays with the Jones family, but I enjoyed spending them at home. There was never a dull moment.

Chapter 14

As with all sports, it takes years of practice to reach one's potential as a runner. The reason I overcame my disappointment at not making the Olympic team, as well as the World Championships fiasco the year before, was because I had hope: the hope of improving over time as I continued to develop as an athlete from consistent training and by gaining experience, whether good or bad. Learning from failure and how to overcome that failure was the only way to succeed in the future. I was certainly learning a good lesson in failure.

I told Benji that I wanted to run faster than 2:32 in the marathon in 1989. "I'm slowly improving," I told him, "but only seconds at a time. Running 2:32 isn't hard, I just don't have the strength to hold a faster pace for 26.2 miles."

"You have plenty of speed. So now we need to work on strength and stamina," Benji agreed. "That would mean more mileage. Do you think you can handle that?"

Benji knew that I thrived on my recovery days, and needed them to take care of everything else in my life and spend more time with the girls. I suggested adding to my second runs on the afternoons of my hard days, to keep my easy days the way they were. "I could run 8 miles in the evenings three days a week instead of the 5 miles I'm running now," I said. Again he agreed, and said we should try it.

"Let's see how you do through December, then run the Houston Marathon in mid-January off of strength only – no speed sessions, just mileage. Amie and I will run, too."

Having Benji and Amie there for their support and camaraderie sounded reassuring. Steve decided to run, as well. He was slowing down a little and needed a goal to keep him training and running more consistently. He was putting on a little belly after a year of being wined and dined at the races and enjoying home cooked meals.

"Houston will be a practice marathon for Boston in April," Benji said. We had a plan.

I'd always enjoyed the challenge of an extremely hard/extremely easy training schedule, and I thrived on it both mentally and physically. Nevertheless, it was still tough, and on some days seemed almost impossible. On the hard days, after running 13-26 miles on rolling hills in the mornings, I had to eat a lot to keep up my caloric intake, take an hour's nap to recover, and then get right back out there for 8 more miles. There were days after waking up from my nap when I *really* wanted to stay there and rest.

That was when I felt my worst. But I stuck with it, sometimes almost crawling through the second runs. My body was tired, even throbbing, from all of those miles in that one day. Even so, I could tell that the discomfort was a good kind of hurt, just sore and achy muscles. They were adapting to hard work by breaking down just enough to handle the stress before repairing from rest, food and massage.

There's a fine line between breaking down to gain strength and breaking down with injury, yet Benji knew what I could take and never pushed it over that line. I was tougher and more resilient than most women. Many of my competitors experienced stress fractures from so much pounding, whereas my bones were so strong that I never experienced skeletal pain or a fracture. My crooked toe was an issue, as always, but I figured out that if I wore new shoes every 120 miles they would have enough cushioning for my toe to sink in. After that, the foam insoles would compact and become too hard. I sure went through a lot of Nikes, a pair every two weeks or less. It was a good thing that Nike sent me all those free shoes.

By the time Houston rolled around, I was averaging 90-100 miles a week. That was low for most marathoners, but high for me. And I did it the hard way, with 75-80 miles covered in just three days of each week.

Houston Marathon ~ January, 1989

I was usually good about pre-race jitters. I had confidence in my ability and didn't get all worked up about my races. But that time was different. I didn't have those special workouts and practice races to prove to myself that I was ready to go. I was stronger than I had ever been, but that was the extent of it. I knew I wasn't "race ready."

The night before the marathon, while Steve and I were watching an HBO movie in Benji and Amie's room, I couldn't help myself and said, "I really hope I can run under 2:40." They all laughed at me.

"I'm serious."

They laughed harder, and Benji wasn't one to laugh easily. "I'd be surprised if you don't run under 2:35," he said.

That caused my anxiety level to soar. I honestly didn't think I could run faster than 6-minute pace after only running slow, easy mileage for months, with no speed sessions to wake up my fast-twitch muscle fibers.

Benji said impatiently, "Just get out there and run as if it were a hard training run with no pressure."

I woke up to a perfect morning to run a marathon, foggy and cool. It was going to be so nice to run on pavement after leaving our Spokane winter wonderland. I hadn't seen bare pavement in weeks. After my talk with Benji, I felt more relaxed. It was just a hard 26-mile training run ahead of me, not a race.

If I was trying to trick myself, it worked. A British runner, Veronique Marot, took off from the beginning and won, while I just loped along with ease to place second. I couldn't run any faster, though I felt good and strong all the way. I finished second in yet another 2:32, but I was thrilled. I ran 2:32 off of base work and slow mileage, with no speed training at all, and it seemed effortless. That was a big indicator of things to come. I knew I would run well in Boston that spring. If all went well, I would run under 2:30. Only a few American women had achieved that.

I went home cheerful, and eager for the 1989 race season. Jamie asked, "Why awe you so happy? You wewe second and wan a 2:32 again." Even so, after that marathon I had renewed energy and hope. I was ready to do what was needed for a stellar racing season, and I knew how to accomplish it.

Just like my "Montana Chug Upside Down" or becoming the best pinochle player in our family, I practiced my workouts and training skills to perfection, or as close to it as possible. I wanted to be ready for my first Boston Marathon. I really wanted to "shoot the moon," as in pinochle, and run a sub 2:30. That was my goal, a goal I thought about every day, especially during those 8-mile second runs in the cold, dark, wintry nights when I walked out the door saying, "This had better be worth it."

Then I would get out there and thoroughly enjoy the run, even on legs that were tired and beat up from my earlier workout. I powered through my workouts and didn't miss a beat to the drummer. I moved to a higher level that winter.

Other than working out, joining the girls for their functions and tending to things at home, I didn't have the time or energy for what most would consider a normal life during that intense training and racing period. But I needed to balance my time with Steve.

At least once a week I joined Steve for a leisurely lunch at our favorite place, the Thai Café around the corner from the Paulsen Center. On our "date," on an easy day while the girls were in school, I had the chance to relax and enjoy Steve's wit and dry humor – not to mention his striking good looks in a suit and tie. Eventually, we became good friends with the owner, a sweet and kind man who was my age and loved visiting with us. He told us a lot about Thailand, and even offered to go with us and show us around if we ever wanted to visit. We called him Val for short because nobody could pronounce his Thai name. Val served the best Thai food I ever had.

The girls loved that place, so we had dinner there often. Val made us special dishes with extra treats and made sure we ate well. It pleased him to see Americans with our healthy appetites. "Val, you're the only person I see these days outside my small running circle," I told him. After that, he invited us to all of his special family gatherings.

On Thursdays, Steve would often order and pick up from Val's on his way home from the office. Thursday was my long mileage day of 30-35 miles and the only day I did nothing but train and pamper myself. That didn't always happen, but that was the plan anyway. There were some weeks when I ate more of Val's cooking than my own.

After becoming a partner in his law firm, Steve spent a lot of time in his office at the Paulsen Center. As busy as he was there, he was also in charge of all our finances and even worked as my agent, negotiating deals with race directors, setting up my travel arrangements and working on my contracts with Nike and Oakley and other sponsors. A few times a year we both met with John Woodhead about our IRAs and my former TAC TRUST investments – TAC TRUSTS themselves were a thing of the past now that prize money was accepted openly – even then I was pretty much in the dark about our finances. It probably wasn't a wise decision, but it allowed me to focus on training, racing and the girls.

I ran two races in Florida in the early spring, leaving Steve and the girls at home. First came the Jacksonville River Run 15K, where I ran a personal best. Afterward, Rob de Castella and I stayed in Gainesville with Keith Brantly before running the Red Lobster 10K in Orlando the following week. We had a great time running, taking turns cooking or going out for a few meals. Rob, the great Australian distance runner, was bigger than most marathoners and had to keep his weight down during racing season so he was watching his diet. He was astonished at the amount of food I put away. I was eating even more after my training mileage was increased to 90-100 miles a week, but it really wasn't that much considering my energy output. I told Rob that he was restricting too many calories from his diet, and possibly slowing down his metabolism in the process. "This may be why you have a weight problem during racing season," I told him.

"Kim eats more than I do," he told everyone when we arrived in Orlando.

For the second week in a row I ran a personal best, when I brought my 10K down to 32:21 (5:13 pace). Mary Level-Menton competed there as well, steadily improving after Benji started coaching her earlier that year. She was still my little follower. We had a good time after the race while joining a group of runners for a few beers at the pool and hot tub. A *Running Times* magazine photographer managed to sneak in a good photo of Keith, who won the race, lounging in the hot tub with all of us women in our bikinis. That boosted Keith's reputation. A good looking Floridian, green-eyed and blond, Keith was considered a ladies man and boy, could he put on the charm, which led to constant teasing from his peers, especially when the photo turned up in the magazine the following month.

It seemed that after a big race we could always count on somebody to do something crazy or stupid, probably to let off steam after the stress of the race and the pressure leading up to it. That time, John Tuttle, who ran for the U.S. in the 1984 Olympic marathon, had finished one too many beers and started eating his glass!

"Why in the world would you do that?" I asked in horror.

"Sweetheart, somebody's gotta liven this place up," he said with a smirk.

Later, after a few idiots encouraged him, he ate a light bulb.

After running a hard race and then enjoying the pool and hot tub, it wasn't easy going out for my 8-mile second run. I persuaded a few runners to join me, but it was 89 degrees and humid, and having had a beer in the hot tub didn't help. They turned back after only a few miles. "How can you do that?" Keith asked, surprised.

I arrived home on a beautiful early spring afternoon in Spokane and was walking in from the garage when I looked up to see feet dangling way up on the third-level roof of the house. I backed up to get a good look. There sat Rachel smoking with Jamie right next to her, holding Punky with one hand and fanning the smoke away from her face with the other. They were talking and laughing, and getting along so well. Even Punky seemed to be enjoying it. I didn't want to spoil it, but called up to them anyway, "How's the view from way up there?" They both went scurrying through the window back into Rachel's bedroom. I had to smile.

I went inside and waited for the girls to gather enough courage to come and talk to me, wondering what excuse they would come up with *this* time. Finally, a half hour later, they slowly came walking into my bedroom as I unpacked.

"Are we in twouble?" asked Jamie, after they hugged me and told me how much they missed me. "We had a welaxing visit outside togethew." Rachel chimed in, "Sitting out on the roof is our time to get away from it all and relax with Punky, just like you did with Blondie."

"Nice try. Even if that were true, I wasn't breaking the rules and puffing away on a cigarette when I was relaxing with Blondie."

I had just come home from a long trip and really didn't want to punish them. Instead, I sat them down and talked about all of the destructive things that smoking cigarettes can cause, like early aging and cancer. It was Jamie who taught Rachel the most valuable lesson of all by posting "before" and "after" photos all over the house of smokers aging over a ten-year time span. That made Rachel angry and she tore them down, but she wasn't caught smoking as much after that.

In late March, I was nervous about the Boston Marathon and needed to have a good solid race to prove I was ready. I always did a specific workout and ran a race a few weeks before a marathon, for feedback on what I was capable of and, hopefully, to boost my confidence.

My pre-marathon workout: 8 x ½-mile repeats in 2:30-35 (5 to 5:10 pace) followed by 4 x ¼-mile repeats in 70 seconds or faster (4:40 pace), with a ¼-mile jog between efforts to regroup. I did that with ease six days before running the Nike Cherry Blossom 10 Mile race in Washington, D.C. I took off with the leader, Anne Audain, but she ran just under 5-minute pace for the first mile and that was way too fast for my marathon trained legs. I slowed down to 5:23 pace and finished third, running 53:41. It was yet another personal best. I was ready.

Boston Marathon ~ April, 1989

I was thrilled about running Boston, and I was treated extremely well by the Boston Athletic Association. Steve and I were put up at the Copley Plaza, where there was a hospitality room filled with snacks, drinks and anything else we might need.

During the days leading up to the marathon, Steve made plans with our friends, giving me the quiet time I needed before my big race. Saturday morning, I woke up in a darkened room to find Steve dressed for a run with one shoe on, in search of his second shoe. As I lay in bed and watched him, I thought about what a kind and caring person he was, though I wished he could open up and talk about his passions and feelings. He was extremely knowledgeable, some people even considered him a genius. I had learned so much from him, but I wanted to learn more about him. Then he looked under the bed again. *Maybe he isn't quite a genius. A genius wouldn't look in the same place twice for a missing shoe.*

"Why don't you open the drapes and let some light in?" I asked. "That way you can see your shoe peeking out from under that newspaper."

He smiled. "Did I wake you?"

"No, I've been awake for a while."

"I'm going for a run with Keith and Jeff. Then I plan to go to the marathon technical meeting and spend the rest of the day at the expo. Do you need anything while I'm out?" he asked as he put on his shoe.

"No, I'll order room service and do some reading. Maybe I can find a good movie on HBO or one of my silly TV shows."

"There's an article in the paper about the women's race, listing the favorites to win. They weren't very kind to you."

"Hmmm. Then I had better not read it, eh."

"You'll show them on Monday. I have no doubt about that," he said as he kissed my forehead.

Steve was heading for the door when he advised, "Make sure you eat enough."

"There's no need to worry about that," I replied.

He turned around and smiled. "I'll bring you some bagels with cream cheese, just in case."

For the next two days, I carbo-loaded, went for short runs, did a few press conferences, and then waited for Steve to return with my friends and take me out for dinner.

Little did they know, alone in my room, I went way above the carbo-loading limit!

The marathon started at noon on Monday, the Patriots Day holiday in Massachusetts. I woke up and topped off the loading process with a full breakfast of oatmeal with maple syrup and milk, a bagel with cream cheese, a banana, and a pot of coffee with cream and maple syrup. That breakfast was going to have to last me awhile. I sipped on some Gatorade while being bussed out to the start in Hopkinton, 26.2 miles away, with the other elite athletes.

From the bus, we were led into a special building to rest up before being herded out to the starting line. Several minutes before the gun, I watched all of the skinny elite runners (some beyond skinny) zipping along doing strides. I panicked. I felt like a lump of lard. Not only had I overdone the carbo-loading and hydrating, I also had the five pounds of water retention I get from PMS. I looked down at my pudgy legs.

What the hell? I can't run a marathon like this!

When the gun went off, I felt like a big turkey trying to take off with dozens of light and lean sparrows fluttering around me. The sparrows were soon well ahead of me as I tried to lug my turkey body down the road. I fell behind right away. *Damn, I shouldn't have eaten so much.* I felt like Blondie looked after I fed her too much rabbit grain.

Just before the halfway point, I approached Wellesley College. I knew the stories about the crowd support there, how the cheering by hundreds of women lining the road was so exhilarating for the runners. But I was finally getting the chance to experience it myself. There was a low rumble in the distance, growing louder and louder until the roar grew deafening as I closed in.

Those women woke me up. No, they jolted me into high gear. I felt a rush of adrenaline as I ran by, and my ears wouldn't stop ringing. *Now I know why everyone talks about this cheering squad.* The spectacular roar faded back to a rumble as I ran on.

I started passing a few runners, going through the half-marathon mark in 1:14:15. That's not bad, but I was still struggling with my carbohydrate overload and knew that the course had been mostly downhill for those first 13 miles so I didn't get too excited. Besides, I was beginning to feel hot from the direct sun.

By the time I made it through the Newton Hills, from 16 to 21 miles, and over the famous Heartbreak Hill, I started feeling better – losing the water I'd retained and burning off all those stored carbohydrates. In the final 5 miles, I felt like one of those light sparrows.

Boston Marathon spectators aren't the normal crowd. Besides the women of Wellesley, there are the hardcore Red Sox fans. The Sox play a morning game at home every year on Patriots Day, and with Fenway Park near Mile 25 it makes for an unusual mix of people lining the street. Some were puffing on cigars as they cheered, and surprisingly I found the faint smell nostalgic, even comforting. Cigars or not, running fans in Boston are knowledgeable, well informed about the competitors and the sport. They don't urge you on gently, they order you: "Get going! You have to do it!"

Thanks partly to their firm encouragement and partly to my finally burning off all the turkey fat, I ran effortlessly, feeling stronger as I went along. With each woman I passed, I felt a surge of energy. Between 15 and 19 miles I moved up from seventh to fifth place, and by 22 miles I was in third.

Ingrid Kristiansen, the world-record holder, was well ahead of everyone. No chance of catching her. I was getting closer and closer to second place in the final straightaway on Boylston Street with less than a half mile to go. Despite trying with all my might, I could never quite catch the New Zealander, Marguerite Buist, in front of me.

As I hit the finish line in third place, the clock read 2:29:34!

I was overjoyed. A sub 2:30 marathon was huge ... my dream, and I had reached it! Even though I took great pride in my accomplishment, I walked away quietly. That wasn't quite "shooting the moon."

One thing I had learned was that carbo-loading really works. Perhaps I developed into an excellent carbo-loader while growing up poor and hungry, becoming depleted when there was little or no food and then eating like crazy when the opportunity presented itself. I remembered Grandma Helen's Swedish coffee rolls, and how I ate as many as I could to last me awhile, just in case.

I went back to Spokane, ready to continue my heavy-duty training plan. My performance in Boston made me the fastest American so far that year, which drove me to bigger dreams, giving me more hope and ambition, and the desire to work even harder. I recovered from the marathon quickly, springing back like a tough weed, and was right back to racing in no time.

Three weeks after Boston, Steve and I took the girls with us to the Nike Women's 8K in Washington, D.C. The day before the race, Nike sponsored a panel on balancing family and a running career, featuring my family answering questions from the audience after I gave a 10-minute talk. By then I was considered one of the top marathoners in the world and I was being asked to attend more press conferences and give talks, which I hated as much as I did when I was a child. Giving those talks in front of the Jehovah's Witness congregation over the years came in surprisingly handy – I did well after all of that practice.

Rachel sat there trying to avoid any attention, answering "yes," "no," or "maybe." Sometimes she just shrugged her shoulders while making everyone smile, including me. Jamie, however, was quite the comedian. She started warming up to the crowd of several hundred people, trying to be cool and getting into answering the questions in her goofy way while showing off for Rachel. When a woman from the audience asked, "What do you want to be when you grow up?" Jamie was handed the microphone and replied without hesitation, "I want to be a wunnew when I gwow up. Then I won't have to go to wowk." Everyone started laughing. The moderator asked, "So your mom doesn't work?" Jamie replied, "No, she wuns."

After the girls and I ran the Nike Women's 8k the next day, they were rewarded for all of their hard work with some sightseeing adventures. Even Rachel seemed to get into the tourist scene. We met the governor of Washington State and went to the White House, although our favorite part of the trip was sitting on the hotel bed together, eating pizza and snacks while watching pay-per-view movies, talking and laughing. Rachel confided, "I really didn't like running the race. It was hard."

Jamie informed her, "You would if you quit smoking and twained once in a while."

The next day, Steve and the girls headed back to Spokane while I stayed to do a photo shoot for Nike. It was a long and tiring week. The many shoots included one where I had to run up and down the steps of the Lincoln Memorial until the photographers were satisfied they had the perfect shot. That was quite challenging just a few weeks after running the hilly Boston Marathon and then an all-out 8k race the day before.

Afterward, the whole crew of us flew to Boston, where we met up with Bob Kempainen, Judi St. Hilaire, Richard Nerurkar and Terry Brahm, some of the other top Nike athletes, for another series of photo shoots. They wanted us to run as a group, which was a challenge since all five of us had to look perfect at the same time. There was one shot where the photographer wanted all of us running fast, with our feet off the ground all at the same moment. "Oh, and try to kick up some dust while you're running!" I actually managed to kick up the dust, and it even ended up in the advertisement.

Richard, Terry, me, Bob and Judi ~ *Courtesy of Nike*

Once we finished shooting all day, we enjoyed our free time with great food, drink and company in the evenings. Several times, we overdid it on all three. My spring marathon was behind me so I didn't worry about the consequences – until I had to fly from Boston to Seattle, and then drive directly to Port Townsend to be there in time for the Rhody Run. Then I was a bit concerned.

When I finally arrived at my parents' house, I attempted a short run to loosen up from the long travel day and reckless behavior throughout the week. My legs felt like rubber. Jamie would have called it "jogging at Grandma pace."

I went to the officers' house, turned hotel, at Fort Worden that night to find all of the Joneses there, settled in and eating dinner – 15 of them, plus Jamie. Most of the adults planned to run the next day. It was a busy sight to see and a lot of commotion. There was Steve right in the middle of it, smiling and happy to see me. I knew I needed to carry on conversation, and I did enjoy their company, but it was hard giving my energy away. I realized that I desperately needed to stay calm for my race the next day, especially after my alarming rubber-legs run earlier.

Once I finished visiting a while, answering their questions – "How fast can you run tomorrow? Who is your main competition? Can you win? What did you do in Washington and Boston? Where did you go, anyplace exciting?" – I went to our room and took a nice hot bubble bath. Jamie came in and sat on the toilet to have her own private visit with me. "You need youw space, Mom. How are you going to win if you can't welax?"

I looked at Jamie. "I have no idea."

After tossing and turning all night with worry, I woke up late to the sound of all the kids running through the hallways and up and down the stairways, overly excited for the race. Not that I expected them to keep quiet. It was supposed to be fun. I was just glad the race didn't start until 11 a.m., giving me more time to get focused and into a race mindset. Steve knew I needed some quiet time and was kind enough to bring my coffee up to our room. By that time he knew that it had to be perfect – three large cups of freshly ground dark roast, with cream and pure maple syrup. "I know this is hard on you," he said softly. "This has been a crazy year. So many races, photo shoots and appearances, all while adjusting to a new family. Things will settle down soon."

"I hope so," I replied, and laughingly added, "Nike certainly knew to feature our family on that panel last weekend, balancing family and a running career."

In the hours before the start, I knew I wasn't ready to race, and several elite women showed up who could easily beat me in my post-marathon and post-fun condition.

My warm up felt terrible so I cut it short, and then had to make small talk as I was putting on my racing shoes. Everyone meant well and didn't realize I needed to focus, especially that year. I ran up to say hello to my family down the street just before the start. They were all there eager to see me win for the sixth time in a row. *Hmmm. It was time to face some music.*

I took off fast, challenged by two women in the first three miles, and then put it into another gear. I ran away from them, feeling free and invigorated. *This isn't possible.* I went with it and loved every step of the way. My legs were moving smoothly, my body was in sync and I felt no fatigue. Even my crooked toe wasn't bothering me. *How could this be?*

I won the race in 41:31, a course record, running a 5:30 pace despite the extreme hills. I was stunned, and then relief rushed over me. Of course, I gave my family a "thumbs up" as I ran by in the final straightaway, as if it was a cinch. *Right!* They had no idea how much worry I went through for that race.

It's not easy to race, even for an elite athlete. Nerves cause anxiety levels to soar and use up all the adrenaline needed to carry us through our many races throughout the year. Racing is a job and we had to find a way to keep things under control.

The only time I allowed myself to get worked up for a race, thinking constantly about strategy and the "what ifs," was before a marathon or the Rhody Run. The marathon was my event, the #1 focus of my career. I usually ran only two a year. On the one hand, that gave me ample time to recover, refocus, and go for it 100 percent every six months without stressing my adrenal glands. If you overwork them, a kind of fatigue sets in that can be detrimental to your career and your health. On the other hand, running only two marathons a year made each one extremely important, which can cause anxiety. It's a delicate balancing act.

Then there's the Rhody Run. I couldn't imagine losing it. It was the race that I needed to win, whether or not I was rested and regardless of who else was in the race. I never set myself up for a good race there, it just happened. It was truly a miracle.

That year, I'd just run the Boston Marathon and broke 2:30 for the first time, and I still ran a course record in the Rhody Run. A year earlier I ran the Olympic Trials only two weeks before yet still won, beating women I shouldn't have. It takes most drug-free athletes months to recover from a marathon and much longer to regroup and race well again. I could do all of that in two weeks, if the race was in Port Townsend.

But then, Port Townsend is a magical place. While racing the Rhody Run, I ran past all the landmarks of my early life.

Fort Worden is the spot where I return again and again for strength. It was where I spent most of my childhood running on the beach, playing in the bunkers, having wonderful adventures with my siblings and friends. It was my savior, a place to heal, overcome and reflect, a place to be alone and regroup, to endure whatever happened in my unstable young life, to grieve and move on from the tragedies I have seen as an adult. On Fort Worden beach, I knew everything was going to be OK. My dad fishes there almost every day. Charlie and Stanley are there, a part of everything I do. I feel their spirits with me as I run in the Rhody Run.

Their ashes are scattered in the water near the lighthouse, alive in that water where I once showed off and played. I will join them some day in that wonderful place.

That afternoon we had our usual post-race barbecue at Mom and Dad's, with my family and the Joneses. Poor Dad was busy barbecuing and being a great host while Mom cooked in the early morning, went to the race, then returned to finish preparing her feast before everyone else arrived. They weren't used to hosting so many people, and it was tiring for them, but the Joneses were grateful as they enjoyed their meal on the deck while watching the kids play croquet and badminton in the backyard. There were kids running everywhere.

I noticed little Chaz, who was barely 3 and looking even more like my brother, watching everyone with that look he gets in those bright blue eyes when he's about to do something "special." He still enjoyed shocking people, and knew how to wait for the perfect opportunity to get the job done. He figured out that the Joneses were very proper. While everyone was within earshot, Chaz yelled at a chipmunk on the telephone wire just above the deck.

"Get down here you goddamn asshole chipmunk!"

"Ohhhh," gasped several of the Joneses. They looked at Chaz as if he were a terrible little creature. Rachel, who was playing badminton with Jamie, gave a big belly laugh. I held mine back, but it wasn't easy.

Dad turned his back to us and faced the barbecue. Mom tried to smooth things over by saying in an overly sweet voice, "Oh Chaz, that's not a very nice thing to say." Of the Joneses, only Harlan smiled and let out a small little chuckle.

"I mean it you little f...ing asshole chipmunk, get down here right now!" Chaz yelled, pointing to the ground.

Dad and I ran into the kitchen with Bradley – from whom Chaz had learned that language – and the three of us laughed so hard we had tears streaming from our eyes. The Joneses were horrified. Everyone stared at Chaz, which of course was just what he wanted. Then he ran off, so proud of himself. I'm sure Steve's family thought we were barbaric, but we were just a normal family whose kids had strong personalities. Very strong at times.

⁓

Because I spent so much time training and then traveling to races, we didn't go on many traditional family vacations. Instead, Steve and I took the girls to several races, where the three of them had a grand time while I rested up. I enjoyed taking them along, although it could be so much work that sometimes I completely forgot about my race until the alarm went off, reminding me I had a job to do in a few hours.

We decided to take Mom, Jamie and Rachel to Portland, Oregon, for the Cascade Run Off 15K in late June. Mom and the girls stayed in an adjoining room. They loved getting together and having Mom there to help me out seemed like the perfect plan.

After checking into the hotel I went down to the lobby and ran into Jon Sinclair; his coach, John Davies; Anne Audain; and Mr. Steve Jones. We were all catching up when the bellman came walking in with Rachel. She had a scowl on her face and boy, was she mad. But not as mad as the bellman.

"Is this your daughter? She was outside the front doors to the lobby, smoking. I told her once to stop, that she's too young to be smoking. I leave only to come back and find her *again* smoking like a chimney! This is not good for the hotel or her."

He left, and everyone was quiet. First I wondered what they thought of my 14-year-old daughter smoking. Then I wondered what in the world Rachel was thinking. I took her upstairs. "You need to stop that. This is way out of control, Rachel."

As always, she agreed and apologized. Then she asked if she and Jamie could go down to the pool and relax for a while with Mom. I didn't want to punish her; we had just started our weekend together. So off they went. Not long after that I was looking out the window a few floors above the pool and couldn't believe what I saw. With Mom asleep in her lounge chair on one side of the pool, there were Rachel and Jamie lounging side by side on the other, Rachel smoking away and Jamie holding the book she was reading in one hand and fanning the smoke away with the other. What a pair.

When they came up later I asked Rachel, "How was the smoke?"

Her eyes widened and she said, "Sorry, Mom." I said, "Hmmm." Jamie was ready to say something clever about how they were relaxing together but I cut her short. Things were uncomfortably quiet for everyone, so I told Jamie and Rachel to start unpacking while I lay on their bed visiting with Mom. Jamie started taking out all of her stuffed animals. First she pulled out Chablis, then Rose, Cabernet, Chardonnay, Shiraz and Blush.

"Jamie, where are the clothes we packed?"

She reached inside and pulled out Zinfandel. "I took them out, othewwise I wouldn't have woom for Zin."

"Where's your toothbrush and underwear?"

"Oh Bwothew, I don't need a toothbwush for just thwee days. And when my undewwear get dirty I'll just tuwn them inside out." Her hands went in the air, "It's only thwee days, Mom."

Rachel let out the biggest belly laugh I'd ever heard. Mom and I had to join in. I'm not sure what Steve would have thought of that, although I have a pretty good idea. It was a good thing he was out enjoying the sights in downtown Portland that afternoon.

The next morning, I marched Jamie the few blocks down to Nordstrom and bought her new underwear and an outfit. Of course, Rachel didn't think that was fair. "Why should I be punished for packing like I was supposed to?" So I bought Rachel a new outfit, too, and then thought ... *what the hell, let's shop.* We all walked back to the hotel loaded down with shopping bags and many choices of things to wear that weekend and beyond.

When we came back to our rooms, Jamie's blanket was missing. She ran all around, crying and searching frantically for the rag she called a blanket. Our room had been cleaned while we were shopping. I wondered aloud, "Maybe the maid threw it out?" Rachel chimed in, "Yeah, Jamie, it was like a big fuzz ball."

I looked at Rachel and she looked at me. *Hmmm.* I had a feeling Rachel knew more about Jamie's missing blanket than she was letting on. After Jamie had a long crying fit, I heard Rachel tell her, "It's a good thing that disgusting blanket is gone. You were way too old for it and the kids at school were making fun of you."

That night, as we were all crawling into bed, I could finally focus on my race the next morning.

Not quite. Jamie came running over to my room, crying again. I took her back to her room and tried to comfort her, telling her about my blanket burning in the fire when I was only 7 years old, how I had nothing left, only my family to comfort me. That seemed to help. Then Rachel said, "Tell us another story to make Jamie feel even better." I told them about my Baby Doll with the unpleasant odor being thrown out during our move from Enumclaw to Port Townsend, leaving me with nothing to cuddle but a Midge doll with a pixie cut.

"You have all of these special stuffed animals with you. You should be happy that you have so many to pick from." Jamie agreed, saying, "I feel bettew," and crawled back into bed after gathering all of her stuffed animals around her.

An hour later, Jamie was back in my room. "What is it, Jamie?" I asked impatiently. "You know there's nothing we can do about your blanket!"

"It's not my bwanket," she cried. "I left my retainew at the westauwant. I lost it again."

I couldn't believe it. *This is the third time in just a few months. Now we have to go back to Moto again.* I said calmly, "Let's get some sleep. Don't worry about it now; you've had a tough day."

Needless to say, I wasn't too focused on the race the next day. It wasn't a total disaster however. I managed to place in the top 10, running 5:20 pace in a 15K. Not bad, considering.

The best thing that happened over the weekend was the maid – or was it Rachel – throwing out Jamie's blanket. Whoever it was did her a big favor. She forgot about it soon enough, and then quit sucking her thumb in public shortly after that.

Steve and I were happily married and I knew he loved me, and I adored and respected him for being a wonderful husband and a great father to the girls. But, as with every marriage, everything wasn't perfect, although we both knew what we were getting into.

Steve liked to look at women and let that look turn into a long gaze. Women loved it. I appreciated it when he looked at me that way, too, in the beginning of our relationship. Not everyone saw it that way. Staffan would laugh and say, "Steve's at it again" when we were all out to dinner or at a party together. Rachel would say, "Why does he do that? It's embarrassing." Of course Jamie had to chime in. "Oh Bwothew, Steve." I learned to smile and enjoy the show, knowing there was nothing behind it. But as Rachel said, it was embarrassing, and also demeaning. I put up my protective barrier early on, which helped me adjust to that behavior, but after a few years of marriage it was getting old.

Steve was being far too attentive to a talented regional runner named Orrine. She had made several comments about Steve being attracted to her and she became obsessed with him. She followed us everywhere and showed up at the Rhody Run, along with many other races that year.

After she had followed our family to another race that summer, and to a restaurant afterward, I was alarmed and told Steve as we were getting out of the car, "I'm concerned about Orrine. There's something terribly wrong with her. She looks as though she's going to do something crazy."

Steve smiled. "She's harmless."

Rachel piped in, "She's shadowing us, Steve. It's creepy."

"I think she's demonized," said Jamie as Steve walked away chuckling. He turned around and told all three of us, "You girls have quite the imaginations. There's no need to be worried about Orrine."

However, Steve was quite concerned when Orrine became a suspect in the murder of her husband. Pete, who eerily resembled Steve, got into his car one day and was shot to death, point blank in the face, with a rifle through the driver's window. Steve wasn't as attentive toward women after that.

I wasn't perfect, either. Steve had concerns about me as well, specifically, my neatness and need for a germfree environment. I know he rolled his eyes when I picked things up immediately for no reason. I wore myself out cleaning up after everyone until, with Steve's encouragement, I figured out a way to save myself. I let the girls take care of their own rooms. Whatever happened in their rooms, stayed in their rooms. I just closed their bedroom doors when needed. Fortunately, Jamie was neat and clean, so her room usually sparkled. Rachel wasn't so concerned. My other solution was putting a basket for all three of them at the bottom of the stairway where they, or usually I, put their belongings instead of leaving them all over the downstairs. I had to use three large baskets for all of their "stuff." Then the house always looked neat and tidy.

Even with our minor issues sorted out, toward the end of summer I was completely worn out from our two hectic years together and finally told Steve, "I've never trained and raced with such intensity, and life has been so chaotic that my body is shutting down. It's not working with me here."

"Why don't you back off on your training?" he suggested.

"It's not just that. I feel like I'm suffocating and need to get away, put my responsibilities aside. I need a mental break."

As I was packing, Jamie asked, "Are you leaving because Steve is a big fwirt?"

"No, not at all, he's just very kind and extra nice at times."

"Is it because we're messy?" asked Rachel.

I hugged them both, "No, everything is fine. I'm just going to Port Townsend to visit Grandma and Grandpa for a week to *just* run and relax. Your mom needs a rest."

"Should we come along and take care of you?"

I smiled, "No, you girls need to stay here and take care of Steve."

Mom was thrilled to have me to herself. She had coffee ready in the morning when I woke up, and then we visited for a while before I went out for my training run. I came back to a big breakfast with eggs, venison steak, crispy hash browns and toast. I would take a nap, run again, and come back to an extraordinary dinner of fresh salmon, Crab Louie, whatever I wanted. Dad barbecued all kinds of fresh seafood when he came home with his Catch of the Day.

Dad was up at 5 every morning to go to work or fish, depending on the day and the tide. I didn't see him until dinnertime. Dad had worked his way up to supervisor on Indian Island, Chuck's old job before he retired, so he had some say over his work hours.

Laurie seemed to be doing much better. Mom and I went to lunch with her in Bremerton at a favorite restaurant. Aunt Jan joined us and even Debbie came across on the ferry.

I was apprehensive about seeing Laurie after our last encounter but, much to my relief, she seemed calm after spending some time in a drug and alcohol treatment program.

Her reasoning for my success and her past behavior was simple. "You're the lucky one, Kimmie," she said. "The rest of us care too much, we feel so deeply that it cuts into our heart. You've hardened over the years and you hide behind your running."

Debbie jumped in. "Running is your drug." Her eyes were as wild as could be. "We all medicate our pain and sorrow with drugs. You're just as addicted as we are."

"I suppose I am," I replied. "Though I'm not destroying my family or hurting those I love because of it."

Then Laurie said slyly, "So you agree. You're no better than we are."

"No, I'm not, but I've managed to turn my drug into something positive. It's not harming anybody. It has helped me through the bad times and enhanced my life. I would say it has saved me."

"No, you're just lucky."

Mom stepped in. "Now girls, let's enjoy our lunch."

I had a wonderful visit with Chuck. I saw him off and on during my trips to Port Townsend, but we never had quality time when my family was with me. Finally ... I had time to really enjoy catching up with him for hours. He was much older, but still happy and jolly like Mr. Cunningham on "Happy Days."

I told Chuck how so much of what I had done, and still did, was because of him. "Learn the ways of the world," he had said, encouraging me to go to college, "and see what the world has in store for you." We laughed and reminisced about our morning hot chocolate and donuts after Debbie and I finished our paper route. And about how he first met me when I knocked on his door thanking him for the ice cream bars my brothers and sisters were enjoying. And our trips to Port Angeles and all those burgers, fries and milkshakes I ate before buying the troll dolls and getting in huge trouble later.

"I had never been happier than I was with you kids," said Chuck. "You were my family." He worried about us like a father: cringing when we came flying down Morgan Hill on our cardboard or doing horse tricks for him on Taboo in the lower school field. He was always there to bandage us, talk some sense into us and encourage us.

Not long after that, Chuck passed away. Losing him left a huge void in my heart, as if I'd lost a big brother. I was grateful to have had such a long "Chuck visit" on that trip.

When I wasn't enjoying my time with old friends and family, I went for many long runs to prepare my base and strength for the upcoming Twin Cities Marathon. "I saw Kimmie running around the lighthouse while we were fishing," one of Dad's fishing buddies told him. "We called to her and she waved. Then when we were heading home we passed her running on the highway, and we saw her again out on the country road over an hour later, still running." Dad laughed and seemed proud when he told me that over dinner.

I decided to run the 13 miles out to Grandma Helen and Uncle/ Grandpa Harold's in Port Ludlow. The plan was just to get a drink there before heading back, making it a 26-mile run. When I got there I asked Grandma for a Coke or something else sugary to drink. She looked at me in horror. "Kimmie, did you run all the way out here?" she asked, clicking her tongue. "Shame on you! You need to eat something."

"Grandma, I have to run back. All I need is a couple of Cokes. I'll eat after my run."

"You are crazy, Swede," said Uncle/Grandpa Harold, while Grandma sliced up some ham and put it on a plate with her Swedish rolls. She put the plate in front of me as I was drinking my Cokes. I knew I couldn't argue with her, and I knew she would worry if I didn't eat. So I ate six slices of ham and six rolls, then ran the 13 miles back to town, feeling slow and sluggish with an overly full stomach. I'd never do that again.

I couldn't remember the last time I felt so good, like a carefree kid again, having "alone time" for more than just a day or two. My body had been crying out for it so badly that it went on strike. After my break, we were working together again and I was ready to go back to Spokane, recharged from my leisurely visit and ready for whatever life had in store for me.

Twin Cities Marathon ~ October, 1989

Before I knew it, it was time to run Twin Cities in October. I wanted to try to break that 2:30 barrier again. I did everything right in my training. I had it down. I was ready.

It was a lovely day as we took off on our 26.2-mile journey over the beautiful and familiar course. Once again, Benji and Amie were there.

Benji was running 2:25-2:30 marathons easily, so my goal was to run close to him. At 15 miles, I was way out in front and close to Benji's 2:25 group. I was just about to tuck in behind them when I spotted a port-a-john and, all of a sudden, I had to desperately use it. *Maybe it's the power of suggestion.*

It wasn't a long break, maybe a minute at most. I was still in first place when I returned to the course, but as I started re-catching Benji's group I suddenly needed to stop again! I had to go so badly that I couldn't wait to come across another port-a-john. *This definitely is not the power of suggestion.* I couldn't believe it was happening to me in a race ... *what did I do wrong?*

I went into the bushes and stayed there for well over a minute. *Damn, I know! I ate Fig Newtons as part of my carbo-loading.* There are a lot of carbohydrates in Fig Newtons but also *way* too much fiber. I'm sure I would have been OK had I just eaten a few like most human beings, but as always I overindulged just like Blondie, enjoying them so much that I ate the entire package.

Lesson learned, but it was time to start running again. After jumping out of the bushes, I asked the spectators if I was still the first woman. "Yes, but get going!" said a man with a radio. "The next woman is Janis Klecker, and the last report was she's two minutes behind."

That was just what I needed to hear. It spurred me into competitive overdrive and I ran strong to the finish. I won by five minutes (almost a mile), in 2:31:42. Janis was second and I was happy to see Jane Welzel come in fourth, especially after calling her an "ass" the year before.

I finished three minutes behind Benji and, considering the circumstances, was pleased with my time. Not bad, but no sub 2:30.

I went home to enjoy a week of snacking and eating the many chocolates sent by friends, family and fans. Jamie loved that part of my marathons, and we ate box after box of chocolates. Rachel would get sick of them after just one box, but not us. "That's not normal," said Rachel with a scowl. "How can you do that? I can't eat another chocolate, ever."

"Good! That means more for us!" Jamie and I said in unison.

With three good marathons – including the 2:29:34 in Boston, the fastest time by an American so far that year – and 17 successful road races, I could have ended 1989 satisfied. Then, a week after Twin Cities, Lisa Weidenbach ran a 2:28:15 in Chicago. *Hmmm.* I put away my chocolates.

New York City Marathon ~ November, 1989

The New York City Marathon was just three weeks away. It is absurd to compete in another major marathon just a month after running 2:31. It's even more ridiculous to think of competing in New York, a tough course that I'd never even seen but was told had potholes; five bridges, with climbs as long as a mile; and a final three miles of serious hills in Central Park.

Why not? I thought.

"Go for it. It will be fun to visit New York and see everyone, then go to my friend's art show," said Steve.

"Go ahead if you think you will be happy with a 2:36 marathon," said Benji sarcastically.

"You've run three fast marathons already this year," said Don. "Do you think you can run another marathon so soon?"

"I feel a conviction that I'm going to do well," I told them all.

I called Fred Lebow, the race director, who said he would be thrilled to have me join the elite field but that he was out of appearance money. "No worries, Fred," I told him cheerily. "All I ask is that you fly Steve, Benji and Amie in with me and put us all up in the race headquarters hotel. That's it." He agreed.

Then I added, "If I place in the top three and run under 2:30, you double my prize money."

"Kim," he said, "If you place in the top three and run under 2:30, it will be well worth it."

Once we arrived in New York, the bold Kim who told everyone, "I'm ready to go, no problem!" wasn't so brave anymore, wondering, *how in the world am I going to pull this off?* My shins were throbbing for the first time since slicing the tibias while running with Benji in Florida, years before. My carbo-loading and hydrating were magnifying my aches and pains. To make matters worse, reporters at the press conferences questioned my decision. "I am going to explore the unknown," I told them. They didn't look convinced. When I was about to walk into the elevator the night before the race a respected athlete agent pointed his finger at me. "You shouldn't be here," he said.

Now I had to run the marathon. Hmmm.

Fred and his New York crew were taking excellent care of my entourage and me. I had their support, and that's just what I needed. "Don't worry, Kim, we'll have you back even if it doesn't work out for you this time," the elite athlete coordinator said. I felt reassured. All I had to do was run.

I planned to carry $20 for cab fare, just in case.

New York is always alive with energy, and in running circles it's buzzing during marathon weekend. For an elite athlete, it's like being at the "Oscars," or as close as it gets. "There's Kim Jones! I hope she wins," people would say, pointing. Others asked for my autograph, or gave me good-luck cards. Even before the race, I was given flowers and presents galore.

On the morning of the race, I was sitting on the elite-athlete bus on the way to the start thinking, *if I don't do well, it's not the end of the world. Nobody expects me to run well. I have 20 bucks in my pocket. It would be a miracle to run a sub 2:30 on this course after running a fast marathon four weeks ago. I won't feel badly if I run poorly; I'm not getting appearance money. No problem. I'll just hope for the best.*

When we arrived at Fort Wadsworth, near the starting line, we were led off the bus and into a huge, heated tent stocked with all kinds of snacks, coffee and anything else a marathoner could possibly need. While waiting to be taken to the start, I sat with Benji, stretching, sipping coffee and watching the elite runners scurrying about.

"Hello, Mrs. Jones. I'm surprised to see you here," a familiar voice said, in an ever-so-pleasant Welsh accent. I turned and said, "Hello, Mr. Jones." Steve was back in New York as the defending champion.

"You ran a great marathon in Boston and then another good one just four weeks ago," he said. "Don't you think you should rest now?"

"I really think I can run another fast marathon. I know it sounds crazy but I feel it. I *know* it. And for some reason if it doesn't work out, I have 20 bucks right here in my shorts pocket for cab fare!" I said, showing him my $20 bill.

He gave out a big laugh, "Only you, Mrs. Jones."

Just before the start I was led on to the Verrazano-Narrows Bridge, where I waited with Ingrid Kristiansen, Laura Fogli and the rest of my competitors. There were so many good elite runners there that I figured I'd be lucky to place in the top 20. I stayed relaxed, enjoying the magnificent view of the Statue of Liberty and buildings off in the distance. It was an overwhelming sight, something I never thought possible to see years ago when I was living in my little town on the Olympic Peninsula.

"Seeing what the world has in store for me." That was what Chuck was talking about. I was in awe, feeling empowered with that "big city" energy flowing though my veins.

Suddenly I knew I wouldn't need the cab fare.

The gun went off and I was running as I had never run before – relaxed, elated, feeling in the moment. Everyone went out so fast that I was way behind, yet I didn't care. The conditions were perfect for me. No wind, no rain, a cool and cloudy day. I've never liked running or racing on sunny days. I had always found the many cloudy days in Port Townsend comforting, and I felt comforted again on that day.

At 10 miles I passed 44-year-old Priscilla Welch of England, one of the top marathoners in the world, who had won two years before. She gave me a "thumbs up" as I went by. It all seemed like a relaxed training run with Staffan, Don and the boys. As I crossed the Queensboro Bridge, not even noticing the uphill at 15 miles, I was alone. The bridge is one of the few spots on the New York course that isn't lined with spectators, and it was so quiet I heard nothing but my own heart pounding.

Then I heard one loud, exuberant voice. "Keep it going, you're running strong! It's your day!" It was Benji.

As I turned off the bridge onto First Avenue in Manhattan, I ran out of the silence into the most deafening roar I had ever heard, even louder than the crowd at Wellesley College in Boston. It felt like the ground was shaking. Spectators called out my name, shouting, "You're in fifth place."

I was shocked. The course was so crowded with fast men that I hadn't been able to keep track of how many women I passed.

There was a lull in the noise, and I could think again. *Why was Benji on the bridge? He's supposed to be racing. And he sure seemed enthusiastic for Benji.* I put it out of my mind and focused on passing Laura Fogli near 19 miles. Laura was an Italian runner who had run under 2:30, and had placed second twice in New York. At 21 miles I passed the Russian star Zoya Ivanova, who had won the Los Angeles Marathon that spring and was a 2:27 marathoner.

I was in second place, running so effortlessly that I couldn't feel my feet hitting the ground. It was a dream race, why we run, what propels us to a new level.

From the slowest to the fastest, marathoners dream of their "perfect" race. Every now and then I was startled when I realized I wasn't in a dream, but reality. I ran into Central Park, floating over the challenging hills, not realizing that I was working even though I was running as fast as I could. Thousands of spectators crowded both sides of the street, screaming and yelling, thrilled to see an American run so well. It was as if New York City had closed down just for me. As I crossed the finish line, the ground was vibrating with the noise of thousands of people cheering – for me! It was surreal, as if I were in a place closer to heaven.

That was my day, but Ingrid Kristiansen had a better one. She won, in 2:25:30. I finished in second place in 2:27:54.

None of it was sinking in yet. I was taken immediately for drug testing to Tavern on the Green, where Benji and Steve were waiting for me. Benji had been so worried about me that he couldn't focus on his own race, so he gave it up on the quiet Queensboro Bridge and waited to be sure I was OK, then ran to the finish line.

After the drug testing I called the girls, who had watched the race on TV, before being whisked off to a press conference packed with reporters from all over the world. The top three finishers – Ingrid, Laura and I – answered questions for over an hour. Everyone was stunned by my time, which made me the fastest American female ever on the New York course and the fourth-fastest American of all time. I was asked about everything imaginable. Someone asked, "What do your daughters think of your amazing effort today?" I replied, "Rachel was thrilled and Jamie said second is pretty good, that it's a lot better than third."

The top three runners had photos taken with the charming Fred Lebow before being driven back to our hotel. I was having a hard time walking on my crooked toe, which was killing me. It's strange ... it didn't bother me at all when I was running, but right when I crossed the finish line the pain started shooting up my foot, into my leg, and right up to my knee.

After a shower, I lay on my bed and was finally able to think about what just happened. An intoxicating rush of relief and pride flooded through me. I realized what I'd accomplished with the odds against me, having the courage to go through with it and make it all happen. I was lying there in my towel, my body pulsating with pain, waiting for room service to bring up my ever-so-needed post race meal: two bacon cheeseburgers, two plates of fries and two chocolate milkshakes. Steve was sitting in a chair reading the newspaper, exhausted from the stress he went through running all over New York, worrying about me and hoping I would come through OK. "I can't believe I just ran a 2:27 in the New

York City Marathon! It's a dream come true," I told him. Steve looked up and smiled. People don't realize what a support crew has to go through. I think it's harder on them.

As I was eating my meal, I realized ... *this is what I ordered with Chuck during our outings years ago.* I felt like he was celebrating with me. I wished he had been. I missed him terribly.

The awards ceremony was incredible. Almost everyone was dressed to the hilt. I managed to squeeze into my heels to wear with my black ankle-length dress for the evening. I decided that next time I would be sure to pack a pair of high heels a size too big in D width. I was presented with a beautiful crystal vase from Tiffany's and a crystal trophy shaped like an obelisk. As we walked off the stage with our awards, Mr. Jones told me, "I can't believe it. You're amazing Mrs. Jones." That came from a world-record holder and the man who had won the year before.

After the ceremony, I was invited to several prestigious marathons and races by the many race promoters and athlete agents from all over the world waiting to talk with the athletes.

At long last, my year was complete. Well, almost. On Monday, Steve and I went to his friend's art studio, where we were given a deal on a $20,000 painting. That one, I loved. It was an "egg tempera," consisting of colored pigment mixed with egg yolk. These paintings are long lasting and the colors are tantalizingly bright. It was a large painting, about 6 feet x 4 feet, a scene with many different types of people walking in New York City through the shadows from the many surrounding buildings that darkened the street. Steve asked, "Should we buy it?" instead of taking action on his own. Perhaps it was one of the reasons I liked the painting so much.

We went home to another chocolate-eating heyday for Jamie and me, while Rachel made a feeble attempt before watching us in disgust. Fred Lebow and the New York Road Runners sent two-dozen roses, several presents, more chocolates and a nice card. It was the perfect ending to my 1989 season.

Chapter 15

Just as 1989 was coming to an end, I was unexpectedly invited to run in a 5-mile New Year's Eve race put on by the New York City Marathon organizers. Ken Martin, the men's second-place finisher that year, and I were going to be flown in as the featured attractions. I was hoping Steve wouldn't find another piece of artwork he couldn't live without.

Ken, Steve and I went to an extravagant dinner party early in the evening on New Year's Eve, where we were seated with Fred Lebow and several big corporate sponsors of the race. Everyone was served champagne and then a five-course meal including steak, lobster and cheesecake. After that, the three of us were taken back to the hotel to prepare for our race at midnight, only a few hours after the dinner party. Ken and I were the only elite athletes invited, so we were expected to win even on full stomachs.

Many runners in the New Year's Eve event dressed in costumes and drank champagne along the course. They were there to have fun and ring in the New Year. Unfortunately for me, in a Central Park race with over 4000 participants, there will always be some fast runners who come to race.

I was hoping for the best until I saw Inge Schuurmans, an elite American track runner. Inge had never beaten me ... *she certainly could now that I was stuffed with steak and lobster.* We took off together in the pelting rain, but my stomach was so full that I soon let Inge go. There was nothing I could do. It was worse than the time I ate the ham and Swedish coffee rolls during my 26-mile run to Grandma's house.

After the turnaround I began to feel better. *What the hell, it's New Year's Eve*, I thought, and took a sip of champagne at the aid station. I looked up and saw Inge, then passed her with a mile to go. I couldn't believe I won the race – on little training since the marathon seven weeks earlier, stuffed from a huge dinner and being way too relaxed after a few glasses of champagne.

Afterward, we went to a New Year's Eve party at the beautiful apartment of Larry Rawson, the track and marathon commentator. After appetizers and more champagne, I was saying silly things that made people laugh without even trying, just like Grandma Helen did. "I think I've had way too much champagne," I told Larry. "Kim, you're drinking non-alcoholic champagne," he told me. Then, everyone laughed even harder.

I went home and took a much needed, solid timeout from running. Life had finally caught up to me. After four marathons in 10 months, averaging 2:29, I needed some serious R&R. I made a lot of money in 1989, but 21 competitive road races in one year was quite a challenge, especially when I had more important things on my mind …

It was time to talk to my 15-year-old daughter about birth control.

I started by telling Rachel about my first experience in Chetzemoka Park and how I was totally unprepared, even going into detail about sneaking out. I told her how she was conceived on that very night. Her eyes widened as she listened intently before thanking me for sharing my story. I let her know that it wasn't totally Brad's fault, that it was just as much mine. We were young, he was worldly and used to such things, and I was trying to impress him by pretending I was something I wasn't – an experienced girl.

"Sex can happen when you least expect it," I told her. "You aren't going to come running to me just as it's about to happen. So, let's go over a simple form of birth control." Jamie came running up asking, "Can I listen?" I looked at Rachel, who smiled and said, "Yes, but Mom's talking to me, not you." I figured Jamie would be OK.

We went upstairs and I showed Rachel a box of condoms. I told her I was putting them in the top cabinet drawer in the hallway. "You know where they are if you ever need to use them. Now, do you know how to use a condom?" She said no. I decided to show her.

I went into the bathroom and brought out a curling iron, the only thing handy on such short notice. Rachel looked at me and laughed while Jamie watched attentively. I unwrapped a condom and began going through the process of putting it onto the curling iron, "This is the boy's penis, and you put this on the tip and then roll it all the way down the shaft to the very bottom," I instructed. "Be sure it's totally covered." Rachel laughed timidly while Jamie giggled. Then I had Rachel try it. She mastered it after several attempts.

Jamie had a bewildered look on her face. "Is that what a boy's penis is like? How in the wold can a boy walk awound with something like that between his legs?" Rachel was roaring with laughter. "They're only that big when they're excited," she told her.

Later that winter, we threw a big party at the house while Benji and Amie were visiting Spokane. There I met Ania Stang, a beautiful, tall, dark and charismatic woman. She was close to my age, half French and half Polish, who mixed up her phrases like Grandma Helen and I did. Ania was finishing up massage school, and had been a three-hour marathoner – coached by Benji – until back problems forced her to stick to shorter distances. Her knowledge of the wear and tear a runner goes through gave her deeper insight into how to work with marathoners. Ania had a gift – she could read people and balance their energy. She had an incredible calming effect on those close to her.

Staffan and his friend, Chuck Strickell, had opened Intermountain Physical Therapy, and Ania worked there to accumulate the hours needed for her massage license. Staffan felt I needed another good massage therapist because he was leaving town for several months at a time on contracts with hospitals around the country.

Ania was the perfect person for the job. "I need to come to your house with my table to work on you three days a week," she announced. "With my therapy massage and your talent, you'll be the best marathoner in the world." I said OK. I didn't have any choice. Ania was the boss, and it was the best thing that could have happened to me. She could dig down as deep as Staffan and was just as relentless when necessary, but also became my best friend and confidante.

Ania came to my house on my hard days, working on me for two hours after I finished up with my second runs. Chuck would tend to any injury-related problems "from one of those crazy accidents she gets herself into," as Staffan put it. Later Steve Shirley, a chiropractor in Spokane, joined "Team Jones," and I was set.

Boston Marathon ~ April, 1990

After some serious training in early 1990, a lot of massage and a confidence-boosting personal best of 53:31 at the Nike Cherry Blossom 10 Mile race in April, I was headed to Boston for another try at the marathon.

I arrived in Boston early to get away from the many distractions at home and rest up for the marathon. Steve and Ania would join me a few days later. I was staying in a tasteful room at the Copley Plaza where I would spend the next four days luxuriating in the comfort around me, with an extravagant feather-top king sized bed, feather pillows, soft cotton sheets and a fully stocked mini bar.

John Hancock, the financial services company and major sponsor of the marathon, had invited me into their small circle of elite marathoners. They flew me to Boston first class, picked me up at the airport in a limousine and put me up in a suite at the Copley Plaza. Hancock focused on a few select world-class marathoners, investing in each with a large appearance fee on top of prize money, and treating us like royalty.

Pat Lynch, the elite athlete coordinator for Hancock, took good care of me. "Order anything you want from room service," he said, or I could walk across the street to the John Hancock Conference Center restaurant. "The chef there will prepare whatever you choose, morning, noon and night," said Pat. "Contact me if you need anything." He handed me his card and my special credentials to enter the conference center.

I woke up each morning after a wonderful night of sleep in my luxurious bed and called room service immediately, ordering a pot of coffee with cream, a bowl of oatmeal, pancakes with pure maple syrup, yogurt and a plate of fruit. I ate while watching "Good Morning America," without a care in the world. After eating breakfast and then reading the newspaper, I stretched lightly and went out for an easy run. When I came back I ordered room service again – a hamburger or sandwich, a baked potato with sour cream, a salad and more fruit. Then I put my feet up and watched movies and comfort shows for the rest of the day.

I decided that I should get out for a bit in the evenings, so I walked across the street to the conference center. There, I had an excellent meal with good friends, who were all John Hancock athletes as well: Joan Benoit Samuelson, the woman who inspired me to run my first marathon after she won the first Women's Olympic Marathon in 1984; "Boston Billy" Rodgers, the most unselfish, genuine person I know; and Mr. Steve Jones.

We all ate very well. I had an abundance of rice and beans, half a chicken, steamed vegetables and desserts galore. Mr. Jones laughed and said, "You eat more like a man than a woman." Joanie looked shocked, and Billy asked me tons of questions, "Where do you put all of that? How can one woman eat so much? Do you always eat like this?"

"I'm carbohydrate loading, you all should eat more," I said, as I kept eating. I was full, happy and enjoying the high life.

I was also wearing bib #1, which puts some pressure on a person.

Patriots Day arrived. In the race, everything was going well until someone spilled water all over my shoes at the first aid station. My feet were soaked. I hadn't raced with socks since Dr. Dave discovered I was able to get a better push-off running without them. Soon my feet were blistering from the movement of that sockless forceful push-off.

By 10 miles, the blisters were getting worse. As I was running up and down the Newton Hills and toward Heartbreak Hill, they started bursting, and by 20 miles I felt searing pain as the skin on the bottoms of my feet began to peel away. My shoes were soaked in blood. I crested the hill trying to land differently, on the outsides of my feet, taking some of the pressure off my mid-foot. That helped the blisters. Unfortunately, it also put all my weight on my crooked toe. It was the only way I could finish.

The pain grew to such a level of torture that I thought I might black out. I was so focused on the finish line that it never entered my mind to drop out. All I could do was put my head down and endure as the misery intensified. By 23 miles I knew there was no skin left on the soles of my feet. I was running on raw meat.

Once I finished, the most painful experience of my life – worse than labor pains – my entire body was sickened. There was a wheelchair at the finish line and I headed straight for it. After being wheeled to the elite medical room in the Copley Plaza I lay on a cot, with Steve brushing my hair back and wiping the cold sweat from my brow as Ania worked with the doctor to take my shoes off. The insoles were embedded into the raw meat on the balls of my feet, stuck so tightly that I had to put my feet, shoes and all, into a bucket of water to soak before the doctor was finally able to pull them off. My feet were a horrid sight, like skinned chicken. The other athletes in the room had to turn away.

There was a tight sickening feeling in my throat. I remembered being dizzy in a spinning room once before, when my dad cut his fingers off. I passed out, but not for long enough. When I awoke, the doctor was cleaning my feet, putting on disinfectant and bandaging them. My sprained, black-and-blue crooked toe was throbbing as well, the least of my worries on that day.

I had no idea I'd finished fifth, in 2:31:01, until Ania told me.

They wheeled me to the press conference, where a reporter asked, "Why do you think you blistered so badly?" I mentioned the water being spilled on my shoes and about running sockless, and then told him, "Suffering terribly is sometimes what life has to offer. I've taken so much from my sport. This was a big payback day for me."

The scripture Dad read to me on that beautiful fall day while sitting on the dilapidated steps of our old prostitute house popped into my head: "We rejoice in our sufferings because we know that suffering produces perseverance; perseverance character; and character hope." I was certainly his tough little Swede on that day.

That night, Keith Peters and Steve took turns carrying me the few blocks to the awards ceremony and helped me onto the stage. Once I received my awards and a beautiful crystal vase there was an awkward pause as I tried to maneuver my way off the stage, walking on my heels with toes straight in the air, until a very handsome Italian marathoner asked, "May I be of some assistance?" Then Gelindo Bordin, the winner of the Boston Marathon earlier that day, carried me to my seat.

I overcame. I healed. I would run with more vigor later in the year thanks to my talented support crew. I was the tough Swede that continued to thrive and kept coming back stronger. I wasn't going to go away that easily.

~

During the summer or holidays, we often drove to visit our families. While I healed, we traveled to Seattle to meet up with Steve's family, then farther north to the Jones' family cabin in Birch Bay, just this side of the Canadian border at Vancouver. It's a stunning place, with views of the San Juan Islands that fall between Birch Bay and Vancouver Island. It's fairly close to Port Townsend, a short but adventurous drive over moss-covered bridge crossings and winding hills alternating with green valleys dotted with lakes and flowers. The shadowy green forest is so lush in places that it's like driving in the dark before reaching the ferry at Whidbey Island that took us directly to Port Townsend.

After our stay in Birch Bay, we were on the hour drive to my parent's house when Rachel threw her apple core out the window as we were going over one of the bridges. "Rachel, that's unacceptable. You're littering and it's dangerous. There could be people below," Steve scolded her as he drove. Rachel, in the back seat with Jamie, rolled her eyes. Steve continued to talk about being responsible, going on and on.

Finally, Rachel said in a decisively slow, mocking way, "It was just a fricking apple core." She was in a seriously rebellious stage. Jamie piped in, "Yeah Steve, an apple cowe is biodegwadable."

Steve's eyes narrowed and his hands tightened around the wheel. Not another word was spoken for the rest of the drive. I looked out the window, enjoying some peace and quiet, admiring the view and thinking. *Rachel needs to work on being respectful and Jamie is getting better, but I'm going to have to take her to speech therapy soon if she doesn't quit talking like Elmer Fudd.*

During our drive, I reflected on how our two families were so different, like night and day. The Joneses rarely turned up the thermostat in their homes, feeling that 65 degrees was plenty warm. They were careful to recycle, and weren't worried about keeping everything shiny clean and in its place. My family strived to be warm, with the temperature in the house above 70. They threw all their trash – plastics and all – into a burning barrel, and liked having things spotless and perfectly tidy. During our trips, we went from one extreme to the next.

Steve's family was very calm and stable with similar personalities, making for a predictable, placid lifestyle. One time, Jamie, Rachel and I were playing cards at the kitchen table with Steve's mother and brother David, waiting for the salmon to finish baking for dinner. "It seems fishy in here," said sister Sarah when she walked in. We laughed. "It seems fishy in here," said brother Evan, when he walked in a little later. We chuckled to be polite. "Something's very fishy in here," said sister Carol when she opened the oven to check on the salmon. We smiled. "It seems awfully fishy in here," said Steve when he came in. We all rolled our eyes. "My goodness, it's very fishy in here," said Harlan in his sweet voice as he walked in, humming. We laughed again. Harlan was like Angel Clarence in "It's A Wonderful Life," trying to earn his angel wings by helping Jimmy Stewart find his way. When he said something "funny," you had to laugh. He was just too delightful.

Our favorite activity with the Joneses was going to Chinatown for dim sum, a midday Chinese meal of light dishes. We all sat at a round table, sometimes all 18 of us, and ordered dish after dish of the many selections brought around to tables on a cart. Rachel and Jamie loved it, especially the pot stickers and siu mai pork dumplings. Everyone had to use chopsticks, so while we waited for our food Steve patiently taught the girls how to use them by trying to pick out the ice cubes from their water glasses. We could always expect an outing to Chinatown, usually at the King Café in Seattle. For the Joneses, that was about as wild as it got.

In my family, at least one person was always out of control. There was never a lull, and if there was, something bad happened quickly to fill it. Once there were six members of my family in the Port Townsend Jail, all at the same time.

By then Laurie was doing all kinds of crazy things. Once she called me from a telephone booth in Bremerton, telling me that she was surrounded. People were watching her, she insisted, and she was afraid for her life. She begged me to come and get her. She was 300 miles away, not counting the ferry ride. But I had no idea where she was, and neither did she, really. I told her to figure out her location and call me back. When she called again, she said, "Never mind, Kimmie, they're my friends now."

Mel was in a state of gloom, looking miserable and embarrassed, but went along with Laurie's shenanigans. She was downright scary at times. Mel started drinking to excess. They lost their beautiful home and spent all of their savings on drugs and alcohol. They lost their self-respect, everything.

Laurie was disassociated from the Jehovah's Witnesses. Mel lost his position as an elder, but remained a brother in the congregation as he kept trying to pick up the pieces and do right by the boys. He still had a good job working on a tugboat and was always a hard worker, constantly trying to be a good person, but he wasn't strong enough to keep away from Laurie. He loved her too much.

We all loved Laurie. The good Laurie was so caring and giving, and we always hoped she would stay. She had the power to pull those close to her into her beautiful mind, wondrous thoughts and powerful observations. She guided us when we needed it most. From the age of 8, she took care of all her younger siblings, and as an adult pulled Mom out of the gutter, figuratively and literally, after Charlie and Stanley died. But we didn't see that side of her much anymore. Laurie's actions had become way out of line, and her power was pulling those closest to her into peril.

Then there were Debbie and Bradley, pulling a few stunts of their own, only to miss their court dates and be in worse trouble. Bradley was put in jail several times for really stupid things. Once, he and his drunken buddies were driving past a cyclist in downtown Port Townsend when one of his friends dared Bradley to lean out the window and give the rider a big wedgie. He did, pulling the cyclist off his bike by the seat of his pants and frightening him to death. The man ended up badly injured from the crash.

Even though he was the sweetest and the most tenderhearted member of our family, Bradley was easily swayed to do things, including steal for drugs if he didn't have the money to pay for them. Debbie could easily talk him into that. He also had a terrible temper, beating people to a pulp if they "deserved" it. He truly didn't seem to realize the ramifications of doing such horrible things. It only took a few drinks or some kind of drug to alter his thinking, which was the only time he found his way into trouble. Maybe, like Pa Seelye and Grandpa Jeffries, Bradley couldn't handle his liquor either.

When he was the sweet precious baby of the family, Bradley was overlooked during the chaotic times in Enumclaw. I was the middle child, yet Bradley was the most neglected. My heart aches when I remember all the precious things for which he deserved to be recognized. He needed the self-esteem that comes when loved ones make a fuss and appreciate the special things you do. Charlie was the only one close enough to his age to play with him then. He tried to be a part of everything, but we all ignored him while fending for ourselves. I wished I could make it up to him.

Bradley did manage to attract our attention when he said something funny. Maybe that's why he ended up with such a great sense of humor. He wasn't a rocket scientist, but he worked hard with a tutor to get through high school. Bradley was clever in a different way, always quick-witted. Once when the tutor was working with him as he struggled with spelling, she asked him to spell "handsome." "B-R-A-D," he answered loudly. Mom and Dad were in the next room and tried hard not to laugh.

I was worried about him, sickened that he might end up in prison with all those hardcore criminals. I couldn't bear the thought of it.

Debbie went through another divorce and had her third child, Jimmy, with a man who abused her. She was escaping his abuse and threats by taking drugs, and she was seriously into crystal-meth. We had been noticing the telling changes. Debbie had kept out of serious trouble so far, but was beginning to associate with some hardcore drug dealers and told us some frightening stories. I was worried for Debbie. I wished there was something I could do or say to save her, the way she had comforted and saved me over the years. I wished I could sing "Angel Baby" to her and make everything better.

... "Steve. Steve." ... Rachel broke the long silence when we drove off the Port Townsend Ferry, bringing me out of my deep, poignant thoughts.

"Steve, would you please drop me off at my friend Michelle's house on the way to Grandma's?" Rachel asked. Then she added softly, "I'm sorry about the apple core."

"Sure thing, thanks for the apology," said Steve, mollified.

Rachel still had many close ties in Port Townsend, and was off visiting all of her old friends during our stay while Jamie made friends with my parents' little neighbor girl named Rochelle. The girl, who lived with her grandparents, resembled all three of Bradley's kids and was the same age as little Bradley. We had our suspicions, and found out later that she was Bradley's daughter. Back in high school, he'd managed to get two girls pregnant within three months. It seems Bradley was a busy boy.

During a big family get-together, Jamie and Rochelle had everyone come out on the deck to watch them perform dance skits to the band "New Kids on the Block." They dressed in hideous outfits, with Jamie wearing the usual bright scrunchies all over her head and striped half tights with underwear over the top, and did silly dances lip-synching to the songs "Please Don't Go Girl" and "Hangin' Tough" over and over again.

Rachel complained when she was forced to watch with the rest of us, "Why would they do this? It's ridiculous and a waste of time."

Mom and Dad started laughing. "You should have seen your mother and her sister in action with their friend Rene – they were even a few years older," Mom said. "They did dance routines wearing their bikinis. Your mom was in her green and pink polka-dot bikini, as skinny as could be, dancing to 'Raindrops Keep Falling on My Head,' 'Leaving on a Jet Plane,' and my favorite ... 'Aquarius.' What a treat!"

"Yeah, the three of them come out twirling around like orbiting planets, hands in the air and turning and turning while singing at the top of their lungs," said Dad.

Rachel laughed. "I guess this isn't so bad then."

Back in Spokane, Jamie was turning into quite the runner. She had run – or sometimes walked, depending on her mood – in the Junior

Bloomsday race every year since she was 6. It was a mile race just for kids, focusing on their fitness and giving special attention to each finisher, and it became a huge success over the years. Kids "trained" for the race in a school program that had them run three days a week. The race had a big role in making the youth of Spokane fitter as well as developing future track and cross-country athletes, along with many future Bloomsday runners. Jamie was beginning to reap its benefits, enjoying her track races, and also running in the one-mile cross-country meets in grade school.

At age 11, Jamie was one of the fastest grade-school girls in the city. I took pleasure in watching her run. She was finally coming out of her turtle shell, feeling confident and making many new friends.

She still had her friend Bo, but only saw him on weekends when she went to Kelly's or when we took Bo with us to races. That summer we took him to the Miracle Mile race. We drove two hours down to Kennewick, Washington, where the race put us up in a nice hotel with a pool for the kids. After frolicking in the pool for a few hours, we all ran the mile races that evening, finishing right in front of the hotel. The kids and fun runners went first, so I was able to watch Jamie and Bo in action, running down the street as fast as they could, as if the hornets were right behind them, trying to beat each other. They were all over the place, elbows flying everywhere while running side-by-side, looking at one another to see what the other would do. Bo was so proud of himself for staying up with Jamie. That is, after he was done bending over with dry heaves.

Then it was my turn. There were always women there who could run under 5 minutes, but I had won the race several times without too much trouble, usually in 4:45. That year, the prize money for first place had jumped to $1700, while second place dropped dramatically, to $500. The winner would take it all. I arrived at the start knowing there would certainly be somebody to race.

Suddenly, I heard a strange voice say, "Kim Jones is here." Then I heard a very familiar voice. "Don't worry about Kim. She's just a slow marathoner, not a track racer with mile speed like you." It was Damien Koch, the bun-hugger-wearing guy from Colorado, talking to Libbie Johnson, a great track racer whom he was coaching.

Hmmm! That got me fired up. I turned and gave them a look. "It's good to see you, Kimmie, you look great," Damien said, giving me a big hug and congratulating me on my recent marathons. I really liked him and knew that as Libbie's coach he had to build up her confidence. But ... he did say I was slow. He introduced me to Libbie and I liked her immediately. But ... he did say I was slow.

At the gun I took off like a bat flying from hell, running 64 seconds for the first quarter mile, 64 seconds for the second quarter mile and 68 seconds for the third quarter mile, way ahead of everyone. The final quarter was slightly uphill, and I began to slow. Then I began to really slow. My body was flooded with lactic acid ... all the way up to my neck muscles. Just then Libbie came up on me and tried to pass, but I heard Jamie and Bo screaming and cheering at the top of their lungs and I reached deep for that extra gear to beat her, running a 4:38 – the hard way, finishing the final quarter in 82 painful seconds.

Libbie and Damien joked later about never again calling me a slow marathoner just before a race. (It was an excellent point – the following year Libbie beat me.) Afterward, Jamie and Bo played in the pool for hours while I enjoyed the post-race party with the runners and enjoyed some excellent Columbia Valley Riesling with Bridgid Kardong. I liked the wine so much that the race director sent a case home with me. *Great. Now Jamie has another name for a stuffed animal.*

I loved our time with little Bo. He was so thrilled with racing that he joined his school's track and cross-country team, and I took joy in watching him compete throughout the years.

During the week of Labor Day, we usually did something special as a family with the McDermotts. They drove from their home in Shelby, Montana, and we drove the five hours from Spokane to meet at their cabin on Lake Five, near Glacier National Park. Vivian and Gary had three boys. Mac and Carl were close to Rachel's age, and Ryan was Jamie's age. Ryan and Jamie had something in common. Ryan couldn't pronounce some of his R's or L's either. *Now we have two Elmer Fudds on our hands.*

At the time I was in deep training for the New York City Marathon. I tackled 15-24 mile runs every other day, towing either Gary or Steve along as they took turns running with me in grizzly country, while the other rode on a four-wheeler or in the car. They needed to take shifts since neither could run at my pace for the entire distance. I smiled as I ran along, thinking how sweet it was that two brave men were protecting me. On my second run, Mac or Carl rode the four-wheeler with me because the men were too tired after the first one. The boys made sure to rev that four-wheeler as often and loud as possible, and not just to be cool; they were trying to scare away the bears and cougars.

That was the best training situation I could have hoped for. I had a great support crew on my runs, and Vivian cooked a lot of delicious and nutritious food. Vivian was like a combination of Carol, the mother on "The Brady Bunch," and their maid, Alice. She was small, gung ho, and always ready to go. She made sure there were plenty of snacks for the kids – licorice, M&Ms, popcorn and chips galore – all of my favorites. She and the men cleaned up around the house and took the kids on outings: waterskiing, boating, hiking and on trips to pick out the many movies we watched in the evenings. The two Elmer Fudds often went off into their own little world, taking a small rowboat around the edge of the lake to catch crawdads and escape the teasing of the older kids.

After my morning runs and lunch, I would take a nap. Before drifting off to sleep, I lay there listening to the chatter of the kids down at the lake with Steve, Gary and Vivian laughing, their voices echoing in the background as they took turns waterskiing or swimming out to the dock. I rested well, completely content that the kids were living their lives to the fullest. The sound of them playing happily was as comforting as hearing the train off in the distance.

~

It seems that when things are going well and life couldn't be any better, I'm always shocked back into reality. That fall, Grandma Helen was diagnosed with ovarian cancer.

During my last visit I had noticed her feet were always elevated because of swelling in her ankles. Her stomach was bloated, but I assumed it was just something one goes through at the age of 76. She had never been sick, and still seemed herself, happy and jolly with a great appetite. In just one shocking moment ... she was facing cancer treatment.

My heart dropped. I couldn't imagine going through life without Grandma Helen there, offering her support and strength, along with her magical power of just knowing. I needed to do something. I wanted to make her happy and proud that year.

I decided that I would win the 1990 New York City Marathon for my grandmother.

That was an ambitious goal considering that Grete Waitz, who had won nine times, and Katrin Dorre, the Olympic bronze medalist were among the many top women entered. But I had trained perfectly all summer, and after my Montana training week I knew I had a chance. Most importantly, I knew that Grandma Helen would be watching on live television. The networks did an impressive job of televising the big marathons back then, and seeing it live would make it even more exciting for her. I would be running for my family, and that's always when I run my best.

New York City Marathon ~ November, 1990

Fred Lebow offered identical appearance fees to Ken Martin and me, both coming back after finishing second the year before. I accepted, but Ken wanted more, and the press made a big deal out of it. Fred ended up giving him more. Frankly, as top Americans, we probably did deserve more. Worried that I would be upset, or maybe make an issue of being denied the same appearance fee, Fred called me personally.

"I'll keep to the appearance fee you offered," I told him, "but if I place in the top three I earn triple the prize money plus the time bonuses."

"OK, you've got yourself a deal," he said, chuckling over the phone. Of course, "Team Jones" was also flown in first class and put up in nice hotel rooms, along with being given per diem to take care of expenses for the long weekend.

Two days before the race, I was offered a modeling job in conjunction with the marathon and one of its major sponsors. They asked me to join two other elite runners modeling evening gowns on one of the major bridges in New York, giving me the expensive gown as a bonus. It was tempting, but the weather was so warm and the shoot would have taken too much time and far too much energy.

Instead, I did what I normally did while resting up for a race: I stayed in my room and read, or watched reruns of "Andy Griffith," "Bonanza," "I Love Lucy," "The Waltons," "Little House on the Prairie," and sometimes "Leave it to Beaver" and "Hazel," depending on the stations. I enjoyed my programs and felt comforted by the nostalgia while dozing off and on, a calming habit that stuck over the years. I really hated giving up that elegant evening gown; however, I needed to be totally focused on the marathon if I wanted to win.

Steve was off with friends, giving me space, and Ania brought me little presents and special snacks of chocolates and fresh pastries while I rested. She showed up with an "Ania first aid kit" stocked with everything imaginable. "Are you planning to operate?" I asked. She laughed and explained in her French accent, "This is for you. We want to be ready for blisters this time." Ania gave me a heavy-duty massage on Thursday night when we arrived, then several mild, relaxing massages over the next two days. I never felt so ready to race while being so comfortable in the process.

The night before the marathon we prepared my special fluid bottles as we always did: mixing just the right amount of electrolytes with water, taping my number and name on the sides, then taking the bottles down to the hospitality room. From there, race organizers would take them out to the course and place them on tables every four miles. Then we were off to dinner four blocks from the hotel, at my favorite Italian restaurant. I always ordered the Jackie Mason special of penne pasta with mozzarella cheese and spinach, plus one giant Italian sausage. I tried not to eat the entire sausage, but I couldn't help myself.

It was already hot as we lined up on the Verrazano-Narrows Bridge for the 10:45 a.m. start, women on one side of the bridge and men on the other, separated by a large median. I was glad I had 24-ounce fluid bottles out on the course, because it was going to be a tough day. I saw Grete for the first time since my trip to Florida with Mom five years earlier. "Hello, Kim. How's your mother?" she asked quietly. I barely noticed my other competitors, sharing as little small talk as possible. We took off slowly, at a reasonable pace for the conditions, so I ran with the leader, Susan Sirma, from Kenya. Grete, Katrin, Margaret Groos, Nancy Ditz, Julie Isphording and the others were behind us.

Suddenly, somebody I didn't recognize came up on us near the 6-mile mark. The women wouldn't merge with the men until 8 miles, so I had no idea who it could be. I glanced over and was bewildered, then took another look to be sure the runner was wearing a women's number. She was! *This is the strongest woman I had ever seen!* I moved ahead to get a good solid look at her. She was wearing bright red lipstick and wearing number F-5.

The F stood for female. *She's a woman all right.* She was running with two men. The men were on the wrong side of the road. *Hmmm.*

I ran with them for a few miles, but the pace was too fast, under 5:30 per mile. In the sweltering heat, I had to back off, and my quad muscle was cramping a bit. They finally left me at 9 miles. I ran alone until Katrin came up beside me on a bridge near 13 miles. I had to make a decision quickly, to either settle in and run with Katrin or go after that unknown woman, whose lead had grown to over a minute. I ran to the table, grabbed my special 24-ounce bottle, guzzled it down perfectly without spilling a drop – all that Montana Chug practice – and picked up the pace.

I was focusing so hard that I paid no attention to the roaring crowd as I turned off the Queensboro Bridge. While running up First Avenue, I even ignored the motorcycle film crew beside me, though usually I try to listen to what they're saying about me on live television because you never know what you might learn. At 20 miles I gulped down another bottle and pressed on. I couldn't think about the rising heat and humidity, and I had to put my miserable experience in Boston out of my head. That was always the point in a marathon when those negative thoughts started to creep in.

My tight quad kept my pace under control, so I was running as hard as I could while not worrying about blowing up. I went to the fluid table at 24 miles for my final bottle, once again drinking it down perfectly without spilling a drop. The women's press vehicle kept coming back to me, and I could hear Kathrine Switzer talking live with the camera on me. I immediately thought of Grandma Helen at home watching, and a surge of adrenaline shot through me like a lightning bolt.

At 25 miles I heard a spectator yell, "Wanda Panfil is 25 seconds in front of you!" At that moment I thought, *I might actually be able to win the New York City Marathon! I can do this!* Another bolt of energy went through me. I worked my way up a mild hill, getting closer and closer to the leader. *I can catch her, I can!* Little did I know at the time, at that very moment, Grandma was on her couch watching the coverage with Mom, Dad and Uncle/Grandpa Harold, her feet up on a pillow from her swollen legs, yelling at Wanda, "You sit down damn you Wanda, just SIT down!"

Unfortunately Wanda didn't sit down, although she looked like she was ready to. As we came up the last hill toward the finish line, she wobbled and kept looking over her shoulder as I pulled closer and closer. The gap was ten seconds ... nine ... seven.

Wanda hit the finish line five seconds in front of me. Five seconds, 2:30:45 to 2:30:50. It was the closest women's finish in the 21 years of the New York City Marathon.

At the press conference, they asked me the question I was expecting, "Are you disappointed in placing second again?"

Everything had been so hectic since I crossed the finish line that I hadn't had time to think, but as I answered I realized that I really wasn't that disappointed. "I ran as hard as I possibly could today," I said to the large group of reporters. "I ran a perfect race. There was no way I could have gone with Wanda's surge between 9 and 14 miles. She outran me." Of course they wouldn't let it go there, and continued to ask about the "what ifs" as Grete waited to take the stage. She had finished fourth, the first time she had finished the race without winning.

I finally told them about my usual telephone conversation with Jamie right after the race. "Second is pwetty good, Mom. It's a lot bettew than thiwd or something," she said.

As I passed her on the stage, Grete said softly, "We should have worn hats filled with ice." We both smiled.

After the press conference, Marty Liquori surprised me by asking if I planned to protest Wanda's victory. "Wanda had two men running with her, going to the table to retrieve her drinks and bringing them to her the entire race," said Marty, a middle-distance Olympian who had been a television commentator for the race. "If she had to go over to a table herself just one time, that's five seconds. She was being aided."

"She ran the distance on her own," I told him. "She *was* being aided, but no one impeded my race. Sometimes women have no control over men handing them water." I added, "She's from Poland; maybe she doesn't know race protocol. I know I would sound like a poor loser if I complained. I wouldn't want to win the New York City Marathon because of a protest."

I laid awake all night thinking about the marathon and being the loser standing tall. In the marathon world, there's only one winner, and the winner takes it all when it comes to fame and celebrity status. Though, I didn't feel sorry for myself for long ... *there are worse things in life*. Carlos Lopes, the 1984 Olympic gold medalist from Portugal, once summed it up perfectly: "Second place is not a defeat. It is a stimulation to get better. It makes you even more determined."

Between the triple prize money and bonuses, I won a lot of money that day. "I'm glad you're an athlete and not an agent or I would go broke," said Fred Lebow with a chuckle. He was impressed that I let my legs do the talking, settling my worth.

Steve found another painting in his friend's art studio. I should have known. Our visits to New York wouldn't be complete without returning home with a piece of art. It was a beautiful painting of a New York City park scene in late fall on a dark, dreary day. The colors were spectacular. It was my favorite painting of all.

Jamie and I were looking forward to our usual post-race "eating day," piling up all of my chocolates on the dining room table as the gifts kept pouring in throughout the week. Our overindulging was cut short when Jamie dove into a box of expensive chocolates sent from a race director in Germany. She took a big bite out of the largest, most impressive chocolate in the box. Right away she started crying, then screaming. "Mom, this tastes like "Off" spray!" I quickly looked at the box and sniffed the chocolate. It was filled with liqueur. Rachel gave out her usual belly laugh and I joined her. Once Jamie rinsed her mouth with water several times, she laughed, too.

I didn't see Grandma Helen again until the holidays, but she hadn't changed her mind about the last half-mile of the marathon. "You ran well, Kimmie, but that Wanda should have just sat down!"

～

December proved to be a good month. I found my true love. His name was Bud.

I spent at least an hour every day with Bud that winter and sometimes I saw him twice a day. I skipped runs with Don and the boys for weeks at a time to be with him. He was my dream.

Bud could go up to 12 miles an hour, up to a 12% incline and 3% decline. I could program him for 30 courses from 10-30 miles, and his glimmering display panel gave me all the feedback and control that I would ever want or need. I never thought a treadmill, even a top of the line model like Bud, could make me so happy. There was an added bonus, I could heat train in the middle of winter without feeling claustrophobic under layers and layers of clothes. By turning the thermostat up to 80 degrees and the humidifier to 80% in the small room, I was set.

There was one stretch in January where I didn't step foot outside for three weeks, preferring to run on Bud. When I finally joined the boys for a Sunday run, it was only because Benji was visiting and my face was pasty white from lack of sun. Nonetheless, I ran fast, strong and smooth, keeping up with the boys without a problem. "How can you possibly run 100 miles a week on a treadmill?" they asked in surprise. "It's better than slipping and sliding all over the icy roads," I told them. They seemed even more impressed with my faster pace. Don told me, "You've moved to a higher level."

After watching "Ghostbusters" over and over with his two young daughters, Don came up with the bright idea to play a trick on Benji and have "Benji Busters" shirts made up for our long run during his visit. Benji was coaching Rob and me, and he gave us our workouts based on time, not mileage. Whenever we had a 2 hour and 20 minute run planned, we went exactly 2 hours and 20 minutes, to the second, running around the parking lot until we hit the exact time. Don, Staffan and the boys rolled their eyes. "What's the big deal? Who cares if you run 2 hours 19 minutes and 55 seconds or 2:20? This is ridiculous." Rob was a stickler for detail, always being exact, and I did it because it drove them crazy and I enjoyed their frustration and cynical comments. At last, they were going to get back at Benji for starting it all. Rob and I were happy to help.

Don silkscreened Benji's face onto the front of white long-sleeved T-shirts, and then added a bright red circle with a slash across it. When we all met down by the River Road, we took off our jackets without saying a word and prepared to start our run. "What's this?" asked Benji. "What're you wearing?" He looked closer. I noticed he was holding back a smile. Everyone ran the River Road on winter Sunday mornings. Therefore, it was a perfect opportunity to display our Benji Busters shirts, with Benji present.

During their visit, Benji and Amie were treated to a few glimpses of the girls' unique personalities. Jamie's tantrums were something else. It didn't happen often, but if she had a stressful night at her dad's, or was overtired or had too much sugar, Jamie changed on us. She would fall to the floor, kicking and screaming until she went hoarse. "See what you'ew making me do (cough cough), I'm choking to death ... my thwoat is so sowe. Fogive me and I will stop cwying. Please fogive me please," and on and on she went. It wasn't pretty. Only the special few, other than Steve, Rachel and me, were privileged enough to see her in action. Staffan would just walk away, sometimes even leaving the house. Benji and Amie would watch in amazement.

Rachel was my little rebel. She decided to continue smoking and hanging out with the wrong group, skipping school and failing in most of her classes. Restriction didn't work. Talking to her worked at times, and giving her the silent treatment after a "Hmmm" seemed to do the trick, but not for long. She hated seeing me upset and would try for a while, but then fall back into her usual pattern.

Jamie started saying, "I love you lots. You're the best in the whole world. I love you so much. I don't know what I would do without you. Sorry, thanks for everything. Please be careful, I love you. Goodbye," before going anywhere, even if she was just going outside to play. She substituted "goodnight" for "goodbye" at the end of the whole spiel if she was going to bed. Every time she said it, she expected us to say it back to her. If we didn't, she would cry and insist it was bad luck and something terrible would happen. Steve and I had to go through that all the time. Every. Single. Day. And. Night. Rachel didn't fall for it, but if we didn't repeat every word we couldn't get Jamie out of the house or to bed.

Jamie would say it all during the most inopportune times, including the middle of interviews, even during live television interviews at home. "Would you please say goodbye after the interviews, instead of when I'm right in the middle of one?" I scolded her. Then she would sit there waiting and staring until the interview was over, which made me nervous. If she really wanted to make things interesting, her little finger would come into the picture and tap on my shoulder when I was on live.

It didn't take long before Steve came up with the brilliant idea to shorten it to: "Ditto, be careful, I love you, bye (or goodnight)." The phrase continues to this day.

Chapter 16

I didn't get out much in the early months of 1991. I was training for yet another Boston Marathon. I really wanted to win, which meant more sacrifice, focusing solely on my family and training. The only people I saw other than my family were Ania, three times a week for massage; Val, when we went to the Thai restaurant once a week; and my training buddies, once in a great while, now that I had Bud in my life.

I saw one other friend, named Wally. He was spectacular, with his own room upstairs near Bud's. He was sleek, clean and all chrome, with three stations surrounding his beautiful silver weights. Three days a week, I spent an hour with Wally while listening to 50's and 60's music and sipping a glass of wine as dinner was cooking downstairs. The wine was my new candy bar, enticing me up there. After each weightlifting exercise, I had a sip of wine as my reward.

Several months before the marathon, Dick Patrick, a sportswriter for USA Today, traveled to Spokane from Washington, D.C., to write a feature article on me, following me around for several days. He and Jamie became instant friends. They played basketball in the driveway, battled at Nintendo and talked while I was taking my nap or needed a break. Who knows what she told him. Dick really enjoyed her and Jamie tried to take charge of him, getting jealous whenever he spent time with me while I prepared dinner, followed me on runs, or watched me run on Bud and lift with Wally. What seemed to impress him more than anything was the glass of wine. "Do you always drink wine when you're lifting weights? Unbelievable."

"It lures me up here," I told him, as he watched my weight/sip routine.

It was Dick's last night in Spokane and we needed to finish up the interview. After Jamie brushed her teeth, I told her a bedtime story. She always wanted to hear the one about Debbie and me stealing the quarter, coming home with chocolate on our faces and being restricted for two weeks to our room. I guess it made her feel better about only having to go to bed. Plus, it was one of my longer stories.

A few minutes after I went back down to the living room to finish the interview, Jamie called from the top of the stairs. "Mom, I want to come down and visit with Dick." I told her no. "I need a dwink of watew." I told her no. "Go to bed, Jamie." She was back at the top of the stairs a few minutes later. "Please, Mom. I'm dehydwated. I need watew and elect-wolytes for my cwamping muscles."

Dick started laughing, "Only your daughter would come up with something like that." I told Jamie she could come downstairs, where she had some Gatorade before climbing the stairs back to her room, smiling and so proud of herself, saying, "Goodnight, Dick."

Early that spring Jamie's friends became more curious about me. As the Boston Marathon drew closer, they watched me on the news, saw my photo in the newspaper and heard their parents talking about me. "What does your mom *do* all day?" they asked Jamie, who was so proud that she decided to show them.

Instead of going to juggling class one day after school, they all headed over to our house a block away. In a rush to squeeze my second run in before she came home, I woke up from my nap, put on my running shoes and hopped directly onto Bud. While gazing out the window at a couple of squirrels scurrying about in the tree branches as I listened to the soundtrack from "Cats" on my Walkman, I suddenly had the eerie sensation that somebody was watching me. I looked to my right. There were half a dozen 10-year-old girls in the room with big eyes staring as I ran, the fan blowing my short satin nightgown out behind me.

By the time I yanked my headphones off, they were already on their way out but I could hear Jamie say, "See, I told you that's what she does all day."

That wasn't the only thing Jamie showed them. Her best friend's mom was driving them home one day when she made a quick stop at Rosauers to pick up a few groceries. While the girls were waiting in the car, one of them needed to use the restroom. "Let's do what my mom does before some of her waces," Jamie suggested. When the mother walked out of the store, she found six little girls squatting behind the potted plants in the parking lot, peeing.

When she scolded them, Jamie explained. "My mom does this before her impotent waces. She says it's impotent to feel bettew and not hold it in."

The mom brought Jamie home and told me what had happened. I explained, "I had to go so badly *once* before a race that I ended up going in the bushes because the port-a-johns were full. It wasn't meant to be standard procedure in a supermarket parking lot." I was relieved when the woman started laughing.

Around that time Jamie stopped speaking like Elmer Fudd. Her retainer was doing its job, correcting her slight overbite as well as her improper speech. The braces later finished the job.

There was never a lull in our life, especially when my focus was supposed to be on an upcoming marathon. My concerns shifted to Rachel's behavior. She was on a slippery slope, more into being cool and hanging out with the kids the copper had warned her about than in going to school. She was failing classes and becoming more disrespectful to Steve. While sitting on her bed, I asked, "What can we do, Rachel? What's this all about? I will do anything within my power to help you."

"You and Steve are good to me, but I'm not happy in Spokane. I miss my friends in Port Townsend. I know that Laurie and Mel aren't the same, and I know I can't live with them, but I miss Mel, Danny and little Charlie." She started crying, which she never did.

"Mom, I don't want to leave you, but I want to be where I belong. I wish we could all move to Port Townsend together."

I didn't know what to think, let alone how to react. Instead of jumping to a quick reply, I said, "Let's think about this. Your happiness is my main concern, and that you give yourself a chance in life. I really want to see you graduate, Rachel. This is so important. Please work to graduate for me. This is all I ask."

"You mean you're thinking about letting me go back to Port Townsend?"

"We'll see."

"Mom, I swear, I will work really hard and do my best, and I *will* graduate with my friends in Port Townsend."

I told her about having to miss my junior year while pregnant with her, then coming back and still graduating on time. "It can be done. You're a smart girl if you focus. You also need to give Steve some respect and listen while he tutors you. It will take some discipline, a lot of it."

Rachel vowed, "I'll do it, Honest to Jehovah God." I believed her.

I talked to Steve. We agreed that if Rachel could bring her grades up by the end of the school year and go to summer school to make up for her missed classes, we would pay her way to move in with a friend to start her junior year in Port Townsend. That seemed to be our last chance to persuade Rachel to work hard, achieve a goal and, more importantly, get that much-needed education. As Steve said, "We've tried everything else."

I said to Rachel the same thing Chuck had said to me, "Go out in the world and see what the world has to offer you." She was thrilled, but I was torn. Jamie, no doubt after some coaching from her sister, told us, "It'll be good for Rachel. She needs to move to Port Townsend." Steve seemed happy with the solution. She was terrorizing him.

It would be up to Rachel from that point on.

I began to enjoy traveling to races for my timeout from "real life" and to meet up with friends, as well as to race. I chose to spend my time with intelligent, humorous and interesting people, the people I respected and could learn from.

During my several races in Florida, I spent most of my time with Mr. Jones and Mark Plaatjes, who had recently moved to Boulder with their families, and four incredibly intriguing masters runners: Nick Rose, another tough and talented Brit who was running extremely well, even in his 40s; and Carol McClatchie, Laurie Binder and Barb Filutze, all sarcastic and witty women who could, and did, beat many of the younger runners. I could always con one, sometimes all, of them into running a long second run after our races. We were all fierce competitors, focusing solely on our races beforehand and racing hard when the time came, but we also couldn't wait to be done with it and have our downtime before heading home.

We did everything together. We ran, had meals, went to movies or just sat around and talked while waiting out the few days before our races. Afterward, we went to dinner and the race parties. I was quite naive compared to the old-timers. They talked about the days in Florida before I had even started running, when they stayed at HoJo's for weeks during the winter racing season. I pulled a Grandma Helen and finally asked, "What's it like there? Is it close by?"

"Yes, fairly close, and it's very comfortable, with a pool," Nick answered in his strong British accent. "Who is this HoJo?" I asked. "Is he a good friend of yours?" They were still laughing when I asked again, "Who is he?" I had no idea they were talking about the Howard Johnson hotels. They educated me, and taught me the ropes over the years. Being so sheltered from the world while growing up in a Jehovah's Witness family, then going from one marriage to the next, I had a lot to learn, even at the age of 33.

I enjoyed catching up on our families and friends and having dinner with Joanie Samuelson and Lynn Jennings when they made a rare appearance at a road race. Joanie was surprised more than once at how I managed to persuade the waiters to bring me the exact pre-race food I wanted in the exact way I wanted it, regardless of what was on the menu. Eventually, she just decided to order what I did: a glass of wine; a big plate of steamed vegetables on the side, with no butter; tons of whole grain rolls; and pasta galore with a touch of meat in the marinara sauce on the side.

Besides Dick Patrick from USA Today, I became friends with Barbara Huebner from the Boston Globe and several other "special" sportswriters and photographers. I looked forward to seeing them when they were covering the big marathons and meeting with them after press conferences, personal interviews, for meals, even a glass of wine or a beer after my race.

Once, I tricked Barb when she came to Jacksonville to cover the River Run 15K and interview me for the upcoming Boston Marathon. At the press conference Doug Alred, the race director, announced that the first runner to reach the 10K mark would receive a bonus. When it was time for questions, Barb put him on the spot by asking, "Since the first runner is sure to be male, does the first woman get a bonus, too?" Doug was flustered as he stammered through an answer in front of the athletes and journalists.

The night of the race I asked Barb, "Do you want to go to the post-race party? We'll be served a nice dinner." We were on the guest bus and almost there before she asked where the party was. "It's at Doug Alred's house," I told her. "Oh, great," she said. "I just embarrassed the guy in front of everybody yesterday, and now I'm going to his house for a party." Doug not only was fine with it, he even decided to give the first woman through the 10K a bonus the following year.

I met some unique and delightful people because of my racing over the years and some have become lifelong friends. That was much more rewarding to me than a satisfying race. My career would end someday but my friends would always be there for me.

After my last two Boston and New York performances, I had become more popular, doing more live interviews, press conferences, and up-close-and-personal TV feature stories. People started asking me where I was from – sometimes even what country, much less what region.

I don't have an obvious accent like a Southerner or a New Englander. I don't really have an accent at all. It's more of a speech pattern, a bit of over-pronounced Canadian – I say "eh?" all the time – mixed with some special words I picked up during my childhood from watching too many episodes of the Cartwright boys, Andy Griffith, Jed Clampett, Fred Flintstone and, later, John Boy Walton. I use the word "reckon" a lot, sometimes "varmint" for an undesirable, and "critters" for animals. I often catch myself saying, "You're in a heap of trouble." Then these words are combined with the made-up phrases I picked up from Grandma Helen over the years. A normal sentence for me is: "I reckon she'll run like a light breeze and astonish us all. She's not one to lollygag around, eh?"

Over the years I've tried to tone it down. It could make for a stressful interview, especially in Boston with so many reporters and foreigners around during marathon weekend. They would give me a sudden, odd look as I caught them unawares with some of the things I came up with. I must have sounded like a proper hick from Canada having a "gay old time."

Boston Marathon ~ April, 1991

Boston 1991 was the perfect day for a marathon. Cloudy with maybe a slight cross breeze but no headwind. Everyone was in the race: the Polish women, led by Wanda Panfil, along with Ingrid Kristiansen, Joanie Samuelson and Uta Pippig, to name a few. Just before the start, masters star Laurie Binder turned and whispered to me discreetly, "You can beat Joanie, Ingrid and Uta," along with several other athletes. "Kim, you're ready."

"I'll cook their asses," I said jokingly.

Laurie was still laughing when the gun went off. Then I realized something. *She didn't mention Wanda.*

All went as usual. I had to play catch-up when the others hightailed it out of there at a pace way beyond my asthmatic tolerance. I passed Ingrid on the second Newton Hill after the firehouse turn, around 18 miles, and was gaining on Uta and Joanie. Wanda was way out in front.

Just as I was passing Uta, a wheelchair toppled over directly in front of us. I was startled into reality and out of my focus zone. I had to do something. I glanced at Uta to see what she had in mind and at that moment we both put our hands up, making a nonverbal agreement to help. We did, and then got right back into our race. Joanie was well ahead of us by then, so we had some work to do. I finally caught her at 25 miles, but passed her so quickly that I didn't have time to warn her that Uta was coming up on her as well.

Wanda won easily, in 2:24:18. I placed second in 2:26:40, a personal best, and was very impressed with myself – not just for running over a minute faster than I ever had before, but for the way I ran and for helping somebody out in the process. I quickly turned around to see Uta 12 seconds behind me, and Joanie two seconds behind her. Kamila Gradus of Poland was just one second behind Joanie. I found out later that it was the closest finish of the top five in Boston history.

Laurie Binder came up to me after finishing her race. "I forgot to tell you that you could beat Wanda." Then she added, "It's kick ass, not cook ass."

After the press conference, Bert Rosenthal from the Associated Press came up to me and asked what I wanted from my running. What, he asked, was my ultimate goal? I told him, "Bert, I want to shoot the moon."

He laughed. "So placing second in Boston in a personal best of 2:26 and becoming the third-fastest American of all time isn't shooting the moon?"

"No, I would call this playing all of the trump cards, but I was missing the ace. Wanda was holding that card." Bert smiled.

I was constantly teased about yet another second place when my friends took me out for a fantastic Thai dinner that night. The 14 of us were eating, drinking and toasting my finish when the owner of the restaurant came up and asked what we were celebrating. Don said, "Kim just placed second in the marathon today."

"Oh, congratulations," he said. "You are the second winner."

From then on everyone called me the second winner. A few weeks later I received a wonderful gift from Jeff – a red terrycloth bathrobe with "Second Winner, Boston 1991" embroidered in white on the right upper corner, and "Kim" embroidered on the lower left pocket. I treasured that robe and wore it every morning.

One morning shortly after, I was lounging in my Second Winner robe when it occurred to me ... as much as I was dedicated to my running the girls came first, my running second. Perhaps that's why I placed second in many of the major marathons.

One month later, my childhood dream – to someday be "The Most Important Person in Town" – from way back when I was the fool of Port Townsend, the *laughingstock* for all to tease, was about to come true. I was asked to be the Grand Marshal of the Rhododendron Parade.

Even grander, I was going to be able to share my moment with some of the people most important to me. I asked Grandma Helen, Mom and Rachel to join me in the parade – four generations of VIPs.

Or at least it was supposed to be. Rachel ditched us and I wasn't pleased. Had I known earlier, Jamie could have joined us instead.

Grandma, Mom and I sat up high on the back of the convertible and led the parade through uptown, where I first hatched my dream while I was being humiliated by Sambo the tomcat peeing through the pillowcase in the pet parade.

We threw candy to the cheering crowds as we rode past the movie theater where I used to show off for the boys and Shamrock threw me off for all to see. Then continued past the big hill, the place we stashed our stolen beer before lugging it up and across town to our clubhouse. We led the way downtown past the Rainier Brewery where we escaped the coppers, and along the downtown streets before turning into Memorial Field. I relished every moment, especially sharing it with Grandma Helen and Mom. I saw Rachel peeking around a corner as we went by. *Hmmm.* Later that afternoon she told me, "Mom, I would have been way too embarrassed sitting on top of that car in front of my friends."

"I can understand, but I think you might regret this someday."

"I do already," she replied as she glanced over at Grandma Helen.

Afterward we went back to my parents' home and ate an enormous amount of delicious seafood. Grandma Helen was overjoyed with our day of being VIPs. I was glad to see her appetite back as she ate several bowls of clam chowder. The color was returning to her cheeks after just going through a strenuous course of chemotherapy. I knew she would be with us a while longer.

It was the best present I could have ever shared with her. And then, to top it off, I won the Rhody Run in a course record the next morning to clinch my imaginary title of "The Most Important Person in Town." There was a big photo of Mom, Grandma and me in the next issue of the *Port Townsend Leader*, along with a nice article about us and about the race. Grandma Helen was a star and felt like one, sending clippings to our many relatives and all of her friends. "I'm as pleased as a big pie," she told everyone.

Seeing her so happy made up for failing to win the New York City Marathon for her or not making the Olympic team in 1988.

It was a big summer for the family. Soon after, Dad won the big Port Townsend Salmon Derby and $3000 by catching a 29-pound, 15-ounce salmon, and won $1000 in another derby for the same fish. The headline of the Port Townsend newspaper read: "PT Salmon Derby becomes family affair," and a story ran with a photo of Dad and the two runners-up proudly holding their salmon. A smaller photo of Dad, Grandma Pat and Mom ran on the same page, with Dad holding his gigantic salmon and Mom, who had netted the fish, holding up his big trophy. Mom had won the derby in 1985 and Grandma Pat, Dad's mom, had won in 1978 – with Dad's help.

Everyone was so proud of him, especially Grandma Pat.

The previous fall, Mom had received some good press as well when she was featured in an article, with a photo, in *Northwest Runner* magazine. She talked about how the Rhody Run inspired her, and how I gave her a pair of running shoes and a watch in 1984. "I'm really grateful to Kimmie," she told the interviewer. "The best gift Kim ever gave me was running." She talked about the tragedies of my brothers' deaths; how she, Jamie, Rachel and I all won our age-division medals in the Cane Dwellers' race in Hawaii; and that she was running a few miles several times a week. Of course, she also managed to talk about Jehovah and her religious beliefs, in a tactful way. She was doing God's will and preaching the good news to thousands of readers.

~

While I was preparing my base, 90-100 miles per week, for the upcoming 1992 Olympic Trials, one thing was happening on top of another.

Harlan became very sick that summer, and was later diagnosed with acute leukemia. He faded quickly, and there was nothing anybody could do. He chose to die at home with his family near him. During his lucid times he talked, chuckled and made silly Jones jokes. He was so kind and caring, trying to ease the suffering of loved ones while comforting those around him. The family was distraught. Nothing like that had ever happened in their family.

Just before Harlan slipped into death, he told the doctors, "I want to live long enough to see my daughter-in-law make the Olympic team." I was startled. I had no idea it meant that much to him.

Harlan passed away that same summer. He is deeply missed.

The Joneses came through. Their family pulled together, rather than fall apart as my family did after so many tragedies.

I felt so much compassion for Steve. "Your dad was such a wonderful man in so many ways," I told him. "I understand what you're going through. I've learned the hard way about the process of coping with the loss of a loved one. First the horrific shock, and now the denial."

He nodded, seeming extremely uncomfortable. I stopped there. He would find out for himself: the anger, the depression, having no desire to get back to normal. Finally comes acceptance for those fortunate enough to reach that point. I have learned that we all go through the process differently. Death changes our perspective, as we have to endure and go forward in life, learning to live without our loved one. Steve would find his way.

On top of losing his father, Steve was watching our friend, Moto, struggle with colon cancer. I knew how Steve felt but he wasn't willing, or maybe able, to show or talk about his feelings. He became quiet and moody, even less tolerant or willing to communicate.

Even before Harlan's death, Steve and I had never had a deep conversation. He was aloof and didn't like confrontation, walking away while scratching his head, then shaking it if he was unhappy or uncomfortable with a situation. We never even had an argument, which was frustrating because I knew it could lead to bigger problems. Appearances were important to him, as were things that made him stand out, like his bright pink shorts with the black polka dots. I knew there was much more to him, and I was continually watching him and observing his interaction with others as I tried to figure him out.

Steve was a man of routine. He did the same thing every evening when he came home from the office. He walked in with a swagger as he sashayed into the kitchen, through the dining room, and directly into the living room to find the mail neatly stacked on the corner of the couch. Without saying a word he began to sort through it, carelessly tossing each letter every which way, taking only what he needed and leaving the rest scattered all over the couch. Then he sauntered upstairs, put on his running clothes, and went for a short run before dinner. Jamie, Rachel, and I rolled our eyes each time, and then I rushed to pick up the mail and put it back into a neat pile.

Despite all that, we could count on him for anything. Steve was our mainstay, always ready to take on the challenges. He enjoyed a demanding and stimulating situation, as long as it wasn't a confrontational one.

A perfect example was when Rachel was learning to drive. Steve bravely agreed to be in charge of her lessons. He stayed calm and relaxed, giving her great feedback. He actually enjoyed the lessons, while Rachel scared me to death when I took her out. My right foot and calf were so sore from putting on my imaginary brake!

Rachel was the worst driver in Spokane. Flying down the streets, swerving around cars, running red lights, you name it. She failed her driving test several times and boy, was she mad.

During that disorganized time, I knew I had to synchronize the challenges – my intense training, showing up at races in one piece and being mentally prepared – along with the disruption at home. At that point I suggested to Steve, "Maybe I should put my summer training on the back burner for a few months before gearing toward the Trials." Steve wouldn't hear of it. He knew it was an important training period, plus he thrived on the excitement of the running world and loved to be right in the middle of it. The busier the better.

Because I'd been running so many hilly races in Boston and New York, we decided I should run the flat, fast Berlin Marathon in the fall. Berlin's course was similar to the Houston Marathon, where the 1992 Olympic Trials were going to take place four months later.

A lot of athletes weren't thrilled about the timing of the Trials, in the middle of winter. It's tough being fit and 100% ready to go in January. To make matters worse, the Trials were supposed to be in Long Beach, Calif., but had to be moved at the last minute because of sponsorship issues. Everything just seemed a little out of whack; however, getting in a good, flat marathon beforehand would help.

Five weeks before Berlin, I was sprinting down a cobblestone street in Flint, Michigan, during the Bobby Crim 10 Mile race, battling for second place with one of my favorite people, Anne Audain. After moving ahead, and just before the finish, pain sent me jumping straight in the air. I'd pulled my hamstring. I quickly turned back to see Anne sprinting toward me, and I hobbled over the finish line just in time.

I had to heal quickly. Ania and Chuck Strickell worked on me every day under Staffan's direction from afar, and whenever I was sitting down or sleeping I used a special micro-current machine that was supposed to speed the healing process with a current running through two electrodes placed above and below the injury sight. The pull was bad, with bruising and all; even so, I was ready for a practice race three weeks later, two weeks before the Berlin Marathon. If my hamstring held up in the Philadelphia Distance Run, I would go to Berlin.

"You're too damn tough to let something like this slow you down," Chuck told me. Then I heard him talking with Ania in the other room. "This is a bad hamstring pull. I've never known anyone to heal in three weeks from something like this, and certainly not be ready to race a half marathon."

Ania replied, "She's more resilient than you know."

It was 80 degrees with 80 percent humidity in Philadelphia at the start of the half marathon. That steam bath would keep my damaged hamstring warm and loose. Laurie Binder was at the start and she wished me luck. I told her, "Go cook some asses."

Off we went. I was running at marathon pace, to test my hamstring and to pace myself in the heat. All was good. I slowly picked up the pace and started inching closer to Anne Audain and Diane Bussa, who were leading. At 8 miles, I was a minute behind. I was feeling strong but tiring from my effort to catch them. Fortunately, Anne and Diane were tiring more than I was. I knew I had to make my move as we crested the hill between miles 11-12 before the final downhill mile to the finish. Off I went, passing them like they were standing in mud, going on to win the race.

I turned around to see Laurie running in, cooking many young girls' asses as she broke the U.S. Masters record.

Commentator Toni Reavis came up to me to do a live interview for ESPN, which televised the race. "How did the race go for you, Kim? Tell us about it." I didn't mention my hamstring, but told him, "I started out conservatively because of the heat and humidity, well aware that it was going to be a tough day. I paced myself and ran within my comfort zone so I'd have the strength and energy to finish strong. On the final hill at mile 12, I made my move ... and I made it count."

The race and that interview were included in a monthly road race wrap-up show on television. Jamie recorded it and watched it over and over.

Not long afterward, Jamie had the big All City cross-country meet, where she would be running against the best grade-school girls in the Spokane region in a mile race. Steve and I were there as usual, watching her excel in her sport.

The race was two laps around a park. Two girls bolted off from the start. Jamie let them get well ahead of her. I watched, very nervously. She ran by and I yelled, "Get going Jamie, try and catch them!" She continued to plod along. When she passed again, well into their next lap, Jamie was still behind. Then, with a quarter mile to go, Jamie put on her jets and passed them as if they were standing in mud as they crested the final hill before the long downhill straightaway to the finish.

Hey! That was my strategy in Philadelphia.

She sprinted to the finish, winning the race. When the TV and newspaper reporters covering the race interviewed her, she told them, "I paced myself and ran in my comfort zone so I'd have the strength and energy to finish strong. On the final hill, I made my move ... and I made it count."

Hey! That's exactly what I said after I won the half marathon. I knew to be careful what I did and said after that. I had a little imitator on my hands.

Berlin Marathon, Germany ~ September, 1991

Two weeks later, I went to Berlin with Ania, Staffan and Steve, treated first class, as I was growing accustomed to. I placed second in 2:27:50, 14 seconds behind first place. Mark Plaatjes placed second in the men's race, just four seconds behind the winner.

"Kimbo, your race was impeded," Mark told me while we waited for drug testing, his hands flying in the air. "This is *not* acceptable. Those male pace setters for that Polish woman kept you from winning the race! I saw the footage at the finish."

Mark was right. The men running with Renata Kokowska kept push-ing me off the course and away from the shortest route. They prevented me from reaching my drinks at the aid stations, and blocked me every time I tried to pass her as she went on to become the winner who takes it all.

I told Mark, "It's Europe. They asked me if I wanted my own pace setters. Now I know why – as bodyguards!"

Mark protested for me, which was sweet but useless. Mark is a "go getter" and always wanting justice. I got an apology from the race direc-tor, but that was the extent of it. "Kimbo, you are too nice to win a mara-thon," Mark told me. But I told Mark, "*You're* too nice to win, too. You did all the leading from the start, allowing second place to use you and save himself to pass you in the final half mile."

We laughed. We were both too nice.

I had a sick, unsettling feeling after that second-place finish. I accepted my past seven second-place finishes in major marathons, fully aware that I was outperformed. But after my Berlin experience, I felt there was an injustice done to me, and my sport. However, life isn't always fair and "life goes on."

Before heading back to the States, Steve and I picked out gifts for the girls: a sweatshirt and a pair of Doc Marten boots for Rachel, and a German made "Steiff" stuffed animal for Jamie. The fawn was close to life size, and from afar the sitting animal looked real. "Please, will you name it something other than a wine?" I asked Jamie. She named it Shinobi, for no reason that I could figure out. *Maybe that will be the name of a new wine someday.*

Soon after we returned, I had a *Running Times* cover shoot. Steve was there to run with me in some shots, which made him more energetic and animated than I had seen him since Harlan's death.

They say there's a "cover jinx" for athletes so I was wary – my next endeavor would be the Olympic Trials. I was on the cover of *Running Times* in 1987 before my World Championships fiasco in Rome, and another magazine before my asthma attack during the 1988 Olympic Trials. The upcoming cover photo was scheduled for the December 1991 issue, a month before the 1992 Trials.

Nevertheless, my focus all year was on the Trials race and didn't stray. I trained extremely well. I balanced everything perfectly. I was ready.

We had one snowstorm after another in December, and there was ice under the snow. I didn't dare run outside. That was my excuse anyway, in order to spend more time with Bud. I thoroughly enjoyed running miles and miles on the treadmill. Six weeks before the marathon, I ran for three hours in the morning: 27 miles, with the middle 10 miles at 5:40 pace. Then I ate a lot, napped, and went right back on the treadmill two hours later for another 9 miles in the afternoon in the tiny room set at 80 degrees and 80% humidity. That was a significant confidence builder for the Trials.

However, running on Bud could be dangerous at times. One day, while I was running 12 mph (5 minute pace) during a mile speed effort, Bud abruptly stopped. I went flying forward, flipping off the display panel and toppling toward the window. The power had gone off. I went marching down the stairs to the basement, only to find Steve walking away from the power box. "Oops," he said, looking anxious and his face red.

Sunday, December 22, 1991. It was Don's birthday, and nobody wanted to run with him. The roads were snow-packed and it was cold and snowing, but I'd been running on the treadmill for 10 days straight. My skin was almost gray from lack of fresh air and vitamin D ... *I should be running on land*. I decided to make my way outside to join Don for his birthday run.

It was a 20 miler along the River Road. We decided to run down one side, cross the bridge at 7 miles and head toward the college on the other side, which was blocked off to traffic and more like running cross country. Steve planned to pick us up in the car once we made our way back. We were having our usual interesting and entertaining conversation until 17 miles, when I became blinded for a moment from running on the white snow for so many miles. I was too close to the edge of the road, above a small cliff leading down to the river, when I stepped on a loose rock covered in snow.

My ankle and I went off the side and I stumbled a bit down the embankment. "Are you hurt?" Don asked anxiously as I made my way back to the road. "I'm OK," I assured him. Once we continued to run, however, I realized that there was something terribly wrong with my foot. We ran for another mile to the main road before I told Don, "I don't think I should be running."

I told him that it was a strange pain, something I'd never experienced. Instantly Don's expression turned to concern. Steve came driving up and jokingly asked, "Do you need a ride?" I said yes, and stopped in my tracks.

Then Steve looked worried. I never stopped during a run, especially when running with one of the boys.

I went to visit Dr. Wigert, who suggested I see James Perry, the best orthopedic surgeon in our area. Dr. Perry took X-rays and did a bone scan. Nothing was obvious. For a week I kept trying to run, but could barely make it out the door before I had to stop from the pain deep within my ankle joint.

Luckily, Dr. Perry had read about a rare ankle injury that wasn't easily detected. He went back and studied the X-ray, finding an anterior calcaneal hairline fracture at the ligament attachment. When my ankle violently twisted, the bone remained strong but the ligament connecting to the bone was injured, causing bruising and a slight hairline crack.

Unfortunately, the ligament I had injured is the one I need for my forceful toe push-off. Most marathoners don't run on their toes, so for them, the injury would mean nothing more than a little rest for a strained ligament. I needed extra rest to give the hairline fracture more time to heal before the Olympic Trials in four weeks, so I couldn't run. Not even a step.

But I had to keep trying. I had many Ania massages. I did pool running to stay fit, which I had never tried before and thoroughly despised. I hooked myself up to electric and micro-current machines, and received physical therapy from Staffan and Chuck. Just before I left for Houston, Dr. Perry gave me a cortisone shot, hoping it would reduce the inflammation and pain enough to help me through the marathon. The shot was extremely painful, but I was willing to try anything.

Of course, while I was going through all of that therapy, Jamie had the "same" injury. She iced when I iced. She used the portable micro-current machine while I used the big one, placing the electrodes in the same places on her foot, while we watched "Murder, She Wrote" and "Matlock" and played solitaire next to each other. She even walked with a slight limp, although she sometimes forgot which foot to favor. Smiling and winking at me, Ania even gave her a therapy massage.

Olympic Marathon Trials, Houston ~ January, 1992

Until we arrived in Houston, I didn't run a step. Four days before the Olympic Trials Marathon, I tried it for the first time. My foot hurt with a deep, dull pulsating pain. I couldn't even get up on my toes to push off. Reality struck. I wouldn't be able to run the Trials.

I was in a dark place, "all alone" ... my dream of the last four years was out of reach. I'm not one to give up. I was not being negative. I was facing reality head on. None of that hard work and sacrifice was going to pay off.

I had to deal with it quietly up until the marathon. My injury was no secret, but I wasn't ready to tell the media that my practice run had been a failure. Instead, I made jokes about all my pool running and feeling like "a fish out of water" on my test run. I went through my pre-marathon routine, right up to the starting line. *Maybe enough endorphins will kick in to mask the pain. Maybe there will be a miracle.*

As always, I was hoping for the best. Only ... I was expecting the worst.

At the starting line I was worried, unsure of what was about to happen. There had been no positive reinforcement of any kind leading into the race. The gun went off and so did I – for a while, anyway. My fitness was good, but my foot was killing me. I've run in pain many times, but I couldn't run with that pain, so sure that I was about to do some serious damage and fearing that I might never run again if I continued. I grabbed some water at an aid station, to give myself a moment to think.

"Good luck," I said to my competitors as I pulled off the course at 3 miles – in a very bad part of Houston – and sat on the curb. A wino came over and sat next to me. *If Anne Audain could see me now, sitting in the gutter again, with a wino this time.*

"Why did you stop?" he asked me. I told him about my injury and how disappointing it was.

"Do you need a drink?" he asked, handing me his wine bottle wrapped in a brown paper bag.

I smiled, shaking my head no, then asked him, "Do *you* want a drink?" as I handed him my bottle of water. He smiled, shaking his head.

Just then, the motorcycle cop following the final runner pulled over, asking me if I was OK and whether I needed a ride back to the hotel. I hopped on after saying goodbye to my wino friend and handing him my bottle of water. "You should drink this. You must be dehydrated," I advised him. He smiled and waved as the copper and I drove away.

At the hotel, I was alone. Everyone I knew was either running, watching or on the press truck. It gave me a chance to sulk, cry and think things through as I cleaned up before going out to cheer on my friends at the 25-mile mark, just outside the hotel. The race was settled by then, so I congratulated the soon to be Olympians – #1 Janis Klecker (2:30:12), #2 Cathy O'Brien and #3 Francie Larrieu Smith – as they went by, hoping to bring some good energy flowing back my way from watching them enjoy their moment. It was bittersweet.

Then, I went directly to the pressroom to face some music. I needed to get it over with. I was devastated and didn't know what to say without breaking down, though it was almost a relief to be out of my lonely dark place and face reality in public. Steve, with some of his family, appeared miserable and couldn't even look at me. Poor Harlan would have been disappointed in me. Ania was there along with other friends who had come to see me make the Olympic team. Of course they thought I would. I was ranked #3 in the world, an American hadn't beaten me for several years, and my qualifying time was almost a minute faster than my closest competitor and minutes faster than most.

Most of the sportswriters were my friends by then, and some really cared for me, taking my disappointment to heart. There was silence. Many seemed almost as devastated as I was.

I felt the need to cheer them up, and it was the best thing that could have happened. I came up with the funny things Laurie Binder, Ania and I said before the race, like Laurie telling me to show up at the starting line with an underwater face mask and snorkel, wearing fins instead of racing flats, after all my time in the pool. I described Ania laughing so hard that she was snorting, saying, "And you can wear a nose plug and do synchronized swimming moves for your warm up before the race. And when they say 'runners set,' you get into a diving start, hands behind your back like you're ready to dive in." Then I told everyone about the wino sitting with me in the gutter, wanting to share his bottle. They laughed and seemed to feel much better, which made me feel a little better – for a short while.

I could tell that I let everyone down. I think it took the wind right out of Benji's sailboat. He was quiet and didn't have the words of wisdom he usually had right after a bad race. He even let his own running slip.

Steve was quiet and unsure of what to say. Jamie and Rachel watched me closely and were extremely good for several weeks.

I received many cards saying things like, "May the comfort of God help you through this difficult time," and "Our hearts go out to you in your time of sorrow." They were condolence cards! Everyone was treating it like a death.

Should I retire? I'm 34 years old and have been at the top for eight years, much longer than most top elite marathoners. I pondered the thought as I jogged 4 miles every other day, at Ania's urging, ("Cheer up, Kimmie, you must get in the pool and exercise, and start running again!") My ankle was taking so long to heal I would have been better off breaking it.

I was sitting in Big Red watching the news when I noticed Punky sitting in her usual place by the radiator, waiting for a pat of encouragement to jump on my lap. She was there in an instant, even before I could put my hand down on my leg. She sat there, seeming to know I was in distress. "Punky, we're getting old," I told her. "You're eight, 48 in human years, and I'm 34. Should we settle in and give up?" She looked at me with knowing eyes, just like Grandma Helen.

The very next day, I was heading out the kitchen door to go grocery shopping when I heard a racket in the backyard. I looked over to see Punky sitting on the grass at the base of a big pine tree. There was a squirrel running down the trunk, taunting her, and then scurrying back up as it chattered away.

"What are you doing?" I asked Punky. "You'll never catch that squirrel just sitting there."

I left for Rosauers and shopped for at least an hour, then visited with Bridgid Kardong for a long while before going home to find Punky still sitting at the bottom of the tree. I brought my loads of groceries into the house. Punky wouldn't even acknowledge me. I called her name and she glanced over, but stayed as still as a rock.

Suddenly, I heard all kinds of screeching and commotion. I ran outside to find Punky with a big, fat squirrel in her mouth, ready for the kill. I grabbed the broom from the back deck and started whacking at both of them until Punky let go. The squirrel went hobbling up the tree. Punky looked defeated, lowering her head as she stalked right past me and into the house.

Punky was right back out there in the yard several days later, watching and waiting ever so patiently for a squirrel. She caught another one! She came trotting up to the sliding glass door with the squirrel in her mouth *after* the kill, so she wouldn't be thwarted. She saw me and paraded around on the deck with her prize – my beautiful white fluffy cat was trotting around so proud of herself. That was my feisty 48-year-old.

Right then, I decided, *it's not time to retire just yet. I'm not ready to give up. I still have some fight in me.* The year before, I'd become "The Most Important Person in Port Townsend" and made Grandma Helen prouder than she ever dreamed possible, but I still had some other goals left to fulfill – winning Bloomsday and an Olympic medal.

I knew that the rest of 1992 was going to be a test. I was going to have to be persistent and press on. *Something is coming, something promising.*

～

It was a rough winter for me, and it took its toll on everyone. For a positive distraction, we went to Disneyland with the McDermotts during the girls' spring vacation and had a fantastic time. It was always like a "Brady Bunch" vacation with that fun and energetic family.

We were the typical vacationing families in Disneyland, staying in a hotel with a nice pool, the tired parents sitting in the loungers drinking beer and laughing after a long day in the park while our kids played and sometimes splashed the annoyed childless couples.

At the park the kids went on every ride possible, over and over. While we parents were on some ride similar to a Ferris wheel we spotted our two spirited 11-year-olds, Jamie and Ryan, running through the park, hand in hand, barging through the crowds and maneuvering their way to the front of the lines. We were way up in the air and helpless, watching our youngest pushing, crowding and thinking they were the most important kids in the park.

Once we staggered off, we couldn't catch up to them as they darted from ride to ride. After deciding to just let them have their fun, we went into line for the most exciting ride in the park, the Matterhorn. We had been waiting in that line for over 45 minutes when all of a sudden Jamie and Ryan went running by. "Come on, Brother," we heard Jamie say. "I know our parents must be up here waiting for us. They must be worried." Everyone let them by, thinking they were looking for their parents! It was their trick to get to the front of the line for all the rides. They went on each ride several times before Rachel, Carl and Mac managed to get on once.

I found solace in watching the kids having the time of their lives. It was the nourishment I needed to repair, to put my running aside and appreciate what life had to offer. Not many athletes realize, right in the middle of their careers, there are more important things in life than making an Olympic team or striving to be the best.

Come to find out, one thing positive came from my injury. It was meant to be, a divine intervention – I had an abundant amount of time, energy and patience to work with Rachel, and we spent many hours together working toward her goal. She managed to catch up in all of her classes during the school year. She really came through. I was extremely proud of her, and she was so proud of herself. It was her first big accomplishment and she put herself to the test, risking failure, only to succeed. Finally, she had some confidence. Moreover, she was getting what she wanted ... moving back to Port Townsend. I would miss her terribly, but I knew she would be happy and work toward a good life there. I gave her up early again, a big sacrifice.

After many tries and a few timeouts, Rachel eventually got her driver's license – barely passing – so I gave her my old red Buick. She packed up and moved to Port Townsend as pleased as a big pie.

It was the best thing we could have done. Rachel excelled in everything she did. She gained self-esteem, a sense of self-worth and felt like the queen of Port Townsend. Everybody wanted her in their lives. Her charisma charmed and drew people toward her.

Rachel became close to her father and his family. Brad was a good man and wanted to make up for lost time with his beautiful daughter after excluding her from his life for so long. He was too young and immature when Rachel was conceived to understand or take responsibility. He had another chance, and Rachel had another family. She was spending time with them as well as with her Grandfather Claude. She adored this big, strong and gentle man as much as I did many years ago.

Rachel also had her cousins and friends, and all of her grandparents. She even started spending time with her adopted family from years ago. They were all there for her. Rachel not only looked like a thin Miss Piggy, but she started acting like her as well, with her head held high and nose in the air with importance. I took pride in seeing her transformation. She still had her moments, though.

Chapter 17

Dr. Perry gave me the OK to race in May. Since I wasn't able to train much and my foot wasn't 100% pain free, I could have skipped the Rhody Run that year, but I needed something positive moving forward. I needed to be brave and face my fears of running on a bad foot, and worse, of losing the race. I didn't know how I was going to pull it off.

The evening before the Rhody Run I went down to the beach, as I always did, to be near Charlie and Stanley. While taking in the fresh sea air and standing in the ankle-deep waves, soaking my poor foot in the healing and soothing ice-cold water, suddenly I knew ... I was going to win.

And I did!

Like most athletes, after a long layoff from injury or illness, I desperately needed to regain my fitness and my lost time from the racing scene – immediately. I became manic, like a colossal wave as it aggressively hits shore, reaching out for everything all at once. That is how I lived out the rest of 1992.

Hokkaido Marathon, Japan ~ August, 1992

I was invited to Japan to run the Hokkaido Marathon in August. It was just what I needed, a new goal.

Jamie, Ania, Steve and I flew across the Pacific Ocean in first class. Jamie decided Shinobi had to join us. How embarrassing. Shinobi was too big to stuff into a suitcase, which meant Jamie carried him throughout our trip. Actually, I was the one carrying him around most of the time while Jamie did cartwheels in the subways, acting like a normal 12-year-old American kid. Since she was almost my height, the Japanese gave her dirty looks assuming she was an adult behaving in such a childish way.

We stayed in a beautiful hotel next to a large park and the marathon finish line. It had a zoo, rides, food stands, ponds, and pathways to run and walk. Jamie and I were the only blonds around, and people stared. Even the crows thought we were something else. When Jamie and I did a mile jog around the park, gigantic crows began diving for our blond ponytails. Everyone threw French fries from the food stands to them for treats, so maybe they thought our ponytails were big fries. The crows grabbed hold of our ponytails and pulled on them until realizing they weren't going anywhere. We decided to wear hats after that.

Ania and Jamie stayed in a room two doors down from Steve and me. Ania gave me long massages in their room while Steve and Jamie went out for adventures in the few days leading up to the marathon. Jamie didn't like the authentic Japanese food so she and Steve went out into the busy noisy streets, all looking the same, with thousands of people all seeming to look and dress alike, to find a corndog stand. They were on almost every corner, and Jamie lived on corndogs while we were there.

The afternoon before the marathon, I was in Ania and Jamie's room getting my final pre-race massage. Steve must have thought I'd be back soon, and ordered room service – sushi for 12 – before sending Jamie out to find her own corndog stand. *Sushi for 12 the day before a marathon?*

That wasn't the worst of it. Hours later, Jamie was nowhere to be found and Steve wasn't answering the door. Ania and I thought he might have eaten so much of the raw and sodium-rich food that he was poisoned or gave himself a heart attack.

The door was bolted from the inside. Security came and tried to help us force it open, with no success. Finally, after what seemed a very long time, Steve came to the door, red faced, with a bloated stomach and soy sauce all over his chin. He had just woken up from a long nap. My hands shot into the air. "Unbelievable!" I said, exasperated. "What were you thinking? And where's Jamie?"

"She left a while ago to get a corndog," he said, still half asleep.

Then the search was on for Jamie. We eventually found her frantically running toward the park from one of those mazes they call streets, upset and crying. After enjoying the zoo and playing in the park, she had gone off in search of her corndog and became lost. She told us that she had been running to people asking, "Where's the hotel? Where's the park?" Finally somebody pointed her in the right direction.

I almost had to laugh. The Japanese must have thought Jamie was quite odd. There she was, towering over them, running around wildly with Shinobi and wearing one of their coins tied to a string around her neck as a necklace. Poor thing. No wonder they ignored her for hours.

That distraction took my mind away from what was looming. I had to run a marathon at noon the next day, with no shade, in 85-degree temperatures.

Running Hokkaido was my first big challenge since hurting my ankle. *Will I be able to run a marathon? Will my ankle hold up? The Japanese expected so much from their only invited American. They gave me a suitcase full of appearance money. Will I fail?* In the hours before the race the elite athletes were bussed out to a large stadium far from the finish line. There, I lay in the only patch of shade, next to the medical tent in the middle of the grass infield, gazing into the sky, readying myself while the runners went through a medical checkup. I'm sure my heart rate was sky high. I had never been so terrified before a race. When the time came, I rose and we were escorted to the starting line on the track. I closed my eyes, inhaled deeply, trying to settle my quivering nerves. Waiting on the line, head down, I watched my knees shake slightly, until the gun went off.

I made a conscious effort to be calm, knowing how far I had to run, and for almost 10 miles all was going well. My height advantage helped ease the stifling effect of being in such a large crowd on a hot and humid day.

I was leading the women's race, feeling pretty good and even thinking I was going to win with ease, until I did something really stupid at the 15K aid station. I bent over to pick up my dropped water bottle. The crowd of runners behind crashed into me, with one runner pushing on my lower back to avoid knocking me over. I felt a big strain from my back down into my hamstring.

What do I do now?

First things first. I picked up my bottle and chugged the entire 36 ounces without spilling a drop, Montana-chug style. I had to hydrate, since I'd missed the first two aid stations because of the crowds.

I was right back in the race, in fourth place. Olga Appell from Mexico and two Japanese stars were in front of me. I was taking such small steps to avoid pulling my hamstring that my stride was as short as that of the 4'10" Japanese runners. I remembered taking tiny steps like that as a kid, when I practiced walking daintily like Japanese Lady while carrying my stick with the paper plate stuck on top. Back then it might have looked sweet, but during a race it must have looked hideous.

Suddenly, my attention was diverted toward two idiots coming at me on bikes. They were out of control, almost hitting the many spectators along the street. It was Steve and Jamie. Jamie nearly crashed into a baby stroller and was so out of control at times that she would ride her bike right out onto the course. It took my mind off the misery I was in, but it was hard to watch them terrorize spectators as they rode to the viewing points along the course.

I managed third place, receiving a hefty bonus and good prize money from the generous Japanese organizers, which at least made the stressful experience worthwhile.

New York City Marathon ~ November, 1992

Next stop, the New York City Marathon. TV wanted to do an up-close-and-personal story on me beforehand. They came in full force, with a reporter, a camera crew and all the equipment involved. Of course, they wanted to get some shots with Jamie, who showed them her immaculate room with all of her stuffed animals neatly displayed on her bed, telling them their names: Chablis, Chardonnay, Cabernet, Shiraz, Merlot, Zinfandel, Riesling and Blush. *I don't even drink blush!* Chablis' ear was rubbed off after spending every night with Jamie, as she still sucked her thumb and rubbed the soft satin on his ear over the years. After being complimented on her neat room she told the reporter, "My mom likes everything in neat piles and everything put in its place."

They just "had" to film Jamie riding her bike alongside me during a run, with a cameraman hanging out the window in a car – very dangerous. Jamie decided to fix herself up for *this* one: a side ponytail with a giant, bright-pink scrunchy; clown tights of assorted colors; and an overly baggy Nike T-shirt that she kept pulling back over her shoulder as it fell off during her ride, almost running into me and the car in the process.

The pressure was on in New York. I wasn't feeling well. My heart rate was high, and I felt tired and achy all weekend and into the morning of the race. It may have been the undercooked game hen I ate the night we arrived. I was starving and ate it anyway. Steve kept telling me, "You'll be fine. It's only nerves." I knew from the start that it wasn't going to be pretty.

I was freezing during the race, even though it was a warm day and I'd been racing for 16 miles. At 17 miles I couldn't even lift my legs, and stopped. A live television camera was right there, and a commentator put a microphone in my face. "What's going on? What's happening?" I was confused and said I didn't know. I walked to the side of the road where one of the cyclists following the top women gave me his warm clothes and radioed for help. A John Hancock limousine came and picked me up on the spot.

Back in the hotel, I lay in my bed with a fever. I was sweating, chilled and absolutely miserable. After running hard for 17 miles with apparent food poisoning, my immune system became so compromised that I was sick and weak for months.

My disappointing year wasn't quite over.

I needed to go to Port Townsend in December. It was time to say goodbye to Grandma Helen. She had survived for several long draining years, but was nearing the end in the later stages of her ovarian cancer. She died the day after I arrived, after sitting up in her bed and telling Dad, "Take care of my Geraldine. Take good care of her." She left us, and our world would never be the same.

Mom and Aunt Jan took it hard. For a brief time, they mourned the loss of their mother by spinning out of control, drinking too much and throwing caution to the wind. Grandma Helen would have clicked her tongue. Losing Grandma Helen was different from the other deaths we experienced. It wasn't sudden, and it wasn't a shock. But for some reason, hearing the news that Grandma Helen was gone felt like a giant lightning bolt striking me.

1993 was going to be a tough year.

It was time to do some altitude training, to challenge myself in more extreme conditions, away from the distractions and comforts of being home. Time to "live to train" in solitude for the first time ever.

It was also time to pick myself up, come back from adversity and go for it in the 1993 Boston Marathon.

I went to Boulder to train under Benji's guidance. I would also be near Mark Plaatjes and his family, Mr. Jones and his family, and Arturo and Joy Barrios. I wouldn't be too lonely. Benji and Amie were like family, and I managed to rent a condo a few blocks from them. I mainly trained alone, occasionally running with Benji as he showed me the favorite routes in the area.

Boulder is a beautiful place, a runner's paradise with many dirt, bike and mountain trails on which to train. It's located at the base of the foot-hills of the Rocky Mountains, at 5,430 feet. Mountains and the Flatirons are in full view. The Flatirons are large slab-like rock formations along the east slope of Green Mountain, named by a pioneer woman after the flat, metal irons used to press clothes. It was impossible not to feel motivated to train every possible moment in a place like Boulder, and that's what I did – in snowstorms, windstorms and on the mostly sunny, blue-sky spring days. Training hard was all I focused on for eight solid weeks. I got out there without hesitation, knowing that I had to come through in Boston.

Mark Plaatjes, who had become a physical therapist and worked on my diaphragm every few weeks, told me during Easter dinner with the running gang, "Just get back out there, Kimbo. You can do it. It's in you. When you're uptight, your asthma acts up and that's why I have to work on you." He was right.

Boston Marathon ~ April, 1993

I tried not to worry the night before Boston, but Mark came to my hotel room to release my diaphragm just in case. Not a good idea after my final carbo-loading meal. We had to laugh, Mark saying with his hands in the air, "This is ridiculous! Your stomach is too full, Kimbo!"

With all of my Boulder friends planning to race or be there, I was in good company. Mr. Jones, Mark, Nadia Prasad and I all planned to run, and our families were there to support us. It took some pressure off. It helps to know there are others going through the same emotions.

Still, as I stood on the crowded starting line in Hopkinton, I was alone with my thoughts. I didn't know what to expect. I hadn't been able to run fast or hard in a race for a long time. I hadn't been able to do the kind of speed sessions I normally did. *Can I do this?* The only way to find out was to face my fears head on.

Here we go again.

Of course, it was a hot afternoon race in Boston. I started passing people early from my usual position way behind: Joanie and Nadia at 9 miles; Olga Appell, who beat me in Hokkaido; and Wanda Panfil before 16 miles. Along the way I also passed many of the runners who beat me in my practice races leading up to the marathon. After a while I just quit paying attention, trying to avoid any distractions. Then, before 20 miles, I passed Manuela Machado from Portugal, and I was in second place.

Suddenly, a heavy wave of sadness and despair rushed over me. The crowds were cheering, but I didn't hear a word they were saying. At that very moment, I missed my Grandma Helen more than ever. I felt a tugging at my heart; tears came flooding out as a wave of memories of my brothers flowed through me. I was thankful to be running alone.

Then, after my lonely cry, I had a vision of seeing all of them again someday in a wonderful place.

The crowds grew larger and louder, and miraculously ... Grandma Helen, Charlie and Stanley were right there with me as I was running down Boylston Street toward the finish line with tears still in my eyes.

Reality forced its way back in. Just like that. Just like it always happens ... and will always happen.

I came running in alone in second place, in 2:29:59. Of course, they rounded it up to 2:30:00. Olga Markova from Russia won in 2:25:27. *Damn, I wasn't expecting her to win.* Markova hadn't been racing and rumor was she was injured. The third-place finisher, Carmen De Oliveira from Brazil, was more than a minute behind me.

Two weeks later I was in the headquarters hotel on Bloomsday weekend when Jon Sinclair came up and gave me a big hug. "Congratulations on a great Boston Marathon," he said with his boyish charm and energy. "It's so good to see you come back after such a big disappointment last year. I'm proud of you ... I know how hard it must have been to work your way back." Jon was genuinely happy for me, as were many of my peers. It isn't easy to impress the best in the world.

I didn't impress everyone, though. It was time to renew my contract with Nike. Keith Peters had moved up in the company and was replaced by Alberto Salazar, who wanted to talk to me directly about some changes. That was strange, because they usually dealt with Steve.

Alberto had some news for me: "We need to cut back on your contract this year. Way back." Alberto is my age, and his career was over years ago. *He's telling me I'm 35 now and we all slow down as we age!*

"You need to start running against the best in the world and be capable of running under 2:30 before I consider giving you a decent contract."

"What? I just placed second in Boston, running 2:30. I've run five sub-2:30 marathons!"

Then he told me I was getting older and wasn't going to improve or be a factor in big races in the future.

I hated leaving Nike. I had never run in any other shoe. But Alberto left me no choice. Even worse, he showed me no respect. Reebok offered me a two-year contract for even more than I had been receiving from Nike during my "younger years."

World Championships, Stuttgart, Germany ~ August, 1993

I continued to push forward, feeling the need to prove myself, especially after Alberto's news.

That summer while preparing for the World Championships, for which I qualified at Boston, I was running on one of my favorite Spokane trails when a mountain bike came flying down as I was hammering up the hill. We collided. My natural reaction was to put my arm out for protection instead of falling off the cliff, and in the process I injured my shoulder, torqued my back and strained several ribs.

"How did you manage to get yourself run over by a mountain bike?" Staffan asked, as expected. Then he became concerned. "This is pretty messed up." He did his magic and I was ready to go even with a stiff shoulder and a tight diaphragm.

Mark Plaatjes, Rolando Vera, Steve, Staffan and I went to Amsterdam 10 days before the World Championships. The event would be in Stuttgart, but Michelle Lukien, a Dutch coach who was a good friend and generous person, invited us to his home for a training camp. While there, he talked to us about our marathon strategies. "Mark, be more patient," he said. "Kimbo, be more aggressive." That was basically switching our usual strategies.

It was a dream situation for runners. All we had to do was walk out the door to a hard-packed cinder trail system, miles and miles of mildly rolling trails disappearing deep into the forest and winding alongside a stream. Michelle's wife, Manna, cooked us nutritious meals, with a huge selection of our favorite foods every day. We were set.

We played a Dutch shuffleboard game called Sjoelen as often as possible. It's a game of great skill that is played competitively in Holland. Each player is given three chances to slide wooden disks along a 6½-foot board atop a table in an attempt to get them through 4 arches at the other end. A few twists that earned you more points made the game even more engrossing.

Of course, I practiced during all of my free time and learned the tricks, becoming excellent at it. We all became good players and had our own championships at the end of our stay. I was in the final championship playoff game with a Dutch athlete. I ended up being the second winner.

On the last day of camp, Michelle had a big party in his large and perfectly manicured backyard, with food galore. It was an extravagant social gathering with many of their friends, neighbors and several athletes from the area. He even hired a famous Dutch artist to draw caricatures of each World Championships competitor.

The next day, Mark, Steve, Staffan and I loaded into Michelle's van and he drove us across the border to Germany as we made our way to Stuttgart. After a five-hour drive, we came to a narrow and steep road with many switchbacks. We drove up and up, and continued climbing, until we finally reached a horrifying-looking compound on the outskirts of town. It reminded me of a movie, creeping up to the Frankenstein castle ever so slowly. Michelle, Steve and Staffan dropped Mark and me at the gate in the barbed-wire fence with our bags, and went to find their hotel.

This is the athlete's village? Hmmm. The gigantic, rusted wrought-iron gates slowly opened, squeaking ever so eerily, as Mark and I looked at each other with wide eyes. At least we had each other, not that two 5'7", 117-pound marathon runners could do much to protect each other.

We walked into an old abandoned German Army complex that was crumbling before our eyes. I wasn't sure it was sturdy enough to hold so many athletes. We walked toward row after row of pathetic buildings. We couldn't use the water system right away because rust poured out of the faucets. We had two options: either take a rust shower immediately; or keep the water running, clearing some of it out, and then take a semi-rust shower the next day. The toilets were usable, but filthy and full of rust stains. After a few days, we pushed enough rust through the system to clear the water a bit, but I wouldn't dare drink it. We had to have bottled water brought in.

Jane Welzel was my roommate. We had decided earlier in the year that we would enjoy our experience together being that we had become good friends despite my calling her an ass in our first encounter. With four other women, we shared a so-called suite of three bedrooms, a kitchen, a living room with no furniture and one bathroom. At least there were two cot-like beds in each bedroom, even if there was no air conditioning in the miserable August heat. "It's not so bad, Jane," I said to cheer her up. "We can open the windows this evening to allow in the cool night air."

"Right, Kim," she said sarcastically in her strong Boston accent. "With all of my travel over the years, these are the worst housing conditions I've ever seen."

Jane and I made the best of it. We sat outside on a porch swing in front of our building for most of the day, until our room cooled off in the evenings. It was a perfect place to view the many athletes walking by.

We thought our room was bad until Mark showed us his. It was on the fourth level, a tiny and stifling attic room. I felt claustrophobic the moment we walked in. As in our room, there were bits and pieces of plaster and building debris all over the floor. Mark's room had the added feature of holes in the wall, some caused by the crumbling building and others by mice. You couldn't walk barefoot without the risk of cutting your feet or stepping on some small living critter.

To top it all off, our building was right next to the compound's beer garden, where the host Germans made sure there were many kegs of beer and plenty of loud music to enjoy. Mark raced the next day, and Jane and I the day after that. Mark threw his hands up in exasperation. "This is ridiculous!" I gave Mark a pair of earplugs and said, "Let's hope for the best."

Later, we helped Mark carbo-load in the cafeteria, located in a big tent next to the beer garden. We decided that we would enjoy that garden in two days, after the women's marathon.

The next day, I watched the men's marathon on television in the massage room while a therapist worked on my shoulder and back. I couldn't believe it! I told her, "Mark's taking the lead after sitting patiently for most of the race! For the first time ever!" He was alone, running toward the stadium to win the gold medal.

Sprinter Michael Johnson was on the table next to me, and overheard. "Wait a minute, how is he winning this race?"

I told him, "Mark relaxed for the first 90 minutes of the race, then worked his way up to the lead pack in the next 30 minutes, before taking the lead and pushing it in for the final 15 minutes." His laugh sounded like Eddie Murphy. "Wait a minute. How in the world can you relax in a race for 90 minutes, push hard for 30 minutes, and then go for a win for another 15 minutes?" It sounded unreal to a sprinter whose longest race was over in less than 45 seconds.

The next afternoon it was our turn. Jane and I bravely took our positions at the starting line. As expected, it was hot and humid. After a few laps around the stadium, off we went out into the streets of Stuttgart.

Nobody was willing to take it out, and I couldn't be messing around in a pack of women with my bad shoulder and back, so I finally took the lead. It wouldn't bother me if I ran smoothly without too much jarring and pace changing. That was not my usual strategy, but the pace was slow enough and I was the fastest and strongest runner in the group.

Some of the other runners seemed to have a different strategy. Two of the Japanese runners kept clipping my heels and kicking my Achilles as we ran. As I led the pack through every water stop, they kept pouring water on my shoes. *Unbelievable!* I was starting to develop blisters, but that was the least of my worries. Each water station turned into a wrestling match while everyone elbowed, pushed and shoved for, of all things, carbonated water. *ASSES!*

It continued through 16 miles until one of the Japanese stepped on my heel, ripping off my shoe. That was all I could take. I lost it.

It would have taken maybe 20 seconds to slip my shoe on and work my way back into the pack. Instead, I picked up my shoe and threw it at the Japanese woman as hard as I could. It went right over her head, which was probably a good thing. I could imagine the headlines: "Raging American marathoner throws shoe, knocks out competition." I'm sure I would have hit her easily if my shoulder had been in good form.

Damn, now I have to find my shoe, put it on, and get back into the marathon. I was out of medal contention, but had to finish. It was tough after I had lost my focus and was noticing every little ache and pain, especially the blisters.

As I continued to run, I began to appreciate what most marathoners go through while struggling through the final miles. We elite athletes have something in us to push, run strong while in a zone, and not notice the effort or pain involved unless disaster strikes. Then we complain, "poor me." We're pampered, even treated like royalty at times. We're rewarded with money, presents and attention. At that moment, during a World Championships race, I was respecting and admiring people who go out and run a marathon while living a normal life, working a "real" job, but still finding the time and energy to train for and endure the marathon.

As I was running, I thought about Punky being so patient with that squirrel, doing everything right while biding her time. She attained her prize. Lesson learned. I needed to be patient, keep my cool and never lead a World Championships race again. Let the pack beat up on somebody else. *I guess my "come from behind" strategy is best after all. It certainly worked for Mark.*

I finally reached the finish line, in eighth place, then sat down right there on the track and waited for Jane to finish. Walking arm in arm, together we faced the reporters waiting for us in the press area.

I will always be disappointed in myself, not so much for losing my temper, but for allowing somebody to break me down.

Afterward, a Japanese team organizer apologized for the incident, explaining that the Japanese run as a team, working together and for each other until the pack dwindles. Then it's a race for the medals. That particular group took it one step beyond.

1993 World Championships at 15 miles with two
Japanese on my heels (literally)
Left to right: Akemi Matsuno, Japan (11th); Katrine Dorre, Germany
(sixth); Kamila Gradus, Poland (ninth); Junko Asari, Japan (gold medalist); me; Tomoe Abe, Japan (bronze); and Manuela Machado,
Portugal (silver) ~ *Courtesy of Victah Sailer*

We took Mark to a *Runner's World* surprise party that evening in honor of his win. Then the three of us, along with Mr. Jones, who had a bad race, and Carol McClatchie, who didn't compete but was the team leader in charge of us, all went to the beer garden. There, after many hours of celebrating Mark's victory, they taught me to say the F word. I was 35 years old and had never said it. Jane and Carol said it all the time, Mark said it freely, and the gentleman Mr. Jones said it away from the ladies. They kept after me until finally I said, "Mark, I'm not going to say f...k!" It just came out. It was liberating. It actually felt good to say f...k after my frustrating day.

Before flying back to the States, we returned to Holland for a few more days. Mark and I needed to find a Sjoelen board, and Mark wanted to buy gifts for his three little girls and wife, Shirley. We found the Sjoelen board and then Rolando's wife, Sandra, and I went with Mark into a lingerie store to help him pick something out for Shirley.

"How about this lovely bra and panty outfit?" Mark said, holding it up to show us. "What breast size is she?" the saleslady asked. "The size of Kimbo's kneecaps." We put the bra over my kneecaps for the fitting and, sure enough, Mark was right. When Shirley tried it on later at home, it fit perfectly.

New York City Marathon ~ November, 1993

It was three months later. After my last New York City Marathon fiasco, dropping out sick at 17 miles, I wanted to go back and redeem myself in 1993. Like Punky, I wanted to endure. Try and try again, until I got it right.

Once again TV decided to do another special story on me. *They sure put a lot of faith in me, especially after last year's disaster.* For two days in Spokane, the camera followed us everywhere. They even filmed Jamie running in a junior high cross-country meet. She was getting used to the attention and wasn't too stressed, but her competition was. She won.

They filmed the three of us playing Sjoelen on our dining room table, and me playing "Indian Song" on my accordion as Jamie sang made-up lyrics to the Indian beat and recorded them as a new answering machine greeting: "I know what the Joneses know, I go where the Joneses go. I want to know what you wa-aant, I want to know what it is ... leave it, leave it, leave your mes-sage, leave it, leave it, leave it nowwww." Then the beep. I couldn't believe I was doing a skit for national television with my daughter, and with my accordion of all things. Unbelievable! I reckoned they were in desperate need of new material. I answered the telephone once, and it was Dick Patrick calling. "I just called to listen to your message on the answering machine." He wasn't the only one.

There was an inversion during the 1993 New York City Marathon — a layer of cooler, abnormally polluted air trapped close to the ground – but at 13 miles I decided, *I am going to go for it this time and push beyond my asthma symptoms.* I had never tried it in a race before. *Maybe I can do it. Maybe if I had pushed through in past races I would have won a few more.*

The next thing I knew, at the 17-mile mark, my eyes opened to the sight of the sky. I was on the side of the road, on my back and gasping for air. Medics were hovering above me and I was on a nebulizer, a device used to administer medication in a form of mist inhaled into the lungs. I heard one medic say, "She's not responding. She's not oxygenating." I felt heavy ... things were foggy. I slowly faded out.

I woke up in the emergency room of the hospital. I felt nauseous, and my head and lungs hurt. My body ached. I was disoriented.

A doctor, who was a runner and knew of me, came in. "You're going to be just fine," he told me, smiling. "What happened out there?"

"I made a huge mistake. I had to try to win the marathon today. I wanted to see if I could run through my warning signs instead of giving in as I always do."

He scolded me. "You're an asthmatic. You should never push yourself beyond that threshold." Softening his voice, he added, "But it's understandable, you're out there running for a prize."

I replied, "Do you not know that in a race all the runners run, but only one gets the prize? Run in such a way that you attain the prize. First Corinthians 9:24." He let out a big laugh and said, "Very good."

Both Steve Joneses rushed in to be sure I was OK. I felt safe. My aching body relaxed, and I fell asleep.

Chapter 18

That winter we bought a two-bedroom condo in Boulder, right next to the South Boulder trail system. I could walk straight out my door to running and biking trails along the South Boulder Creek and a golf course, or go up into the more rugged mountain terrain of the Mesa Trail, just below the Flatirons.

The condo was a second-floor end unit, facing southwest with a full view of the Flatirons and mountains beyond from every window. When I saw a storm creeping eastward over the mountains like a white glove slowly gripping the foothills, I knew I needed to hightail it out for a run before it hit.

I had a recliner like Big Red facing the gas fireplace and angled so I could look out onto the tranquilizing view under the clear blue skies. Almost every day while drinking my morning coffee I enjoyed the bright orange-red reflection of the sunrise on the Flatirons, changing to a deep rose before sending long crimson shadows westward behind the rock formations.

In the evenings, I sat with a glass of wine at cocktail hour, gazing upon the brilliant Colorado sunset, the blinding yellow becoming the color of my merlot just as the sun slipped behind the mountains and turned the rock formations into a tantalizing deep violet.

It was just what I had always dreamed of, a peaceful place to get away from stressful situations, always perfectly clean and germfree without a crumb on the floor; where the girls could join me for some quality time. Starting in 1994, I trained there for several months each year.

While in Boulder I began training with Mr. Jones, who had just turned 40 and was running a bit slower. Of course Arturo Barrios, Mark Plaatjes, Mark Coogan and all the other boys training in Boulder just *had* to give Steve a hard time for ditching them to train with a girl. "Wah, wah," "Ma, ma," they would cry like a baby whenever we ran past or worked out on the track after they'd finished and were standing around. They could be brutal. Steve is fun to tease, with his quick-witted replies in a strong Welsh accent making him an easy target.

I also gave Mr. Jones a hard time, ordering him around far too much. "Why don't you make yourself useful and run in front to shield me from the wind?" I would say jokingly. Or, "Go run in lane 4" when we did our half-mile speed efforts on the track, while I ran in lane 1 as hard as I could in each turn, forcing him to work harder to make up the extra distance. "It's really hot, why don't you take your T-shirt off like the other boys?" I would ask him, fully aware that he'd put on a few pounds over the winter. Everyone laughed. When he finally did drop the weight and take off his T-shirt, he showed off a suntan line straight from Hank Hill on "King of the Hill." It still looked like he was wearing a white T-shirt. We laughed even harder. He could take the teasing, though. I think he even enjoyed it at times.

Mr. Jones and I quickly became good friends. He is the most caring person out there. As Ania said one time, "He wears his heart on his sleeve." I could see that. Once, when I was tired, miserable, and ready to be done toward the end of a 25-mile run, we saw a dead bird on the side of the road. "Oh, look at that poor little bird, he was hit by a car," said Steve. As he stopped to be sure it couldn't be saved, I shot my hands into the air. "It has eyes, doesn't it? It's his own fault! He should have seen the car coming!" I declared as I continued on, "orbbing" and with no patience. Steve looked shocked, but had to laugh.

One of the favorite routes in Boulder for serious cyclists and runners ran right by our condo. I would go out to Cherryvale Road, a nice old country road with rolling hills that wound through farmland, until it came to Marshall Road, long and flat through the middle of Old Town, before turning onto South Boulder Trail and heading back to my place. I ran the seven-mile loop almost every day until a black bird – an aggressive, mean and nasty critter – decided to attack me on Marshall Road every time I ran by. It swooped down like the crows in Hokkaido, but *this* one would actually hit me. It didn't bother Steve, ever.

After many attacks, I grew so mad that one day I picked up some gravel from the side of the road and threw it, scattering it into the air and almost hitting the bird as it flew backwards before soaring down to nick my forehead. Another time, only to protect myself, I grabbed a tree limb the size of a large baseball bat and swung each time it dove toward me. It was like being in a batting cage. Poor Steve looked around nervously, hoping nobody would come running or riding by to see me in action. After that, I had to wait until nesting season was over before going back. That bird was ready to kill me.

Mr. Jones and I trained extremely hard together. Once, after putting Steve in lane 4 during a track workout – 8 x ½ mile in 2:25-7, with the boys teasing us on the sidelines – we were running back to the condo as a long cool-down when I hit the "Golden Orb," big time. Things were spinning and my legs were rubber as I went weaving down the trail. I was dripping in a cold sweat, and starving. After a long silence I finally said, "I would eat a Milk Dud right off the street." Steve laughed, but I was *not* trying to be funny.

Then I saw a green bike. Boulder has a fleet of green bikes available for anybody to use – you ride one where you need to go and then leave it at your destination for the next person. I threw my track shoes in the basket and hopped on, but my legs were toast. I couldn't pedal. Steve ran behind the bike and pushed me home. Of course, some of the boys drove by and watched the show. We never heard the end of that one.

The only other time I "Golden Orbbed" in front of Mr. Jones was when we were finishing a long, hard workout on the country roads outside Spokane, where he had joined me for some training. He followed me as I ran directly to an apple tree, picked up an old apple from the ground and started eating it on the spot. "How did you know to come here?" he asked, amazed. "I do it all the time," I told him. "These apples have saved me all year, but now they're pretty rotten, eh?" Steve shook his head. He was as exhausted as I was, but refused to take a bite. "You're a survivor Mrs. Jones, in more ways than you think," he said.

Steve knew that I wasn't joking around when I hopped on a green bike, or when I ate an old apple or a Milk Dud off the ground. That was no different than eating cattle grain when the opportunity presented itself. In the old prostitute house and during my life in Enumclaw, I learned to survive by being resourceful.

Some say that bad things happen because of bad luck. I say, bad things happen because of poor timing and bad judgment. I muddled through 1994 as bad things happened one after the other. I just kept the faith and continued to persevere. *Something good is going to happen. It has to. I just know it.*

After compromising my immune system with that asthma attack in New York, I had a high fever off and on and didn't feel well for months, which was a clear sign that I was over-training trying to keep up with Mr. Jones.

Steve was driving on our way to a trail run when a taxicab pulled out in front of us. We crashed right into him. I strained my ribs, missing two months of training.

While running in her neighborhood, Ania was attacked and bitten on her right thumb by a big German shepherd. The bite became infected, and she was on an intravenous antibiotic for weeks. I felt so badly for her; that powerful right thumb of hers was never going to be as strong. We were both disappointed that she wouldn't be able to do the deep tissue massage that I needed, and worse, I wouldn't be spending as much time with my best friend. I felt lost without her.

Ania suggested I try Brian Tibbetts, the massage therapist who worked with Dan O'Brien, the World Champion decathlete who lived near Spokane. Brian was close to my age, big and strong in a boyish way, with blond hair and kind blue eyes that lit up when he was amused. He laughed a lot, told funny jokes, and looked so much like "Grizzly Adams" that his nickname was "Bear." Boy, could Brian dig in and get the job done. Ania continued to do energy work and light massage, and could still use those bony elbows if needed, but Brian did most of the work after that.

The weekend Steve, Jamie and I were out of town for the Boston Marathon, our dear friend and dentist, Moto, died after his long fight with colon cancer. I didn't run so well, finishing eighth in 2:31:46.

Other than winning the Rhody Run, not much good came out of the year. I ran 15 decent road races, but it was a struggle. And more disturbing, my family was struggling again, too.

When Jamie and I went to visit my parents and Rachel during her winter break, I found out for myself what was going on.

Laurie and Mel's life continued to fall apart. It was heartbreaking watching them and their boys fall into a deeper, darker place. Laurie was turning into my dad more and more every time I saw her, only worse. She was paranoid and out of control like Dad, but she was cruel. Dad didn't have a mean bone in his body. He was a victim and struggled all through his life. Laurie had more going for her – a nice home, money, family love, good friendships – yet she chose to throw it all away, enjoying the moment and not considering the consequences of her behavior. I knew it wasn't all her doing. Her addictive behavior was inherited, along with other issues. Dad was close to her age, in his late 30s, when he was finally diagnosed with his mentally debilitating disease.

Just after we arrived, I was sitting in my parents' living room when I glanced out the large picture window to see Laurie creeping up the side-walk looking suspiciously coy. She opened the front door and peeked in to be sure the coast was clear before rushing into the chair next to me. After giving me a hug and looking me over, she said, "You look too thin, Kimmie, are you OK?"

"It's been a tough year. Things have been a little out of control. How are you?" I asked, relieved to see her normal and somewhat composed.

"What have Mom and Mike told you about me?"

"I heard you've had some wild episodes. Leaving Mel and the boys for days, sometimes weeks, while off with undesirables, drinking and drugging before being thrown in jail."

"Kimmie, I'm really trying. Every time I get it together and things seem to be almost perfect, I snap and go crazy. I'm so ashamed. I stole Mel's paycheck, leaving him with no money to pay the rent or bills." She broke down, "I hate Mom. It's her fault we're all so screwed up. Debbie and Bradley agree with me. Mom's not perfect, you know. She preaches God's word and condemns our behavior, and then turns right around and behaves just as badly as the rest of us. She was even thrown in jail for a DUI, you know."

"Yes, you've told me … many times," I reminded her. Then she started accusing Mom of terrible things. As I listened, I looked at Laurie, really looked at her. She resembled the actress Susan Sarandon: tall and lean, elegant with a sense of entitlement; her startling brown eyes, intense at the moment – other times warm and placid. It was Laurie who made it possible to keep Rachel in our lives. She'd done so much good in her life. She cared for her younger siblings through-out a lifetime of chaos; the many times she protected us from harm years ago when our step-father walked into our little white house in a drunken rage. Laurie would gather the five of us together and we'd scurry under the bed before the fighting began. She nursed Mom back to health after a devastating beating, slicing her apples and carrots, spoon-feeding her broth. I felt so much love for Laurie. Sadly, she was not the same person when under the influence of drugs and alcohol – just like Pa Seelye and Grandpa Jefferies, she couldn't handle her liquor either.

Laurie asked, "How can you love Mom and be her perfect daughter after what she's done to us?"

"I don't blame Mom. She was, and still is, a victim of circumstances, just like the rest of us. I don't accept everything she or the rest of our family does, but I understand it."

"You know," said Laurie, "I can trick her into drinking and partying with me. Sometimes I give Mel and Mom too much alcohol and drugs, then leave them alone together before sneaking back *hoping* to catch them in an inappropriate act."

"Laurie! You're acting just like our dad! He did the exact same thing to Mom and Mike years ago!"

Her controlled expression and demeanor turned to fright when Mike walked in behind us from the garage door, and for good reason: not long before my visit, Laurie was caught breaking into their house – everyone assumed she had planned to steal Mike's gun collection. He had so many that they had their own room.

She suddenly changed into another person, and pointed at me. "You've had it easy all your life. You are the lucky one!" she shrieked, and stormed out.

Mike caught the tail end of our conversation, and I asked him, "Did Laurie learn this behavior from our first dad?"

"I don't know, Kimmie," he answered, "but I can't take much more of this, it's heart-wrenching." He added as he settled into his recliner, "All of you kids had a tough life, experiencing the same disappointments, so don't let them tell you any differently."

"It's hard to handle as many disappointments as we have. Jehovah only gives us the challenges we can handle, making us stronger for the next one," said Mom when she walked into the room. "We all have our own way of dealing with them. I know your running helped you through a lot of terrible times."

During a long pause, while Mike stared out the window and Mom looked off into the distance at nothing in particular, it occurred to me ...

disappointment is like a piece of driftwood on a beach. Eventually the tide comes in to carry it away, only to leave another in its place. *Are the many disappointments in my life some kind of extensive preparation for things to come – for some calamity that could bring me to my breaking point?*

Mike looked over, "You've come through, Kimmie. You have a good life and two great kids because of it."

I felt deep pride hearing that from my dad, Mike. Then, suddenly, I felt overcome with guilt when they told me what was going on with the rest of the family.

Laurie's boys also struggled. Little Mel and Danny found their way into trouble off and on, nothing worse than any of my escapades at their age, but unlike me ... they were acting out. The boys were lost, insecure and frightened. They were forced into a life they had never known when their parents were disassociated from the JW Congregation. It was a crying shame.

There was still hope for little Charlie. He was smart and aware for his young age. Charlie was more like me. He observed, the way I did many years ago. Charlie was a part of the dysfunction, yet refused to take part in it when he had a choice.

The others chose the easy route. Staying in dysfunction and blaming others is much easier than fighting to get out. I allowed the hardships in my young life to shape my perspective in a positive way, learning how to stand apart from the chaos and dysfunction around me. *Perhaps I was more aware than the others. Maybe I had more courage to fight my way out of this pattern of self-destruction.* I certainly had more luck, with so many good people coming into my life to help encourage me – and my running – along the way.

Debbie and Bradley were in huge trouble again. They were often in cahoots with each other, accused of smuggling drugs and selling them only to be repaid with more drugs. It was another vicious cycle. I heard that they were also involved with a group of hardcore criminals and drug dealers, breaking into storage facilities in the Tacoma area and getting away with thousands of dollars in merchandise. Later, Debbie started making methamphetamines, once setting the kitchen on fire. She narrowly escaped, burning only her hair and eyebrows.

A bounty hunter once showed up at my parents' house looking for Debbie. He explained not only the trouble she was in, but also the danger that was lurking. "These people will end up turning on her," he said, "or she'll end up in the middle of the crossfire once our group or the law finds them."

The drug dealers did turn on Debbie, threatening her and her family if she didn't play their game. In the end, Debbie was afraid for her life. Finally, she was arrested and thrown in jail.

We could never get a straight answer from Debbie about how she managed to get in such trouble. When she ended up in prison for something else entirely, she wrote to Mom, "Please understand that this case in Lewis County was supposed to be dropped to trespassing, but instead they changed my sentencing date, which I was unaware of, and when I missed it they sentenced me to here. My lawyer quit during all of this and this is where I ended up." She went on to say, "It was pretty harsh for just walking through a field and just looking at a claw-foot bathtub that had been used as a horse trough."

Debbie wasn't finished trying to convince Mom of her innocence yet. "Jehovah God moves in mysterious ways and I think he needed to bring me back to His Will. I actually allowed him back into my heart and feel his love for me." Of course Mom fell for the con job. Debbie clinched Mom's sympathy when she told her, "I'm reading the *Watchtower* and *Awake* magazines and love them. So I guess this all happened for a reason."

Her answer to me was shorter, but no more specific. "I don't know, Kimmie, they did me wrong. I shouldn't be here. My attorney is going to get me out of this," she said, wide eyed and fast talking as always.

Bradley was sent to prison for a few years and later ended up back in prison for several more. He is the strongest, toughest looking man you will ever run across, with the kindest and most caring heart. Just don't make him angry. Eventually, he was put in a California penitentiary that had an especially bad reputation. He found his way into a group, as most prisoners do, while working out and becoming a big and even stronger Swede who nobody would want to mess with. If they did, they would have to face not only his temper but also his pack of prison brothers.

Debbie was smart and knew how to work people, how to charm them to get what she wanted, so I wasn't as concerned about her. I'm sure she had everyone under her thumb as the queen of her Washington State penitentiary. I worried more about my baby brother. I was hoping that his quick-wit and humor would help ease the harshness of fellow prisoners.

I was sickened by the circumstances my brother and sister faced. I couldn't sleep some nights, knowing that two people I loved dearly were in hardcore prison with dangerous criminals, their lives in peril, locked up in a place far worse than Debbie and I had imagined back in our room when we were under restriction years ago.

"This is what prison must be like. I will never, *ever* go to prison," I told Debbie back then.

Debbie looked at me with her big blue eyes and said, "Me either, Kimmie."

—

While my siblings let their obsessions rule them, I chose to rule my obsession – running.

Not that luck was always on my side in 1995, either. I focused all winter on running the Osaka Women's Marathon at the end of January. I would receive an enormous appearance fee, with the chance to win an exorbitant amount of prize money and bonuses if I ran well. Then on January 17, 1995 – 12 days before the marathon and just four days before my flight – the Great Hanshin earthquake struck, killing more than 6,000 people. The marathon was cancelled. Generously, the organizers sent me $10,000 for my trouble.

London Marathon ~ April, 1995

I shifted my plans to run the London Marathon. Two weeks before the race Jamie caught a terrible stomach flu. The day I flew to London, I came down with it, too, and was nauseous all week. I couldn't carbo-load, not even for a day. I ended up running, but without any fuel could manage only a 2:31 and sixth place, which wasn't too disappointing. However, without being able to carbo-load, I learned how vital it was. I would never again second-guess my heavy body at the start of any marathon, no matter how pudgy my legs were.

After the marathon, Steve and I took a short train trip with Mr. Jones to his hometown in Wales. We ate bangers and mash, and drank some Guinness at his buddy's pub while many of his old friends asked me about my marathon. They had watched me lead the race through 15 miles and then falter toward the end. One friend asked, "You certainly found plenty of energy just before our hometown favorite passed you down the final straightaway. What sparked you?"

"As I was making my way to the finish, the crowd suddenly began cheering so wildly that for a moment I thought I was really popular and I reacted, until I saw the tropical shadow on the pavement and realized it was Liz McColgan, your British athlete."

They were laughing violently. Then I added, "My friend Ania and I nicknamed her 'Palm Tree Head' because she always wears her short ponytail right at the top of her head, making it sprout like a palm tree. I couldn't miss her."

We finished up our visit to Wales at Mr. Jones' favorite bakery for an assortment of pastries before heading back to the States.

World Championships, Gothenburg ~ August, 1995

My 2:31 in London qualified me for the 1995 World Championships Marathon in Gothenburg, Sweden in early August. I was excited about the marathon, but even more so about visiting my Swedish relatives after the race. I was really looking forward to meeting them, learning their lifestyle and hearing more about my heritage.

Jamie, Steve and I stayed with Staffan in a house that, with his Swedish connections, he set up for us in the hills, away from the athletes' village. I trained in the nearby forest for the week leading up to the marathon. Staffan joined me for a few runs and told me, "You're ready. You can win. I've never seen you this fit." I was definitely among the favorites to medal.

As the week went on, the days grew warmer and more humid. For the most part I stayed in the house during the day, resting up, while Staffan took Jamie and Steve on sightseeing trips. One evening Steve came back with a big bag of fresh shrimp boiled in salt water. Not something I should have been eating two days before a marathon, but I just couldn't help myself. I ate beyond my share.

The morning of the marathon I woke up bloated, my skin the color of the brick powder I tried to wear for my school picture when I was a little girl. But *this* I couldn't wash off. *Damn. This food thing has always been my nemesis.* My legs were fat and my stomach was so swollen I had to cut the elastic around the waist and leg holes of my racing shorts to put them on. I felt ill, my kidney area hurt, and my stomach and diaphragm squeaked when I took a deep breath.

I wished that I could throw up like most human beings, but I've never been able to throw up. *Damn Ass in the Stinkweeds. The shrimp must have been tainted. Or maybe it was the salt water they were boiled in.*

I didn't realize that shrimp can have your daily requirement of sodium in just four small servings, and I'd eaten many times that. Did I have sodium poisoning or food poisoning?

Why do I always do this to myself?

I looked like a big orange ball bouncing three laps through the city of Gothenburg. An agent from England asked afterward, "What happened to you?"

Still as orange as can be, I came bouncing in on live television to finish 16th – just ahead of Sweden's star, so of course I was on display for all to see. I wondered if my Swedish relatives were watching. How embarrassing. Not only was *my* marathon a disaster, so was the marathon itself. It was a quarter-mile short. I knew right at the start that we were supposed to run one more lap before leaving the stadium.

I became silently furious with Steve. *Why did he bring those shrimp to me? I was doing just fine on my pre-marathon diet.* By this time he knew that I would eat anything that looked good and sometimes too much of it, especially when I wasn't supposed to.

Then I came back to reality. It was a colossal combination of errors, all mine, and I was to blame.

A few days later, we took the train for a day trip to Linkoping, southwest of Stockholm, to visit several dozen cousins. They were all at the train station to greet us, looking a lot like my family back home. There was even one with dark auburn hair like my brother Charlie and Little Chaz. They showed us around their lovely, quaint neighborhood. It was just what I imagined, clean and orderly with many fine bakeries, lovely shops and wholesome and friendly people.

We had a big meal at the home of my oldest cousin, the head of the clan. She was in her 80s and very much in charge, making sure we ate and drank to excess. We ate dinner, the most wonderful Scandinavian food I ever had: Swedish meatballs and pickled herring with cream sauce, sausages, fishballs, mashed potatoes, potato dumplings filled with pork, pickled cucumber and lingonberry jam. We finished off with Swedish cheesecake; a hollow cake shaped like a cylinder; an assortment of pastries, rice pudding served with dewberry jam and, naturally, some strong Swedish coffee. We ate for over three hours as the entire family sat around a gigantic table, until we were stuffed to the gills.

One of my cousins not only looked a lot like me, we even had similar mannerisms. We rested our hands on our chins, sometimes at the same time; smiled and sipped our coffee in unison; and used our hands the same way when talking with passion. We even used our silverware alike, cutting with our right hand and using the fork with our left. *Strange ... this is my great grandfather's side of the family.* I had always thought I resembled and had the mannerisms of my great grandmother, Anna, and Grandma Helen.

We had a wonderful time visiting while sharing our meal together, and my cousins certainly thought I was pretty special beating their Swedish star in the World Championships. They went on and on about how great I was. They didn't mention the fact that I was orange on TV and still orange during our visit. Maybe they thought I was wearing Q.T., the self-tanning lotion.

When we returned home, Jamie thanked me for taking her to Sweden. "We had so much fun because you always find something good in all your races, even the bad ones," and then we started laughing about my being orange.

"I can't feel hopeless because I've always believed that difficult times lead to better days. That's how I've survived in this marathon world. Every cloud has a silver lining."

The phone rang. "Will you accept a collect call from Brad Seelye?" asked the operator.

I paused. "Yes."

"Kimmie, will you send me a running photo? Your magazine cover shot? I want to hang it up on my cell wall. I brag about you all the time, and the guys in here don't believe that I have a famous sister on the cover of *Runner's World*. Make sure you write 'to my handsome brother Brad.' Not Bradley."

It was as if a bucket of ice water had been poured over me. It was crystal clear at that moment. I had to keep running, strive for better things, for my family if not for myself.

"Mom, are you OK? What did he say? Is he OK?" asked Jamie when we hung up.

"I don't know. Bradley's sense of humor is how he survives." I began to cry. "I sure hope it helps him cope in the prison world. I'm sickened from the thought of what he must be going through ... what might happen to him."

"He'll be fine, Mom."

"I sure hope so."

Chicago Marathon ~ October, 1995

Nine weeks after my "orange incident," I ran the Chicago Marathon in October, hoping for a little more luck than the last time around, and to get in a decent marathon before the Olympic Trials in February. I ended up the second winner, in 2:31:24.

Later that fall, I did a photo shoot for the cover of *Running Times*, mainly training at Riverside State Park and along the Bloomsday course. The photographer, Tim Hancock, also shot me with my family while the writer, John Parker, talked with me for several days getting an in-depth interview for his story.

Punky hid because she didn't like the photographer. So we used Burt as our prop, pretending he was sweet and nice for the camera while he scratched us to pieces after each shot. Burt was a brat, a spoiled tomcat who used us for meals and a place to crash when he wasn't cruising around the neighborhood, hoping for – and usually getting – better treatment at a neighbor's house. He was the neighborhood Fat Cat, abusing the system, as sweet as a big pie until he got what he wanted. Then he moved on.

Burt had a heart-shaped collar with his name and our address printed on the back. At least once a week a car would pull up and the driver would get out and walk over to the passenger's door to let Burt out, as if he were a king. Then that little operator would come bounding up the front yard, expecting treats. Of course he got them. However, Burt had to earn his treat that time, when he came charging right into the middle of the photo shoot.

Once again, Jamie had to deal with a photographer at her cross-country meet. Talk about pressure for a 15-year-old girl! Steve enjoyed the process, as always, helping Jamie deal with the pressure but she was used to it by then. Good girl, learning from past experiences. Her competitors suffered, though.

Of course, by then I really knew about the curse, firsthand, of being on the cover of a magazine going into the Olympic Trials. But I told Steve, "That's just superstition, eh?"

Olympic Marathon Trials, Columbia, S. C. ~ February, 1996

The 1996 Olympic Trials came up quickly. By my third Trials, I had learned a few things and had a good handle on everything I could control. Jamie did her part in trying to control things, as well. After catching the stomach flu before the London Marathon, she was so worried about anybody coming over with germs that she sat down at the computer and designed signs to hang at the doorways: "Stop (stop sign)! Do not come in unless you wash your (picture of hands). You are not allowed inside if you are sick (tongue sticking out). You and your germs (picture of bugs) must stay away."

Every time Steve walked into the house that winter, Jamie nagged him, "Wash your hands, STEVE." She was constantly after him to cover his mouth when he coughed and sneezed. He just rolled his eyes and ignored her, coughing and sneezing all over everybody and everything. A week before the marathon, Steve came down with a serious virus. By the morning of the marathon, I had the virus.

It was the Olympic Trials. I had to give it a try. Unfortunately, I couldn't run without severe stomach cramping and having to make a pit stop every few miles, until finally I couldn't go any further. My Olympic hopes were foiled, once again.

I went home destroyed, feeling sickened – and it wasn't from the flu. I was sitting in Big Red, musing about my future, when Punky came and sat on the floor close enough to jump up. She was waiting for the pat of encouragement to join me, shifting from paw to paw as she crept closer.

"Go away," I told her. "I don't want you up here."

I was angry and disgusted with everything. Punky's persistence was becoming annoying, so I picked her up and put her outside before going upstairs to get ready for bed.

Suddenly, the motion lights flashed on and I heard a racket through my open bedroom window. I ran to look. Six enormous raccoons were on our deck, probably the same ones that had been terrorizing our neighborhood, killing small dogs and cats in their quest to find food. Frantically, I looked for Punky.

At first I couldn't see her anywhere. Then I went closer to the window and was surprised to see her headfirst in a large overturned bucket, her big white fluffy bottom sticking out and her tail tucked under. The raccoons didn't even notice her. I rushed down the three levels, almost breaking my neck, and out to the deck. "Get away, you little asses," I yelled at the raccoons. They looked at me, and then charged forward! I grabbed the broom and started whacking at them. They kept their ground. I turned the hose on them – using the power spray – and they waddled away. Punky slowly backed out of the bucket and then rushed toward the edge of the deck as if *she* had frightened those raccoons away.

"You're a survivor, Punky," I told her as I carried her into the house. "We were all put on this earth to survive."

I thought long and hard about my Olympic Trials disaster. Everyone was treating it like a death, again. It wasn't that bad. I experienced misfortune and had to get over it – heal and continue, or quit.

"We need to learn from our mistakes and move forward," I'd told Rachel more than once. I'd made many mistakes, sometimes more than once, but I always tried to learn from them. It would be a shame to call it quits after I had learned so much. I still knew how to survive thanks to Punky for showing me the way – again.

—

Jamie started high school and quickly became popular, striving to be the best at everything. She was an honor roll student and a track star, running the same events that I did in high school. I thoroughly enjoyed going to her meets and working with the track and cross-country coach, giving him workout plans, encouraging the girls and helping them with running hills – showing them that training could be fun. They especially enjoyed the time when I joined them on a team relay from downtown Spokane, climbing 30+ miles to the 5,853-foot summit of Mount Spokane. We dressed alike in plaid boxer shorts and our hair in pigtails, with a big picnic waiting for us once we reached the top. It was quite refreshing; doing something different that took me out of the marathon mode. I met some great kids in the process. There was one girl I wanted to take home and protect.

Teresa was a beautiful, thin black girl with startling green eyes and weaved-in long braids that Jamie and I sometimes helped her maintain. It was a pain taking those things out. Small and lanky for a sprinter, Teresa had a feisty little attitude. She was a tough smart aleck with a good heart, and the best sprinter in the state as a freshman, which I'm sure is why she was so self-assertive and full of self-esteem. Teresa called me Momma Jones, always running up to hug me and then show off, no matter what she was supposed to be doing on the track.

Jamie and Teresa became close friends. But Jamie wasn't allowed to go to Teresa's house after a frightening encounter near her home. The day was turning to night when we drove right into a gang of young men, in our white Mercedes of all things. We instantly locked the car doors and tried to keep driving, but they wouldn't move out of our way. Jamie turned gray with fright and I was ready to have an asthma attack. They pounded on the windows. "Come on out here. Let's see who we have here in this nice car." I told Jamie, "Hang on, we're out of here," and drove right through. The gang moved away as I made our way out. Jamie didn't say much, but she was moved to become Teresa's "guardian angel" after that and became more and more protective of her best friend over the years.

During that drive, we found out Teresa lived in a bad neighborhood, in the middle of Spokane's drug scene. Some of her family used drugs and there were all kinds of people running in and out of their house selling, using, and who knows what. Her mother was there off and on. Teresa was at our house a lot and stayed with us when things were bad at home. We took her on trips, shopping, out to dinner and enjoyed her thoroughly. She needed tutoring to pass her classes and Jamie helped her with that, among other things, taking Teresa under her wing.

Jamie and Teresa

I truly enjoyed watching my two little track stars, traveling to all of their meets. I turned into my high school track mom, Betty Level – the mom who had everything the girls needed during a track meet, including words of wisdom. Jamie and Teresa would come rushing up to Steve and me after their races to talk about themselves, wanting to hear what we thought about their performances. It was something I needed as much as they did.

Being around the track gave me the urge to try for a qualifying time in the 5000 meters at the Olympic Trials, despite being marathon trained. The U.S. Track and Field Trials were in mid-June, and I had only a few weeks left to qualify. I would have just one shot at running a good 5000-meter time.

A lot of people doubted me. But Jamie and Teresa were behind me. So were Mr. Jones and Keith Peters from Nike, and Lynn Jennings, who gave me some pointers on how to race on the track at that level. I knew that no matter what happened, training for a shorter distance was my way to improve, recharge and bring myself out of the doldrums.

To run a qualifying time for the Trials I had to pick a huge competitive meet. I chose the Oregon Track Classic where I would be pushed to a fast time. Unfortunately, I would also be on display, and that meant the pressure was on, especially when it would be the first time I had raced in spikes in 20 years. Nonetheless, I strode like a metronome, clicking off 76-second laps and qualified in 15:43:04 (5:03 pace) as the spectators watched in disbelief. Everyone had considered me a slow marathoner over the years, but after all, I was really a sprinter at heart.

I took the entire gang to Atlanta for the Track Trials and ran fast enough in the first round to automatically qualify for the final, where I placed seventh. Jamie loved watching me race on the track. Because she had just experienced the same protocol in her state meet a month earlier, she knew how stressful it was just to make it to the final, and even knew the tactics and strategies involved. She became so emotionally caught up in the moment during the final, not only from the possibility that her mom might make the Olympic team in the 5,000 meters, but the bravery it took to even step on the track.

The faster racing was going to pay off later. I hadn't touched base with my speed in so long and it was a sure way to get faster in the longer distances, especially since I was creeping toward the big "4-0." I was running out of time. I wasn't going to give up, even after two years filled with bad luck and struggling through one disappointing race after the other. I had to keep going.

I felt a strong conviction that something was coming, something great.

New York City Marathon ~ November, 1996

I finished the year off by going back to the New York City Marathon in November to run a good solid performance and redeem myself after my last two disasters. I just had to try again. Despite running into a gusty headwind for most of the race, I ran strong. I despise wind! I detest it! I ran past the dreaded "17 mile-mark" without a problem, placing fourth. After that ... I felt redemption.

~

In 1997, I was back with Nike. Alberto had moved on to another part of the company, so I was treated better and with more respect when Mark Nenow took his position. That was all I asked for in the first place.

Fred Herlitz, who was in charge of the sunglass department in Nike promotions – we called him "The Sunglass Guy" – gave me an outstanding contract, which included bonuses for placing well in big races and among the top three in U.S. Championship races. It even doubled the bonus money if I won a big race while wearing Nike sunglasses. It worked out well for me since I rarely raced without sunglasses, though I was sorry to leave Oakley.

I decided to run in as many U.S. Championship races in 1997 as I could, to take advantage of the speed I'd tapped into the year before on the track and maybe win some extra money. The sunglasses deal was a big incentive.

First came the U.S. Championship 15K in Jacksonville in March, on the familiar River Run course that I had run eight times. After my warm up, I was sitting on the curb at the starting line, ready to put on my racing flats, when I realized I packed the wrong shoes. I had Jamie's racing flats! Jamie, of course, had the same exact shoes as me, except that she wears size 11 and I am size 8. On my way out the door I had grabbed her shoes, which were always right next to mine, off the shoe rack.

Carol McClatchie sat down next to me and laughed. "What are you going to do?"

"I guess I'll just have to wear them. I can't race in my heavy training shoes!"

"Good luck," she said sarcastically as we approached the starting line. I did a couple of strides in the oversized shoes, slapping down the street for all to see.

"What in the hell do you have on your feet?" exclaimed Keith Brantly. "They look like elf shoes."

As I toed the starting line, many of the elite runners were laughing. I was the fool again. Some things never change.

I slapped my way through the first part of the race, smiling as I remembered wearing Debbie's oversized shoes for most of my childhood. *This is no different.* The slapping sound made me smile more, bringing back other funny memories. The next thing I knew, I was climbing the final hill at 9 miles and catching the leaders, with Lynn Jennings pushing the pace. I was sneaking up and gearing up for the pass until my slapping gave me away and Lynn and Kristin Beaney took off sprinting in the final half mile to beat me. I placed third in 50:36. Not bad for wearing clown shoes.

Boston Marathon ~ April, 1997

That spring, I was still feeling hopeful, thinking I had a reasonable chance to win Boston.

It wasn't to be. I had a mediocre race, passing many runners, but it was a constant struggle. The night before the race, a huge rainstorm they call a Nor'easter came through, and again I was fighting a head-wind all the way. Not once did I feel like I was able to roll along feeling free and strong. Every time I caught up to a man or group of men who might shield me from the wind, they slowed down and I had to move on to another. The time went by quickly, but it didn't feel like a race. It was more like a resistance run.

Toward the end of the marathon, I passed a poor woman who seemed to be struggling into the headwind as much as I was. Darren De Reuck, a South African and husband of Colleen De Reuck, one of my competitors, said to me afterward, "That wasn't very nice, passing her while she was suffering and struggling to the finish."

"Ass!" I replied, my hands shooting into the air. "And I wasn't?" Darren was more shocked than I was by my reply, fueled by stirred-up emotions post-race.

"Sorry, Darren, but you always say the wrong thing at the wrong time."

"No, I'm sorry." He laughed, "Though we've become good friends from the many times you've straightened me out." Later that night, I called him "anal" because he was being far too bossy and particular about everything. He was taken aback and defended himself, "I'm not an anus!" I replied jokingly, "You're that, too." Our laughter eased my disappointment.

Even though most felt I ran a respectable time, I wasn't satisfied. I placed ninth in a deep and competitive field that included the Olympic gold medalist, Fatuma Roba, and Uta Pippig trying to become the first woman to win Boston four times. I earned a decent appearance fee and made some good prize money. But 2:32:52 was my slowest Boston ever.

Still, that slower pace into a headwind meant that I didn't physically beat myself up, so I decided to go for a good performance in Bloomsday 13 days later.

Winning Bloomsday had been my dream going all the way back to 1982 when I was sitting in the gutter with Anne Audain. Back then, it really *was* only a dream. It certainly wasn't a possibility in my mind. If I could win Bloomsday at age 39 – that would be more wondrous than winning any marathon – it would be miraculous.

I'm not being realistic, how can I expect to win Bloomsday? I'd just run Boston – my legs weren't beat up, but they were definitely tired from the hilly course and wind resistance. Most of the Joneses were staying in our home over the weekend and, to top it off, I had to give an hour-long speech in the ballroom of the race hotel to a convention of physicians and caregivers on Saturday – the day before the Bloomsday race.

Steve was all smiles. "No need to worry, just ignore everything." *Hmmm.*

The Joneses took over my house, flooding my marble bathroom trying to fix something in the sink that didn't need fixing, and the house was turned upside down, crumbs everywhere. I had no control. I packed up on Saturday morning and went to the hotel where the invited elite athletes were staying, and Don put me up in a room for the night.

I was literally sick to my stomach with worry about my speech on Saturday. Steve suggested, "Just start off with a joke. Tell them how nervous you were, expecting to be up on stage in front of everyone, until you pictured them all in their underwear."

"You've got to be kidding me," I said. "You're joking, right?" He wasn't.

The drug company Glaxo Wellcome was one of my sponsors. They were paying me well to give that talk and were there to grade my performance. I trudged up on stage, no notes, nothing. I looked out into a full ballroom, not really sure how to start off.

Suddenly I said, "My husband Steve told me to get up here and start with a joke. He actually wanted me to tell you that I'm picturing all of you in your underwear." They laughed, really laughed.

Then I went right into my asthma story. I told them about my first serious asthma attack, showing off when I was rushing home for dinner, and how Mr. O'Meara, the town's milkman, revived me but I ended up missing dinner anyway. I described the way my siblings and friends treated my symptoms, pushing on my back as I lay flat on my stomach to force the air from my lungs, or rubbing my back gently while saying things to calm me down and feel safe enough to relax and allow the trapped air to release on its own.

I began telling them how it all played into my development as a distance runner. My siblings and I ran for miles to get to places we wanted to go, and I instinctively knew I had to slow down, sometimes walk or even stop when I experienced asthma symptoms: pacing myself. Or, I ran really fast to get far ahead of everyone, took a short rest, and ran fast again before they caught me: speed intervals. I talked about running up Morgan Hill, then sliding down on cardboard over and over again: hill repeats. Skipping rope and beating kids on the playground bars for their milk money and a little respect: strength training. Chasing Kayla all over town when she escaped: long, slow distance runs. Sprinting down to the end of the dock before jumping into the freezing water and then swimming as fast as possible back to shore before running on the beach and doing it all over again and again: circuit training. Through all of that, I learned how to back off when needed and not show off all at once. I learned how to be a marathoner.

I'd realized it long before I began my speech, but I had never really put all the pieces together until then. I talked for the entire hour, telling them many funny stories from my childhood. They loved the stories. I finished up talking about the asthma medications I was taking, the dosage, and how I hoped it would work for me the next day in Bloomsday.

My last words were, "I'll hope for the best and see what happens."

Afterward, it was time to get ready for the race. Steve Shirley, my chiropractor, went into his office after my speech, just to give me a much-needed adjustment even though it was a Saturday. Brian Tibbetts gave up his Saturday night and came to the hotel to give me a massage, working on my diaphragm and ribcage to open things up after my stressful day. To add a little more pressure, I was given bib #1.

Then I lay awake all night. *I really want to win. How can I expect to win?*

In the morning, I jogged over to the Paulsen Center for my warm up and then went inside where the elite runners could relax until the race started directly outside the front doors. I sat on the floor and admired this fine building, the brass elevator doors, the elegant woodwork, the crushed-tin ceilings and markings. Then I was totally relaxed. *Whatever happens, happens. There's no need to worry about things I'm not in control of, especially now. I don't want to waste any energy. I'll save all of my energy for the race.*

It was 15 minutes before the start when I took my racing flats out of my backpack to put them on. They were two different shoes. I was in such a hurry to leave my messy house that I didn't pay close enough attention. One shoe was red and white and size 8, and the other was purple and white and size 9. *Hmmm.* At least they fit OK, they were both Nikes and, thank goodness, they were racing flats. Most importantly, I had a left and a right shoe. So, no problem. I put them on and went into the line for the restroom before going out the door to face some music.

Bloomsday 1997 would be the fourth year the elite women started 15 minutes before the elite men and rest of the 50,000 runners. That meant it would be a tactical race. No woman could take off like a blazing bullet, then tuck in behind men and be pulled to a fast time. It also meant that if I won, I would actually be the very first runner to cross the finish line, something I couldn't do if winning Boston or New York.

I'd never finished higher than fifth in Bloomsday, and it would almost certainly be my last chance to win. The competition was strong: Gladys Ondeyo, a top Kenyan; Martha Tenorio, an Olympian from Ecuador; and three tough Russians, to boot. It would be a daunting task.

We took off on a cool blustery morning, as cloudy as an early spring morning in Port Townsend. The lilacs were out, their fragrance as comforting as it was in my high school track days, their delicate purple and white blossoms peeking out from every yard as we ran through the neighborhoods, calming my fears of the unknown that lay before me.

Aware that I needed to ease into it, I was thankful that we started slowly. I had no idea what my legs had in store for me. A local runner, Kari McKay, took off like a bat flying from hell, faster than she was capable of running – or so I hoped. The other women were watching me, and let her go. An American, Carole Zajac, was leading our pack and well prepared to win the race. She'd been excelling in shorter events on the track, making her faster than most.

I wasn't worried until we went through the first mile in 5:38. *Now that's slow for a slight downhill mile.* We ran another 5:38 downhill mile. *What should I do now?* I continued to follow the American, who started picking up the pace just in time for the uphills. *Hmmm.* The pack dwindled to eight: Carole, the Russians, the Kenyans and me.

We passed Kari like she was running through molasses when we began our 5:10-5:15 miles. I was tired every step of the way, but there was no taking a rest, mentally or physically. I *really* wanted to take a breather and slip behind the pack. My legs were heavy and I was working just at my threshold, but I knew I had to stick with the leader and stay in the moment, no matter what, if I wanted to win. There was a high-school track team working the aid station at 3 miles, chanting "Kim Jones, Kim Jones, Kim Jones," loudly and without pause as we ran by. I felt good, proud to be recognized by the young, up-and-coming athletes in Spokane. They gave me the encouragement I needed to persevere and remain grounded, and to work through *this* unpleasantness some call pain.

When we hit Doomsday Hill at 5 miles, Carole took off. I wanted to stay back with the pack, hoping she would fade later, but I couldn't. She was running strong. I was hoping for some sign of weakness, for a boost, to know she was working beyond her ability level and hurting, as I was. Just before we crested the hill, she faltered, hunching her shoulders and landing hard as she stayed on the ground a bit longer. She lost her track form and began to shuffle.

This is it. I have to go.

Just then, I saw my friend "The Vulture" ready for his annual high-five. I didn't do it. I had to ignore him!

I pressed on, fully aware that I had to make my move and make it count, *right now*, before heading into the final 2 miles. *This is going to be a long move!*

Carole followed, but allowed me to get eight seconds on her. I took a couple of peeks each time I turned a corner to make sure I kept that distance, fighting the headwind alone as I worked toward the finish line. I didn't want her drafting off me. She stayed eight seconds behind me right to the final uphill into the finish. I wasn't sure how my legs were going to hold up on the last hill. They were feeling that hilly Boston course from just 13 days earlier.

As I ran toward the finish line, I began to realize I was about to win my hometown race in the biggest moment of my career. I'd played my cards right, being patient and working with the players throughout the entire game, matching their every play with a trump card only to come out throwing the ace at the end.

I'm shooting the moon!

It was the most triumphant moment of my life. I savored every single step, hearing the crowd roaring just for me. That crowd seemed bigger and louder than the ones in New York and Boston – at least they did to me that day. There was no discomfort during that flash of glory. I was the first runner to cross the finish line, breaking the tape, arms flung overhead in exhilaration, and it was the biggest thrill of my life.

I ran the perfect race, making my moment even more rewarding ... and I rejoiced. I never knew what rejoice really meant until then. Everyone was ecstatic. In the finish area, I gave Curt Kinghorn a big hug. Then, I saw Jamie standing there with tears in her eyes, so proud of me. She knew what I had to live through, not just over the past few weeks with the chaos around the house, but throughout my entire career. Jamie was the only one who really knew how much it meant to me. She rejoiced, too.

Any American placing in the Top 10 was awarded double prize money. I received a big bonus for wearing Nike sunglasses. A huge photo of me ran on the front page of the Spokesman-Review, arms spread wide as I broke the tape with joy, relief and exhilaration on my exhausted face, my thin legs buckling a little, and my two different shoes for all to see. And, naturally, wearing my sunglasses.

My Bloomsday win made a big impact on the younger generation of Spokane. Parents and teachers told me little girls were running around with ponytails and wearing their parents' sunglasses, sometimes even wearing two different shoes, saying, "I'm Kim Jones!" as they ran as fast as they could through their houses, in their yards or at recess. I was their superhero, for a few weeks anyway. Many people in Spokane felt they knew me after watching my long and eventful 15-year career, my trials and tribulations as well as my successes. The *Spokesman-Review* and the news stations followed almost every race and many of my personal struggles. To some, my career became a soap opera or reality show as they eagerly waited to hear the next installment and hoped that I would someday win this big race in their hometown called Bloomsday. I made them proud.

~

In running, like "shooting the moon," I've found that the desire for an ultimate challenge continues after attaining the grand prize.

I recovered quickly and continued my quest to run U.S. Championship Races. The Old Kent River Bank Run 25K in Flint, Michigan, was just six days after Bloomsday, and 20 days after Boston. I was on a roll, feeling invincible, and I wasn't getting any younger. Even though another good race so soon was improbable, I needed to take advantage of the situation.

It was a battle from the start as I worked against Russian Alina Ivanova the entire distance. I was in a fight for 15½ long, hilly miles in blustery winds. It was the year of the wind, which was there to greet me in every single race. I played my cards to perfection, as I did in Bloomsday, winning the open division, the American prize and then receiving that nice bonus from "Fred the Sunglass Guy." *I can't believe I'm actually doing this, at age 39!*

I won the Rhody Run a week later, for the 12th time, and then took a long rest. However, I was rapidly approaching 40, another good reason to enter the Tufts Health Plan 10K for Women, the 10K U.S. Championships, in October. It was another windy race – no surprise there – so I ran behind a pack of 14. It dwindled from seven, to five, then I took a little rest and a mental break. Big mistake – when the pack dropped me, I was stuck facing the wind alone. I crossed the bridge at 4½ miles, 20 seconds behind Libbie (Johnson) Hickman and the leaders. Her coach, Damien, called out, "Go, Kimmie, you're beautiful ... you're running great!" It gave me a little boost, and slowly I caught the others, passing all of them with less than a half mile to the finish.

There was one problem, though. I was so occupied watching on the left for the shadows of the Americans, just in case I needed to make another move, that I dismissed Kenyan Gladys Ondeyo on my right, whom I'd defeated soundly at Bloomsday. She zipped right past me. I won the U.S. Championship but Ondeyo won the race in the final 50 meters.

What a colossal mistake! I've always focused on the finish line, pushing hard all the way in. I let my guard down, assuming I had the win. Another lesson learned the hard way. I ran a 32-minute 10K, won another U.S. Championship and clinched the 1997 USA Running Circuit title, but I was not pleased that I had failed to heed Mr. Royce's warning from years before: "It's not a win until you cross that finish line."

On the awards stand, Libbie said jokingly, "I thought you were just an old, slow marathoner."

"I *am* old," I said with a smile.

New York City Marathon ~ November, 1997

I was feeling good and wanted to finish the year strong, so naturally I had to end my year with the New York City Marathon in November. I ran a decent time of 2:32:00, placing sixth. Finally, my year was complete, or would be after celebrating with Mark Coogan and Mr. Jones. Just after the awards ceremony that night, we were carrying our crystal vases back to the hotel when Mark wanted to stop in at one of the popular runner pubs. "We can't go in like big showboats with our crystal!" I told him.

"It's packed with celebrating marathoners," he assured me. "Nobody will notice."

One bartender filled the vases up with beer. I'm surprised we didn't chip our teeth on those things. Everyone teased Mark because he was sitting at the bar with a Tiffany vase, and the fact that his vase was smaller than mine made for some good jokes.

1997 was my most successful year of all. I worked hard for everything, taking it beyond what most consider hard training. My appreciation was tenfold, knowing I had worked beyond my limits and played my cards to perfection.

It was the year when it finally dawned on me, *this is what I was training to do my entire life* ... giving talks at the meetings in the Kingdom Hall and learning the skills of communication, developing as a distance runner from my active childhood, taking advantage of what was offered in life, healing and then toughening up from the many traumas thrown my way. Some never grasp what's offered in life, never recognizing their learned skills from the past. Some even consider their childhood a disadvantage, blaming it for their inadequacies and reason for their failures. I considered myself lucky to be able to use everything life dished out to me – good and bad – working hard to become the best I could possibly be with the abilities I had.

"I'm a great believer in luck, and I find the harder I work the more I have of it." ~ Thomas Jefferson.

Chapter 19

Rachel

We spent a lot of time with Rachel in 1997, and I was thrilled when she made plans with us for the holiday season. She joined us for Thanksgiving with Steve's family in Seattle, where most of the Joneses, Jamie and I ran the Seattle Half Marathon on Saturday morning. I wasn't sure how, but I managed to win after an over-loading carbo session at Thanksgiving dinner. Then Rachel, Jamie and I headed to Port Townsend early Saturday evening to visit my family, leaving Steve with the Joneses.

Because of the holiday weekend, the Seattle ferry was packed. Rachel drove farther north to the Edmonds ferry, but traffic was even more backed up there. Even if we waited for hours in line we might not have made the last boat. It was late and we needed to get to Mom's for her amazing clam chowder.

There was no time to waste. Rachel yelled, "Hold on!" as she hightailed it, passing all of the patient travelers in two long lines waiting their turn. She was going 30 mph, speeding almost all the way to the ferry before quickly squeezing into the line, bringing her red VW convertible to a sudden stop between a large truck and a motor home that were inching ahead.

Our heads lurched forward. In the back seat, Jamie was laughing so hard that she was sputtering and snorting. Rachel and I looked at each other, eyes as wide as could be. My hands shot into the air. "Unbelievable, Rachel!"

"We do need to get to Grandma's in time for dinner," said Jamie, jumping in quickly. "Nice going, Rach!"

It was comical, but I warned Rachel, "That was really dangerous! You can't be taking chances like this. You're not invincible."

We drove directly onto the ferry without waiting, but I was too embarrassed to get out of the car and go up to the main deck for snacks. We had some pretty irate people behind us. It was worth it, though. Mom's clam chowder was magnificent, and she even made her special fried oysters with garlic bread.

A month later, Rachel brought her new boyfriend, Cooper, to Spokane over Christmas. They were living together in Seattle, which meant it must be serious. Cooper was tall and lean, handsome in an Irish way with reddish-blond hair and blue-green eyes. He fit into the family right away, with a good sense of humor and a decent belly laugh. He even liked just hanging out eating snacks and watching rented movies with Jamie, Rachel and me while making quick-witted comments.

That winter, running in Spokane turned from serene to scary when we had a serial killer on the loose. I ran across several taped off crime scenes while running along Hangman Valley Road and the trails near our Thorpe Road loop.

One day as I ran, detectives were in the midst of taping off a murder scene. Most of them knew me by then, and they told me to avoid the area. I did. Those crime scenes contained the dumped bodies of murdered women. Later, Robert Lee Yates was arrested and convicted of 13 counts of murder in Spokane involving prostitutes in the Skid Row area on East Sprague Avenue. He would have sex with them and sometimes do drugs before shooting them in the head and dumping their bodies in rural locations. Unfortunately for me, I ran in those rural areas.

The River Road and trails leading off it weren't the safest places to run either, but I loved that area west of the city and chose to run there anyway. A young girl's body was found in a cardboard box under some brush deep into the State Park where I did my 20 milers. The girl was raped and then bludgeoned to death, and left at my 12-mile mark. It was shocking to find it happening around me in the most beautiful areas of Spokane.

While running along the River Road one day, I came across a large group of people congregated in a dirt parking area next to the river. I sensed danger ahead, but it was too late. They started to come out to the road. As I ventured closer I saw they had shaved heads and were dressed in T-shirts and black Army boots, some in jackets and Army pants. They were covered in tattoos and wore chains with Nazi emblems. There are several groups of white power skinheads in the Spokane area, mostly in nearby northern Idaho, and it looked like one of them.

Three guys walked toward me while punching their brass knuckles into their fists as I was running toward them. The others circled behind me.

I was between the devil and the deep blue sea. *There's no place to retreat. No escape!*

I slowed to a jog, looked the lead guy straight in the eyes and asked in a pleasant voice, "Good morning, how's it going?"

The skinhead's demonized look changed to surprise as he moved to the side and let me pass. "Good morning," he grumbled.

My legs were weak and I was on the verge of an asthma attack, but I stayed calm and did the right thing. I had learned from my past not to allow victimizers to feel in total control of the situation, but to show them that I wasn't afraid and they were not "the boss of me." It took them off guard, as it always did, long enough to give me a chance to escape or at least a moment to think.

I did all of my speed workouts out there on the River Road, running back and forth on a flat two-mile stretch that had quarter miles marked off to allow for a timed effort. I was older and the fewer speed workouts I did on the track, the less wear and tear on my aging body. It was the perfect alternative.

I was on my own during my workouts, and constantly teased about injuring all of my training buddies. Staffan broke his ankle while running too fast down one of the trails, Don had a hamstring problem and Steve was struggling with minor injuries. The other boys in our group not only had aches and pains, but they had "real" jobs and couldn't get away during work hours.

Over the past few years I had been noticing a small blue car either driving slowly or parked along the River Road, but that winter while I ran back and forth on the same stretch of road, the car kept cruising back and forth at almost the speed I was running. A guy with long dark hair, a beard and beady brown eyes gawked at me through his open window as he drove by.

However, that time was different. It was the same creepy guy, but strangely the car had switched from an Oregon to a Washington State license plate. I memorized the number and ran back to my car, skipping the rest of my workout. Steve immediately called a friend on the police force. He checked out the plate and felt we needed to catch the guy in the act.

I was going to be the decoy in a police investigation. I had to smile. It reminded me of an "Angel Investigation." My roommates Kelley and Claire would have been proud. I was to go down to the river, park in my usual spot at the same time as always, and go through my normal routine. I told the officers that my plan was to warm up on the side trails and then do mile repeats, running back and forth on the road.

When I arrived, they had already stopped the guy. It was a relief, but I was disappointed that I wouldn't be a part of the operation. Apparently, the guy was a stalker. He knew my name, where I lived, my daily routine and details of my past that most people wouldn't know. He even had newspaper photos. He came right out and told the police all of that, adding that he had the right to drive anywhere he pleased on the public streets and wasn't doing anything wrong.

There wasn't enough evidence to arrest him for anything, but the police told him, "If anything ever happens to Kim, we're coming after you."

I still saw him out there after that, but he didn't gawk at me as long or drive quite as slowly.

Perhaps I should have stayed away from those danger areas, because I wasn't setting a very good example. My little 17-year-old follower decided she liked running along the River Road, too, and had a few encounters of her own. Once when I was out of town, a man followed her at dusk and kept driving back and forth, gawking as she ran alone. Maybe it was the same pervert? Jamie ended up running way too far, dusk turning to dark, before finally making her way along trails to the main road.

As the New Year began, Mr. Jones came to Spokane to do some winter training with me. Maybe the fact that there was a murderer out there and that Jamie and I had a stalker had something to do with that.

Houston Marathon ~ January, 1998

I had completely recovered from my long and successful year in 1997 and was training better than ever. I told Mr. Jones, "I'm seriously thinking of going to Houston for the 1998 U.S. Marathon Championships in January." He coughed and his eyes widened. "That would be tough after running New York and winning a half marathon in November, but I'm sure you can do it. You never cease to amaze me."

It wasn't as easy as I had hoped. That was the only race in my career in which I chose to ease up. With only 1.2 miles to go, where I usually come charging in, I decided to shut down my jets. It wasn't a good day. I had wanted to stop from the beginning, and think I would have if Jamie hadn't been at every 5-mile mark cheering for me. I couldn't drop out in front of her! At 20 miles, Carol McClatchie's husband, Jim, who was a coach in Houston, asked if I was OK. "I don't know," I said as I ran toward him to stop for a break. "Keep running!" he shouted. "Gwyn Coogan is just ahead of you."

I could see Gwyn, Mark's wife, but every time I picked up the pace my head felt like it was going to pop off. I stayed at 5:50 pace counting down the final miles while Gwyn stayed the same distance in front of me. When I made it to 25 miles I knew I wasn't going to catch her. I took a look behind me. Linda Somers Smith had faded so badly after taking an early lead on that day of miserable 95-percent humidity that I didn't even see her, so I settled for being the second winner. I started jogging and finished the final 1.2 miles in 10 minutes. It usually takes me seven.

We had a great time at the pub afterward, with Jamie playing darts, eating burgers and thoroughly enjoying the McClatchies. Later that night, while lying in our hotel room beds, she said, "Mom, this was the most fun I've ever had! I always thought you went to races and just came home. You and your friends have more fun than any of my friends, even at our parties."

"I don't always enjoy myself so much after a race. Sometimes I do come straight home, depending on what you're up to."

"I was worried about you running in the heat today. How can you race like that?"

"The training is usually harder than the racing, although this marathon was really tough, Jamie, really tough!"

"How can you do this all the time, for so many years?"

"The hardest part for me is trying to keep our life under control as I train and race. I don't do a very good balancing act." I looked over at her. "Can you tell?"

"No, everything is perfect at home."

Steve was already sound asleep next to me – he had a rough day as well. Just as I was ready to doze off, Jamie asked, "Do you think I can be as tough as you are in my track races this spring?"

"Absolutely."

"Do you think I can win the mile and 800 at state this year?"

"Absolutely, but it will take a lot of work and dedication, even sacrifice. You'll need good sleep and a good diet, and you will have to skip a few of those rowdy parties some of your friends have. Those early morning runs at 5 a.m. you persuaded me to do with you this winter will really pay off. We should keep that up."

"I'll do whatever it takes, Mom."

"Then your hard work shall be rewarded."

"Ditto, be careful, I love you, goodnight."

"Ditto, be careful, I love you, goodnight."

Once we returned home, Jamie kept ditching her friends to spend time with me, sometimes doing nothing more than watching TV, having snacks or quietly reading. One Sunday evening, after Jamie had skipped out on one too many parties, her friends decided to find her. She came running down the stairs while Punky and I were sitting in Big Red watching "60 Minutes."

"Mom, turn the TV off, quick," she yelled as she grabbed the controls. "My friends are here to make me go out with them! Hurry, we have to hide!"

With no time to think, I bolted out of Big Red as Punky went flying off my lap, and we hid behind the lattice on the stairway just as 10 of her friends came walking up to the front door. Jamie turned and said, "Mom, look at Big Red! The chair's still rocking!" and we started laughing. I had jumped out of the chair so quickly that it was still going back and forth like crazy. We laughed harder when we saw Punky sitting on the stairs hiding and peeking through the lattice with us.

After ringing the doorbell and getting no answer, all 10 faces looked through the picture window with big eyes riveted on Big Red rocking madly. Our big old house looked scary enough already, but I'll bet that made for some good ghost stories.

⌒

On a terribly windy morning in March, I was at the starting line of my first spring race, the St. Patrick's Day Dash in Seattle. I was a favorite to win, and a local television station wanted to do a quick interview on live television just minutes before the start of the race. "Please stand a little closer to the press truck," the interviewer asked. "A little closer." Suddenly, a big gust of wind hit a signboard on the truck just as a guy was getting ready to secure it. The sign fell from the top of the truck and skidded down my ankle, landing on my foot.

In that one dreadful moment, reality shone through to me as brightly as the sun's ray through a freshly washed window. In just one instant, my elite running career was over. My right foot was crushed.

The doctors told me what I already knew. The extreme trauma caused a severely dropped foot. There was no way I could ever again run up on my toes and use the forceful push-off that made me a standout runner. No more running on my toes, no more powering forward. Once again, I would have been better off breaking a bone, but my strong bones caused the soft tissue, ligaments, tendons and muscles to take on too much damage.

After my foot healed, I could walk just fine, I could even run, but I had to run low to the ground and almost flatfooted. I would never again race as I used to.

I had been planning to retire while on top of my game, before the slide in performance began as I grew older, although I hadn't decided on a date. *Now I don't have to make a decision. It was made for me.*

Surprisingly, I wasn't devastated. There are worse things that can happen in life in just one instant.

It was time to move on. I could still train and race, much slower, and after turning 40 in two months I could run a few masters races and take care of my race and appearance commitments through the year while easing into my retirement. I was ready. As Heraclitus of Ephesus once said: "You cannot step twice into the same stream."

I was thankful the accident wasn't worse. I was thankful that my running wasn't taken from me completely.

Steve would barely talk to me. He didn't want to discuss my injury and would shake his head and walk away when I wanted to talk about my future. I guess he was avoiding the issue and felt sorry for me. He realized I wasn't going to be the same athlete, on top of the world, anymore. He perked up right away when I decided to take the girls on a late spring vacation to Hawaii, however. He decided that he also needed a distraction and wanted to go with us.

"What's up with Steve?" Rachel asked after we arrived in Hawaii, noticing his moodiness. I told her about his change in behavior since my injury. "Mom, that's not right, he needs to be supportive. This happened to you, not him." Jamie piped in, "Yeah Rach, he's worse at home. He won't even talk to Mom. He's much better here."

"I don't think Steve knows how to handle this," I told the girls as they sat on the beach beside me, their hands clasped around their knees as they listened intently. "Our relationship was built on a fairytale world from the beginning. He came into our lives just as I was becoming one of the top marathoners in the world. We were treated with grandness, became famous and money was easily accessible – all I had to do was go run a race if needed." I pushed my feet into the sand. "Now he doesn't seem to want or maybe know how to live a normal life with me." The girls pushed their feet into the sand.

"I'm to blame in a way. I put you girls first, ahead of my running, and Steve was a close third. I'm sure he sensed that."

"He's been a good father to us, hasn't he? Even when I was an ass living at home," said Rachel.

"Yes, he's a good man."

Jamie suddenly seemed concerned. "Do you talk about *anything?*"

"Never. There's no connection or communication between us, and most of the time he just leaves without a goodbye. This has always been his way of dealing with unpleasant situations. If he didn't confront it, it wasn't happening." I pushed my feet deeper into the sand. "I really think our marriage is over."

They agreed, especially after watching him for the next 10 days in a place that most people would consider paradise. Steve made the vacation more stressful than it should have been, but I had my girls to bring me out of it with laughter.

We were on the beach a bit too long the first day in Maui, so I told the girls that we should give our skin a rest. "We have Indian in us, we'll be fine," insisted Rachel. I threw Jamie the sunscreen and headed up to the condo, asking Rachel if she wanted me to bring her sunglasses. "NO Mom, I'll be fine! I'm 22 now!" That night while we were all eating pizza and watching movies in the condo, Rachel came out of the shower with an incredibly swollen sunburned face and white lines across her forehead from squinting in the bright sun. Even Steve had to chuckle.

While we were grocery shopping to stock the condo refrigerator, Rachel and Jamie started fighting over mustard. Jamie wanted yellow and Rachel wanted Grey Poupon. I finally asked Jamie, "Do you like Grey Poupon?" and she said, "no." "Rachel, do you like yellow mustard?" She replied, embarrassed, "yes." Then they started fighting over Rachel feeling that Jamie was my favorite. I walked away and let them solve it on their own. They picked out the yellow mustard and kept apologizing to me all the way through checkout. We all laughed after getting into the car when I said, with my hands in the air, "You guys are 17 and 22, and you're fighting over mustard?"

The next afternoon, the girls were diving into the huge waves on a big surf day while I was sitting on the beach watching. Steve lounged on the sand beside me with his forehead on his hands, when I asked, "Do you think that's dangerous?" Steve raised his head and looked out to see the girls being thrown headfirst into shore, then came running out of the water with sand in their mouths, ears – and bikini bottoms, which would droop and begin to fall off. "It looks like you have a big load in there," I heard Rachel say between their laughter and screaming.

"No. They seem OK," said Steve.

"Are you sure? Those waves look threatening!"

"They're fine."

I went out with them to see for myself. The girls were so worried when I went crashing down. "Mom, are you OK? You need to be careful!" They loved me with all their hearts and I had the deepest love for them. I was blessed having two beautiful, healthy and caring daughters.

As we were leaving the beach, we noticed a big, bold sign: Danger. Stay Out.

Back at home, Steve was off in his own world. Thoughts that he could leave me in my moment of defeat circulated like a shark spiraling in on a target, and so it went on and on until I was certain that he truly did not care anymore. Although I was disappointed, I knew that he must have been struggling, too. I had no regrets spending those 11 years with him. Steve truly is a good man and had always been supportive of me and my running career in every way possible, and he helped me raise two lovely, yet demanding daughters; however ... our life as we knew it was over.

Steve made new friends and began training with the ultra-marathon runners in Spokane. They were a great group that ran for many hours at a very slow pace while training for 50- and 100-mile races on trails and roads. It was good for Steve, who was dealing with minor injuries and had slowed down quite a bit in the shorter distances. He needed a change from mainstream racing. But, running all those miles gave him an extra boost of confidence.

Trying to spark a conversation, I searched for something we still had in common. I even tried talking to him about his plans to run a 50 miler in Montana, the Le Grizz Ultra Marathon, near Glacier National Park. He would say one or two words and then walk away. That clinched my decision – our marriage was over. I wasn't going to live like that for the rest of my life. I had to figure out a good time to talk to him about a divorce.

Now I was the one avoiding confrontation.

In May 1998, I turned 40 on the weekend of Bloomsday, and decided to run the race and go for the masters title. Even with my foot taped up tightly, I managed it without too much trouble and my time of 42:17 was a new U.S. Masters record. Even so, it was intensely painful and two minutes slower than the previous year. I will always have a deep passion for running, but the thrill of racing was gone. Running Bloomsday on my birthday launched my career, and sadly, 16 years later, I was saying farewell on my birthday.

Spring and summer passed quickly. The time had come for my final commitment for the year: signing autographs and making a few appearances for the Chicago Marathon in October, before running it as a masters competitor. It would be my last big race, no matter what Punky did to impress me. It was time to shut down my engines and figure out a plan for retirement.

Chicago Marathon ~ October, 1998

I knew when I stepped on the starting line that it was my last attempt at survival in the marathon world. My sore foot was swollen and achy from the humidity, and both feet were blistering in the first few miles as I twisted around trying to avoid stepping on my crooked toe, running flatfooted in the hard-packed untested racing flats. I thought about how absolutely miserable I was in my first college cross-country meet when I ran directly into that tree and decided to quit running. I felt as I did then, only my foot was sore the entire way and my crooked toe went numb. Even worse, the race was 26 miles, not three. I had a long way to go.

My body was rebelling and kept telling me it wasn't willing to be out there. My mind kept ordering me to stop. I kept forcing myself to go through the motions despite the agony. *This isn't what running should feel like!* It didn't help knowing that I could run faster if I could just get up on my toes and press forward. Johnny Cash's "Ring of Fire" kept playing in my head. I felt like I was burning in that ring of fire. My feet did, too. I struggled to the bitter end, and even managed to qualify for the 2000 Olympic Trials, but I wasn't enjoying racing anymore. That miserable experience clinched the deal. It was time to call it quits.

After fulfilling my last commitment in October of 1998, I retired. No second thoughts.

A few days later, it was time to face some music and confront Steve. While he was in the Red Room, reading, I cornered him so he couldn't slip out the door and walk away from me.

"We need to talk."

He scratched his head, apparently realizing there was no escape. "Yes, we do." There was a long silence.

"Our marriage isn't working," I finally said. "Have you even noticed?"

"Yes," said Steve. "What do you think we should do about it?"

I thought for a minute. "I feel there's nothing left between us ... we have nothing in common." I explained how I felt until Steve asked, "Should we seek counseling?"

"It's only worth going to counseling if we have one thing that we can build on, just one thing we enjoy doing together."

We both thought for a long while, and I couldn't come up with one single thing. Then Steve piped up, "I like traveling with you to races."

As infuriated as I was, I calmly said, "You know that when we travel together, you're treated first class along with the elite athletes. We stay in elegant hotels and eat at the finest restaurants, everything is paid for, and you are out with our friends while I'm resting in my room. Then, after I work my ass off in the race you're too tired and go to bed early, leaving me on my own. That's not togetherness. My racing was the glue to our marriage. There's no more glue."

"I guess we should get a divorce then," he said.

"Hmmm, I guess so."

Sadly, that was that.

It helped keep the tension down in the house when Rachel and Cooper came for a visit again over Christmas. We followed our tradition of just sitting around and talking, eating snacks and watching movies. For our "lying around watching movies all day" program, we each picked out something from Blockbuster. Rachel found "The Texas Chainsaw Massacre" and Cooper chose "A River Runs Through It," which was filmed in Bozeman, Montana, not far from Spokane. Jamie picked out the most idiotic movie I had ever watched, "Can't Hardly Wait." We all suffered through it for her sake, and after that started saying mockingly, "Can't Hardly Wait!" whenever we were eager to do something.

I chose "The Horse Whisperer." Steve walked in just as we were watching a scene with Robert Redford. "Chaps, how nice. Especially when he's wearing them, hmmm," I said. Then as we all saw Steve standing in the room, I added nervously, "Chaps? What are chaps anyway?"

When Steve left the room, Rachel asked, "What was that all about?"

"I have no idea. How stupid. I guess I don't want him to think I like chaps and decide to surprise me by wearing a pair," I said as they all chuckled.

Cooper and Rachel started calling me "Chaps."

Chapter 20

Divorce isn't a pleasant experience. I realized that the first time, but it's *really* not easy divorcing an attorney. We weren't hurting for money by any means. I just didn't know how much we had or where it was.

Steve never asked me how I felt about the many decisions he made regarding our finances. I knew all along that he was shielding me from those stresses, allowing me to focus on my running career. So there I was, without a credit card or checking account. I had rarely used the checkbook during our marriage. I never even saw the statements for any of our accounts because Steve took them directly to the office.

I had a lot of work to do. It was my own fault and I alone was to blame for my ignorance.

I asked a mutual attorney friend, Tim Harkins, to handle our divorce. Tim was a good and fair man who handled my divorce from Kelly 12 years earlier. He watched his son compete for the Ferris High School track and cross-country team while I cheered for Jamie and her Lewis and Clark team, making it convenient for discussing things outside the office.

Steve and I divided everything evenly, except for his business. I didn't ask for half of his partnership. Stupid, some would say, but it would only have made the divorce proceedings more difficult and expensive, losing more assets after attorney costs. Besides, I wasn't out to ruin Steve. I still cared too much about him to do that. The only thing we went back and forth on was who would be stuck with the newly leased Mercedes. I knew part of Jamie's college fund was secure through Kelly, and I would figure out the rest later. Once again I was ready to go out in the world and see what it had to offer.

Steve was getting the Spokane house in the divorce, but Jamie and I planned to stay there for several months until she graduated in June of

1999. Steve lived in a friend's condo until I moved to Boulder, where I kept the condo and where Jamie planned to go to college. It was a good setup.

I traveled to Boulder and stayed for a couple of weeks to set things up for my move. I also went out with Jon Sinclair a few times. He had a combination of John Denver's boyish charm and strong beliefs and MacGyver's methodical intelligence, making clever, incisive comments when warranted. As many of Jon's friends said, "Jon is brutally honest." He's a realist, and he'll tell you the truth as he sees it, even if he offends you.

That was when I met Wiley, named because he looked a lot like "Wile E. Coyote" in the Looney Tunes cartoon, "Road Runner." Wiley was a precious, kindhearted mutt with the gentle face of a beagle and the body of a medium-sized golden retriever. Over the years, Wiley ran with Jon for many miles. Some days Wiley would cover 30 of what Jon called "dog miles," running back and forth and up and down hills. Wiley ran a lot farther than the guys he ran with.

In 1993, *Runner's World* did a photo shoot of Jon and Wiley running in the foothills of Fort Collins, and when the two appeared together on the September 1993 cover the staff told Jon that Wiley was the first "Cover Dog" in the magazine's history. Jon loved that dog the way you love a child. They went everywhere together in his collector 1973 dark-blue Bronco, and Jon would cover him with a blanket when they sat on the couch watching the "Today Show." Wiley was spoiled in a good way, getting a treat when he did something special, sometimes just for looking especially cute.

Their interaction told me a lot about this man I was falling in love with.

During the many months of sorting out my own life, I watched Jamie excel in her last year of high school. She was a straight-A student and won the Scholar Athlete Award from the Greater Spokane League, which each year recognizes students who excel in the classroom, community and athletics. She was in the newspaper a lot, and one sportswriter wrote that she "finished the league unbeaten with a come from behind win." *I wonder where she learned that?*

Jamie was undefeated in cross country that fall before leading her team to the regional meet, where my little follower learned to handle her only defeat when she had a bad race and placed eighth. I was proud of her for accepting failure without making any excuses ... always willing to work harder.

Jamie following me (stride for stride) as I pull
her through her indoor mile PR ~ 1999

With Jamie coming off the cross-country season stronger and more powerful than ever, I watched with great pride in the spring when she and Teresa showed their "stuff." They were running the best times in the state at their events and walked around as if they owned the track. How funny ... just like Sarah Level and I did in our heyday. We were even the state leaders in the same events.

I trained with Jamie several times, pushing her through some great workouts, enjoying every moment as she continued to grow stronger and faster. She became the queen of middle distance, winning the district and regional meets in all of her events.

At the state meet, with all eyes on her, Jamie made a rare mistake. In the 800 final, she was feeling invincible despite facing one of the fastest 800-meter girls in the state, just like the Jezebel I used to race in high school – in the same event and the same situation. Jamie had beaten her in the past, using her come from behind strategy. However, Jamie made her move, but she didn't make it count. After passing the other girl and thinking she had the state title, Jamie eased into the finish and lost when the sprinter out-leaned her. Why didn't she learn what *not* to do from my Tufts 10K loss to Gladys Ondeyo? Instead, she just had to follow suit! The girl beat her by eight-tenths of a second.

Jamie walked off the track in tears. I had to do something. I went to the corner of the track where she was alone and crying. I gave her a hug. "Jamie, you ran a great race, 2:13 is fantastic!"

"Mom, I should have won. I'm so stupid," she said, still in tears.

"Jamie, what do you think people are going to remember you for right now, that you were second in this race or how you acted in defeat? You were the second winner."

I went on, "A true champion is the athlete who accepts defeat honorably, giving her competitors respect and showing good sportsmanship."

She looked at me, wiping the tears from her eyes and attempting a smile.

"OK," I told her. "Now you need to regroup, focus, and use what you've learned from your mistake in this race for the mile in a few hours."

Jamie took my advice and walked back to the stands with her head held high, smiling and accepting congratulations from everyone. She was remembered for that as much as she was for a heart-stopping mile race a little while later.

Knowing she had the most speed, Jamie stayed at the back of the pack as she let everyone else fight for the lead early in the race. Suddenly, with just a lap to go, she took a tumble. My heart sank. But Jamie didn't panic. She got up, caught everyone in a dramatic sprint and burst ahead in the final 100 meters to win the state title in 5:03. She was thrilled, and learned a valuable lesson about perseverance.

Like mother, like daughter.
If you can endure bad luck, good fortune is right around the corner.

Teresa won the 400 and the 200. Their mile-relay team placed third and Lewis and Clark High School placed third in the state.

~~~

The following week was a whirlwind. I signed the divorce papers, Jamie graduated from high school and I had to be out of the house by Sunday night. Plus, it was time to sort out Jamie's college fund, the money set aside by Kelly over the years. That, along with a partial track and cross-country scholarship from the University of Colorado, and she would be set for the time being.

I asked Kelly to transfer the money from Jamie's college fund into her Boulder account.

"Whaaaat, what do you mean?" asked Kelly when I called him.

"The child support money you agreed to put into an account for her college during the past 12 years."

"Whaaaat? What do you mean? Whaaat money?"

It was like reliving our divorce.

I went right back to Tim Harkins, who wrote up the necessary papers and filed them in the court system immediately, before Jamie graduated in just days, to be sure Kelly would be responsible for back child support since he hadn't lived up to his promise on the college fund. Jamie was already 18, and if we didn't hurry Kelly would be off the hook as soon as she received her high school diploma.

Kelly called Jamie the next day, the night before her graduation, and told her that he couldn't afford to pay that amount off in four years and that I was ruining his life. She came crying to me. "Mom, please don't ruin Dad's life. Don't make him pay the money. I don't need it."

I told her. "You do need it. Your dad needs to take responsibility for this." Suddenly, even after experiencing so much unpleasantness with him, I began to feel sorry for Kelly. I couldn't have lived with myself had I made his life miserable as he struggled to fulfill his agreement. I softened. "I'll work something out with him ... so his *life* won't be ruined." After a few meetings, Kelly agreed to pay $250 a month for eight years to pay off the minimum of what he would have owed in child support. It wasn't even close to the amount it could have been, but at least Jamie was happy again. However, I was responsible for her college. Steve didn't offer to help. He didn't have to, but that $250 a month wasn't going to go far.

I would figure something out.

Mom, me, Rachel, and Jamie (in front) ~ June 1999

Mom and Rachel drove to Spokane together for the graduation. Jamie was beautiful in her graduation gown. Her cheeks bright and rosy, her eyes sparkled with excitement and happiness, not only because she was graduating, but also from experiencing an amazing senior year. I told Jamie, "You're going to be something special. I feel it. With all that bottled-up energy and your kind heart, you're going to go a long way." I realized later, *this is what Grandma Helen had told me 33 years earlier, when I was just 8 years old.* Afterward, the four of us celebrated with dinner at the Thai Cafe. Val served us so much food he was shocked to find that we'd eaten it all, but still came back with his special dessert for us, black rice pudding with ice cream and coconut sauce. We were in heaven with Thai food galore. Val knew we needed a big meal to carry us through the long weekend.

We had no time to dillydally. The next day, I had to finish packing while Mom and the girls helped me prepare for the graduation party; Mom even did the yard work. Then after a successful party, I had to be out of the house in less than 24 hours.

Rachel and I packed everything in the bedroom, and then had a well-deserved snack in bed together after a long day.

"I'm really proud of Jamie," said Rachel. "She's so special. Nobody understands her like we do."

"I'm proud of her, too, but I'm just as proud of you."

"Why?"

"You worked hard and graduated with your class. That was a huge accomplishment and gratifying for all of us. You even worked on an Alaska salmon fishing boat that summer, not too many women could do that! Through all of your ups and downs in life, you've become a smart and extremely strong woman. Sometimes you're too headstrong, though."

I thought a moment ... then added, "You take too many chances, Rachel. I worry about you. Jamie worries just as much, but dismisses her worry knowing that you're, as she calls you, her Superwoman."

"She really calls me that?" she asked proudly.

"All the time."

Just after turning the light off, Rachel asked, "What will you do now that you can't race anymore?"

"I'm not sure yet. I still have a few talks lined up. Maybe I'll write a book."

"You can do *anything,* Mom!"

"I hope so. Maybe I should write my autobiography. I'll write everything. Things you and Jamie don't even know about me. It will be our story. Yours, Jamie's and mine."

"Mom ... that would be perfect! When will you start?"

I thought a moment, "I'll start right away."

"It will be the best book *ever,*" she exclaimed.

"We shall see. People won't pick the book up because of my fame as a marathoner."

"You're one of the best marathoners in the world!" Rachel proclaimed.

"I used to be."

Suddenly, we heard noises outside. Blustery winds were blowing the tree limbs, casting shadows on the bedroom walls to make the situation even spookier. "Follow me," I whispered to Rachel as I ran to the closet window that looked down to the sidewalk leading up to our front door. Rachel clumsily followed me, half asleep and stubbing her toes on every packed box between the bed and closet. "Ouch, Ouch, Ouch, OUCH!" was all I could hear in the dark room. Peering out the window, we spotted two boys looking around and then disappearing into the bushes to get closer to the house.

"They're up to no good," I said. "Let's teach them a lesson. Watch this."

In a loud and shaky male voice I yelled out the window, "Harriet, Harriet, where's our crazy son? He's escaped from the attic!"

The boys came out of the bushes and back onto our walkway, looking up toward the attic.

"Be Harriet," I told Rachel, but she was laughing so hard she couldn't speak. I carried on, in a shrieking female voice.

"Our son has a knife out there behind the rock! He's going to do something CRAAAAZY."

The boys stood frozen in their tracks. In a cackling demonized voice I screeched, "We should have left him in the asylum! He's INSAAAAANE, he's going to KIIIIILL somebody!"

Just as the wind picked up, blowing the shrubs and trees, and casting eerie shadows everywhere, the boys took off like rockets. "How did you know to do that?" asked Rachel, laughing so hard she could barely speak. "You scared the hell out of them."

I was laughing just as hard. Finally I said, "I don't know. It's a gift."

"It felt good to laugh like that didn't it?" said Rachel once we were back in bed.

"It did. Sometimes it releases the anxiety we build up inside."

"Like moving?"

"Exactly."

"Goodnight, Mom. I love you."

"Goodnight, Rachel. I love you, too."

Somehow, that silly act eased my fear of the unknown that lay before me. Mom, who was downstairs and slept through the whole thing, loved our adventure story when we told her the next day, wanting to hear it over and over again. She laughed every time. She needed laughter for some reason. We all did.

It was time to say goodbye to Spokane. I was leaving everything behind – my friends, my support crew and, except for the few belongings that I could fit into a U-Haul utility van, my life as I knew it. Rachel planned to drive the van while I drove my Mercedes full of whatever else we could hastily throw in before Steve arrived at 6 p.m. sharp to claim his property. I was leaving Bud, Wally, even Big Red. I had no room for them in my new home.

Several weeks earlier, Punky had decided to leave as well, even before I could figure out if I should take her with me or let her stay behind in the home she had become so comfortable in. I wondered if she knew that Jamie and I were leaving, and that it was time for her to do the same. After sitting with me for an extra long time, purring away and nuzzling, she walked out the back door, across the yard, and into the abandoned lot behind our house. There, dandelions were growing wild in the tall grass. She turned back, taking a good solid look at me, and then continued on without hesitation.

Punky left us that day forever. She was an old cat, living her 16 years of life in earnestness and devotion. It was time to find a place of her own, a place where she could have her alone time to die gracefully.

I will always miss Punky.

At 5:30, Mom and I were frantically unplugging and dismantling the computer. We started out being careful, but the clock was ticking toward 6:00. Finally I said, "Mom, just unplug the damn thing. Whatever you choose to do is fine." She was shocked. "Oh Crumb, Kim. Will we ruin it?"

"I'll find out when I get to Boulder," I said. Then we started laughing until we cried.

Mom and I shoved the computer into the back seat of the Mercedes and then Mom drove off, back to Port Townsend. Jamie and Rachel hugged for way too long as the clocked ticked to 5:57. Then I gave Jamie a hug and kiss, saying, "I'll see you in a few weeks," when she planned to join me after saying goodbye to her friends. We would start our new life in Boulder together.

Steve pulled up just as I followed Rachel out of the driveway.

My life in Spokane was over.

While driving toward Idaho, I finally had some tranquil time to think. I felt lost. I had no control over the things going on around me, nor did

I have my racing to shelter me from harsh reality. After 22 years of marriage, Mom and Dad were separating. Mel and Laurie's marriage ended in divorce – and Bradley and Debbie were in trouble again. I was sick with worry about them, but more so for their kids, who were living their lives with no direction. I was making some big changes myself, unsure where the road might lead.

I hoped I was doing the right thing.

Suddenly, I was abruptly awakened from my deep thoughts. It was Rachel on the walkie-talkie that we'd bought for the trip. My code name was Chaps and hers was Harriet. After some annoying static I heard, "Chaps, do you read me?"

"Chaps here, I read you," I replied in a tough voice.

"Mom, you're free!" Rachel yelled ecstatically, just as we were crossing the Idaho and Montana border, just over an hour out of Spokane. "Doesn't it feel good to be free?"

"It's great," I said, trying to sound enthusiastic. "Over and out and 10-4."

On our two-day drive we talked constantly on those walkie-talkies in our tough trucker voices. Sometimes a real trucker would comment on our conversations. "Slow down!" I told Harriet a couple of times, when she was rolling along at 100 miles an hour in the van. "Copper on your right!" she warned me just before we passed a speed trap.

On the second day, after turning off I-90 and heading south on I-25, just after crossing the Montana and Wyoming state line, I heard the static. "Chaps, Harriet here, is your car radio on?" Rachel told me to turn to an oldies station. "Listen to this song. It reminds me of us." I turned the volume up and listened to B.J. Thomas singing "Rock 'n Roll Lullaby."

Tears began to well in my eyes as I thought about our life together, and how similar it was to this special and meaningful song. *I was just sixteen and all alone when I had Rachel. We grew up together. When she was afraid and crying, I would sing her a rock 'n roll lullaby to let her know it would be alright. I hope she felt all my love come through when I sang it to her.*

I began to cry. I wondered what would have happened if I'd kept Rachel when she was a baby. There were times when I was so hard on myself for giving her up. After a long break I radioed back, "This song was meant for us. Are you crying like me?"

"I'm bawling my ass off," she said.

Then ... "Mom, we made it, didn't we? We made it through, after everything, didn't we?"

I smiled to myself. "We're survivors, Rach."

"Mom, you did the right thing." There was a long silence.

We hit a big swarm of miller moths just before we crossed the Wyoming border into Colorado. Long after the moth incident, I finally heard static and then Rachel's voice. "How about those moths?"

Jon and Mr. Jones helped us unload the van when we arrived in Boulder, and then Rachel stayed for a week to help me unpack, but mostly for comfort.

Jamie called from Spokane and gave us a few good laughs before Rachel left. "Mom, you didn't pack your clothes from the bedroom closet. I'm wearing a cool red vest with a top that matches perfectly."

"I know I packed everything in that closet," I said. "And I don't have a red vest. Jamie, I don't think those are my clothes you're wearing."

"Whose are they?" she asked. "Do you think they're Steve's new girlfriend's?"

I started laughing. "You had better change before Steve sees you wearing his girlfriend's clothes."

Rachel couldn't contain herself, letting out her usual belly laugh at Jamie's expense.

Jamie called again a few days later, frantic after having a big party at the house while Steve was away for the weekend. "Mom, I'm in huge trouble. I had too much to drink and not thinking we drank Steve's Big Bear Beer!" It was Steve's "prize" trophy from the Le Grizz 50-mile race, a gigantic bottle of beer with a special label made up just for the award winners. Steve was so proud of it and his accomplishment that he placed it in the china cabinet for all to see. "This was his favorite award EVER!" she cried.

"Jamie, do you have the bottle?" I asked calmly.

"Yes," she answered, barely able to breathe.

"Is it intact?"

She was calming down. "Yes."

"Is there any leftover beer from the party?"

She perked up a little more. "Yes, some Bud Light."

"OK, this is what you do. Pour the Bud Light into the Big Bear Beer. It will take several bottles. Then, search through the garbage for its original bottle cap."

She came back to the telephone. "OK, I have it."

"Now get some pliers and crimp the bottle cap tightly around the Big Bear Beer. Be careful not to break it."

Jamie hung up the phone and went to work. She soon called back as pleased as a big pie. "I did it, and it looks pretty good."

"Now put it in the china cabinet and hope for the best."

Poor Steve. I wonder if he ever noticed. I assume the Bud Light in the Big Bear Beer bottle must have evaporated eventually. There's no way Jamie could have totally sealed it with those pliers.

Later that year, Steve married, and soon after had a child. I was pleased for him and truly happy knowing he was living the wonderful life he deserved.

—

Over the winter months, I began writing my autobiography. The words started pouring out. My mind was sharp and my memory clear, as if it were meant to be. As I wrote, I immediately began to realize that my major role in life was to create happiness in my family, to please them and make them laugh by doing special tricks and funny acts, like making my sad father laugh while somersaulting straight into the lake full of frogs, cleaning the house until it sparkled for Mom, jumping off the crane on the high dock to impress them all, and then later, through my running. Even though I enjoyed the special attention that I never received as a child and the escape it gave me, for the most part, I ran for my family, to give them a sense of pride and share in my thrill along with the rewards.

I was still carrying out my role in life through writing my story. I wanted to show Mom and Dad that they did the best job they knew how as very young and tormented parents, a better job as time went on, and that they are wonderful parents now. I also wanted to show my siblings that there *is* a reason – though *not* an excuse – for their disruptive and dysfunctional behavior, as I tell our story through my perspective. I believed my words would enlighten them, help them come to terms with their present lives as they find peace and in all hopes ... heal.

I've found the meaning of what I am.

Even though my reason for writing was for Rachel and Jamie, it shifted to crystallizing the differences between my family and me. Why did I come out OK? Why did Jamie and Rachel turn out to be prosperous, caring and strong women? How could I have been such a focused and consistent marathoner in the midst of so much disorganization and trauma throughout my career, with 26 career marathons averaging under 2:33?

My running career was as steady as a ship sailing on a calm sea, though nobody knew about the rough current beneath. I learned to deal with turbulence while remaining calm and staying on a steady course from the time Old Mole became lopsided and died with the nails in his side.

I learned all of this through life experiences, good or bad, and these valuable lessons helped me overcome, and become who I am.

Julius Caesar summed it up perfectly: "Experience is the teacher of all things."

When I wasn't busy writing, I spent my time with Jon Sinclair. What drew me to Jon, besides his captivating charm, was his hair. It had the same texture and smell of my blanket that burned in the fire. Oddly, from that moment on, I felt comforted and safe with him.

Jon was attentive and caring. He respected me as well as my opinions. Better yet, he thought I was the best thing since sliced bread. Wiley thought I was even more special than Jon did, and instantly became my dog. He followed me everywhere and wouldn't leave my side, which didn't help my allergies – he had more hair falling off of him than any animal I had ever seen, the canine version of Charlie Brown's friend Pigpen in "Peanuts." Hair came flying off even when he sneezed.

Jon and Kent Oglesby, his business partner, invited me to join them as a coach at Anaerobic Management. He and Kent started what may have been the first online coaching business for runners. They each had about 30 clients from all parts of the country and a few outside the States, designing personal training plans for each individual via email for a monthly fee. They had several athletes in Fort Collins whom they met on the track to guide through workouts, and others who were fast enough to train with them.

It was the perfect job for two retired professional athletes, doing what we loved to do most – run and work with athletes. With Jon's 30 years of running and an extraordinarily successful 15-year career, and my successful 15-year career filled with many failures from which to learn, we had an abundance of wisdom and experience to share. I built up to 25 clients online and enjoyed working part-time while living the retirement lifestyle.

Kent and Jon had been friends for years. They went out to dinner and movies and even shopped together. They were often sighted walking through the Old Town of Fort Collins after dinner or beers and were considered the bachelors about town. They were adorable: two small runners, Jon walking and talking tough, Kent more relaxed and seeing the lighter side of things. They balanced each other perfectly.

Kent fell in love and married Dawn about the same time Jon and I got together. Dawn looked so much like me that people thought we must be sisters, even twins. Dawn behaved more like me than my cousins in Sweden did, with the same taste in style, ordering the same foods and even using "the hands." We appreciated one another.

I was in Fort Collins a lot and establishing new friendships. Once a week I trained with Jane Welzel, who was getting ready for the 2000 Olympic Trials. Even though I'd qualified, I was sure I wouldn't run the Trials after my Chicago fiasco and subsequent retirement. Whenever I tried to run fast enough to train properly, my foot took a beating.

Jane found three unsuspecting men close to our age to be our training partners: her boyfriend, Doug Mason, and two others, Bob Brustad and Bruce Pulford. We planned our first run together for New Year's Day 2000.

After celebrating New Year's Eve with Jon for most of the night, I was so hungry when we went out to breakfast that I ordered Deep Fried Cornflake French Toast, six scrambled eggs and six pieces of bacon before heading to meet my new friends for what Jane had called a rolling 13-mile run. Off we went, straight up a hill that wouldn't end. Finally, I complained to Bob, a funny and kind man who could pass as my brother, "What the hell? When is this hill going to end?"

"Sister," he answered, "Where I come from, we call this a 'candy ass' hill."

"OK, Candy Ass," I said, "lead the way." But boy, was I hurting with all of that food in my stomach.

During the next run, Jane was named "Tight Ass" when she complained, "My ass is tight." I was named "Hairy Ass" after sitting on Jon and Wiley's couch earlier that morning in my black tights.

The next week we were back on the Horsetooth Hills for another tough workout on a cold January morning when we looked over at Doug. In his black thermal tights and top, he was sweating profusely as he crested a big hill. He became "Sweaty Ass." It took several more runs until I said, with my hands in the air, "What ass name are we going to come up with for Bruce? He has no ass." That was it. We all said in unison, "No Ass." Later that year, Tom McKernan, "Smart Ass" and John Harris, "Chili Ass," joined our group.

Though it seemed silly, the joking was our way of making the runs less daunting, creating a strong bond among us, just as I had done with my Spokane training partners. Perhaps I learned it from the Cartwright boys, who developed a strong sense of group loyalty and camaraderie through their jesting and horsing around.

It's odd, my first word to Jane was when I called her "ass" at the 1988 Olympic Trials, and 12 years later ... *here we are in an "Ass Group" together.*

Besides the Asses, I had some wonderful girlfriends in Fort Collins. Jane, Dawn and I – all Taurus women – celebrated our birthdays together in the month of May. Jane and Dawn brought in three more Taurus women, who were also in their 40's. Judy, Linda and Sue were attractive, intelligent and energetic women, making for an enlightening and uplifting time together. They were the girlfriends my mother told me I needed in life. "Men come and go, Kimmie, but your girlfriends will always be there for you, no matter what." We comforted one another when going through a rough patch, we were there for each other when tragedy struck, and we were all full of advice for each other. I spent my free time with them, meeting for coffee, having wine and dinner parties, and even going on road-racing trips together.

Developing those new friendships after a lonely year in Boulder, I was feeling better about leaving my good friends and family in Washington State.

With Jane Welzel during an Ass and Taurus party

One summer day while Rachel and Cooper were visiting us in Boulder, Jon wanted to share his love of rock climbing.

His good friend and climbing partner Matthew, whom everyone called Lucky, joined us near the Flatirons to help Jon with the daunting task of teaching us. Rachel was brave and climbed right up and came down without a problem. While Cooper and Jamie were taking their turn, Rachel and I were sitting on a soft grassy patch, leaning against a big boulder and watching, when she asked, "How's the book coming along?"

"Great, I'm about to divorce Steve, although there's a big gap to fill. I need to divorce Kelly first."

She let out a big laugh, "I can't wait to read it."

"You'll love it, Rachel. You and Jamie are stars." I smiled. "Seriously, I have learned so much while writing it."

"Like what?"

"There's always a calm before a storm. In our family it's usually a disastrous storm. I've managed to weather the storms better than the others over the years, but knowing that, I'm always wary about being too happy and content."

Then she became totally engrossed. "How did you do that?"

"Mom told me long ago that we lived a schizophrenic life because that's what people do when you live with a lunatic. After Dad died, everyone carried on that crazy lifestyle, causing some kind of turmoil when things became too placid, yet they didn't know how to handle the real disasters, becoming even more manic. Through all of this, I learned of ways to deal with it, and later escape it."

"Tell me," she begged.

"Later," I told her. "I'd rather have you read my story and find out for yourself. You're going to understand a lot more about our lives, and the many questions you may have will be answered. You know, this is one of the reasons I'm writing this."

"When will you be finished?"

"Soon."

We looked up to see Cooper attempt his climb. He was harnessed, tied in to the rope, while Jon was instructing and Lucky belayed, using the rope to protect Cooper from a fall. Cooper was moving cautiously. "This could take a while," I told Rachel.

She scooched close to me, hugging her knees up to her chest ... then leaned in even closer. With eyes as wide as could be, she asked eagerly, "Tell me more, how did you survive?" I had never felt so much love for Rachel as I did at that very moment. I grinned, "This reminds me of the time I instructed you on how to put a condom onto a curling iron." She blurted out a big laugh. "I forgot about that!"

"You definitely possess the main ingredient for survival," I told her. "What?"

"Laughter." I went on to tell her, "I survived because I surrounded myself with good people, learned to endure bad luck, and took advantage of good luck when it was on my side. I had an uncanny sense of danger lurking and could act on it in an instant. Most importantly, I've always hoped for the best and cherished everything good in my life. Don't take *anything* you care about for granted, Rachel ... it could slip away from you in an instant."

"Kimmie, it's your turn," Jon called out. After watching Jamie climb up the rock wall and then struggle on her way down, I was hesitant.

I put on the harness, tied in to the rope, and climbed up just fine but wouldn't come down. All I could see was one small metal device wedged into a crack in the rock as an anchor above me. "This is supposed to support me?" I called down.

"Just back up and drop off the overhang, and we'll lower you down," said Lucky.

"I don't think so, Lucky."

"Come on, Kimmie," Jon hollered. "The chances of that anchor coming loose are as slim as a bolt of lightning striking you."

"That's what you said about the golf ball that hit me while running near the ninth hole."

I heard laughter. "Come on, Mom," the girls encouraged.

"I don't think so."

Jon gallantly climbed up the rock wall and brought me down to safety.

Not long after that, Jon was using one of his anchor devices during a climb and it broke in two pieces.

"Maybe you shouldn't go out in a lightning storm after all," he said.

Rachel and Jamie adored Jon. Rachel stared at him for a long while one day shortly after our climbing adventure and then whispered to me, "I can see why you like him." Jamie said, "He's the perfect guy for you, Mom, and he'll be a great stepfather for me someday." Jon treated the girls like daughters, and Jamie liked to tease him. When he was doing something important or with a group of friends, she would call out, "Daddy, Daddy, I've missed you, Daddy." Of course, serious Jon said, "Yeah, yeah" in his tough voice, though I would notice him holding back a smile.

Later that summer, after several telephone calls, Laurie persuaded me to come to her wedding in Bremerton, where she and her fiancé Jeff were living. She promised to be on her best behavior, and she had been the good Laurie for a while.

"I really want you here, Kimmie. Would you come over the night before my wedding and stay with Jeff and me, so we can talk, just like old times? I miss you so much."

I had my reservations, but I couldn't say no. Jon and I went to Seattle to pick up Rachel. "Are you sure you want to come with us?" we both asked Jon several times before catching the ferry to Bremerton. I gave him one last warning, "You don't have to come with us. This may be stressful." Cooper even invited Jon to stay in Seattle with him.

"No, I'll go with the girls," Jon said. "Come on, how bad can it be?"

Jeff was waiting for us at the very end of the driveway when we arrived, seeming far too eager. He was a big man, with long, dark hair down to his shoulders and dark eyes. He looked like he could be a rugged biker. He welcomed us and showed us where to park, being incredibly nice yet suspiciously animated and far too anxious. "Let's see what happens now," said Rachel as we got out of the car and then, here came Laurie. She looked great and was dressed perfectly, looking thin yet healthy. She hugged Rachel while Jon and I grabbed our travel bags out of the trunk of the car, and then Laurie hugged me, way too tight, saying, "I've missed you so much. I love you, Kimmie."

Then she pushed me away, saying, "I hate you. I have always hated you."

Jeff stepped in, telling Laurie that she promised to behave. She grabbed me again for another hug. *Hmmm, I'm not feeling very good about this.*

We went into their nice clean condo, not a crumb on the floor. But it was in a bad and violent neighborhood, with drug dealers next door and prostitutes below. Laurie asked Jon, "So, are you gay?" Jon, calm and showing no sign of alarm, responded, "No, Laurie, I'm not."

"Oh. Well, did you know that watching your interview after running Bloomsday one year is what inspired Kimmie to run? Now you're together. It's amazing! Jon Sinclair is actually dating my little sister! She's not what she seems, so be careful." Jon told her, "I think I know her well enough" and then Jeff nervously changed the subject. Rachel looked at me with big eyes. She didn't seem to be feeling very good about *this* either.

We all talked awhile and after Laurie made a few more uncalled for comments she suggested, "Let's walk down the street to the bar and celebrate our wedding tomorrow."

Jeff had a young daughter sound asleep on the living room floor. "We can't leave her here all alone," said Jon.

"It's OK, we do it all the time," said Laurie. She was only 7 years old.

"Rachel and Kimmie will go with you guys and I'll babysit," Jon volunteered.

So the four of us walked down to a rough bar. "Don't drink much," I told Rachel, "only a light beer. We need to be up on our toes here." Laurie was already picking fights with the biker women while sitting on their boyfriends' laps.

"We're in huge trouble, Mom," said Rachel. Then she ordered a double whiskey on the rocks. I panicked and said, "me, too." And I don't even drink hard liquor.

By the time we'd been there an hour, every single person in that bar was ready to kill us. I had never seen Laurie so evil. She was making horrible comments to everyone, even calling the big gnarly women "fat asses" among other things. We were finally asked to leave.

Five guys, some with knives and one with a gun, followed us out of the bar. I had an asthma attack right there. Rachel frantically searched my purse for my inhaler while Laurie rubbed my back to calm me down. Then Jeff scurried us across the street to a safer place, the bowling alley. While we waited for the undesirables to disappear, Jeff ordered a round of beers – not what I wanted or what Laurie needed.

"So Rachel, who's your mother? Is it her," she asked, pointing across the table, "or is it me?"

I whispered to Rachel, "Do us all a favor and say it's her."

But Rachel never backed down from anyone. "You're not my mom. She is," she said, pointing to me.

Uh oh. Now we're in for it.

Laurie began screaming in her demonized voice. "I took care of you when she didn't even want you. She never wanted you. Nobody wanted you, Rachel! You were unwanted from the beginning and we were stuck with you because your mom was a tramp in high school."

Rachel started crying. Rachel never cried. I didn't care what Laurie said about me, but I wouldn't stand for that. "Let's go," I told Rachel.

"You can't walk home alone," Jeff insisted, even though the condo was just across a busy four-lane street and up a dirt road.

Laurie went crazy, accusing Jeff of caring more about us than about her. She ran out. All five undesirables were still out there waiting for us. Jeff took my hand and Rachel's as we walked toward the busy street.

Suddenly ... Laurie jumped out from behind a parked car. "I'll show you!" she yelled, running into the busy street and trying to get into cars stopped at the red light. She almost made it into one before the person pushed her out and sped away. As the light turned green, Laurie was almost hit by passing cars as she fell to the side of the road in a heap. By then Rachel and I were both in tears. Seeing Laurie that way was heart wrenching.

Jeff rushed to Laurie and pulled her to the dirt road. I grabbed Rachel's hand and headed for the condo. The next thing we knew, someone was shining a large spotlight on us. "It's the coppers!" said Rachel.

"Get back here!" they ordered, with their guns on us. It was just like the TV show, "Cops." We walked back and they questioned us. "This crazy woman is my sister and she celebrated way too much before her wedding tomorrow," I told them. One of the coppers warned, "Go ahead but be careful, this is a rough neighborhood." Rachel and I rushed back to the condo, in tears. We told Jon the story as we grabbed our bags to get the hell out of there.

But not soon enough.

Laurie showed up screaming and yelling, accusing me of being after Jeff and pushing me down the stairs. On our way out I told Jeff, "You'd better think twice about marrying this person who's supposed to be my sister. Think about your 7-year-old daughter, who needs you."

Suddenly, Laurie popped up from behind the couch, her dark eyes boring right into me, like Pa Seelye's when he tried to entice me to sit on his lap, like Dad's eyes when he took his gun out, and even like Uncle/Grandpa Harold's when he would look right through me into his troubled past. I feared, just as I had years ago with the demons, that she was seeking her victim.

We quickly grabbed our bags, ran for the car and escaped back to Seattle.

Laurie and Jeff canceled the next day's wedding. Mom called me and asked, "What did you do? Laurie said Jeff is in love with you and you're to blame."

"Right," I said sarcastically. Jon and Rachel, hovering over the phone, laughed and then Mom had to laugh, too. "It didn't sound right," she admitted.

Cooper was glad he stayed in Seattle.

Laurie and Jeff ran off soon after to get married on their own.

Before we flew back to Colorado, I took Jon to meet my parents. It was sad going back to the Port Townsend area. Uncle/Grandpa Harold had died after enduring 80 years of pain and sadness, and was finally able to join Grandma Helen in a better place. Though we missed him, I knew he was at peace and happy there. Things would never be the same, especially since Mom and Dad were in the process of divorce. Dad and I were both worried that Mom wouldn't be able to take care of herself.

Dad really liked Jon, which was huge considering he didn't usually accept people immediately. Jon is his own man with strong opinions, and is a respectful person who doesn't put on airs. Dad admired that and found Jon interesting, intelligent and forthright. "What you see is what you get with Jon," Dad told me. "He's a good man, Kimmie."

Chapter 21

The Old Town of Fort Collins is a lot like Spokane. It has a river running through it, a charming historic downtown with many nice restaurants and coffee shops, even a train track that goes right through the middle of the city. Jon's house was only half of a mile up Mountain Avenue, the center of the running community.

Mountain Avenue is lined with many restored homes and majestic trees, some over 100 years old. It has a vintage trolley car running up the grass median from downtown, past Jon's house and then up another mile to the City Park, a golf course and a cemetery. The historic trolley has a smoothed grass path between its tracks, leading to some of the best running routes in town. The cemetery is where many runners do their speed workouts, on a shady, hard-packed dirt road a mile around the perimeter where Jon has every quarter mile marked off.

All of those wonderful places reminded me of Spokane, and sometimes I forgot I was in Fort Collins, thinking I was back in Spokane running in one of my favorite parks. It felt like home.

I decided to move to Fort Collins, and began looking for a house to buy in Old Town. Jon had two parrots and Wiley. My asthma could handle Wiley, but was highly sensitive to Brutus and Jake. Plus, I didn't like Brutus, a neurotic ass of a bird who did nothing but screech, causing Jake to chime in. Jake was wicked, spoiled and could act just as obnoxious as Brutus, even chasing poor Wiley around in circles through the house biting at his tail. He even bit my toes when I walked past him barefoot. But Jake had quite a personality and for some reason I liked him. When Brutus died suddenly, Kent and Dawn bravely offered to take Jake so that Jon and Wiley could move into a bigger house with me.

We found a house one block down and across the street from where Jon had lived for 20 years. Jon took a lot of teasing about his big move, from the 700 block of Mountain Avenue to the 800 block. Everyone loved teasing Jon, who was much more serious than his jokester friends. I called him "Mr. Peabody," after the genius dog from Rocky and Bullwinkle who was always instructing Sherman. Jon would educate anyone on any subject when asked a simple question, his voice growing louder and louder as he described things in detail. "Why don't you get your charts and pointer stick out, and show us how it's done," I would tease.

We moved into a historical house built in 1901, a smaller version of my home in Spokane with the original woodwork, stairway and all. It even had a small, basic apartment in the basement for the girls to stay in when they visited us. I felt like I was home again. Wiley had no trouble leaving 700 Mountain Ave behind. During his walks he trotted quickly by his old house without giving it a glance.

Because of my asthma, Wiley wasn't allowed upstairs but he had the main floor as his own, with a bed in Jon's office, a bed in the dining room and a dog couch in the living room. A dog in the kitchen isn't sanitary so I didn't encourage him with a bed in there, but that's where he spent most of his time anyway. He could even "nose" open the screen door to the backyard, where he walked his perimeter each and every time he went out. Wiley was set.

On our front porch with Jamie, Jon and Wiley dressed for Christmas

We had a good life in Fort Collins. Jon and Wiley were early risers and downstairs waiting to greet me every morning. As I walked down the stairs, there was Wiley at the bottom of the steps and Jon in a big over-stuffed chair sipping his coffee. They would look up at me as if I was their queen. I felt special and beautiful as I was sauntering down the stairs in my flannel pajamas with my hair a mess. They truly adored me and I treasured them.

Poor Wiley had to celebrate all of the holidays with us. He posed for our Christmas photos, which he hated. There was company and noise, which he hated. But Easter was another story. I hid treats all over the house for the "Wiley Easter Snack Hunt," making a trail for him by start-ing in the dining room and dragging each snack to the next hiding place to create a scented trail. Once we opened the door, he would come charg-ing in, sniff out the first snack and gobble it down, then follow the trail until he began to feel full, skipping over the Scooby snacks in favor of the Snausages.

At that point he was stuffed, passing up all the rest to find his favorite, the Beggin' Strips, and gulping them down before falling into his nearest bed to take a rest. Later, once he had some time to regroup, he would go back for the less-popular snacks.

I took pleasure in sitting on the front porch swing, drinking my morn-ing coffee, with Wiley by my side, waving to our friends as they ran along the trolley tracks. I enjoyed waiting there for Jon and his boy friends to finish up their group run at our house. I could hear them coming for blocks, as Jon would get louder and louder and his training buddies fol-lowed suit. It must have been a testosterone thing. Pretty soon they were all talking so loud it sounded like a noisy parade coming down the street. Wiley, who hated any noise and especially raised voices, rushed back into the house. I began to realize how adorable both Jon and Wiley were with their unique personalities.

Jon and I were paid to travel to races for speaking engagements and appearances, and even to run in a few. Organizers would get a two-for-one deal with us. I ran some local races with friends, usually with Tanya Poel, whom Jon was coaching toward qualifying for the 2004 Olympic Trials. Tanya was Lucky's wife. They lived in Boulder and were both air-line pilots. Lucky and Jon were off rock climbing a lot, leaving Tanya and me to train and enjoy our time together, which Jamie joined in on. We had so many laughs together, sometimes over the stupidest things.

Tanya became like a sister to me and Lucky became my good friend, "Luck." Jamie started calling them her "Boulder mom and dad."

Jamie was running for the University of Colorado cross-country and track teams. She wasn't putting a lot of energy into her running but was excelling in her classes, becoming a 4.0 student. Kelly had become a responsible and supportive father as he mellowed with age, and Jamie was much happier as they began to develop a loving father-daughter relationship. I knew it was in him.

Jamie had adjusted to her new life in Colorado, as I did.

A year had passed and in October 2002, Rachel called. She and Cooper had moved into their new condo in the Queen Anne district in Seattle and she couldn't wait to have us over for a visit to see it and meet their new puppy, Samson. Jamie and I dropped everything, headed for Seattle, and stayed for a week. The condo was beautiful, on three levels with a view of the Space Needle from the deck.

Surprisingly, the place was immaculate. "Mom, now I know why you like to have everything perfectly clean and in its place. It makes me feel good about myself," she told me. Then we met Samson, a tiny Jack Russell who streaked up and down the stairs like lightning, and would occasionally sneak out of the condo to trot across the street to Rachel and Cooper's morning coffee shop. There, after somebody opened the door for him, he waited for a treat.

Rachel was so proud of her new life.

She and Cooper took us out to Salty's in West Seattle, where Cooper was manager and part owner. They wined and dined us until the restaurant closed. Then, Jamie began eating all the cherries from the drinks. Cooper went to the bar and brought her more ... and more ... and more. Rachel crinkled up her nose and shook her head. "Why does she do that?" she tried to whisper discreetly.

"We both know Jamie's quirky behavior too well. She's always trying to impress her big sister. Why does this surprise you?" I asked.

"She ate 60 cherries, Mom!" Rachel laughed.

We glanced at Jamie across the table, with a big grin on her face and 60 cherry stems lined up neatly in front of her.

After dinner, Rachel drove us home like a crazy woman, zipping in and out of traffic, through yellow lights and speeding through the streets as if she owned the place. As we sped across a bridge, we swerved around two cars and came inches from the guardrail. In the back seat, Jamie said, "I don't care if we crash. At least we'll all die together." That's how I knew she felt the same way I did. *We're going to die.* "Rachel, slow down," I pleaded, as my foot kept hitting my imaginary brake. "Oh, Mom, I know exactly what I'm doing," she said with her Miss Piggy attitude.

Toward the end of our visit, Cooper showed Jamie and me an engagement ring. He planned to surprise Rachel on November 4th. We promised not to say a word.

"Guess what?" Rachel said that night, when he left the room. "Cooper bought me an expensive engagement ring. I found the receipt in his wallet, and then I found the ring. I wonder when he plans to propose. Can't hardly wait!"

Poor Cooper, he should have known. You can't surprise Rachel with anything.

That night, we talked until 5 a.m. about everything in our lives – the old days, the future and what we wanted after we pass away. Rachel, Jamie and I all agreed to be together, wanting to be cremated and have our ashes scattered off the Fort Worden beach in Port Townsend to join Charlie and Stanley, and the rest of my family when the time comes.

A day later, Rachel drove us to the airport at 6 a.m. Thank goodness there wasn't much traffic to zip through. We hugged goodbye for an extra long time. I smelled her soft baby hair and I felt so much love for her. Then she hugged Jamie for just as long.

"I don't want you to leave," she said. "We have so much fun together. I love you and Jamie so much."

"I love you too, Rachel"

"Me, too," said Jamie.

On our flight home, Jamie asked, "Do you think Rachel will be OK? I worry about her, Mom. She drives like a maniac and does daring things. I just keep reminding myself that she's my Superwoman and nothing will *ever* happen to her."

"She'll be fine, she knows how to survive in this world," I reassured her.

However, I was worried myself.

Then I started to think about how lucky I was, and began to appreciate everything I had gained throughout my lifetime ... *I have a deep love for my girls, deeper than I could ever have dreamed after my dad and brothers died. I'm completely and unconditionally in love with Jon, removing the "wall" that's always been there with the men in my life. I'm surrounded by good, strong, and caring people I can trust. I feel safe. I have a lovely home, plenty of food, a fine life. I know that I'm being rewarded for standing strong and going forward, for making more good choices than bad.*

I turned to Jamie in the seat next to me and said aloud, "You know, I could die tomorrow, knowing I have lived my life to the fullest. I have made a difference in this world, Jamie. I paid a price and now God is rewarding me tenfold. Just like Job."

She smiled.

Jamie and Rachel ~ October 2002

Friday, November 1, 2002, two weeks after our visit with Rachel, Jamie came over for the weekend during our first big snowstorm of the year. The three of us went cross-country skiing in City Park. Jon skied, Jamie did a little skiing and I tried to ski without falling on every downhill. I have taken two hours of lessons just on learning how to stop, and still can't master it. I ended up chipping a front tooth when I fell on my ski pole. *Damn, now I have to wait until Monday to see the dentist.* It made finishing up the leftover Halloween candy from the night before a bit challenging, but I managed. I looked like a hick with my broken tooth, but Jon said it was sexy and that I looked like the singer "Jewel."

The next morning, November 2, 2002, we were snowed in by almost two feet of snow and decided it would be best to stay in our pajamas all day and make snacks galore – eggs and ham in the morning, then on to popcorn, nachos and sandwiches, even a cake as the day went on. We were watching the Hannibal Lecter movie trilogy, starting with "Red Dragon," moving on to "The Silence of the Lambs," and finishing with "Hannibal." Jon was in his office, ear distance away, typing on the computer and making comments when he felt we needed to know something important, but came out to watch a few of the better scenes with us.

The snowy day was turning into night, and there we were, nice and cozy, still in our pajamas and snacking away. Right in the middle of "Hannibal," the telephone rang. I ran to the kitchen. "It's Mom," I called to Jamie and Jon.

"Hi Mom! You wouldn't believe the perfect day we're having …

She interrupts. "Kimmie, something just horrible has happened. It's Rachel."

Her voice said it all.

There was a big rock in my stomach. Hornets were stinging my body. I sank to the floor. Jon rushed in, then Jamie. "What happened?" Jon picked up the phone.

Everything moved in slow motion after Mom's call. Jamie, Jon and I sat together on the couch in the darkened living room, stunned, with "Hannibal" on mute but still flashing on the TV screen. Wiley laid his head on my lap, sensing our distress. "She'll be OK, she's on life support," said Jamie, through tears. I wanted to hug Jamie. *I can't. If I hug her, it will be admitting that Rachel is dying.*

"She'll be just fine, she's tough," I reassured Jamie as I searched deep from within for hope.

"Kimmie, it's not good. They don't think she's going to make it," Jon said softly.

Time went by, a time I couldn't measure. Rachel's grandfather, Claude, called from the Seattle hospital to tell us they were going to turn off the life support machines. "No! Don't! I need to say goodbye to my baby, please wait," I begged.

"No. No. No," cried Jamie as she ran through the room, her palms raised toward heaven.

"I'm sorry, Kimmie, so sorry."

Jamie and I began to weep, and our weeping turned into wailing. To wail is different than to cry. It's a horrible sound, an eerie and shrill sound. A sound nobody should ever have to make, a sound I choose never to make again.

I hugged Jamie. I held her tight. I didn't ever want to let her go.

Rachel made a big mistake. She had taken one too many chances, choosing to stay out with an old friend and use cocaine instead of going home with Cooper when he left the bar to walk Samson. All we know is she was slipped a speedball, heroin mixed with cocaine. The two drugs amplify each other, the cocaine a powerful stimulant that causes a rapid heart rate and the heroin a depressant that slows it down. The two together can make the heart lose its rhythm, increasing the risk of heart failure. Rachel had used cocaine before, but she probably didn't know about the heroin – or that she was pregnant. Her body rejected the drugs and her organs slowly shut down.

There was no hope for her baby ... or mine.

Rachel died that night.

I am in hell, and now Jamie is here with me.

By the next day, we were in Seattle. Lucky and Tanya were there before we could even think of what to do next. When they walked into the hotel, relief rushed over us. We were still numb. Jon was our rock, but he became despondent. Lucky, Tanya and Cooper's friends helped us through the horrific details of dealing with a death, accompanying us to talk with the funeral home to make plans that I could never make. Jamie, Jon and I were in shock. We listened, but we couldn't hear.

Jon, Lucky and Tanya made sure Jamie and I went outside for some fresh air and a run. We were reluctant but went a few times. I think it helped. Tanya insisted that Jon take me to a dentist to fix my broken tooth, instead of following Lucky's suggestion that we fix it ourselves with one of those tooth-bonding kits from the drug store.

All five of us traveled to Port Townsend and stayed in a hotel there before going back to Seattle for the funeral the following weekend.

We shared a luxurious room at The Tide's Inn with two gigantic beds, a rollaway for Jamie, and a view of the ferry making its rounds. The inn was made famous from a suicide scene in the movie "The Officer and the Gentleman." Tanya managed to bring a smile to my face when she exclaimed, "This room is like being in Candyland," as she pointed out the designs on the candy colored, pastel-green-and-pink furniture. Even the lamps looked like icing on a wedding cake.

It was late once we settled in for the night. Jon, Jamie and Tanya were sleeping, and Lucky was reading. *Lucky knows how I feel.* Before he married Tanya, he had a daughter who would have been Jamie's age. Melissa was only 12 years old when she was thrown from her horse while out riding with her father. She died in Lucky's arms.

I lay there pretending to be asleep. It was soothing to have the light on and listen to Lucky turn the pages as he read.

Then Lucky turned off the cake-frosting lamp.

My mind started racing as I lay there in the dark. *How can I live without Rachel? How's Jamie going to handle this?* I glanced out the window and noticed the lights of a boat sailing into the harbor. *I wonder what they're up to, being out on the water so late.* Suddenly, I realized that Rachel died the night before the New York City Marathon. I began to feel guilty ... *this must have taken the wind right out of the sailboat of our friends and the athletes we coach who ran the marathon. This was their moment to shine. Now, their moment is tarnished.*

There was a sense of ease and comfort as I listened to the low rumble of the ferry pulling in to dock for the night, the heavy breathing of my friends sleeping in the bed next to me, of Jamie in the rollaway at the foot of our beds, and of Jon beside me. My mind and body went heavy. I fell into sleep.

Rachel's funeral was held in West Seattle. Mom was sitting with her new boyfriend, Jeff, in the front row and Dad was with his girlfriend, Cindy, across from them. I had seen that look on their faces before. It made my heart sink. Mel and the three boys were in the back row, but

Laurie wasn't there. I'd heard she was in jail. I saw Steve and some of the Joneses.

Brad and his family were there. It was the first time I had seen Rachel's father since high school.

"I am so sorry, Kimmie, more than you'll ever know," he said through tears as he gave me a hug. "I'm sorry I didn't help you when Rachel was just a baby. You were all alone." He began to break down. "You're the lucky one. You've always had her in your life. I missed out on a lot, but I was blessed with nine years of having Rachel in mine." Rachel was right. He had turned into a good man after I knew him as an immature boy so many years ago.

The church was packed, and some people had to stand. It was all I could take, hearing the funny and touching stories everyone had to tell, for their own sake as much as ours, and watching the slide show of Rachel's life set to her favorite songs. "Easy" by the Commodores was her all-time favorite, and was also her special song with Cooper. As it played, I remembered the many times I sang it to her when she was just a baby, over and over. *I know that's why she loved it so much.* I broke down quietly, and stayed broken.

We went home to find that the Taurus women, the Asses and our many other friends in Fort Collins had left us cake, flowers and cards while we were away. I'm grateful that most of them had the chance to meet Rachel and see for themselves how special she was. Jane liked her immediately. She loved Rachel's spunk.

I stayed home. I cried. I didn't want to see anybody or go anywhere ever again. I couldn't listen to music. Everything I heard reminded me of Rachel and I broke down even more. Every morning I hoped to wake up and find out it was all a terrible dream, but when I woke up my stomach still had that rock in it and the hornets were stinging me.

I'm mad at Rachel, really mad. Why did she make that stupid mistake? What was she thinking? She was being carefree one too many times. Then I felt guilty for being mad at her, and I felt guilty for everything I didn't do for her when she was alive. *Could I have done more? I should have. Was I a good enough mother? I wasn't. I hate myself.*

Months go by. Jon, the Taurus women and the Asses wanted me to go on a weekend trip. That made me mad. *Why can't they just leave me alone? They keep badgering me to do things when all I want is to stay home. Why would I want to go on a trip? It's as if I'm supposed to have fun.* I finally agreed. We drove four hours way up in the mountains, to tiny Columbine, where there's tons of snow with several cabins and one small store, nothing else. The 14 of us rented a large cabin, planning to snowshoe, cross-country ski, and spend time together, talking and playing games while the snow falls outside our windows.

We all took turns cooking big meals for each other. I laughed at the funny things they said, especially Candy Ass's comments and jokes. *I'm not really laughing.* I played our silly games, and seemed to be enjoying myself. *I'm not.* I showed them how to Montana Chug Upside Down and they were intrigued, especially Sweaty Ass and Smart Ass, the engineers in the group. Sweaty even asked me to do it again, so he could get low to the floor and watch each step in order. I felt guilty for being there, *but it's kind of nice to be with my friends. It's comforting, but then I feel guilty for feeling comforted.*

The winter comes and goes. "Maybe you should work on your book a while. It might help you feel better," Jon suggested as he handed me my laptop. Reluctantly, I opened it up, only to find that my story had vanished. My computer had crashed and there was no way of retrieving it. The look on Jon's face was heartbreaking.

March 30, 2003. Jon, Jamie and I went to Port Townsend to say goodbye to Rachel on her birthday. Cooper was there to meet us, and so was Samson, scurrying all over the beach, enjoying the refreshing feel of the sea breeze and the cool sand on the warm, partly cloudy spring afternoon. We hugged, cried and said goodbye to Rachel in our own quiet ways. We said nothing aloud as we gently tossed her ashes into the heavy waves on the Fort Worden Beach to join my brothers.

She won't be alone.

If Rachel were alive, she would be 28 today. She would be six months pregnant. Cooper would be a father soon. I would be a grandmother.

I wish it would rain.

We walked up the beach where there were many friends and family. Everyone took a white rose and tossed it into the water. There were tears of sadness along with the tears of joy celebrating Rachel's life. I was hoping it would ease our pain and help us heal.

It didn't.

A month later, I was lying in bed on my 45th birthday, staring at a spider crawling on the ceiling. *I know every crack and mark in that ceiling now*. Jon came in and opened the blinds to let the brilliant spring sunshine into our bedroom. "Get up, Kimmie. You need to get out and run, or at least go for a walk." He left.

My bedroom had green walls and my sheets were yellow. It reminded me of my clover patch. There was even a ladybug crawling on the inside of the window. I watched the ladybug crawl around a while before opening the window to set it free. Then I went back to bed. I had no desire to do anything. I was lifeless and had no joy to share with others. I was even having a hard time watching the "Bonanza" extravaganza, three shows in a row, on my favorite TV channel. Even "Murder She Wrote" reruns weren't helping. Jon checked on me often and brought me snacks. *How annoying. I don't want to eat.*

Weeks go by. Now Jon is being bossy. "Kimmie," he insists, "I want you to eat all of your lunch." He hands me a tray with my favorite lunch of tomato soup, grilled cheese sandwiches with extra cheese, sliced apple and pear, gingersnap cookies and a big glass of milk. He fluffs three pillows behind me, making me sit up. He leaves.

I guess I should eat this lunch Jon worked so hard to prepare for me. I've been in my room for four weeks straight. Wiley is probably downstairs waiting for me.

Maybe I should get up and try to run.

Time doesn't heal. It just gives you a chance to absorb the shock.

It's summer now and I suddenly realize – I've been so selfish. Jamie and I had been constant reminders to one another of our loss, breaking down the moment we saw each other. We found it was easier to stay away.

"I need to comfort Jamie," I exclaim to Jon. "I've been avoiding her!"

I immediately go to her in Boulder.

My stomach aches and my sadness deepens when I see the hurt on Jamie's face, the stress that's taking its toll on this beautiful young girl … her furrowed brow, the deepening dark circles developing under her glossy eyes, the pain etched in her face. She's about to break down. She needs me more than ever now. She needs me to show her the way as I always have, the way to accept our great loss and move ahead, go forward and be happy, as Rachel would want us to do.

I find some matches and go for a run. Near Cherryvale Road, there's an old abandoned barn with a big hornets' nest attached to a rafter under the roof. I've been admiring it for a while.

I light it on fire, standing back to watch while enjoying the roar and the pops that are so empowering. I feel a rush of relief as the hornets' nest burns. I look off into the big field beyond. All around there are dandelions growing wild. Some are going to seed. I remember Rachel as a baby with her dandelion head, then Jamie's, and mine. I can hear Rachel's big belly laugh and I begin to laugh out loud, too.

The rock in my stomach goes away.

I think about the three of us being together in a field just like this. We are those dandelions growing wild. Blondie is there, frolicking in the field. Punky is prancing around with a big field mouse in her mouth, so proud of her catch. I see Dad and Murphy smiling, no longer sad and fighting their demons, with Tippie following them, thrilled to be with them in this wonderful place. Charlie is out there waving while trying to look cool, but I can tell he's happy to see me. I see Stanley smile his special smile, running toward me. Uncle/Grandpa Harold and Grandma Helen are walking together, hand in hand, young again and happier than I have ever seen them.

They are all here with me. They have never left me.

I go to Jamie and show her the way.

"I know Rachel is with us," I tell her as we sit close together on the couch in her small apartment. "She will always be here for her little sister." Jamie begins to cry. "Mom, I'm so mad at her. She was my Superwoman. Why did she die? We warned her to be careful. Why did she make that stupid choice? Why did she leave us? *Why*?"

I guide her gently. "We have to forgive her."

After our long cry with time passing in silence, Jamie looks over, "I love her so much, Mom."

"So do I. Rachel thought she was invincible, just like Miss Piggy," I say with a warm smile.

Jamie is smiling now. "She walked around as if she owned the fricking world and lived a fuller life than anybody I know," she laughed.

"She lived life her way, she did it her way, and she wouldn't have changed a thing."

"She was so tough, Mom."

"So are you, Jamie."

My little follower, who has always learned from my example, follows me out of sadness and despair to a better happier place, healing along the way. She begins to smile again, her gray and pasty skin turning sun-kissed, her eyes sparkling like they used to. The heavy weight crushing down on her shoulders seems to be lifting.

I look in the mirror and notice ... I had made the same transformation.

I married Jon two weeks after burning that hornets' nest, and we're living a dream life with Wiley in our cozy home on Mountain Avenue while enjoying the energy around us. I can hear the train off in the distance as I fall asleep every night to the scent of Jon's blanket hair. I am comforted, feeling safe and happy for the first time that I can remember.

Jamie started student teaching in the fall while finishing her final year at the University of Colorado. She continues to heal in her own quiet way as she follows me on our path toward accepting, rather than fighting, our loss of Rachel. We are laughing again.

We will mend and grow strong together.

Debbie and Bradley have just been released from prison, after several years and attempts to rehabilitate.

They will try, again.

Laurie was recently released from a year in the Jefferson County Jail. She is still troubled, without a grasp on this mentally debilitating disease that controls her moods and behavior. She will try, as she has so many times before.

Because that's what a dandelion does.

A dandelion is a hardy weed with a bright yellow flower that thrives without any attention or care. It will endure all kinds of hardship. It keeps coming back even stronger after many attempts to kill it or tame it down. A dandelion will continue to thrive and grow while making the world a beautiful place for those who see its beauty.

My family is like a dandelion. We were tough yet tender and caring. We were resilient, though on the verge of breaking if pushed hard enough. Instead of breaking or falling apart, we kept coming back stronger and even more resilient, springing back from adversity. It takes a lot of strength and perseverance to keep going and absorb all of the hardships my family had to survive throughout our lives. Some say we cared too much, that we couldn't harden up to become the harsh weed that remains steadfast. We loved too deeply and loved each other too much, making us fragile and easy to break.

Some of us did break, while the others mended in the broken places, making for a tough and hardy weed.

There are only a few dandelions standing strong, thriving. We wait ... hoping for the others to find their roots again and bloom.

Epilogue

Seven years later:

Jamie graduated from the University of Colorado with a bachelor's degree in psychology and a master's in education, becoming a Nationally Certified Teacher. She teaches second grade now at Flatirons Elementary School in Boulder and has shared her love for running by starting a kids' running club in her school. Each year it ends with a race called "The Pebble, Pebble," a takeoff on the popular Bolder Boulder 10K race. The turnout has grown over the years, and now over half of the students in the entire school take part in the program. Jamie is running marathons and races around the country appreciating the "Joy of Running".

Jamie's relationship with her father, Kelly, continues to grow stronger with each passing year. Kelly and his loving wife, Robin, are at Jamie's side in times of adversity, as well as in times of joy and celebration. By her 30th birthday, Jamie had found her soul mate, Tim Roth. They will be married in June 2011, and will travel through life together enjoying all that it has to offer.

Mom married her dream man, Jeff Cleaver, who looks like a young Ben Cartwright on "Bonanza." He is caring, responsible and stable. More importantly, I can see the adoration for her in his eyes. Mom is his true love. Jeff is the perfect Jehovah's Witness man. He is 11 years younger than Mom and has the energy to go with it. There is laughter in Mom's eyes, which I haven't seen since I was 5 years old, before Dad was diagnosed with schizophrenia. Mom and Jeff live in Port Ludlow, only a few streets from where Grandma Helen and Uncle/Grandpa Harold lived. They can view the Hood Canal and enjoy the dandelions and rhododendron bushes growing wild and shimmering in the sunlight along the roadside when they take their daily walk.

After many attempts, Mom has finally set down roots.

Dad is retired now and married a wonderful woman, Cindy. She is funny, charming and full of energy, reminding me of Alice on "The Brady Bunch." She makes Dad laugh, and brings out the man I knew Dad to be. She is his partner in life. They live a quiet life on a beautiful farm in Quilcene, 20 miles south of Port Townsend, with a view of the Big Quilcene River and the Olympic Mountains as the backdrop. Grandma Pat lives close by, still showering him with love and attention. You may see them out in Dad's boat near Point Wilson where he continues going out for their catch of the day, whether that be a salmon, crab, shrimp, or occasionally a gigantic octopus.

Bradley was back in prison for a few more years, but has come back strong, ready to fight this time, after doing some Ultimate Fighting to release his anger as well as to experience that immediate rush of endorphins. He and Sherri, his childhood sweetheart, divorced years ago and he is now living in California with a loving woman, Regina, who has stood by him through thick and thin. I just talked to him on the telephone. "Kimmie, I'm doing good, I have a good job working construction and money in my pocket." Then he broke down a little. "I'm going to fight this, I'm not drugging anymore." Then he broke down a little more. "I'm still the crybaby in the family." With his determination and kind heart, he will make it.

Sherri owns "The Junction Diner," a small Café in Poulsbo, Washington, finally establishing herself after many ups and downs enduring the Seelye family saga.

Brad's daughter, Ashley, became a dental hygienist and she and her brothers help out in their mom's café. She's a good girl and leads a good life. His boys, Bradley and Chaz, have had a few ups and downs of their own, with a few visits to the jail, but are now on the road to leading a respectable life. They'll make it because they have their father's determination and kind heart.

Debbie is living out in The Boondocks, just outside Enumclaw. She has stayed out of serious trouble and continues her struggle to maintain a good life. Debbie tells me that she is working toward a college degree in Occupational Health and Safety. She's still using her magical charm in working the system, though. I saw her on the Seattle KOMO news station a few months ago, speaking out about how Pierce County financial aid money is being tied up and causing her to be homeless. She persuaded the news media as well as the Pierce County Financial Aid Director to take care of this immediately. Her award was approved the next day and she received her grant check of over $20,000 a few days later. She was put up in a hotel until she could get her feet back on the ground. Who knows? Maybe Debbie is still enjoying the comfort of hotel life. I wouldn't be surprised if she is living it up at the Ritz.

Her son, Jade, is working in a security systems business and living a good Jehovah's Witness life in Pasco, Washington, with his young Jehovah's Witness family. Geno, her middle son, has seen his share of trouble. Debbie tells me that her youngest son is struggling with depression, signs of schizophrenia and violent behavior; that at one time he sought help in the same hospital with the wire-mesh windows where my dad was treated many years ago. Debbie is doing her best in providing her boys with food and shelter, keeping them from harm's way.

Laurie is still married to Jeff, and over the past several years they have lived in their cozy home in a charming town on the Olympic Peninsula. Laurie tells me that she is in a good place with herself, sons and husband. "I really like who I am today and the things I did I have learned from." Jamie and I went to visit her during one of her good patches. She looked sad and troubled. "Don't stay in your dreams for too long, Kimmie, your mind will play tricks on you," she warned. "You could get trapped like me and dream your life away."

Mel passed away after a long battle with cancer. Laurie took Mel into her home, nursed him, and was by his side to the end. He is deeply missed.

I will always remember Mel standing strong, smiling his beautiful smile while wearing his Jon Sinclair "racing unit."

Their boys, Mel and Danny, are continually in and out of jail, mainly for drug and alcohol situations, and haven't quite figured out how to fight their way out of the vicious cycle. I believe in time they will follow their brother's example: Little Charlie, who isn't so little anymore, made it through. He was the only one besides Bradley and me to move away from Washington State, away from the sadness and dysfunction. He grew into a beautiful young man with the Norwegian looks, and has his father's wonderful smile. He found a good job working for Northern

Directional Drilling and moved to California with his young family. He has a good life.

Wiley passed away a few years ago after sharing 15 wonderful years with Jon and 8 with me. We miss him terribly. But I know he's out there frolicking in the field with Blondie when he and Tippie aren't too busy chasing Punky around.

Jon and I are still living on Mountain Avenue, coaching while enjoying a leisurely life. I adore Jon and he treats me like a queen. A few things have changed. Now I sit on my porch swing in the mornings and watch a family of foxes trotting across the grass median, sometimes coming into the front yard to take a rest. If I get up early enough I'll see raccoons scurrying across the street after their busy night, causing mischief I'm sure. Squirrels scramble around everywhere, chattering away to make sure we aren't enjoying too much peace and quiet. Where's Punky when we need her? Every morning I look up to the many turkey vultures nesting in the trees above beginning their day, swirling in circles as others join them, darkening the sky before making their way out of town for their daily hunt for dead carcasses and who knows what.

I ran through the cemetery a few days ago and came across at least 10 deer grazing next to some gravestones, like they owned the place. They weren't at all alarmed while they stared at me as if I was the oddity, intruding on them. There's an owl's nest in the corner of the cemetery, and we can expect a new batch of babies each year. Sometimes you can hear them hoot in the middle of the night.

I run through the golf course almost every day. Many of the golfers know me by now and give me a wave, although, there are some who aren't pleased and wave their clubs. Some things never change.

I am happy here. I have a fine life.

My family has tamed down over the past seven years. That's what age and time will do. Maybe they'll tame down even more during the next seven years.

I'm hoping for the best.

Kim Jones and Jon Sinclair ~ 2011

ABOUT THE AUTHOR

Certainly considered one of the best female marathoners in US history, Kim Jones could also be included in a list of the country's top 10 marathoners, male or female. Throughout her career Kim has been one of the most dominant distance runners in the world. She has more high-level placings in world-class marathons than any other US female marathoner in history with 17 performances under 2:33. (Deena Kastor 10; Joan Benoit Samuelson 9; Lisa Weidenbach 7)

Fastest marathon performances:

2:26:40	Boston 1991 (2nd)
2:27:50	Berlin 1991 (2nd)
2:27:54	New York City 1989 (2nd)
2:29:34	Boston 1989 (3rd)
2:30:00	Boston 1993 (2nd)

*** Plus 12 other performances under 2:33 since 1986

5000 meters- 15:43 (1996)

10K- 32:23 (1989), 32:48 (1997)

1/2 Marathon- 1:11:34 (1988)

Marathon- 2:26:40 (1991), 2:31 (1997, at age 39)

Former U.S. 30K (1:47:41) and 20 mile (1:55:29) records

Ranked 3rd in the World in the marathon (1989)

Member of the Road Runners Club of America Hall of Fame

26 career marathons:

Fastest- 2:26:40 (Boston 1991)

Slowest- 2:48:48 (Honolulu Marathon 1984) – first marathon

Average time for the first 25 marathons- 2:33:04

Average place for the first 25 marathons- 4.1

Acknowledgements

I want to thank my editor and friend, Barb Huebner, whom I've nicknamed Huebner P.I. because of her amazing ability to fact check and "get the scoop." Her guidance, advice and wisdom have been deeply appreciated.

Editing a book of this size is not an easy task; in fact, it is a monstrous undertaking. These are my words, this is my writing and I take full responsibility for any mistakes. I was fortunate to receive help and find needed information from many resources: the Jefferson Country Historical Society (Marsha Moratti, Archivist-Research Center), the Port Townsend Public Library, Enumclaw Public Library (Robert Baer); the *Enumclaw Courier-Herald*, *Port Townsend Leader*, *Port Angeles Peninsula Daily News*, *Spokane Spokesman-Review*, *Seattle Times*, *Seattle Post*, *New York Times*, *New York Post*, *Boston Globe*, *Minneapolis St. Paul Star Tribune* and *Pioneer Press*, the *Associated Press* – the many newspapers around the world; *Runner's World*, *Running Times*, *Northwest Runner*, *Track & Field News* and many other magazine publications around the globe; feedback from the Twin Cities, Bloomsday and New York Road Runner's board members.

I am indebted to my dear friend, Donnamarie Barnes. Her contagious enthusiasm and encouragement after reading my first draft gave me the spark needed to move forward – and for her wonderful job of preparing my old tattered photographs for this book.

"Thank you" to George Hirsch for his support, along with his advice and direction throughout the publishing process – and to Bob Yelling for giving me a three-day crash course on how to write an autobiography.

I feel gratitude beyond what I can express to my husband, Jon – my mainstay, my mentor, my treasure at the end of the rainbow. His direction and support have guided me through the hard times and his love has pulled me through the tragedies. His passionate response to my book and his help throughout the editing process brought me to the completion of this endeavor.

I want to thank Jon and my daughter, Jamie Roth, for encouraging me even before I put my pencil to paper.

Jamie's input, support and love carried me through the process of healing as I wrote our story. It was "Jamie and me against the world" for many years and now my husband, Jon Sinclair, and her husband, Tim Roth, are here to enrich our lives, empowering us to move forward and appreciate what the world has to offer.

I have written my story based on my very vivid memories and the information that my mother, Geraldine Cleaver, has provided. I am truly indebted to her for the tremendous help during this enormous undertaking. I couldn't have done it without her encouragement and input, especially on the early years of my life. My mother's ability to transform herself and survive what, at times, seemed insurmountable has been a life-long inspiration. She has always found joy in the good moments.

I am deeply grateful to my family for sharing their memories. My father, Mike Pollard, a man of great strength and integrity, who was just a kid himself when he swept my family away from a tragic place and brought us to the beautiful paradise, Port Townsend, Washington. That wonderful town was our savior ... where we all grew up together.

A loving thank you to my siblings – Laurie, Debbie and Bradley for their encouragement to go forward, generously giving me their blessing to write about our lives. We have many memories of our early childhood and I hope it wasn't too painful for them to go back there. They have enlightened me and confirmed many of the memories I have.

I have a deep appreciation for the people who came into my life at the right time, as I wandered down a bumpy and confusing pathway from childhood through adolescence, unsure of which way to turn: The Jehovah's Witnesses and my neighbor Chuck for helping my family when we needed it most; and my many friends and supporters in Port Townsend, Washington. A special thanks to my high school track coaches Mrs. Kuehl and Mr. Brink. And, most important of all, the man who showed me the joy of running and taught me how to become a champion without realizing I was one, Mr. Royce.

And later, in my adult life: the life long friends who appeared around each blind corner at just the right time; Benji and Amie Durden who have become my family in Colorado. Benji was my mentor in life and running. He empowered me with the confidence and strength to become a world-class runner, giving me the tools needed to go on in life after my competitive years.

I am truly grateful to the man who was instrumental in my emergence into the world-class running arena – Don Kardong, my past advisor and training partner, and a dear friend.

I could never have endured a 15-year marathon career at the top of my game without the attention and care from my talented support crew, "Team Jones": Staffan Elgelid, Ania Stang, Steve Shirley, Brian Tibbetts, Chuck Strickell, Dr. Robert Wigert and Steve Jones.

I was also fortunate to have a tremendous amount of support from the many townspeople in Spokane, Washington, who have encouraged and assisted me throughout my running career – it would take another book to list everyone.

A special thanks to my pre-readers who's input was invaluable: Jamie Roth, Margaret "The Mom" McCarthy, Amy Hayes, Kent and Dawn Oglesby, Tayna Poel, Matthew Trucco, Elizabeth Sinclair, Harry Hackett, Jim Vassar, Susan Landau, George Hirsch, Don Kardong, Mr. Steve Jones, Joan Samuelson and Bill Rodgers.

I must thank my keen-eyed proofreaders: Jon Sinclair, Donnamarie Barnes, Kent Oglesby, Edie Stevenson, Jeff Cleaver, David Blankenship and Tom Sinclair for helping with the final edit. Their contribution was a tremendous help.

~

I am overwhelmed with thankfulness and joy to learn that I will be a grandmother soon.

If you can endure bad luck, good fortune is right around the corner.

Made in the USA
Columbia, SC
15 February 2019